Multiple Job-holding among Farm Families

Multiple
Job-holding
among
Farm Families

EDITED BY

M. C. HALLBERG

JILL L. FINDEIS

DANIEL A. LASS

Iowa State University Press / Ames

M. C. **Hallberg** is professor of Agricultural Economics at Pennsylvania State University.

Jill L. Findeis is associate professor of Agricultural Economics at Pennsylvania State University.

Daniel A. Lass is assistant professor of Agricultural Economics at the University of Massachusetts.

HD
5110.2
U5
M85
1991

© 1991 Iowa State University Press, Ames, Iowa 50010

Manufactured in the United States of America
⊗ This book is printed on acid-free paper.

First edition, 1991

Library of Congress Cataloging-in-Publication Data

Multiple job-holding among farm families / edited by M. C. Hallberg, Jill L. Findeis, Daniel A. Lass. – 1st ed.
    p.   cm.
  Papers presented at a symposium held 5/16–17/88, sponsored by the Northeast Regional Center for Rural Development et al.
  Includes index.
  ISBN 0-8138-0287-3 (alk. paper)
  1. Part-time employment – United States – Congresses. 2. Part-time farming – United States – Congresses. 3. Farm income – United States – Congresses. 4. Rural families – United States – Congresses. I. Hallberg, M. C. (Milton C.) II. Findeis, Jill Leslie. III. Lass, Daniel A. IV. Northeast Regional Center for Rural Development.
HD5110.2.U5M85 1991
331.25′72 – dc20   90–43479

CONTENTS

VI. Policy Issues and Research Needs

PREFACE

This book contains the papers prepared for and presented at a symposium on multiple job-holding among farm families in North America held on May 16–17, 1988, and sponsored by the Northeast Regional Center for Rural Development, the North Central Regional Center for Rural Development, the Southern Rural Development Center, the Western Rural Development Center, and the Farm Foundation. The symposium was intended to provide information useful to researchers, extension personnel, and students interested in the area, and to those agricultural leaders and policymakers involved in the development of policy for rural society. It was designed to satisfy the following major objectives: (1) to review the current importance of and motivations for multiple job-holding among farm families in North America, to examine recent trends in the phenomenon, and to identify the place of multiple job-holding in the modern agricultural sector; (2) to review major theoretical contributions designed to suggest hypotheses about the economic behavior of multiple job-holding farm families and to identify significant limitations of this theory; (3) to review major findings of recent surveys on multiple job-holding in agriculture; (4) to examine important labor market factors impacting multiple job-holding farm families; and (5) to identify the public policy issues relevant to this area. The book is organized into five major sections according to these objectives.

The symposium focused attention on the "multiple job-holding farm family," in which either or both spouses work part- or full-time at some nonfarm activity in addition to farming their own farm. This focus was chosen deliberately to highlight the fact that part-time farming (the more common term used to describe the phenomenon under study) is the product of a very complex and changing set of conditions and motives, and that narrow definitions and research methodologies are not likely to lead to the most useful and satisfactory explanations. Thus the symposium was organized on the premise that the *farm family* is the relevant unit of concern rather than just the farm operator, and that the income of the *farm family* should receive our attention, not just the income of the farm operator.

Although this book is concerned with multiple job-holding in North America, several of the authors indicate that the phenomenon is not limited to North America. Indeed in a recent paper by M. C. Hallberg, "Multiple Job-holding among Farm Families: Implications for Research and Policy," presented at the Fifth European Congress of Agricultural Economists, Balatonszeplak, Hungary, 1987, this fact is documented in detail. In the developing world, multiple job-holding among farm families is now generally looked upon as a necessary component of the process of accelerated growth in rural areas and of income enhancement for rural people. In the developed world too the phenomenon is viewed, in part at least, as a means of enhancing the incomes of rural people. There appear to be no specific geographical, population, or income characteristics that would explain variations in the incidence of multiple job-holding among farm families. Thus we conclude that the phenomenon is motivated by a set of forces common to the farm family regardless of country of origin.

An important premise that may help guide future research and policy responses in this area is that there is a symbiotic relationship between farming and nonfarming of benefit to both sectors. Many farm families could not exist without the nonfarm jobs provided by the nonfarm sector. All farm families need the market outlets, inputs, and business and social services provided by the nonfarm sector. But the rural, nonfarm sector also could not exist if the farming community with its surplus labor, service sector needs, and social and economic institutions did not exist. This symbiotic relationship is beginning to be recognized in some countries (e.g., Western Europe and parts of Asia) but needs to be further explored. To sustain and enhance this symbiotic relationship is a task that will require innovative research, extension education efforts, and public policies. The policy responses to the phenomenon of multiple job-holding might be varied and diverse. In general, though, we might expect multiple job-holding farmers to respond more to the availability of nonfarm jobs and nonfarm wage rates than to the price of farm products established by the market or by government policy.

The editors wish to thank the Regional Rural Development Centers and the Farm Foundation for sponsoring the symposium that led to the papers included here. Appreciation is also expressed to Rose Ann Alters (Pennsylvania State University), the secretary who helped the editors compile this volume. We also thank Maria Kushman (University of Massachusetts) for her efforts in this regard.

M. C. HALLBERG
JILL L. FINDEIS
DANIEL A. LASS

CONTRIBUTORS

Mary Ahearn, Farm Costs and Returns Section, Farm Sector Financial Analysis Branch, Agriculture and Rural Economy Division and Economic Research Service, U.S. Department of Agriculture

Paul W. Barkley, Professor of Agricultural Economics, Department of Agricultural Economics, Washington State University

Peggy F. Barlett, Associate Professor of Anthropology, Department of Anthropology, Emory University, Atlanta, Georgia

James C. Barron, Extension Economist, Department of Agricultural Economics, Washington State University

Susan Bentley, Economic Research Service, U.S. Department of Agriculture

Ray D. Bollman, Statistics Canada, Ottawa

Thomas A. Carlin, Economic Research Service, U.S. Department of Agriculture

Kenneth L. Deavers, Director, Agricultural and Rural Economy Division, Economic Research Service, U.S. Department of Agriculture

Jill L. Findeis, Associate Professor, Department of Agricultural Economics and Rural Sociology, Pennsylvania State University

Anthony (Tony) M. Fuller, University School of Rural Planning and Development, University of Guelph, Canada

Tesfa G. Gebremedhin, Associate Professor, Department of Agricultural Economics, Southern University and A & M College

Christina H. Gladwin, Associate Professor, Department of Food and Resource Economics, University of Florida

Brian W. Gould, Assistant Research Scientist, Department of Agricultural Economics, University of Wisconsin

Milton C. Hallberg, Professor, Department of Agricultural Economics and Rural Sociology, Pennsylvania State University

R. J. Hildreth, Managing Director, Farm Foundation

Wallace E. Huffman, Department of Economics, Iowa State University

Thomas G. Johnson, Associate Professor and Extension Specialist-CRD, Department of Agricultural Economics, Virginia Polytechnic Institute and State University

Daniel A. Lass, Assistant Professor, Department of Agricultural and Resource Economics, University of Massachusetts

John E. Lee, Jr., Administrator, Economic Research Service, U.S. Department of Agriculture

Rosemary K. Mahoney, Agricultural Economist, Agricultural Cooperative Service, U.S. Department of Agriculture

William Saupe, Professor, Department of Agricultural Economics, University of Wisconsin-Madison

R. G. F. Spitze, Professor, Department of Agricultural Economics, University of Illinois

Daniel A. Sumner, Council of Economic Advisers and Department of Economics and Business, North Carolina State University

Luther Tweeten, Anderson Professor of Agricultural Marketing, Policy, and Trade, Department of Agricultural Economics, Ohio State University

Lionel Williamson, Extension Economist, Department of Agricultural Economics, University of Kentucky

Additional Symposium Support

Walter Armbruster, Associate Director, Farm Foundation

H. Doss Brodnax, Jr., Director, Southern Rural Development Center, Mississippi State University

Daryl K. Heasley, Director, Northeast Regional Center for Rural Develoment, Pennsylvania State University

James Holt, Holt, Miller and Associates, Arlington, Virginia

Peter F. Korsching, Director, North Central Regional Center for Rural Development, Iowa State University

Steven Lilley, Department of Sociology, North Carolina State University

Russell C. Youmans, Director, Western Rural Development Center, Oregon State University

PART I

Historical Perspective and Future Prospects

 CHAPTER 1

Multiple Job-holding among Farm Operator Households in the United States

MARY AHEARN
JOHN E. LEE, JR.

Public policies for any sector of the economy are more likely to be effective and useful if they are based on accurate perceptions of the sector. Typically, changes in the reality of a sector are lagged by perceptions of reality, and further lagged by policies and institutions intended to serve that sector. The greater the lags, the less effective the policies, and the greater the likelihood that unintended and perverse effects will result.

U.S. agriculture provides one of the clearest illustrations of this truth. The differences between perceptions and reality for farming may be greater than for other sectors because, in addition to the fact that farming has undergone dramatic structural, technological, and managerial changes, the sector—and our rhetoric about it—continues to be wrapped in a unique cloud of values and beliefs. Since many in our country are still only a generation or two removed from the farm or from rural communities, those values and beliefs about farming, however inarticulate or contradictory, are widely held.

In this time of continuing transition for farming, and as we enter a period of major policy debate brought on by proposals for global agricultural policy reform and the impending 1990 legislation that will replace the 1985 Food Security Act, it is more important than ever that policymaking be based on accurate perceptions of the reality of the farm sector and on a more useful understanding of the policy needs that derive from that reality.

3

Part-time farming and multiple job-holding among farm families are not new. Many of the founding families of our nation, and many ordinary folk of the time, combined farming with a variety of other pursuits. But the trends of this century have been toward greater concentration of farm production on fewer and larger commercial farms, while a growing majority of farm households that add little to aggregate farm production depend primarily on off-farm sources of income to sustain the family. Generally, these trends tend to be viewed with concern, and discussions of part-time farming are couched in judgmental terms such as small, poor, relatively disadvantaged, etc. Often, discussions of multiple job-holding farm families conjure up images of people being forced out of farming or having to seek off-farm work to save the family farm or to supplement family income.

Our tendency to think in such judgmental terms about part-time farming probably has several roots. One such root is our tradition of the idealized family farm as one of moderate size, where Ma, Pa, and the kids own the land they farm and do most of the work, and where most of the income comes from the farm. This was the perceived norm, and other situations were seen as deviations from the norm, i.e., as something less than ideal. In truth, this full-time family farm norm was never the predominant situation in the South, Southwest, West Coast, or the Mountain States. It was probably most prominent in the Midwest and in the pre–dust bowl Great Plains.

Another likely root of our less-than-positive perspective on part-time farming was the socially undesirable situation in which nineteenth-century and early twentieth-century tenant farmers and southern sharecroppers often found themselves. Much of our agrarian policy has had as its goal bringing these tenants and sharecroppers, many of whom had to supplement their farm earnings with other income, up to the idealized norm—the full-time owner-operated family farm.

The prospectus for this symposium stated the often negative connotation of part-time farming another way: "Multiple job-holding among farm families in North America has traditionally been viewed as a transitional phenomenon—either as the first step in the process of entering farming or as the first step in the process of adjusting out of farming. As a consequence policymakers have treated multiple job-holding in agriculture as a phenomenon to be tolerated but not necessarily encouraged." The prospectus goes on to state: "More and more, however, it is being recognized that multiple job-holding among farm families is a rather permanent phenomenon which enables many farm families to pursue a chosen lifestyle, maintain a rural residence, or meet other personal or financial goals."

Indeed, it is time to recognize that U.S. agriculture is, and has long been, a pluralistic sector, containing a great variety of people and businesses seeking to achieve a wide variety of personal and business goals and objectives. Rather than judge this pluralism as positive or negative, we should simply observe it as a fact. Then we can move on to study the conditions of this reality, what they imply, and for whom. In this way we are more likely to identify legitimate policy issues that arise from existing conditions and trends and better understand the likely consequences of alternative policy responses to those issues.

In the remainder of this chapter the terms *multiple job-holding* and *part-time* are used interchangeably. The first section is a review of definitional issues relating to part-time farming and part-time farms. The next section provides a description of historical trends in the extent and characteristics of part-time farming. The following sections provide alternative concepts of part-time farming and describe the subpopulations classified as part-time under each concept. Following a brief review of what the trends suggest for the future, the chapter concludes with some questions about the usefulness of the part-time farming classification scheme and suggests some interests that could motivate alternative classifications of farms and farm households.

Definitional Issues

Part-time farming and part-time farms are concepts which are generally not given specific definitions and oftentimes not distinguished from each other. Part-time farming is applied to individuals or households which include individuals engaged in farming activities, and it relates to the allocation of their time among various activities, including leisure. The term *part-time farm* applies to farm businesses or establishments and generally relates to aspects of production technology. The part-time farming issue is more relevant to questions directly regarding the welfare of people and the part-time farm label is more relevant to the issue of efficient use of scarce resources. The policy issue of transferring income from nonagricultural sectors to the agricultural sector relates both to the part-time farming activities of individuals and the relative efficiency of part-time farm businesses.

Part-time farming could apply to individuals or to households which include individuals who are engaged in farm production activities — farm operators, farm workers, farmland owners, and farm business associates such as partners and shareholders of incorporated farm businesses. However, the part-time farming label has usually been applied to farm operators or farm operator households not depending solely on the farming operation for their livelihood and spending less than a normal work week in farming activities and the remainder of available time at off-farm work or at leisure activities (i.e., multiple job-holding).

Nonoperators are essential to the farm production process, and are oftentimes involved in nonfarm activities or associated with more than one farm. Many farm workers are employed to assist farm operator households with farm activities only during peak production periods. Because of this seasonal nature, the farm workers' group includes many who are employed in farming for less than a full year. Special policy issues relate to this group: adequate supply of farm workers at critical times, immigration reform, and subpopulations with a high incidence of low incomes and low access to social services.

Nonoperator owners of farmland and capital are another very unique group of individuals who are likely to be engaged in farming activities only part-time. This group is sizeable. For example, there are over 4 million owners of farmland compared with 2.2 million farm operators.[1] This group is also of special policy interest. Many individuals in this group, along with farm operators, share in the management and risks of farming and are eligible for payments from the government under agricultural programs (Boxley 1985). The group includes both those landowners who are retired farm operators and those whose only connection to farmland ownership is as a business investment. A thorough analysis of part-time farming should ideally include other nonoperator households which share in the entrepreneurial role with farm operators. The organization of farm businesses has changed over time so that increasingly more than one individual or household has a claim on the residual income of a farm business. This is the case, for example, with partnerships.

The difficulty in characterizing these nonoperator groups and their multiple job-holding is that the data system is extremely weak in coverage of nonoperators. In the 1935 *Census of Agriculture* (Vol. 3, p. 218), part-time farming was described as follows:

> The most popular or prevalent view seems to be that it is a mode of living whereby a family resides on a farm but receives income, in a more substantial degree, from nonfarm sources; briefly, it usually connotes a combination of industry and agriculture. Other restrictions or amplifications are often made.

---

1. A high-quality estimate of the number of farmland owners does not exist. Most analysts estimate about 4 million, in spite of a 1978 landownership survey which estimated that there were 6.9 million farmland owners. The concern that there were nonfarmland owners identified as farmland owners in the 1978 survey is supported by the survey data which indicated that less than half of the respondents reported receiving farm income in the survey year.

Not all interpretations have made an occupation outside of farming a prerequisite, as income from agricultural work not connected with the farm on which the family resides or outside income from nonoccupational sources such as pensions, interest, dividends, etc., may be a part of the interpretation. Or again, part-time farming may be thought of from the standpoint of the amount of farming activity without any reference to an outside source of income.

This view, developed in 1935, is not a single definition of part-time farming, but rather it includes several elements that are, in the main, consistent with the view held today. It is doubtful, though, that an income-based concept is necessarily the more "popular or prevalent" concept. Whether or not the household resides on a farm is irrelevant to the part-time farming definition. In addition, there is likely not strong agreement that to be classified as part-time, an operator household's off-farm income is larger ("more substantial") than their farm income. Finally, part-time farming does not usually connote a "combination of industry and agriculture." The latter is representative of the time in which the view was forwarded. At that time the type of industry located near most farms was more likely to be the goods-producing industries, in comparison with today's more heterogeneous nonmetropolitan areas.

Identification of part-time farms, in contrast to part-time farming, has also been of interest in the past. The motivation here has generally been to differentiate those farms that do not operate at a size large enough to benefit from the most basic economic efficiencies from farms viewed as "legitimate businesses" or of "commercial size." This distinction is generally independent of farm operator household resources, most notably the availability and use of household labor.[2] The difficulty here is that legitimate or commercial businesses are very difficult to define. A definition of part-time farms which is based on some notion of operating below an economically efficient level would have to consider the complete complement of factors of production. This would vary by production specialty, resource quality, and weather.

Since the basic purpose here is to separate small from large farms, part-time farms are often defined in terms of gross sales below a certain level. An early example is the 1955 *Census of Agriculture,* where part-time farms were classified in the standard sales class system. However, operator and operator household off-farm characteristics were relied upon to do so.

---

2. However, consideration of the use of household labor relative to total farm labor requirements is generally critical to discussions of a "family farm." In practice it is impossible to develop an acceptable working definition of a family farm, particularly one that will withstand the test of time.

More precisely, part-time farms were defined as those where the value of sales of farm products was $250 to $1,199 and the operator reported either 100 or more days of off-farm work *or* the other income received by the operator and household members was greater than the value of farm products sold. A noteworthy aspect of this definition is that by accounting for operator and operator household characteristics, allowance was made for either hours-based or income-based concepts. This definition, however, limited part-time farms to those with low levels of farm sales. If a farm had sales of $250 to $1,199 and its operator and household did not meet the above off-farm work or income requirements, the farm was classified as a (Class VI) commercial farm. Similarly, if a farm operator household was more dependent on off-farm sources of income or an operator worked more than 100 days off the farm, the farm was not classified as part-time if it had more that $1,199 in sales of agricultural commodities that year.

At various times, part-time farms have been referred to as those with gross sales below $10,000 or $20,000, and currently noncommercial or part-time farms are most popularly defined as those with gross sales under $40,000. As the price level changes over time there has been a need to change the critical boundary level for definitions of part-time and commercial farms based on gross sales.

Historical Information on Part-time Farming

Data on the farm and nonfarm work activities of individuals involved with some aspect of agricultural production come from a variety of sources. We will briefly describe historical information available for farm operators and their households, farm workers, and farmland owners. By far, the most data are available for farm operators and their households.

Farm operators or farm operator households

Two historical data series which relate to part-time farming of farm operators or farm operator households exist. The *Census of Agriculture* has collected data on the number of farm operators who have worked off the farm. Table 1.1 presents these data beginning with the 1929 census. From 1929 through 1944 the percent of farm operators who worked any days off the farm was rather stable at around 30 percent. The 1930s were a period during which nonfarm job opportunities were scarce as the nation experienced and recovered from the Great Depression. The decline in the number of farms which began in 1921 temporarily halted in 1929, and the total number of farms increased through 1935. The decades since the 1940s have seen the farm sector decline to one with a significantly smaller number of farms and with a greater percentage of farm operators who work off the farm. The greatest increase in days worked off the farm was in the category of 200 or more days per year. In 1929, 6 percent of the farm operators worked 200 or more days off the farm and in 1982 almost 35 percent of the operators worked 200 or more days off the farm. Note that these data only consider the work time farm operators spend off the farm and not the nonfarm income from all sources or the work or income of other members of the farm operator household.

Table 1.1. United States operators working on and off their farms

| Census year | Number working off-farm | | | | Number not working off-farm or not reporting[a] | Total farm operators |
	For 1–99 days	For 100–199 days	For 200 or more days	Total		
1929[b]	1,179,629	326,565	396,704	1,902,898	4,385,750	6,288,648
1934	1,316,702	348,151	412,621	2.077,474	4,734,876	6,812,350
1939	803,612	378,893	564,688	1,747,193	4,349,606	6,096,799
1944	491,303	244,475	834,579	1,570,357	4,288,812	5,859,169
1949	835,672	313,353	943,897	2,092,922	3,292,603	5,385,525
1954	820,012	306,377	1,027,348	2,153,737	2,629,284	4,783,021
1959	556,235	229,787	877,819	1,663,841	2,044,132	3,707,973
1964	448,983	189,027	824,173	1,462,183	1,695,674	3,157,857
1969	391,790	219,687	870,815	1,482,292	1,247,958	2,730,250
1974[c]	196,921	156,584	657,971	1,011,476	1,267,794	2,279,270
1978[d]	252,471	180,770	770,045	1,203,286	1,054,489	2,257,775
1982[d]	223,733	188,797	774,844	1,187,374	1,053,602	2,240,976
				Percent		
1929[b]	18.8	5.2	6.3	30.3	69.7	100.0
1934	19.3	5.1	6.1	30.5	69.5	100.0
1939	13.2	6.2	9.3	28.7	71.3	100.0
1944	8.4	4.2	14.2	26.8	73.2	100.0
1949	15.5	5.8	17.5	38.9	61.1	100.0
1954	17.1	6.4	21.5	45.0	55.0	100.0
1959	15.0	6.2	23.7	44.9	55.1	100.0
1964	14.2	6.0	26.1	46.3	53.7	100.0
1969	14.3	8.0	31.9	54.3	45.7	100.0
1974[c]	8.6	6.9	28.9	44.4	55.6	100.0
1978[d]	11.2	8.0	34.1	53.3	46.7	100.0
1982[d]	10.0	8.4	34.6	53.0	47.0	100.0

Source: U.S. Department of Commerce, Census of Agriculture, years cited above.
[a]Those reporting no off-farm work or not reporting were not always tabulated separately. The combined number is reported in the none or not reporting column.
[b]Excludes days worked in nonfarm self-employed activities.
[c]In 1974, the data were only calculated for sole proprietorships and partnerships. That is, corporations and other types of farm organizations were not asked to provide this information. The total operators column also excludes these farms.
[d]Specified that days worked off the farm are to be included only if the operator worked at least four hours per day.

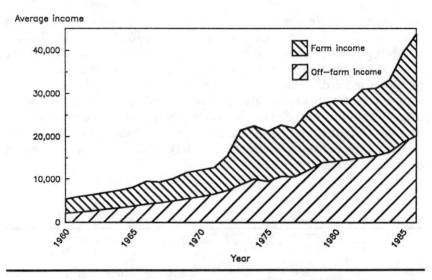

Figure 1.1. The proportion of farm operator household income from off-farm sources has increased over time. Farm and off-farm income include cash items only. (*Compiled from U.S. Department of Agriculture, 1987,* Economic Indicators of the Farm Sector: National Financial Summary, 1986)

The other major source of historical data that relates to part-time farming is the annual U.S. Department of Agriculture series *Economic Indicators of the Farm Sector* on off-farm and farm income of farm operator households (Figure 1.1), which began in 1960. An unfortunate assumption implicit in these data is that there is one household associated with one farm, i.e., all of the farm earnings accrue to the farm operator household.

Data from this source indicates that total off-farm income of the sector increased faster than net cash farm income during the 1960–86 period. In constant dollars, off-farm income increased 43 percent, compared with 10 percent for net cash farm income. These increases in income occurred at the same time that the total number of farms decreased by 44 percent. For several years during the 1970s and again in 1985 and 1986, the average total cash income of farm operator households exceeded that of the average cash income for all U.S. households.[3] Off-farm income has played an important role in closing the historical farm-nonfarm income gap.

3. In making this comparison, the U.S. Department of Agriculture's estimate of income of farm operator households was adjusted to be consistent with the underlying concept of the U.S. Department of Commerce's estimate of cash income for all U.S. households.

Table 1.2 presents 1986 data on the farm and off-farm income of farm operator households by various subpopulations: sales class, type of production specialty, and region. The sales class data are published annually from 1960 forward (U.S. Department of Agriculture, *Economic Indicators of the Farm Sector*), and it is possible to construct a time series for type of production specialty and region using unpublished U.S. Department of Agriculture data. By sales class, smaller farms (annual sales of less than $40,000) receive the greatest average off-farm income followed by the largest farms (sales of $250,000 or more). Mid-sized farms (sales of $40,000–$249,999) receive the lowest average off-farm income. As size increases, off-farm income as a proportion of total income decreases. Note

Table 1.2. Distribution of off-farm income by selected characteristics, United States, 1986

Agricultural subsector	Percent of sector's farms	Off-farm income Average ($)	Off-farm income Total ($000,000)	Percent of total cash income from off-farm sources	Percent of sector's off-farm income
All farms	100	20,212	44,708	46	100
Sales class					
Less than $40,000	73	22,534	36,336	96	81
$40,000–$99,999	13	13,780	4,053	37	9
$100,000–$249,999	10	12,602	2,648	17	6
$250,000 or more	4	17,562	1,670	5	4
Type of farm specialty					
Cash grain	21	16,575	7,824	41	18
Cotton	1	13,711	294	19	1
Tobacco	4	13,912	1,115	60	2
Vegetables	1	18,969	504	9	1
Fruit, nut	3	43,365	3,168	56	7
Nursery	1	17,834	454	10	1
Other crops	8	21,578	4,061	72	9
Cattle, hogs, sheep	40	22,971	19,936	64	45
Dairy	10	6,525	1,495	23	3
Poultry	1	18,737	510	5	1
Other livestock	10	26,333	5,346	109	12
Region					
Northeast	7	23,090	3,592	48	8
Lake States	11	15,090	3,690	39	8
Corn Belt	21	19,070	9,056	46	21
Northern Plains	9	13,770	2,699	29	6
Appalachia	15	18,930	6,419	62	15
Southeast	8	24,600	3,513	44	8
Delta	6	21,280	2,809	56	6
Southern Plains	11	25,410	5,921	60	13
Mountain	5	20,310	2,464	46	6
Pacific	7	25,000	3,975	35	9

Source: U.S. Department of Agriculture, *Economic Indicators of the Farm Sector: National Financial Summary, 1986,* and unpublished USDA data.

that because of the assumption of one household per farm imposed by the data restrictions and because this assumption is more likely to be violated for large farms, the proportion of income from off-farm sources is more likely to be understated for farm operator households associated with large farms than those associated with the small farms. However, the general trend across sales classes is no doubt true.

By type of production specialty, livestock producers generally have high average off-farm incomes, with the exception of dairy and poultry producers. Because dairying is labor intensive, farm operators and their households have less flexibility in their work schedules to work off the farm. Of the crop specialties, fruit and nut producers and their households have the highest average off-farm income, but producers of miscellaneous crops followed by tobacco producers receive the greatest share of their total cash income from off-farm sources.[4]

Off-farm income by region varies significantly as well. The Pacific region has a high average off-farm income, although since farm incomes are relatively high in this region, off-farm income is not a large percent of total income. The opposite is true for the Appalachian region, where off-farm incomes are below the U.S. average but off-farm income accounts for the majority of cash income. This is because farm incomes are also low.

The follow-on survey to the 1978 *Census of Agriculture,* the *1979 Farm Finance Survey* (FFS) (U.S. Department of Commerce 1982), provides unique cross-sectional data on part-time farming characteristics for operators and their households in 1979. As a measure of part-time farming, the FFS uses whether the operator, spouse, or both work off the farm. The data on off-farm work by sales class from the FFS are consistent with the sales class data of off-farm income, i.e., farm operator households of smaller farms are more likely to work off the farm than those of larger farms. This data source also indicates that in 52 percent of farm operator households the operator, spouse, or both worked off the farm. In 47 percent of those households only the operator worked off the farm, in 16 percent only the spouse worked off-farm, and in the remaining 37 percent both the operator and spouse were employed off-farm. Since farm operators are more typically male, these data are consistent with a 1980 U.S. Department of Agriculture survey of women farm operators and wives of male farm operators which found farm men more likely to work off the

---

4. Again, because of the necessary assumption of one household per farm and because fruit and nut producers are generally larger operations, the share that off-farm income is of total income is likely understated since more than one household is sharing in the residual returns from the farming operation.

farm than farm women (Rosenfeld 1985).[5]

Age of operator is related to part-time farming whether part-time farming is measured by any nonfarm employment activity in the household, major occupation of the farm operator, or dollars of off-farm income. The *1979 Farm Finance Survey* reports that those households that had someone working off the farm were more likely to have an operator under 65 years old. The U.S. Department of Agriculture's *Farm Costs and Returns Survey* indicates that in 1986 the average age of operators whose major occupation was farming was 53 years old, compared to an average age of 48 for operators whose major occupation was other than farming.

The *1979 Farm Finance Survey* (U.S. Department of Commerce 1982) provides the only national data on the type of off-farm employment of working operators and spouses. The majority of employed operators and spouses worked as employees at nonfarm private sector businesses. The occupations of operators and spouses were varied. The most common occupations for operators in 1979 were craftsmen (21 percent of those employed off the farm), nonfarm managers and administrators (14 percent), and professional and technical workers (11 percent). The majority (52 percent) of operators worked more than 50 weeks per year at an off-farm job and 72 percent worked more than 35 hours per week. About 15 percent of operators travelled 30 miles or more one way to their off-farm jobs. The most common types of occupations held by spouses of operators differed from those of the operators: 26 percent were clerical workers, 21 percent were professional or technical workers, and 17 percent were service workers. Spouses were less likely than operators to work 50 weeks or more per year off the farm (47 percent), to work 35 hours or more per week (59 percent), and to travel more than 30 miles one way to their off-farm employment (only 6 percent).

Hired farm workers

Historical data on hired farm workers who were paid for farm work anytime during the survey year exist beginning with 1945 (U.S. Department of Agriculture, *The Agricultural Workforce*). In addition, for most years, information is included on whether or not workers had a nonfarm wage or salary job at any time during the year. Since 1945 the hired farm work force has decreased in size, and the percent of hired farm workers with a nonfarm wage and salary job increased during the period (Table 1.3).

---

5. The opposite trend is true for farm residents. Women farm residents are more likely to have nonfarm employment than are men farm residents.

Table 1.3. Number of hired farm workers and percent with a nonfarm wage and salary job, United States

Year	Hired farm workers	Percent with a nonfarm wage and salary job
1945	3,212	NA
1946	2,770	42.5
1947	3,394	33.4
1948	3,752	33.4
1949	4,140	30.3
1950	4,342	NA
1951	3,274	26.4
1952	2,980	NA
1953	. . .	. . .
1954	3,009	28.7
1955	. . .	. . .
1956	3,575	28.8
1957	3,962	25.6
1958	4,212	30.7
1959	3,577	32.3
1960	3,693	35.9
1961	3,488	32.5
1962	3,622	35.3
1963	3,597	31.9
1964	3,370	37.9
1965	3,128	36.6
1966	2,763	39.0
1967	3,078	34.4
1968	2,919	36.6
1969	2,571	37.2
1970	2,488	40.4
1971	2,550	36.6
1972	2,809	41.3
1973	2,671	41.6
1974	2,737	41.6
1975	2,638	40.9
1976	2,766	43.1
1977	2,730	41.1
1978	. . .	. . .
1979	2,652	42.5
1980	. . .	. . .
1981	2,492	40.7
1982	. . .	. . .
1983	2,595	40.1
1984	. . .	. . .
1985	2,522	46.3

Source: U.S. Department of Agriculture, Agricultural Workforce, years cited above, compiled by Victor Oliveira.
. . . = No survey conducted.
NA = Data not available.

Farm landowners and other contributors of capital, land, management, and labor

Data on contributors of land and capital are extremely scarce. A 1978 survey of landowners (which includes farm operators) collected some information on farm and nonfarm incomes, but an annual series does not exist — the previous landowner survey was conducted in 1946. Of the 80 percent of farmland owners that responded to the nonfarm income question, 88 percent reported having received some nonfarm income in 1977. About half of those who reported receiving nonfarm income received less than $10,000 (Table 1.4). Only 16 percent or less of the farmland in the Delta, Southeast, and Appalachian regions was owned by owners who reported no nonfarm income, compared with 40 percent or more of the farmland in the Northern Plains and Mountain regions (Daugherty and Otte 1983).

No data exist on the characteristics, including nonfarm activities, of other contributors of resources to farming who share in the residual income from the farming business, such as partners or shareholders of farm corporations.

Related data sources

The U.S. Department of Commerce collects income and employment data for individuals related in some way to a farm business (U.S. Department of Commerce, *Money Income of Households, Families, and Persons*

Table 1.4. Farmland owners and amount of farmland owned, by nonfarm income of farmland owners, United States, 1977

	Farmland owners		Farmland owned	
	Number (thousand)	Percent[a]	Acres (million)	Percent[a]
Nonfarm income ($)				
None	668	12.3	118.5	28.4
10,000 or more loss	8	.1	2.0	.3
3,001–9,999 loss	36	.7	4.7	.7
1–3,000 loss	33	.6	3.2	.5
0–2,999 income	766	14.0	91.7	13.8
3,000–6,999 income	992	18.2	99.5	15.0
7,000–9,999 income	694	12.7	54.9	8.3
10,000–14,999 income	713	13.1	63.0	9.5
15,000–19,999 income	666	12.2	43.9	6.6
20,000–24,999 income	372	6.8	30.5	4.6
25,000–49,999 income	368	6.8	43.8	6.6
50,000 or more	135	2.5	37.7	5.7
Total	5,451	100.0	663.4	100.0
No response to nonfarm income question	1,182		179.4	
Corporations, unsettled estates, and other institutions	244		95.2	
Total	6,877		938.0	

Source: Daugherty and Otte 1983.
[a]Percentage of owners and acres for which nonfarm income of the owner was reported.

in the United States). These include a series of nonfarm employment data for people who live on farms. This farm residence series is composed of operator households, hired workers, unpaid workers, farm landlords, and others, but does not include all of the households in any of these subgroups. This is a problem since the composition of the farm population has shifted over time among the subgroups.

There are also data series available on those whose principal occupation is operating or managing a farm and those who receive farm self-employment income. The former series omits those operators or managers for whom farming is not their major occupation. The latter series omits farm operators of incorporated farms and includes landlords who rent farmland on a share rental basis. The fact that each of these population concepts does not purely capture any of the contributors to agricultural production—farm operators, farm workers, farm landlords, and other claimants of residual income—is a serious drawback to their usefulness. The small size of the farm samples is also a serious drawback to the reliability of these series. For example, the estimate of the size of the farm self-employment population is considerably less than the size of the farm operator population. We would expect the farm self-employment population to be larger than the farm operator population since the operator group omitted from this series (operators of incorporated farms) is smaller than the nonoperator group that is included (share rental landlords).

Toward a Definition of Part-time Farming

An underlying and critical first step toward defining part-time farming is to identify the unit of observation. We have chosen to focus our data analysis on the farm operator household because (1) the operator is the major entrepreneur and decision maker in the agricultural production process, and (2) the farm operator and his or her household supply resources to farm production and, thus, receive the residual income (after all market factors are paid), making them the most affected by market and policy shifts. We will focus on the farm operator household in the remainder of this paper for pragmatic reasons as well—data limitations are less severe than for other groups.

Recent specifications of the household model combine aspects of both the traditional consumption and production models (Singh, Squire, and Strauss 1986). In the standard economic household model the household is the unit of observation. In that model the consumption unit seeks to maximize its utility subject to a budget constraint. Utility is a function of market goods, and the budget constraint specifies that the household cannot consume more than the sum of earned and unearned income. In the standard economic production model the unit is a firm seeking to optimize a function, such as profit, with respect to inputs. In the "new household economics" or household-production approach, the household is viewed as producing consumption goods for itself with market goods as inputs into the production process. The household utility is then a function of these home-produced goods and, in some specifications, some market goods. Such a conceptual model for the unit of observation is well suited for farm operator household-business units who integrate production and consumption activities in a not-so-subtle way (see Singh, Squire, and Strauss 1986 for applications of this model to agriculture). For the farm operator household-business unit, net farm income is included in the budget constraint.

Income-based concepts

Part-time farming concepts based on income sources have the advantage of focusing on what the operator or household is actually relying on for a livelihood—the farm or another source of income. However, the part-time label implies something about how farm operators or households are spending their work time, and time allocation may not be closely related to the generation of income. In addition, farming is a risky business and one with considerable annual variation. Since major data sources are generally collected on an annual basis and are not panel data, income estimates are generally only available for a single year. The year for which the data are collected may be an exceptionally high or low income year for many farming operations. Similarly, this variation commonly affects whole subsectors simultaneously, such as a region which has experienced a drought or a type of production specialty which has faced stiff competition from abroad.

Two possible part-time farming concepts based on the farm income share of household income have been defined. The income-based concepts are for the operator household. That is, they are not based solely on the operator's income contribution. This approach is preferable, particularly in light of the increased labor force participation of women and the involvement of many women in farm business activities. The income-based concepts differ in whether only earned or total cash off-farm income is considered. Farm noncash income items, such as an imputed rental value for farm dwellings, are excluded from income. We may have wished to consider noncash off-farm income as well, such as food stamps, Medicare, employer-provided insurance coverage, etc. However, our data source only collects cash off-farm income.

The first income-based concept for part-time farming defines part-time farming as a farm operator household whose income earned off the farm from wage and salary jobs or nonfarm businesses or professional practices represents the majority of the sum of these off-farm income sources and net cash income from their farming operation. The second definition defines part-time farming as a farm operator household whose cash income from all off-farm sources (earned and unearned) represents the majority of income of the sum of all cash off-farm income plus net cash farm income.

Hours-based concepts

Part-time farming concepts based on hours spent in farm versus off-farm work activities have the advantage of identifying where the operator or household is expending the most significant portion of personal energies. Hours-based concepts are largely insensitive to yield and price variations, in contrast to income-based concepts. However, hours-based concepts are less relevant for describing how important farming is to the financial well-being of the farm operator and household. The operator and household may depend on the farm for their major income source and still be considered part-time farmers when part-time is an hours-based concept. Another limitation of the hours-based concept is that considerable variation exists in the labor requirements by type of production specialty and, given the specialty, by type of production technology employed. A crude measure based simply on hours with no adjustment for these factors will lead to crude classifications of farm operators and households as part-time.

Three hours-based concepts for part-time farming are used. The first concept is based on whether anyone in the operator household receives any off-farm income from wage or salary jobs or nonfarm businesses or professional practices. The second hours-based concept is based on whether the operator works an arbitrarily established number of hours on the farming operation per year — 1,000 hours, or approximately one-half year. The final hours-based concept defines a part-time operation as one in which the farm operator spends the majority of his or her work time at an off-farm activity. An advantage to the latter concept is its common usage.

The exact part-time farming concept one chooses makes a significant difference in the number and percent of U.S. farm operator households that can be classified as part-time. Table 1.5 compares these differences across concepts using data based on the *Farm Costs and Returns Survey* (FCRS) (U.S. Department of Agriculture 1987) for 1986. These data are known to undercount the total number of U.S. farms by roughly 700,000 in that year. The number of farms in the United States in 1986 was estimated at 2.2 million as compared with the FCRS's representation of 1.5 million

Table 1.5. Part-time farm operator households by alternative part-time farming concepts, United States

Part-time concept	Number of farms	Percent
Income-based		
Earned cash off-farm income is majority of earned cash income	647,410	43
Total cash off-farm income is majority of total cash income	836,210	55
Hours-based		
Someone in household has off-farm wage or salary job or business	939,206	62
Operator works less than 1,000 hours per year on farm	481,052	32
Off-farm work activity is majority of operator's total work time	569,085	38

Source: U.S. Department of Agriculture, *1986 Farm Costs and Returns Survey.*

farms. Furthermore, the undercount is known to be more severe among small farms. Because smaller farms are more likely to be associated with part-time farming households under any reasonable concept, the percent in part-time farming as reported in Table 1.5 should be considered a low estimate. The percent of farms which are part-time varies considerably across the concepts, from 32 percent for households whose operator worked less than 1,000 hours per year on the farm to 62 percent for households which reported having someone in the household with an off-farm wage or salary job or nonfarm business.

Table 1.6 presents additional farm and household characteristics by each concept. Generally, farm operator households classified as part-time (under each of the concepts) differ from the U.S. average farm operator household in the expected ways: the average farm incomes, direct government payments, farm assets, farm equity, and poverty rates are all lower for part-time farming households than for all farms under each concept.[6] Similarly, off-farm incomes are higher for part-time farming households, and the farms operated by these households are much more likely to be small and to specialize in red meat production (beef, hogs, or sheep) and general livestock and crops.

There were some differences among part-time concepts, however. The average farm incomes of part-time farming households under the income-based concepts are much lower than under the hours-based concepts. One

---

6. The poverty line is a simple indicator of a minimally necessary cash income for a single year. The Department of Commerce adjusts the level annually by size of household and age of members. Because farming is an occupation that is financially risky and returns are affected by many factors, farm income is much less stable over time than is off-farm income. Therefore, to the extent that farm households save and dissave over time to manage their average consumption based on their perception of their permanent income, a single year poverty rate is less appropriate for farm operator households than for most other households.

Table 1.6. Farm operator household characteristics by alternative part-time farming concepts, United States, 1986

| | Part-time farming concept | | | | |
| | Income-based | | | Hours-based | |
Characteristics	Total cash off-farm income is majority of total cash income	Earned cash off-farm income is majority of earned cash income	Someone in household has off-farm wage or salary job or nonfarm business	Operator works less than 1,000 hours per year on farm	Off-farm work activity is majority of operator's total work time
Part-time farms					
Number	836,210	647,410	939,206	481,052	569,085
Percent	55	43	62	32	38
			Dollars per farm		
Average farm income	−1,524	−1,998	9,361	2,338	126
Average government payments	1,551	1,498	4,212	1,507	1,089
Average off-farm income	39,321	42,780	34,690	38,691	43,417
Average assets	197,234	183,607	246,755	187,324	195,349
Average equity	165,945	149,450	187,471	160,166	159,374
			Percent		
Sales class					
Less than $40,000	88	86	72	90	91
$40,000–$249,999	8	12	24	9	7
$250,000 or more	3	2	4	1	2
Type of production					
Cash grains, exc. rice	17	15	21	19	15
Rice and cotton	1	1	1	1	1
Peanuts and tobacco	5	3	5	4	4
Vegetable, fruit, nut	5	4	5	7	5
Other crop	10	9	9	11	10
Dairy	3	5	7	1	2
Beef, hog, or sheep	49	49	41	46	49
Other livestock	11	14	11	11	14
Percent below poverty level	16	12	17	19	15

Source: U.S. Department of Agriculture, 1986 Farm Costs and Returns Survey.

income-based concept (based on earned cash income) and one hours-based concept (based on anyone in the household having an off-farm job) included a much larger group of households associated with mid-sized farms. The type of production specialty of part-time farming households defined under these two concepts reflects a greater participation in cash grain and dairy production.

Our major conclusions from the available data with which to determine the significance of part-time farming are that (1) the characteristics of part-time farming households under each concept are consistently different from those of the average U.S. farm operator household, and (2) it is most important to tailor a definition to the question being addressed, e.g., low incomes, local nonfarm employment opportunities, or on-farm labor requirements.

A Joint Income and Hours Categorization Scheme

To better understand the relationship between the way in which farm operator households allocate their time among farm and off-farm activities, we have further categorized households into four groups based jointly on their income from off-farm sources and the major occupation of the farm operator. Again, the choice of concept is arbitrary, but we believe a joint distribution of the two major concept types (income-based and hours-based) for households is most informative. The four groups are described as (1) operator's major occupation is not farming and the household is not dependent on farm income; (2) operator's major occupation is not farming but the household is dependent on farm income; (3) operator's major occupation is farming, but the household is not dependent on farm income; and (4) operator's major occupation is farming and the household is dependent on farm income. Table 1.7 presents the data for each category, Table 1.8 for the poverty population in each group, and Table 1.9 for the nonpoverty population in each group.

As expected, the first and fourth groups are the most homogeneous groups since the majority of their income is from the source where the operator allocates the majority of his or her work hours to off-farm and farm activities, respectively. The households in the first group accounted for a third of all FCRS farms, and would account for an even higher proportion of U.S. farms — probably 40–50 percent — without the FCRS undercounting problem. These farms produced only 5 percent of U.S. agricultural production and operated 10 percent of the acres. This group had the lowest average farm income, the highest average off-farm income, and

Table 1.7. A joint categorization of United States farm operator households by major occupation of operator and income source

Major occupation of operator	Major cash income source	
	Off-farm income	Farm income
Other than farming	492,366 farms (33% of FCRS farms) 5% of FCRS farm production 10% of FCRS acres operated −$2,691 average farm income $48,637 average off-farm income 14% participate in government programs (4% of all payments) $640 average government payments $4,469 average government payments per recipient $139,546 average farm equity 8% below official poverty income level 94% with sales below $40,000 Most common specialty: beef, hog, or sheep (51%) Second most common specialty: cash grain (14%) Third most common specialty: general livestock (13%)	76,719 farms (4% of FCRS farms) 8% of FCRS farm production 10% of FCRS acres operated −$18,205 average farm income $9,919 average off-farm income 25% participate in government programs (4% of all payments) $6,963 average government payments $15,922 average government payments per recipient $286,629 average farm equity 58% below official poverty income level 66% with sales below $40,000 Most common specialty: beef, hog, or sheep (36%) Second most common specialty: cash grain (19%) Third most common specialty: general livestock (15%)
Farming	343,845 farms (22% of FCRS farms) 11% of FCRS farm production 17% of FCRS acres operated $148 average farm income $25,982 average off-farm income 32% participate in government programs (14% of all payments) $2,863 average government payments $8,894 average government payments per recipient $203,748 average farm equity 28% below official poverty income level 80% with sales below $40,000 Most common specialty: beef, hog, or sheep (46%) Second most common specialty: cash grain (20%) Third most common specialty: general crops (9%)	603,248 farms (40% of FCRS farms) 76% of FCRS farm production 64% of FCRS acres operated $36,358 average farm income $5,280 average off-farm income 57% participate in government programs (79% of all payments) $10,496 average government payments $18,544 average government payments per recipient $319,690 average farm equity 33% below official poverty income level 31% with sales below $40,000 Most common specialty: cash grain (29%) Second most common specialty: beef, hog, or sheep (26%) Third most common specialty: dairy (22%)

Source: U.S. Department of Agriculture, *1986 Farm Costs and Returns Survey.*

the lowest average farm equity. More than half were red meat producers and almost all had sales under $40,000. In spite of their low farm incomes, this group had the lowest poverty rate of all the groups (8 percent) due to their off-farm incomes. The farm operator households in this group who

Table 1.8. A joint categorization of United States farm operator households in poverty by major occupation of operator and income source

Major occupation of operator	Major cash income source	
	Off-farm income	Farm income
Other than farming	39,500 farms (3% of FCRS farms) 3% of FCRS farm production 1% of FCRS acres operated −$5,313 average farm income $11,779 average off-farm income 13% participate in government programs (1% of all payments) $504 average government payments $3,789 average government payments per recipient $99,231 average farm equity 97% with sales below $40,000 Most common specialty: beef, hog, or sheep (57%) Second most common specialty: general livestock (13%) Third most common specialty: general crop (9%)	44,597 farms (3% of FCRS farms) 2% of FCRS farm production 5% of FCRS acres operated −$31,982 average farm income $6,063 average off-farm income 14% participate in government programs (1% of all payments) $1,077 average government payments $7,574 average government payments per recipient $265,557 average farm equity 84% with sales below $40,000 Most common specialty: beef, hog, or sheep (43%) Second most common specialty: general livestock (18%) Third most common specialty: general crop (11%)
Farming	97,405 farms (6% of FCRS farms) 2% of FCRS farm production 4% of FCRS acres operated −$3,343 average farm income $8,047 average off-farm income 26% participate in government programs (3% of all payments) $2,069 average government payments $7,809 average government payments per recipient $131,821 average farm equity 84% with sales below $40,000 Most common specialty: beef, hog, or sheep (45%) Second most common specialty: cash grain (18%) Third most common specialty: peanuts, tobacco (8%)	198,331 farms (14% of FCRS farms) 14% of FCRS farm production 25% of FCRS acres operated −$18,722 average farm income $3,239 average off-farm income 42% participate in government programs (13% of all payments) $5,549 average government payments $13,343 average government payments per recipient $238,640 average farm equity 61% with sales below $40,000 Most common specialty: beef, hog, or sheep (33%) Second most common specialty: cash grain (24%) Third most common specialty: dairy (15%)

Source: U.S. Department of Agriculture, *1986 Farm Costs and Returns Survey.*

were in poverty had both greater farm losses and lower off-farm income on average than those not in poverty. In addition, the poverty population in this group was somewhat less likely to be cash grain producers than the nonpoverty population.

The operator households with an operator whose major occupation was not farming but who were dependent on farm income was a small group—only 5 percent of all households. They were also a very odd group,

Table 1.9. A joint categorization of United States farm operator households not in poverty by major occupation of operator and income source

Major occupation of operator	Major cash income source	
	Off-farm income	Farm income
Other than farming	452,866 farms (30% of FCRS farms)	32,122 farms (2% of FCRS farm)
	5% of FCRS farm production	6% of FCRS farm production
	9% of FCRS acres operated	5% of FCRS acres operated
	−$2,463 average farm income	−$87,883 average farm income
	$51,851 average off-farm income	$15,271 average off-farm income
	14% participate in government programs (4% of all payments)	40% participate in government programs (3% of all payments)
	$653 average government payments	$7,970 average government payments
	$4,523 average government payments per recipient	$20,074 average government payments per recipient
	$143,062 average farm equity	$315,885 average farm equity
	95% with sales below $40,000	41% with sales below $40,000
	Most common specialty: beef, hog, or sheep (50%)	Most common specialty: cash grain (30%)
	Second most common specialty: cash grain (15%)	Second most common specialty: beef, hog, or sheep (27%)
	Third most common specialty: general livestock (13%)	Third most common specialty: general livestock (12%)
Farming	246,440 farms (16% of FCRS farms)	404,917 farms (27% of FCRS farms)
	9% of FCRS farm production	62% of FCRS farm production
	13% of FCRS acres operated	39% of FCRS acres operated
	$1,528 average farm income	$63,337 average farm income
	$33,070 average off-farm income	$6,280 average off-farm income
	34% participate in government programs (10% of all payments)	64% participate in government programs (66% of all payments)
	$3,176 average government payments	$12,920 average government payments
	$9,224 average government payments per recipient	$20,200 average government payments per recipient
	$230,597 average farm equity	$359,389 average farm equity
	78% with sales below $40,000	17% with sales below $40,000
	Most common specialty: beef, hog, or sheep (46%)	Most common specialty: cash grain (13%)
	Second most common specialty: cash grain (21%)	Second most common specialty: dairy (25%)
	Third most common specialty: general crops (10%)	Third most common specialty: beef, hog, or sheep (22%)

Source: U.S. Department of Agriculture, *1986 Farm Costs and Returns Survey.*

composed of at least two very different subgroups of farm operator households: (1) households who operate large, successful cash grain and livestock operations, as well as having an operator whose off-farm job is a major occupation; and (2) households who operate small livestock farms that earn low returns and which include operators with low-paying off-farm jobs. Both the poverty and nonpoverty populations in this small group of farm operator households had very high farm equity, $265,557 and $315,885, respectively.

The group that earns more off the farm than on the farm, but with farming as the operator's major occupation, includes almost one-quarter of the FCRS farm operator households. They account for about 10 percent of U.S. production. A large majority of the farms are small and almost half specialize in red meat production. Households could fall into this group for a variety of reasons, including a production failure or a successful farming year but an even more financially rewarding off-farm activity. The group may also include households who are retired from full-time farming but still consider their major occupation as farming even though their major income sources are off-farm transfer payments or dividends and interest income. Households that operate small farms with little or no off-farm opportunities to which they allocate their time would also fall in this group. This latter group is sometimes referred to as limited resource farmers.[7] Households in this group had relatively low average farm income and the lowest average total income of all groups, and 28 percent were below the official poverty level. There is little difference in the farm profile of the poverty and nonpoverty households within this group aside from the obviously lower incomes of the poverty households.

The other more homogeneous group, dependent on farm income and the operator's major occupation as farming, accounted for three-quarters of all U.S. production. This group comprised nearly 40 percent of FCRS farms. Not surprisingly, these farms had relatively high farm incomes and direct government payments, receiving almost 80 percent of all payments to operators. The farms in this group were more likely to be mid-size and large farms producing cash grain and dairy products than the other farm operator household groups.

This group had a poverty rate of 33 percent. The households in poverty in this group were less likely to participate in government programs and those who did participate received lower average payments. This can be explained by both the average size and type of production specialties of the poverty group versus the nonpoverty group, since government commodity programs were designed for cash grain and cotton commodities and payments are linked to volume of production. The poverty group included more small operations. Sixty percent had annual sales below $40,000 compared with less than 20 percent for those not in poverty. In addition, those in poverty were more likely to be livestock producers and less likely to be cash grain producers, compared to households not in poverty.

---

7. Some use the term limited resource farmers to apply only to minority farmers. In this case no such limitation is applied.

What of the Future?

A recent Office of Technology Assessment (OTA) report (Congress of the United States 1986) predicted that by the year 2000, fifty thousand farms will produce 75 percent of the value of all agricultural output. The report estimated that the total number of farms would decline to 1.25 million.

We believe those predictions are a bit dramatic. Earlier projections by the Economic Research Service (ERS) based on data through 1978 suggested that the number of farms will decline moderately to about 2.1 to 2.2 million by the year 2000 (Edwards, Smith, and Peterson 1985). The decline in farm numbers slowed gradually in the 1970s and even reversed slightly at the end of the decade. In the 1980s, farm numbers have declined at rates of from 1.5 to 3.0 percent annually. In light of these developments, we expect an ERS updated forecast of farm numbers in the year 2000, based on more current data, to be closer to 1.7 to 1.9 million, still significantly higher than the 1.25 million farms predicted by the Office of Technology Assessment.

We have no formal projections for part-time farms or farmers. Commercial farm production will continue to become more concentrated with the continued slow decline in the number of farms that produce 90 percent of the value of farm products. More important, we believe there will be a continued increase in the diversity of farm and household employment and income situations. As in the rest of society, there are likely to be more two-career households. Not all farms will be large scale. Some analysts believe the most important future technologies will be the biotechnologies which are likely to be scale-neutral, unlike the past technologies which tended to benefit larger operations most. There will clearly be a place for small farms, especially those that find a unique market niche for themselves, and for part-time farming households.

What's the Problem?

After sifting through an array of alternative definitions and classifications of part-time farms, and part-time farmers and their households, and after a growing sense that the classifications are largely arbitrary, one is led to ask, "What are we looking for? What is the perceived problem that we are trying to address?"

Let us cite some hypothetical, but not unrealistic, cases of part-time or multiple job-holding farm-related situations. Then we can speculate about the issues.

Case 1

A 35-year-old bachelor operates a 640-acre corn-hog farm in Illinois. He nets $45,000 annually. The farm keeps him employed most of the time, but for the entire year he averages working less than 40 hours per week. We would probably classify him as a full-time commercial farmer. Not very interesting for purposes of this discussion.

The farmer decides to get married. He marries a woman who is a doctor, a specialist who works long hours and nets $90,000 per year. Now they are a multiple job-holding household. What's the problem? Why do we care? Her hours of work add up to more than his, and her income is greater. By some definitions that makes them part-time farmers.

Again, what's the problem? Nothing is changed on the farm. We suppose it might be useful to know that the household is doing well financially.

Case 2

A family operates a 1,600-acre wheat farm in North Dakota. Net farm income averages $60,000 a year. They have no livestock. With large tractors, it takes less than a month to prepare the ground and plant. Only a few weeks (or less) are required to harvest the crop, with a few more weeks required for marketing and taking care of legalities at the local ASCS office. In reality the farm requires the effort of the family for only about three months a year. Most of the rest of the time the family lives in Las Vegas. Is this a part-time farmer? Whether part-time or not, what's the problem?

Suppose the farmer decides to work in Las Vegas during his off months. Now we have a multiple job-holding family. What's the issue? Why are we studying this family?

Case 3

Joe Bureaucrat works for the Department of Commerce in Washington, D.C. He makes $50,000 per year. His wife teaches in the Fairfax County school system and makes $30,000 per year. They live in the suburbs. For purposes of this discussion, they don't even appear on our radar screen. We are not interested in them. But Joe saves his money and buys 80 acres of cropland in Westmoreland County, Virginia. He grows corn and soybeans, doing most of the farm work on weekends—just for fun. He has no plans to expand into full-time farming. Now Joe is a part-time farmer and a member of a multiple job-holding farm household. The blinking red lights on our radar screen are going crazy. Why? Why are we interested in Joe now?

Case 4

Now we come to a small farmer in the North Carolina Piedmont region. He has a tenth-grade education and lives on a 180-acre farm he inherited from his father. He raises hogs and some corn to feed his hogs. He has a large garden and some fruit trees, and sells some fresh fruit and vegetables. The family does all the work. They netted $9,000 last year, a typical year. The family earns no other income. The farmer and his family are underemployed, but would be defined as full-time farmers. So are we not interested in them even though the family is poor and has inadequate housing, diet, and medical care? Then he gets a job in a local textile mill and adds $15,000 per year additional income. Now he's a part-time farmer and our interest in him picks up. Then his wife gets a job in the same mill, adding another $15,000 to family income. Now they are a multiple job-holding family. We begin to drool! Why?

Given the endless number of ways one can define and sort farms, farmers, and farm-related households, one keeps coming back to the questions: What difference does it make? What are we looking for? For what purpose are we grouping farms for study?

Are we a conference looking for an objective? Other than for study of household and firm behavior, is there some social or policy objective or perceived problem that explains why we address a two-day conference to a vaguely defined subpopulation we alternately call multiple job-holding households, part-time farms, and part-time farmers—and for which the only clear distinction is that they have some financial link to farming? By the way, does that link include farm landlord income or just operating income? What does the distinction have to do with well-being? Or efficiency? Or any other social objective? How about hired workers? Do they count? Part-time hired workers? Multiple job-holding hired workers?

We suggest that one important result of this conference is the continuing education of policymakers and the general public to the fact that the financial well-being of farm families is not solely a function of farm business income—in fact, it is less important than off-farm income for the majority of farm families. Beyond that, however, if we are to figure out whether the conference objectives (and our ongoing research objectives) are achieved, we have to sort out why we are here. What are we trying to do and why? Are our definitional handles operationally meaningful? By that, we mean, do they help us understand the nature, characteristics, causes, and consequences of behavior or of a problem, and do they provide a workable basis for analysis and policy response? Do any of our delineations of subpopulations tell us about social problems to be addressed? Do they tell us anything about the competitiveness and viability of American agriculture?

By the end of the conference, it is hoped that we will have sorted out our legitimate motivating interests, including research and extension interests, and that we will have determined whether those interests are productively approached via the classifications of farms and households around which the conference is organized. We could conclude that this should be our last conference on part-time farmers, not because we don't care, but because, as a result of this conference, we have found a better way to approach the issues we do care about.

Let us conclude by suggesting three possible interests that motivate us, with brief comments on each.

1. *Better understanding of firm and household behavior.* Some of you are interested in improving our theoretical and empirical understanding of why farm firms, farm operators, and farm households behave as they do. This would allow us to improve our modeling, and hence prediction, of how these units would likely behave under alternative economic and policy scenarios. Our own bias is that our theory of firm or household behavior is quite adequate. There are a variety of ways, however, in which that theory could manifest itself. Contributions in this area are likely to be useful (for example) in teaching entrepreneurship and personal and household resource management and less useful for explaining aggregate behavior.

2. *Concerns about farming as a business sector.* Are there reasons of economic efficiency, competitiveness, or resiliency, among others, for interest in part-time farms or farming? Are we concerned about economies of size or efficient use of labor and overhead capital? Will farm operators and households with diversified occupational and income interests respond differently to economic and policy conditions than operators and households that depend primarily on farming? If there are efficiency and response issues, is the part-time, full-time delineation the most useful way to approach them?

3. *Concerns about people.* Ultimately most of us are motivated by concerns for human well-being. Thus, we are interested in understanding problems such as poverty and underemployment and in the effectiveness of policies to deal with the problems. Again, is the part-time or multiple job-holding delineation the most useful approach to such problems? Recall, for example, that overall, the incidence of poverty is lower among part-time, multiple job-holding farm operator households than for other farm operator households, in part because of the stability of off-farm income compared with farm income.

There are many stereotypes and perceptions relative to part-time farmers and their households. It is important to determine whether rhetoric matches reality. If it does not, it is important that such information—and its policy implications—is well understood by the public.

In general, perhaps what we should be doing is examining the changing character of agriculture, including the apparent tendency toward a more pluralistic farm sector, and the causes and consequences of those changes in the context of society's goals and concerns for farming and for people. This conference can make a contribution to that goal.

References

Boxley, R. 1985. "Farmland ownership and the distribution of land earnings." *Agricultural Economics Research* 37(No. 4):40–44.

Congress of the United States. 1986. *Technology, Public Policy, and the Changing Structure of American Agriculture.* Washington, D.C.: Office of Technology Assessment, U.S. Government Printing Office.

Daugherty, A. and R. Otte. 1983. *Farmland Ownership in the United States.* AGES 830311. Washington, D.C.: Economic Research Service, U.S. Department of Agriculture.

Edwards, C., M. Smith, and N. Peterson. 1985. "The changing distribution of farms by size: A Markov analysis." *Agricultural Economics Research* 37(No. 4):1–16.

Rosenfeld, R. 1985. *Farm Women: Work, Farm, and Family in the United States.* Chapel Hill: University of North Carolina Press.

Singh, I., L. Squire, and J. Strauss, eds. 1986. *Agricultural Household Models.* Baltimore: Johns Hopkins University Press.

U.S. Department of Agriculture. Various years. *The Agricultural Workforce.* Washington, D.C.: Economic Research Service.

_____. Various years. *Economic Indicators of the Farm Sector: National Financial Summary.* Washington, D.C.: Economic Research Service.

_____. 1987. *1986 Farm Costs and Returns Survey.* Washington, D.C.: Economic Research Service and National Agricultural Statistics Service.

U.S. Department of Commerce. Various years. *Census of Agriculture.* Washington, D.C.: Bureau of the Census.

_____. Various years. *Money Income of Households, Families, and Persons in the United States.* Series P-60. Washington, D.C.: Bureau of the Census.

_____. 1982. *1979 Farm Finance Survey, Census of Agriculture,* Vol. 5, Special Report, Part 6. Washington, D.C.: Bureau of the Census.

 **CHAPTER 2**

Multiple Job-holding among Farm Families in Canada

ANTHONY (TONY) M. FULLER

This chapter is intended to serve two purposes. It is designed primarily to describe the patterns of multiple job-holding in Canadian farming. This is attempted with reference to historical patterns of change in the study of the subject as well as with secondary sources of information and data. The second objective is to provide a critical analysis of the implications of such patterns in light of the present debate on restructuring in the global economy.

In attempting a critical analysis, some old traps have to be dealt with. Problems of definition have long mired research on this subject. The term *part-time farming* in particular has led generations of researchers to overlook some of the key relationships which characterize this phenomenon. This has often been compounded by disciplinary bias which has limited the methodological development of the subject and confined it to standard economic and statistical analysis. The sum of this unfortunate trend in our past research, to which I have also made my contribution, has been to focus almost entirely on the agricultural aspects of the phenomenon.

The enduring emphasis has been on trying to define part-time farming as a single, definable entity, i.e., to determine its chief characteristics and to correlate these with key farm indicators such as farm size, enterprise type, or land use. This focused on what part-time farmers do on their farms. When, over time and with a plethora of case studies, it was discovered that most part-time farm operations resemble the patterns of full-time farming operations, it became evident that operators with off-farm jobs do *not* necessarily have farms that are part-time, inefficient, or in any major way different than the range of farming operations in the area. In addition, when it was learned that part-time farmers themselves are also generally representative of all farmers in the area in terms of socioeconomic characteristics, they were dismissed as uninteresting.

What may be referred to as the *production bias* came about not only because of the way the subject was being studied, but also because of the finding that part-time farms (as defined!) contributed little to the total value of agricultural production. This led in turn to part-time farms being seen as synonymous with small farms and referred to as marginal in production terms and anachronistic in structural terms. As a result part-time farming tended to be dismissed as unimportant.

The main problem with "part-time farming studies" is the *operator bias,* which is the practice of defining part-time farming or multiple job-holding with reference to the farm operator only. Whether measured in terms of time allocated to formal off-farm activities (gainful occupations) or by the sources of income, the emphasis has been on the operator so that the farm family has been largely ignored. The main cause of this has been the structure and composition of data bases, particularly the agricultural and occupational censuses which have been the main sources of information. It is interesting to note, however, that even in the hundreds of case studies on part-time farming, it was only the operator for whom extensive information was gathered. Collectively, this has led to gender bias in our research. It has meant that farms have been analyzed and classified on the singular basis of whether the farm operator has an off-farm job or not. If the operator has, then the *farm* has been classified as part-time. Clearly in many cases, operations classified in this way are no different than so-called full-time farms, because the operator's labor is substituted by capital, family members, or hired labor. An operator who has a part-time job does not necessarily run a part-time farm!

The combined effect of the production bias and the operator bias has been to question part-time farming only from an agricultural production perspective. This generally assumed a degree of economic rationality in decision making as well as some unstated virtues of single full-time occupations in farming. This "moral" bias has given part-time farming a bad name and has negatively influenced research and policy in this area. It is therefore important to adopt a better term for the phenomenon and I am delighted that multiple job-holding has been chosen for this conference. In Western Europe, the term *pluriactivity* is being commonly used, largely for the same reasons: to rid us of the biases, poor research findings, and rigidities that have constrained our thinking on this important subject.

I can, however, use these biases to pose some questions. If the history of agricultural policy and the major part of the research effort in the twentieth century has emphasized production agriculture based on the model of the family farm as the production unit with full-time occupations as the assumed labor relationship, then what do we have, in reality, today? Multiple job-holding, however defined, is a common feature of contemporary farming. Why is this so and what does it mean for future policy direction and research? From an agricultural perspective one can attribute the cause of so much multiple job-holding to changing relations in agriculture or one can seek answers by examining the changing structure of labor markets and rural economies. Some would suggest that changing social organization has much to do with it. In this chapter I propose examining multiple job-holding in Canadian agriculture in order to address some of these questions. The aim is to understand multiple job-holding at the household level, to see it as a function of local labor market opportunities as well as conditions in agriculture. I will seek to demonstrate what we have understood well and what we have misunderstood by reference to the history of Canadian research on the subject. The whole is set in the context of agricultural policy and change in industrialized societies.

The Canadian Picture

Multiple job-holding is an integral feature of Canadian farming, however measured and defined. Moreover, I would suggest that it has long been an integral part of the family mode of agricultural production. The full significance of multiple job-holding in Canada has recently been more fully examined and explored, due mainly to the efforts of Ray Bollman, whose work I shall draw upon frequently in this chapter.

There are three themes which I would like to pursue: (1) the historical perspective, (2) the research tradition, and (3) the present level of understanding. This tripartite approach will enable me to describe the Canadian picture and to conclude with a section on the dynamics of change and questions for the future.

The Historical Perspective

Multiple job-holding has long been a common element in the household economy. Farm households in Canada from the period of settlement have been involved in a variety of land management practices, commodity production, on-farm subsistence tasks, and community roles and responsibilities. Wietfeldt (1976, p. 208) expressed it well for the pioneer period in nineteenth-century Ontario in describing the tasks of a settler family in 1840:

> Cutting and clearing forest land, the logging connected with this land improvement, making pails or tubs for the house, repairing tools or making new ones, dressing the flax for spinning, making linen for bags as well as for the house, making boots, mittens, and harnesses from the hides they had tanned on shares, splitting and making shingles for the roof, making cane furniture, melting pewter and making spoons with molds, shoeing horses, leaching ashes and boiling lye to make potash for sale, laboring on public roads as required by statute, slaughtering meat for the household, transporting products to market and hauling in all building supplies, splitting rails for fences, and digging the well.

Over time, the nature of nonfarm and off-farm tasks changed and became more remunerative in a contractual sense. Mechanization in agriculture led not only to excess farm labor but to changes in the disposition of farm family labor especially in certain times of the year and on farms where, due to increased specialization, no livestock was kept. A Dominion Bureau of Statistics Report in 1960 noted the relationship between multiple job-holding on Canadian farms and wage occupations in industry. My point is that diversified household activity has been present for most farming families throughout the nineteenth and twentieth centuries, although the period from approximately 1940 to 1960 did witness the preeminence of full-time farming, when full-time and singular career paths were dominant.

In summary terms, *full-time farming is the aberration in modern farming history and multiple job-holding among farm households is the norm.* What has and will go on changing is the exact nature and combination of activities undertaken. Further study on the nature of pluriactive households may reveal much about the capital penetration of farming by absorbing surplus labor and the proletarianization effects this may have had on farm families.

The Research Tradition

The approach to multiple job-holding in Canada reflects the general approach to research on part-time farming in North America with three important additions. Generally, part-time farming has been approached as something of an anachronistic curiosity, being a feature of regional underdevelopment (Stewart 1944; Zeman 1961), structural rigidity (Brinkman and Warley 1983), marginal productivity (Lerner 1976) and, when not associated with small farms, being mainly classified with hobby farming (Troughton 1976). It is not that these attempts at classification are necessarily wrong, but that few seemed to realize until the last 10 years that multiple job-holding is, to a varying degree, part and parcel of *all* these farming systems and rural situations, and as such is a structural feature of farming and not a temporary or residual side effect. Almost all studies in Canada have focused on the farm operator and have classified farms and farming on standard social and economic attributes of farmer and farm operation (Steeves 1978; Bollman 1979a; Mage 1982; Turnbull 1963).

The 1975 Symposium on Part-Time Farming held at the University of Guelph reflects this research approach. Most papers were based on empirical research at the case study level and largely concerned classification of farms derived from multivariate analyses. Few heard the call by Cavazzani and Sivini (Italy) and Vogeler (United States) that structural approaches would potentially explain the proliferation of part-time farming in western agriculture (Fuller and Mage 1976).

Subsequently, Canadian studies have contributed three small but significant aspects to the multiple job-holding debate. The first concerns the entry and exiting phenomenon which has added more to our understanding of farm turnovers and the mobility of families into and out of agriculture. This was based on access to an excellent source of secondary data facilitated by linking the agriculture and population censuses over three census periods. Two points emerged. First, there has been, since 1960, very high turnover of census farms. This is not revealed when utilizing net figures which reflect only the residual position of farm structures at one point in time and ignore the dynamics of farm population movements (Steeves 1979). Second, much of the mobility of entry and exiting is associated, although differentially, with multiple job-holding. The focus here has been on beginning farmers and there is little information on the dynamics of operators who move into and out of multiple job-holding over time. This work has contributed to what Fuguitt (1959) established earlier in the United States, that multiple job-holding is associated with entry and exiting from farming. For example, Down (1982) found that new entrants to agriculture were particularly associated with multiple job-holding before and during the entry period. *Multiple job-holding helps to explain the mobility process, but mobility alone does not explain multiple job-holding.*

The second contribution is that made to policy issues. The phrase "benign neglect" was used to describe the Canadian policy position on part-time farming in 1975 (Crown 1976). Subsequently, Bollman (1979b, 1980, 1982) has examined several aspects of the policy issue. What emerges from these lines of enquiry is confirmation of the apparent insignificance of part-time farms in terms of agricultural policy as they appear to contribute little to overall agricultural production. Multiple job-holding farm families, however, are a different proposition. The policy focus on productivity and the issue of whether operators with nonfarm occupations are "real farmers" is raised by Bollman. The important point is that only real farmers, however defined, have been of central interest to agricultural policymakers. Issues of the utility of multiple job-holders as contributors to rural development, especially in remote and marginal areas, has not been systematically studied despite the concern on this point raised by the Europeans (Gasson 1977).

The third contribution has been the use of the time variable to describe some basic characteristics of multiple job-holding in Canada. Table 2.1 illustrates that of the 293,089 census farms in Canada in 1986, 60 percent of them were operated by operators who reported no off-farm work. These units produce 80 percent of total agricultural production and are therefore of economic importance to the sector. However, some significant contributions to production also come from units run by operators with some off-farm work (up to 97 days). It is evident from Table 2.2 that the proportion of census farm operators who worked off-farm increased only slightly between 1950 and 1980. However, the average time commitment of those who did spend some time off-farm rose substantially (Figure 2.1), especially in the greater-than-228-days category (Table 2.2).

Table 2.1. Multiple job-holding among Canadian farm operators, 1986

	Number of operators	Percent of total agricultural production
Total number of census farms	293,089	100.0
Farm operations with no off-farm work	177,445	80.0
Farm operations with off-farm work	115,644	20.0
Less than 97 days of off-farm work	82,107	17.8
97 days or more of off-farm work	33,537	2.2

Source: Statistics Canada, *Census of Agriculture,* 1986.

Table 2.2. Multiple job-holding among Canadian farm operators

	1950	1980
	Percent	
Farm operators working 1–228 days off the farm	22	25
Farm operators working more than than 228 days off the farm	6	14

Source: Statistics Canada, *Census of Agriculture,* 1950, 1980.

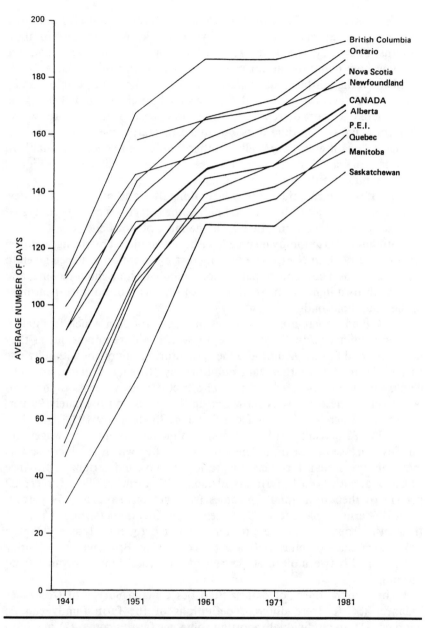

Figure 2.1. Average number of days spent off-farm by census farm operators, Canada and Provinces. (*Adapted from Mage 1982*)

This view of off-farm work in Canadian farming is useful only as a starting point, as many questions arise as to the full meaning of these patterns. First of all, the figures relate only to farm operators. It is essential to know how many of the operators with no off-farm work have family members in the nonfarm labor market. Similarly, the disposition of family labor would reveal a good deal more about households and farming on units where operators do report off-farm work. Because the operator works off-farm some of the time does *not* make the farm operation part-time, inefficient, or different, especially if other family members are available to do farm work and/or management. The question of labor substitution is underestimated in the time approach.

What is required, therefore, when taking this kind of macro-level view is for other variables to be used to analyze the categories already suggested by time spent off the farm. Income is the most obvious choice.

Studies of farm family income have been stimulated by the agricultural crisis of the 1980s in North America. Increasing attention has been given to farm income as a component part of total family or household income, and this has thrown light on the significance of off-farm (or nonfarm) earnings in the household budget.

In Canada, there are two sources of secondary data which facilitate a further examination of the income approach. Both are important, as they deal with total family income and the agricultural component within it. The first is the use of tax-filer data published by Revenue Canada, for self-employed, unincorporated farmers who report positive gross or nonzero net income. These statistics show that in the 1940s approximately 90 percent of total net income was from farming. In the early 1980s, this had declined to 52 percent. Within the nonfarm income component, wages and salaries increased most up to the late 1970s, after which the increase was mainly in investment income. In Ontario, the most industrialized province of Canada, with 114,615 farm tax filers in 1983, farm families averaged 22 percent of their total family incomes from net farm income, 59 percent from off-farm employment, 12 percent from investments, and 7 percent from other sources. Tax filers on farms reporting greater than $50,000 in gross farm sales (commercial farms according to Brinkman and Warley 1983) earned between 39 to 50 percent of their total family incomes from farming.

The second source of data is Statistics Canada Survey of Consumer Finances (SCF). Here different definitions of the farm family can be adopted: (1) one individual reporting some net farm income, (2) one individual reporting farming to be the major occupation, or (3) one individual reporting net farm income to be the major source of income. Bollman (1982) reported that for all three groups, "income from off-farm employment and income from investments have increased their share of family total net income at about the same rate." He also demonstrates that off-farm income is high on all types of farms (enterprises) and sizes of business (gross farm sales). It is also a phenomenon which is regionally diffused, although it is of less significance in the Canadian Prairies. The latter observation does not mean that the farming economy (grains) is doing well there. On the contrary, it reflects a lack of off-farm job opportunities.

Examining total family incomes through tax-filer data and Consumer Finance Survey data has been rewarding, although many problems remain. There is invariably the question of whether net farm income is a meaningful calculation. Small farms (less than $2,500 gross farm sales) inevitably report negative net farm incomes and total family income structures can become muddled when there is more than one tax filer per household. Despite this, income statistics at the total family level and time allocation figures based on the farm operator's off-farm work can provide a general picture of resources allocated to and derived from farming and nonfarm remunerative activities.

In Canada, generally, the time commitment to off-farm work is increasing, while the income derived from nonfarm sources, for most farm households, is proportionally higher than that derived from farming. It seems evident therefore to view the welfare of farm households as not only influenced by conditions in the farm economy, but also as a product of opportunities in the local and regional labor market. The fact remains that in Canada farm income levels are inferior, generally, to nonfarm incomes. Total farm family incomes, on the other hand, are almost on a par with nonfarm family incomes. The critical contribution that off-farm incomes make to income parity is well demonstrated.

Toward an Understanding of Multiple Job-holding

What emerges from this brief description of multiple job-holding in Canada is a very standard picture of western industrial agriculture wherein a strong tendency toward duality in the agricultural structure has already emerged, part-tenancy holdings are on the increase, and land holding for reasons other than commercial farming is becoming common. A series of regional variations across the country reflect local, environmental, and socioeconomic conditions. Multiple job-holding among farm households appears to be associated, randomly, with all types and variations of agriculture, whether farming in the rural-urban fringe or in the agricultural heartlands, whether in grain or livestock farming, or whether on large or small operations. It is evident that multiple job-holding is not exclusively a function of agriculture, as many have assumed, but is the product of a variety of factors. These, as suggested earlier, would include the local labor market and the desire of farm families to want to experience economic well-being and social development not unlike the perceived quality of life of households in the nonfarm sector.

What we seem to have omitted from our research agenda is an understanding of the dynamics of the many human resource situations in agriculture. Not only is there the movement of whole families into and out of farming, but the considerable mobility of families and members into and out of the local and regional labor markets, as well as occasional participation in the informal economy. There are seasonal dynamics too. What emerges is that multiple job-holding is another way of managing land on the one hand, and family resources as they mature and change on the other. Over time, demands and opportunities in farming change, families change as do their aspirations and needs, and the external environment may also change, providing different opportunities and limitations. Multiple job-holding is a simple, flexible mechanism for managing the adjustments necessary to accommodate change in any of the three spheres: the farm, the family, or the external environment. Although some configurations of family labor distribution may not maximize farm production or productivity, the overall benefits of multiple job-holding, for the family, may be optimal in economic and/or social terms.

Within the three blocks of changing circumstances (the farm, the family, and the external environment), the farm family mediates its own course of actions. The family itself is also governed by its own changing structure and needs over time. It is my understanding that a key mechanism for accommodating many of these needs and expectations on the one side, with changing exogenous circumstances on the other, is the perfectly natural tendency toward multiple job-holding.

In Praise of Multiple Job-holding

Multiple job-holding permits the substitution of labor in farming and often reduces the seasonal underemployment problem experienced on many farms in marginal areas. This is an essential but little understood dynamic. Off-farm incomes are significant for family budgets. Several studies suggest that capital is directed into agriculture from off-farm income sources. The direction and patterns of money flows within farm families are little-known phenomena. Off-farm incomes often enable farm families to remain on the land and to retain an effective link with agriculture. These are referred to as survival strategies, and may resemble the characteristics of persistence (Gilles and Cebotarev 1988). Multiple job-holding permits family members to enter the nonfarm labor market and to gain experience, skills, and satisfaction while in many cases exploring different career paths. In some instances, income, skills development, and the entrepreneurship acquired enables people to remain in the countryside, especially if they are able to develop microenterprises on their farms or in the local community. This may be particularly important for women (Reimer and Shaver 1988; Smith 1987). *Multiple job-holding is a flexible mechanism for adjusting to changes in agriculture, family needs, and shifts in the external environment.*

Multiple job-holding may play an important economic function at one point in the family cycle (e.g., when families are young) and a social function at another (e.g., when siblings are developing career paths). It enables farm families to spread income risks and to broaden their social networks. Theoretically, there is no reason to believe that multiple job-holding cannot serve economic, social, and psychological purposes for different household members at the same time, as well as over time. Clearly there are negative aspects of multiple job-holding, such as gender exploitation, stress due to high mobility, and conflict from changing household roles, and these need to be examined.

I mix these attributes of multiple job-holding deliberately because it is important to recognize that we are dealing with a multifunctional phenomenon which cannot be fully interpreted from a singular disciplinary or policy perspective. Multiple job-holding is a key dynamic of rural systems, and probably always has been.

In terms of agriculture and agricultural policy, multiple job-holding is not a particularly valuable concept. As we have seen, it is a mistake to assume that operators with off-farm work or off-farm income necessarily operate nonviable farms. Certainly some do, but so do many so-called full-time operators (those with no off-farm work). In terms of policy it is essential to keep separate the farm as a production unit and the farm household, which is an income/labor unit. Policies that support the *former* are clearly agricultural in nature and those that affect the latter are more social welfare oriented in intent, e.g., income support. Farm families occupy land, but increasingly earn less of their income from the land. This raises the question of whether farms are businesses where only farming can take place.

Future Prospects

It is in this context that some future prospects can be briefly mentioned. If multiple job-holding among farm families has been a useful mechanism in maintaining family incomes and overall quality of life in many rural areas, then it is likely to be even more important as agricultural restructuring continues. In an era of agricultural surpluses, diminishing trade options due to the development of Third-World food-production capacity and further technological revolutions in agriculture (biotechnology), it is likely that further separation between bulk food producers and other farmers will continue such that a functional decoupling could effectively take place whereby the top 15 to 20 percent of the producers become fully integrated into the food system and supply the major part of its needs. Many of these operators and their families will be multiple job-holders, but it is of little consequence. As we know, multiple job-holding serves a social, career-development, and life-satisfaction function which will apply to all families. The remaining farm families—the residuals—who are by far the majority of landholders, will be left to continue as best they can. They will be encouraged to diversify their operations and adopt sustainable farming practices. Both devices will have desirable environmental effects, as operators will be less pressured to produce at the maximum level and to take risks with their land. Many will be multiple job-holders with (relatively speaking) substantial off-farm incomes. Such families will occupy the bulk of the land resources in Canada and may well become seen as occupiers of land, given that their raison d'être may no longer be farming in the commercial or singular sense. Many will find niches in specialized markets (local, organic, ethnic) and others will occupy land as a family heritage, leisure unit, or the basis of a nonfarming enterprise.

Clearly, if such a basic division in landholders does occur, then policy options will also diverge. Multiple job-holding will be crucial to many occupiers of land, and policies that actively promote rural development will be needed, such as rural industrialization, local economic development, rural child care, transportation pools, and the further development of communication infrastructures. Agricultural conservation policies may need to be revised as might land-use planning controls. Agricultural training and extension will also have to adjust to accommodate a myriad of clienteles. Many of these adjustments are already on the way.

Clearly, for the rural residents of tomorrow, the ability to adjust to changing circumstances in farming, the household, and the external environment will depend upon their personal aspirations, flexibility, and institutional supports. Given that over 80 percent of farm families in industrialized nations already engage in multiple job-holding, the choice may have already been made.

References

Bollman, R. D. 1979a. "Off-farm work by farmers." Census Analystic Study, Cat. No. 99–756. Ottawa: Statistics Canada.

_____. 1979b. "Off-farm work by farmers: An application of the kinked demand for labour curve." *Canadian Journal of Agricultural Economics* 27(No. 3):37–60.

_____. 1980. "A comparison of money incomes of farmers and non farmers." *Canadian Journal of Agricultural Economics* Proceedings: 48–55.

_____. 1982. "Part-time farming in Canada: Issues and non-issues." *Geo-Journal* 6(No. 4):313–22.

Brinkman, G. L., and T. K. Warley. 1983. *Farming in Canada and Ontario in the 1980's: Changes in the Nature of Farms, Capital in Farming, and Farm Family Financial Returns.* Ontario: School of Agricultural Economics and Extension Education, University of Guelph.

Crown, R. 1976. "What should be done about part-time farming—implications for policy," in *Part-time Farming: Problem or Resource in Rural Development,* ed. A. M. Fuller and J. A. Mage, 198–206. Ontario: University of Guelph. (GeoAbstracts, Norwich, England.)

Down, J. 1982. "Characteristics of farm entrants and their enterprises in Southern Ontario 1966 to 1976." Working Paper No. 6. Ontario: Agricultural Statistics Division, Statistics Canada.

Fuguitt, G. V. 1959. "Part-time farming and the push-pull hypothesis." *American Journal of Sociology* 64 (Winter):375–79.

Fuller, A. M., and J. A. Mage, eds. 1976. *Part-Time Farming: Problem or Resource in Rural Development.* Ontario: University of Guelph. (GeoAbstracts, Norwich: England.)

Gasson, R., ed. 1977. "The Place of Part-Time Farming in Rural and Regional Development." CEAS, Seminar Paper 3. Ashford, England: Wye College.

Gilles, V., and E. A. Cebotarev. 1988. "Farmwomen's Off-Farm Work Contributions: A Comparative Study of Three Maritime Provinces." Paper presented to the Canadian Association of Rural Studies. Windsor, Ontario.

Lerner, A. 1976. "Classifying Part-time Farmers for Agricultural Policy Purposes." Unpublished report. Ontario: University of Guelph.

Mage, J. A. 1982. "The geography of part-time farming—a new vista for agricultural geographers." *GeoJournal* 6 (No. 4):301–12.

Reimer, W., and F. M. Shaver. 1988. "Les fermes familiales et les agricultrices au Quebec," *Agriculture et politiques agricoles: Transformations economique et sociales au Quebec et en France.* Paris: L'Harmatton.

Smith, P. 1987. "What lies written and behind the statistics?: Trying to measure women's contribution to Canadian agriculture," in *Growing Strong: Women in Agriculture,* 128–208. Ottawa: Canadian Advisory Council on the Status of Women.

Statistics Canada. 1950, 1980, 1986. *Census of Agriculture.* Ottawa: Statistics Canada.

Steeves, A. D. 1978. "The Occupational and Income Diversity of Canadian Census Farm Operators in 1971, Canada." Sociology and Anthropology Working Paper 78–5. Ottawa: Carleton University.

————. 1979. "Mobility into and out of Canadian agriculture." *Rural Sociology* 44(No. 3):566–83.

Stewart, A. 1944. *Part-time Farming in Nova Scotia.* Halifax: Institute for Public Affairs.

Troughton, M. J. 1976. "Hobby farming in the London area of Ontario," in *Part-Time Farming: Problem or Resource in Rural Development,* ed. A. M. Fuller and J. A. Mage, 137–53. Ontario: University of Guelph. (GeoAbstracts, Norwich, England.)

Turnbull, N. D. 1963. "Part-time farming in the North Okanagan, British Columbia, 1960." *The Economic Analyst* 33(No. 3):63–70.

Wietfeldt, R. 1976. "Attitudes of farmers' unions towards part-time farming," in *Part-Time Farming: Problem or Resource in Rural Development,* ed. A. M. Fuller and J. A. Mage, 207–12. Ontario: University of Guelph. (GeoAbstracts, Norwich, England.)

Zeman, J. 1961. "A study of small farms in the Rosetown-Elrose area of West-Central Saskatchewan." *Economic Analyst* 31(No. 3):60–66.

CHAPTER 3

Motivations of
Part-time Farmers

PEGGY F. BARLETT

Why Study Part-time Farmers?

Multiple job-holding has been an important adaptive strategy
to increase family income and spread risk throughout history.
Peasants in ancient China mixed agricultural production with craft work
and retail activities to achieve a higher standard of living (Rawski 1972).
Farm families in Central America combine independent agricultural production with farm labor on plantations in certain seasons, to gain an adequate income (Bossen 1984). In many North American rural communities
100 years ago, doctors, butchers, or other specialists often owned land and
produced crops and livestock for family consumption and for sale (Allen et
al. 1937). As Fuller (Chapter 2, this volume) has said, full-time farming
with no additional off-farm income is the historical exception, not the rule.
Furthermore, as Ahearn and Lee (Chapter 1, this volume) point out, many

This study was supported by the National Science Foundation under grants #BNS-
8121459 and BNS-8618159 and by the National Geographic Society and Emory University.
Any opinions, findings, conclusions, or recommendations expressed in this publication are
those of the author and do not necessarily reflect the views of the National Science Foundation
or the other sponsors.

I would like to express my gratitude to Marc Brooks, Elizabeth Guthrie, and Paul Dark
for their assistance in data collection and analysis. The encouragement and cooperation of the
University of Georgia College of Agriculture, and the Dodge County Cooperative Extension
Service and Agricultural Stabilization and Conservation Service, are greatly appreciated.

multiple job-holding families are not poor. They may not even present a policy challenge or social problem to be addressed.

Why is it important to study these farm families? First, because the North American structure of farming is undergoing important changes at present, and the numbers, types, and sizes of farms that survive in the United States and Canada have important implications for the quality and security of our food supply and the welfare of rural areas. Second, the agricultural sector has had to adjust economically in recent years to a severe slump and rapidly changing government policies as well. The impact of this recession is of immediate national concern, and farm families that also have sources of off-farm income are a substantial component of the farm sector.

Third, the very existence of multiple job-holding farm families is of interest to us as students of current societal change. Also called part-time farmers, a term I shall use interchangeably with multiple job-holders, they represent an important and growing population that uses resources, contributes to the national food supply, and both participates in and affects the welfare of local communities. Their decisions to combine jobs and farming in particular ways provides insight into the interaction of economic, political, and familial changes in contemporary industrial society. Their values and goals clarify the character of this historical moment, and their plans and choices will create a future that perpetuates or alters various aspects of modern life.

The multiple job-holding family is interesting to this researcher because it combines several income sources in order to achieve a desired standard of living. In most cases, the part-time farming husband's off-farm income is sufficient to provide a consumption level comparable to many one-income households in the country. In most cases, women's incomes are lower than men's, but still sufficient to support a family at a consumption level not uncommon nationally. To these two (or more) income sources is added a farm, though its contribution to the total family income does not challenge the primacy of salaries. What is interesting is that usually all three sources of revenue are combined, in spite of the significant increase in workload, risk, and loss of leisure. Why this choice is desirable is the subject of this chapter.

The decisions of multiple job-holding farm families cannot be understood apart from their cultural context. The late twentieth century has seen transformations in many aspects of life, and part-time farming families are responding to these changes

1. in work life, both its daily character, its rewards, and in our societal evaluation of work;

2. in family ties, the meaning of marriage, commitment to the family enterprise, child-rearing, and ties with broader kin groups;

3. in standards of living, expectations about lifestyles, and attitudes toward deferred gratification, consumption, and self-esteem;

4. in notions about class, upward mobility, citizenship, and the role of education, income, and occupation within rapidly changing rural and urban communities; and

5. in beliefs about religion, spirituality, the meaning of life, and a growing cultural ambivalence about the secularization of society, including concerns about stewardship, morality, conformity, and self-actualization.

As they chart their path through these changes, multiple job-holding families are in a highly favored position. As the world faces an ever-growing population, with increasing poverty for many, the citizens of the industrialized nations experience a high and often rising standard of living. Alienation from productive agricultural resources has brought pauperization to many groups in Latin America, Asia, and Africa, but has for the most part been accompanied by job opportunities in industrial societies.

In this context, multiple job-holding farm families in North America can be interpreted to be concentrating income sources to gain a higher consumption level. Not only are one or more jobs combined with working the land, but the family's total work effort is intensified as well. More hours of work and the resources (jobs or land) that might otherwise have supported three families are combined in one—an option available only to a fortunate few. Others (in the United States and other industrial societies) have no access to land for farming nor to even one adequate off-farm salary.

A second interpretation of the part-time farming decision is that it allows families the benefits of stable salaries while also giving them the security of control over productive resources. At a time when many of the world's peoples are forced to accept their helplessness in the face of industrial change and job loss, the multiple job-holding family holds onto family land, recognizing both its monetary value and its ability to ensure survival if other income sources fail. Landownership cements class status as well. These perspectives are not necessarily shared by the part-time farm families themselves, but provide a way of interpreting the phenomenon of multiple job-holding, within the context of global economic development. In this discussion of the motivations of part-time farmers, attempts to express the opinions and meanings of the farm families studied will be combined with interpretations from the researcher's perspective. The purposes of studying multiple job-holders outlined above cannot be achieved without a combination of these two foci.

From Local Studies to Regional Definitions

Given the centrality of agriculture structure in my research goals, this study concentrates on farm families in particular, not rural residents in general. To explore the decisions and motivations of farm families—and also to test the validity of survey measures of farm structure—an intensive study of one county was found to be most useful. A county was chosen in the Coastal Plain of Georgia that was average for the region in its production of row crops (corn, soybeans, wheat, peanuts, cotton, and tobacco) and livestock (hogs and cattle). No study of one county in one state can be used to understand the complexities of the whole continent. But where local conditions show considerable similarity to national processes, some insights can be gained. Dodge County was chosen with the help of many experts to be as typical as possible of the mainstream of row-crop and livestock agriculture in the Southeast. A statistical comparison shows that in 1982, Dodge County was quite similar to the means and proportions of the Georgia Coastal Plain and the United States as a whole (Table 3.1).

Table 3.1. Agriculture in the Georgia Coastal Plain and the United States

	Dodge County sample	Coastal Plain counties[a]	United States[b]
Mean farm acreage	414	409	440
Farms 1,000 acres and over	6%	3%	8%
Mean gross farm sales	$61,373	$73,747	$58,858
Farms with sales			
$100,000 and over	19%	17%	13%
Part-time farmers[c]	34%	39%	36%
Mean age of operator	47.3	50.6	50.5

[a]Mean of 57 counties, from 1982 *Census of Agriculture*.
[b]*Source:* U.S. Department of Commerce 1983.
[c]Farm operators who work 200 or more days per year off the farm.

Because the county was too large to interview all farmers, a random sample of half the farmers in the county carried out in 1982 yielded 124 farms and 156 farm families. Participant observation, formal interviews, questionnaires, and telephone surveys with these families were carried out for nine months in 1982 and 1983 and for eight months in 1987. The analysis of multiple job-holders presented here draws primarily from the results of this newer five-year follow-up in which husbands and wives were mostly interviewed separately (as advocated by Garrett, Schulman, and Herath 1984 and Buttel and Gillespie 1984).

Kada (1980, p. 13) has said that part-time farming is "a highly complex phenomenon," and most researchers stress the great variability within the group (Buttel 1983; Fuguitt et al. 1977; Fuller 1983). This volume explores well the wide variety of definitions used by different researchers to isolate populations for study. Following Fuguitt (1961), who advised narrowing our categories to create a manageable population for study, this study uses a number of empirical findings in the literature to suggest fruitful ways to define a meaningful group of multiple job-holders.

The first issue—*amount of off-farm work*—has been addressed by Van Es et al. (1982), Salant (1984), and Kada (1980), who found that full-time jobs were the most common type of employment by farm operators; part-time jobs are usually seasonal work connected with a larger, full-time farm operation. Given the rising participation of farm women in off-farm, non-agricultural labor markets, to use Kada's definition of 30 days or more off-farm work by any family member would inappropriately deplete the ranks of full-time farmers and unnecessarily complicate the analysis of part-time farming. For some research purposes, such a broader definition of multiple job-holders would be appropriate, but given the goals stated above, multi-ple job-holding families are defined here as those working 200 or more days per year at an off-farm job (full-time jobs).

The second issue—*whose off-farm work*—has also been studied by Salant (1984), Bokemeier and Coughenour (1980), Coughenour and Swan-son (1983), and Cawley (1983). These authors found that whether or not the *operator* worked off the farm had a strong impact on farm size, en-terprise mix, and sales, while the *wife's* off-farm work had a much less significant impact.

These definitional criteria emerged as the most useful in the 1982 study of all sizes and types of farmers in Dodge County (Barlett 1984, 1987). Analysis of these 124 farms revealed three distinct types: full-time farms, part-time farms, and retirement farms. Where operators had no off-farm work (retired operators excluded), median acreage in production whether the wife had a job or not was 246 versus 220 acres. Median sales for both groups fell in the $40,000–$99,999 category. (In this study, there are both male and female operators, but since none of the female operators is cur-rently married, the more descriptive term *wives* is used instead of the gen-der-neutral *spouses*.) When operators had jobs, acreage dropped to nearly a fourth (58 versus 49 acres) and both groups had a median $10,000–$19,999 gross sales. Analysis by size and sales deciles showed a similar pattern (Barlett 1986, p. 295).

Regional and commodity variation must be expected in designing defi-nitions of part-time farming and multiple job-holding. Dairy production requires close family cooperation, and numerous studies show farm women to be active and to consider themselves operators on dairy farms. In con-trast, midwestern row-crop and livestock farms tend to reveal a sharper division of labor between household and domestic tasks and agricultural production for sale. The southeastern crop and livestock farm shares much of its commodity mix and gender roles with these midwestern farms. In areas where few jobs are available for women or men, appropriate definitions must also change. Only a series of detailed local studies can point the way to valid regional definitions.

The Career Choice

Several ideas of the origin of part-time farming have held sway in the social science literature since World War II. Early studies tended to see multiple job-holding as a temporary phenomenon, but that view has been replaced over the last decade by research that notes the persistence of these families over time (Albrecht and Murdock 1984; Coughenour and Gabbard 1977; Fuller 1976; Saupe and Salant 1985). The root of the decision to combine farming and jobs, however, is often interpreted as the farm's failure to "make it" as a full-time operation. Thus, multiple job-holders are seen as *transitional,* downwardly mobile full-time farmers, "squeezed out" by an unfavorable economic climate and competition from larger farms (Buttel 1982; Buttel et al. 1982; Coughenour and Swanson 1983; Gladwin and Zabawa 1987; Molnar and Smith 1983; Rosenfeld 1985; Wimberley 1983; Zabawa 1987). Many studies assume a primary commitment to farming (Buttel and Gillespie 1984; Kada 1980), though Bollman and Kapitany (1981) found evidence in Canada to suggest that more part-time farmers have jobs prior to beginning farming. A few have also argued that multiple job-holding is a transitional stage prior to entering full-time farming (Huffman 1977; Wilkening and Gilbert 1987). Little of this research has been carried out in a way that tests these assumptions about the intentions and motivations of multiple job-holders, in spite of Mage's call for such an approach (Mage 1976).

The Dodge County study revealed that shortly after completing his education, a young man usually makes a career decision whether or not to farm or to seek an off-farm job. Data on part-time farmers' decisions and work histories showed that in two-thirds of the cases (67.4 percent), a commitment to a job became primary, and, as found by Harrison (1966) in England as well, most operators had no intention to farm full-time. Later, half before age 30 and half after, a second decision was made to add farm production to other activities. I have called this group the *standard* part-time farmers. Since the combination of job and farm began as a conscious rejection of full-time farming in most cases, multiple job-holding can thus be seen as based on two decisions: first, the career decision; and second, the decision to add a farm later in life.

Though a minority, there is a group that conforms to the expectations that all part-time farmers are transitional. These are full-time farm operators who obtained off-farm work because they face heavy losses and high debt loads in the current farm financial crisis. In the 1987 study, the *transitional* group made up 18.4 percent of the total. They show differing degrees of acceptance of multiple job-holding; some are sure they will return to full-time farming once their debt negotiations are resolved or the farm economy improves. Others expect to scale back their farming activities over time. In some analyses below, the whole sample of multiple job-holders is used. In other sections, such as when exploring the motivations to avoid full-time farming, the transitional cases are excluded.

There are an additional seven cases in the study who chose originally to farm full-time, but who became transitional prior to the 1970s (most left farming in the 1950s). They are lumped here with the standard type because, with experience, they revised their original career decision and chose stable multiple job-holding instead. Their average duration as full-time farmers was five years. Their reasons for rejecting full-time farming are the same as the reasons expressed by the other standard part-time farmers.

The 1982 study distinguished a third group of part-time farmers, the *investors,* and they have persisted with some distinct characteristics. These operators all employ a full-time hired hand and generally are much less involved in day-to-day operations. Most inherited their land and continue farming for diverse reasons—investment being primary among them. Said one investor: "I'm not a big farmer, nor a good farmer, but I'm proud to be a landowner."

Factors Affecting Career Decisions

Career decisions are affected by a range of factors, including lifestyle aspirations, farm background, attitudes toward farming, parental attitudes and expectations, enjoyment of farm work, available land and capital resources, and job opportunities. The interviews with Dodge County multiple job-holders reveal not only their motivations and career decisions, but also provide insights into the cultural values and aspirations behind their choices.

Most men and women on part-time farms in Dodge County came from farm backgrounds. Figure 3.1 shows that most commonly, they grew up on small to medium family farms; in 45 percent of the sample, parents owned farms under 275 acres. Another 22 percent came from elite farm backgrounds (from 275 acres to several thousand). A small group (12 percent) were children of sharecroppers or farm renters, and in 15 percent of the cases parents did not farm or quit farming early in life. Figure 3.1 shows that wives are more heterogeneous in their farm backgrounds: 80 percent of operators come from farm owner backgrounds, compared to only half (51 percent) of the wives. A third of wives are from nonfarm families, though only 10 percent of operators have this background. These figures confirm that most people who join farming and jobs learned farm skills at home and choose to continue that way of life. That women are more likely to come from nonfarm families suggests that husbands' farm experience may play a greater role than wives'. Van Es et al. (1982) also found that Illinois part-time farm women are more likely than their husbands to be from nonfarm families. The background of part-time farmers also confirms that they are a relatively fortunate group. The majority of Georgia farm operators in the 1930s were tenants and sharecroppers. That the study sample is drawn mainly from landowners suggests that this choice is not so feasible for the larger group of children of landless farm families.

The career decision, whether to farm for a living or rely on a job, is made early in life and reflects the opinions of the late teenage years. Dodge County interviewees were asked to recall their attitudes toward farming

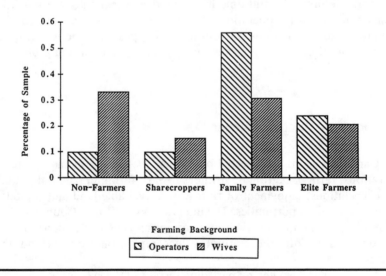

Figure 3.1. Farm background of part-time farmers in Dodge County—operators (N = 50) and wives (N = 39). (*1987 study*)

when they got out of school. Only 43 percent reported having had positive feelings about farming or the farm life. "I loved it; I always wanted to farm" is a typical comment. Slightly more (48 percent) said they had no interest in farming or were opposed or even hostile to the idea. When transitionals were excluded, positive feelings about farming were even more rare. Said one woman, "My whole heart's desire was to do something else besides pick cotton and hoe peanuts. I said to myself, 'I want to get *away* from this cotton patch.' I wanted a better life." Those people with negative attitudes toward farming came to modify them as they grew older, wanted to rear their children in the country, became less satisfied with their off-farm jobs, or as machinery and chemicals made farm work easier.

The historical context must be remembered in evaluating these attitudes. Many Dodge Countians emphasized that farm work was very different "back then." Many had grown up with summers of hot, hard field work, picking cotton, and stacking peanuts by hand. Some remembered working with mules; farm houses often had no electricity or running water. "We weren't *poor*," insisted one such man. "Everybody was the same." Houses without central heat and without bathrooms were common, and farming was identified with this kind of life. Desires to "do better" reflected a judgment that off-farm jobs provided a better opportunity to change that lifestyle. Such desires for upward mobility and affluence are not unique, of course, to the South, as Fink's (1986b) research on nineteenth-century Iowa has shown.

Disadvantages of Full-time Farming

To explore the career choice, three kinds of questions were asked in interviews with multiple job-holding families. First were very open-ended discussions about people's attitudes toward farming as they were leaving school, their aspirations, and their work history. Second, respondents were asked what things they liked and disliked about farming. Third, a composite list of disadvantages of full-time farming and advantages of part-time farming was generated from the 1982 study, and people were asked to indicate which reasons were true for them. The three sources combined to produce a complex picture of respondents' attitudes and changing decisions over their lifetimes. The third, more structured, set of questions gave a sense of the distribution of reasons for multiple job-holding. The more open-ended responses produced some interesting contrasts between husbands and wives, to be discussed later. This section will look at the career decision from the operator's perspective.

Table 3.2 summarizes the disadvantages of full-time farming. Overwhelmingly, financial considerations have priority. The income available from farming was held by 91 percent to be simply inadequate and unacceptable. "You can't make any money," summarized this point of view. A large group also agreed that the risk and uncertainty in farm incomes was troublesome to them; they much preferred the stability of a paycheck. About half also stressed they chose a job because no pension or medical insurance was available from farming. These financial considerations were primary in the open-ended discussions as well: "It just couldn't support the lifestyle we wanted."

Table 3.2. Operator responses on disadvantages of full-time farming

	Number (N = total no. of respondents)	Percent
Inadequate income	30	90.9
Risk/uncertainty	23	69.7
No fringe benefits (pension, insurance)	18	54.5
Capital constraints	14	42.4
Land constraints	10	30.3
Prefer work of job	10	30.3
Desire to do better	10	30.3
Long hours/hard work	3	9.1

Note: Transitional farmers excluded.

In addition to dissatisfaction with farm incomes, 42 percent indicated they had insufficient capital to farm. In most cases, this judgment reflects the fact that the young operator needed to buy land or equipment and was unable to do so. Several pointed out that loan programs to help aspiring young farmers without assets were not available then. As for land resources, about a third agreed that insufficient land was one of the reasons they had rejected full-time farming. This low response was a surprise because one of the hypotheses of the study was that operators judged farm incomes to be inadequate because of small farm size. Further discussion on this issue revealed that most operators felt substantial land resources had been available to them, but — regardless of farm scale — the income generated was inadequate and irregular.

These reasons to reject full-time farming and choose an off-farm career reveal a primary commitment to a certain level of family consumption. Were these families willing to share the standard of living of their parents, farm incomes would not be evaluated so harshly. Instead, married life without a new house, new furniture, a new car at regular intervals, and other household conveniences is not acceptable. Farming is furthermore seen as too risky. Steady income and a reliable consumption standard from year to year are valued highly. Some of the multiple job-holders remember parents or grandparents suffering farm loss in the Depression. Many watched their farmer parents face difficult years when bills were hard to pay. Their choice to depend on a job reflects their changing aspirations in a much more affluent Southern Coastal Plain. Said one: "I didn't want to continue the farm life I grew up with; those were the bad old days!"

This desire for greater affluence was rarely expressed in terms of relative social status. Most part-time farmers did not complain of feeling inferior as children, of wanting to escape the lower rungs of the local prestige hierarchy. Higher consumption was not linked with being taken more seriously by peers or neighbors or changing one's place in society. Quite the contrary, a more middle-class lifestyle is seen as the norm and the multiple job-holding family seeks simply to move along with the rest of society. Farming can no longer provide that level of income and so is rejected as a primary life's work.

For a minority, the rejection of full-time farming is linked to social class aspirations. Some children of small farmers and sharecroppers complained about lower status in school, about not having treats or clothes that wealthier friends had. These people admit that their lifetime goals involve keeping up with the Joneses and giving their children things that other families can afford. The majority of part-time farmers interviewed, however, did not share this more competitive perspective.

The Decision to Add a Farm

It is widely recognized that multiple job-holding combines economic as well as a range of nonpecuniary benefits (Brooks, Stucker, and Bailey 1986; Coughenour and Gabbard 1977; Gladwin 1985; Paarlberg 1980; Rupena-Osolnik 1983), though studies differ in the extent to which a rural lifestyle is the primary goal of the part-time farming family. The decision to take on farm activities in Dodge County reveals the continued centrality of financial concerns, but also addresses several other aspects of changing cultural values, including family life, recreation, and spiritual issues.

Looking at financial reasons first (Table 3.3), the farm is seen by 85 percent of operators as a second job. The decision to add a farm is therefore justified as part of the operator's pursuit of affluence and part of the role of breadwinner. Future income is also important; nearly three-fourths of the sample see farming as a long-term plan to assure additional income on retirement. As one man said, making $2,000–$3,000 on the farm today "isn't making *anything*. But it *would* be if we were retired."

Table 3.3. Operator responses on advantages of part-time farming

	Number (N = total no. of respondents)	Percent
Financial		
Second income	28	84.8
Retirement income	24	72.7
Investment	18	54.5
Security	13	39.4
Inherited land; prefer not to rent	13	39.4
Personal and familial		
Enjoy farm work	31	93.9
Continue family tradition/keep homeplace	24	72.7
Higher quality diet	20	60.6
Rear children in country/rural residence	18	54.5
Inheritance for children	13	39.4

Note: Transitional farmers excluded.

Buying a farm is also a form of investment and forced savings (55 percent). A few couples admitted they would not have accumulated the same level of assets had they not had a mortgage to pay off. Only a few felt they had benefitted from reduced taxes; most felt farm expenses greatly outweighed tax savings. For nearly 40 percent, owning a farm represents security, "something to fall back on if anything should happen to my job." For some, this security guards against a second national depression, though others want the security of assets in being an established property owner. A surprisingly high 40 percent agreed that a significant part of their decision to farm was precipitated by inheriting land. Some were unable to find renters to work the land for them; others were unwilling to risk the possible harm to the land that renters might cause. Many of these cases are in the investors group. They probably would not have chosen to buy a farm if it had not become available to them in this way. In other cases, inheriting the land simply made easy an option that might otherwise have been delayed.

One of the revelations of the 1987 interviews was the central role of family land. Though in the 1982 interviews many part-time farmers stated family land was not a major factor in their decision to farm, further questions about the sources of farmland for rent or purchase revealed that 90 percent of multiple job-holders use at least some family land. In many cases, this is the parents' farm—"the homeplace"—but in others, it is land that belonged to aunts, grandparents, or cousins. Sometimes direct heirs do not want the land and so it becomes available to a nearby but more distant relative. The land is usually purchased, and owners or heirs paid the going price. About a fifth asserted that though a farm had become available from family, they were prepared to buy from nonkin in order to begin farming. This pattern suggests that a desire for the farm life and rural residence is connected in most cases to a particular, familiar piece of land and residence in a well-known rural community.

Turning to personal and family reasons for farming, the recreation and enjoyment of farm work is central to nearly every operator's decision to farm. As found in many studies (Coughenour and Gabbard 1977; Coughenour and Swanson 1983; Van Es et al. 1982), this enjoyment of farm work recognizes the change of pace from the daily grind: "It breaks the monotony of my job." A wide range of operators, from skilled, blue-collar workers to professionals, called the farm "therapy" from the stresses of their jobs. They appreciate the peace of working alone on a tractor and the escape from interpersonal pressures. Some like the physical labor, while all like the satisfactions of being their own boss, seeing tangible results of effort, and being outdoors. Hunting and fishing are also benefits on some farms.

In spite of negative attitudes toward farming when they were young, many agreed they farm in part to continue a family tradition and keep the home place in the family (73 percent). Sixty percent value the better diet of fresh vegetables and carefully fattened hogs and cattle. About half stressed that the farm allowed them to raise children in the country, an environment considered to be sharply superior to trying to keep kids out of trouble in town. Being able to bequeath children the land as inheritance—and even to give them an opportunity to farm for a living—motivated 40 percent of the cases interviewed. Many of these personal and familial reasons combine a lifestyle preference with a financial advantage. For example, rearing children in the country is cheaper, said some, as well as more likely to provide a positive environment.

In addition to these benefits of farming, the decision to add a farm is affected by several other factors. The economic climate seems to play a role; more current part-time farmers began farming during the decade of the 1970s, when farm incomes were high and optimism reigned, than in other decades. Slumps also seem to discourage would-be part-timers. A number of people in the study became multiple job-holders in the early 1950s, but after the recession and drought of 1953, interest in part-time farming slowed. Another factor that affects the decision to add a farm is the family's need for additional income. As children grow older and expenses rise, many operators desire a second job and begin farming. In some cases, the timing of the decision to add a farm was determined by parents' health. Illness or injury to an aging farmer father can force children to help out. This experience allowed several operators to rediscover their enjoyment of farm work, and to take over the farm when their fathers retired or died.

In open-ended discussions with farmers, a religious or spiritual aspect of farming commonly emerged as well as these more tangible issues. Many operators expressed a deep love of nature, of satisfaction in being outdoors, and of "watching things grow." Further discussion revealed they value farming because it allows them a connection to the fundamental issues of life, birth, and regeneration. Many talk about farming as a way to become closer "to God and His works." The fact that these aspects of farming were expressed in spite of cultural prohibitions against self-revelation and emotion shows their centrality in the thinking of many part-time farm operators. Farmers were simply unable to explain why they make these choices without including these religious dimensions.

Farming's connection to deeper meanings of life point out some of the ways multiple job-holding responds to dilemmas facing many in all walks of industrial life. The need for spiritual satisfaction that is met in this case by farming is met by some urbanites in New Age practices or by other rural residents in Christian charismatic churches. As many traditional rural values are tarnished and questioned and as daily rhythms of effort seem divorced from a higher purpose, farming reconnects people to nature and the supernatural.

The desire to add a farm can be seen as a response to the unsatisfying nature of many jobs. Work life is often frustrating, tedious, and stressful for many in our society, and probably no more so in Dodge County. What is unusual is that these workers have access to a type of second job that provides such a sharp contrast to the first. The satisfactions of watching things grow, of tangible production, provide an antidote to the alienations of salaried employment. Employees all over the country seek such antidotes, but mostly in hobbies or recreation — spending money, not making money as farmers hope to do. Part of the passion with which farming is embraced comes precisely from the conjunction of these two dimensions. Part-time farming can fulfill both the cultural imperative to earn more and accumulate more goods while at the same time providing some therapeutic recreation from the primary job. It mixes production and consumption characteristics, lifestyle and breadwinning, masculine work role as well as play.

Parental Attitudes toward Farming

It is commonly assumed that farm parents want their children to continue in farming and highly value farm continuity. Though most part-time farmers in Dodge County grew up in farm families, their parents were not always supportive about farming as a career choice. When asked what their parents' aspiration had been for them, 49 percent of the men and women interviewed reported that their fathers had been negative or neutral about farming full-time. Of their mothers, 54 percent had not been supportive of a farming career. Discussions with some of these parents confirmed these opinions. Parents were sometimes reported to have expressed strong negative opinions about farming: "She saw it wasn't a good life and wanted me to make money." "Farming wasn't his thing; it had held him down too much." Other times parents were neutral: "They put no pressure on us — never encouraged us to farm." "They wanted me to do whatever I wanted." Positive feelings were expressed directly, in affirming a high evaluation of farming: "Farming's the best life there is," and indirectly in satisfaction with children's choice to continue: "There was no pressure, but he was proud I stayed on."

Parents' attitudes reflect the same emphasis the operators place on the financial support a farm provides. One woman reported her mother was very positive about farming and the financial life, "but she saw that the income was limited." Several reported that their parents wanted them to "do better in life." "My father didn't ever want me to depend on farming for a living." In many of these accounts, farming is seen as having a mix of positive and negative attributes but its poor ability to provide a comfortable lifestyle makes many parents urge their children to avoid it. These comments show that a revered farm tradition is not the inheritance of all farm children. Their parents participate as well in the recognition of a rising national standard of living. In half the cases in Dodge County, expectations for children do not include reproduction of the family's agricultural enterprise, and "a better life" in financial terms is a primary goal. Farming has many virtues and the rural life has many advantages that are appreciated, but not at the cost of relative poverty. Thus, part-time farmers' balancing of personal, familial, and financial options does not in all cases represent a sharp break with parental expectation, though in half the cases, it does. These parental attitudes may vary by ethnic group and by region of the country, but this particular southern case, echoed by Fink's (1986a) research in Iowa, provides a caution to simple generalizations about agrarian ideology and the love of "farming as a way of life."

Multiple Job-holding Families and Wives' Farm Involvement

Recent research has emphasized the importance of seeing the farm in a family context, and giving appropriate credit to women's involvement and contribution (Bokemeier and Coughenour 1980; Bollman 1981; Coughenour 1984; Gladwin 1985; Pearson 1979; Tigges and Rosenfeld 1987; Wilkening and Gilbert 1987). These studies vary in the extent to which women are seen as primary contributors to the farm operation, farm helpers, or primarily housewives (Buttel and Gillespie 1984; Gladwin 1985; Rosenfeld 1985; Sharp, Gwynn, and Thompson 1986). Several researchers have begun to explore the ways in which wives' attitudes and goals are different from their husbands', debunking the romantic view that farm families are necessarily of one mind (Bokemeier and Garkovich 1987; Garrett, Schulman and Herath 1984; Fink 1986b; Sachs 1983). Women's commitment to the farm and their participation in and approval of the decision to farm cannot be taken for granted in multiple job-holding families. For example, several Dodge County operators indicated in the 1982 study that the farm was their responsibility alone: "The way I see it, it's my job to provide the living and her job to take care of the house." To clarify the operator's point of view, the 1987 study pursued these attitudes in greater depth, asking among other things, whether farmers saw the farm more as a family project, a personal hobby, or a second job. They were also asked the disposition of farm income; Table 3.4 reveals the results.

Table 3.4. Operator's perception of farm

Farm is mainly a	%
family project	10.3
personal hobby	53.8
second job	51.3
Farm income goes to	
pay household bills	17.9
make special purchases	15.4
farm investments only	87.2

Only 10 percent of the cases interviewed agree that the farm is a family project. About equal numbers saw it as primarily a personal hobby and a second job. (Some felt it was a combination of these options, hence percentages do not sum to 100.) These data confirm that, for many, the farm is part of an operator's breadwinning role; most of the rest see it as primarily his personal recreation. The farm's limited contribution to the whole family is underscored by the overwhelming degree to which income from the farm is reinvested there. Only 18 percent of the part-time farmers said their farms helped with household expenses. This low figure should not be interpreted to discredit the financial goals of farming; it reflects the very poor profit levels of the last decade, and the extent to which financial aspirations have not been realized.

One of the unexpected findings of the 1982 Dodge County work was the extent to which farm women expressed alienation from the farm and, in some cases, their disapproval of the decision to farm. Both open-ended and closed questions were used to explore the extent to which women share their husbands' enthusiasm and commitment to the farm. A few Dodge County women are the primary farm operators, and their opinions were reported in previous sections; the majority of women connected to part-time farms are married to farm operators. In the 1987 study, wives of part-time farmers were asked about their attitude toward farming when they were young adults as well as their current attitudes and the history of their farm involvement.

As would be predicted, many farm women expressed a love of farming and support for the decision to operate a farm, but this group numbered less than half the total (45 percent). Others were more cautious about the value of agricultural production, but expressed enthusiasm for rural life (see Table 3.5). These two groups together make up slightly over half the 40 women interviewed (53 percent). Positive comments include "I'm proud to be continuing my family's tradition." "I enjoy farm work and living *out*." Another 45 percent of wives interviewed were negative about farming for various reasons. "It's just not worth what you put into it," summarizes one of these negative points of view. Financial disappointments and the drain on the family's resources are a big part of this evaluation. The long hours and strain on their husbands, especially during drought years is another component. Referring to the combination of debts and drought, one woman said, "the last five years have been living hell."

Table 3.5. Wives' attitudes toward farming

	Whole sample ($N = 40$)	Transitionals excluded ($N = 33$)
	Percent	
Positive evaluation of farming	53	58
Commitment to farms as family project	45	49
Rural residence highly valued	30	27
Negative evaluation of farming	45	39

As reported in other studies (Barlett 1986; Buttel and Gillespie 1984; Craig, Lambert, and Moore 1983; Sharp, Gwynn, and Thompson 1986; Van Es et al. 1982), most women on part-time farms do relatively little farm work. "I don't fool with the farm at all," said one. "Housework is my job." Especially those who are negative about farming engage in few activities on the farm, and thus the husband's evaluation that the farm is his own hobby is an accurate representation for approximately half the cases. Even where women do little farm work, they sometimes express a joint commitment to the farm. In 45 percent of the cases, wives see the farm as a family project. The fact that this figure is substantially higher than for operators suggests that some women see themselves as supporting the farm or sharing in the overall decision in favor of multiple job-holding. "I try to help him, but that doesn't mean I like it." In other cases, women like farming and would like to do more farm work but are constrained by childcare and domestic or job responsibilities. Others have allergies or other health problems that keep them away from the farm activities, though they would enjoy the work if they were able to do it.

Women's attitudes about farming can combine positive and negative aspects in a complex mix. In one case, a woman who came from an elite farm background expressed strong negative attitudes toward her childhood and farm work. She always wanted to have an off-farm job, obtained the necessary training, and kept a job throughout her married life. Her husband began to operate his family's farm when his parents died, and she supported that decision and still does. In terms of activities, she has no involvement with any aspect of the farm work, rarely visits the farm, and her husband says she'd be unable to identify its boundaries. Yet she articulates strong support of the farm life and states that she would accept a dramatic drop in her standard of living in order to keep from losing the land. She was one of few women of over 40 interviewed who would hypothetically agree to trade some level of the family's consumption for assured farm survival. Though atypical, this case cautions against easy assumptions about the connections between farm attitudes, farm work, and support for the husband's farm activities.

This divergence of men's and women's attitudes is revealed in the responses to the open-ended questions (Tables 3.6, 3.7): What do you like about farming? and What do you like least about farming? In general, women responded less and were more likely to say "nothing" or "I don't know." Their most frequently cited reason for liking farming was to live in the country and raise children there (44 percent). A little over a third (37 percent) expressed the love of nature and of watching things grow that was discussed for operators. Growing a garden and enjoying a better diet were also mentioned by a third. For over a quarter of the women, their favorite thing about farming was that their husband enjoyed it so much. Support of his preference reflects the fact that the farm is much more his choice than hers.

Three contrasts between operators' and wives' opinions stand out. Wives are almost half as likely to value being outdoors and close to nature,

Table 3.6. Responses to open-ended question: "What do you like about farming?"

Most frequent reasons	Operators[a] (%)	Wives[b] (%)
Watch things grow/be close to nature	60.6	37.0
Be own boss/challenge/achievement	39.4	0.0
Rural life, especially for children	36.4	44.4
Have garden/better food	0.0	33.3
Husband likes farming so much	0.0	29.6

Note: Transitional cases excluded.
[a]$N = 33$
[b]$N = 27$

Table 3.7. Responses to open-ended question: "What do you like least about farming?"

Most frequent reasons	Operators[a] (%)	Wives[b] (%)
Poor financial return	51.5	40.7
Risk	12.1	29.6
Long hours	12.1	14.8
Government programs/regulations	9.1	0.0
It's all husband's decision	0.0	25.9
Bad weather/droughts	6.1	25.9

Note: Transitional cases excluded.
[a]$N = 33$
[b]$N = 27$

and none of them counts as a plus the sense of achievement or challenge in farming, the satisfaction in being one's own boss that was mentioned spontaneously by 36 percent of the operators. This response reflects the fact that women are less involved with farm activities and decisions, and have less opportunity to experience those satisfactions. Though men agree that farms provide good food, they never volunteered that fact as one of the reasons they like farming. Women's approval comes more from the aspects of farming that overlap with their domain: the home environment, children's welfare, and the family diet.

Disapproval of farming also reflects different emphases for operators and wives. Frustration with the poor income performance in recent years and the high risk of multiple droughts is shared by both and tops both lists. Wives then go on to complain about the adverse weather, while operators rarely do. They, instead, complain about the long hours and the intricacies of federal programs. The lack of involvement of a significant minority of the women is shown in their response, "It's all his decision." These women were unwilling even to express an opinion about the farm situation, since the decision whether or not to engage in farming is not theirs.

Multiple Job-holding and the Nature of Marriage

These data show that a sense of commitment to farming is not always shared by both husbands and wives in a multiple job-holding family. Several aspects of this gender difference reveal the structure of marriage and spousal roles that guide these Dodge Countians.

First, the majority of husbands and wives feel that the financial support of the family is the responsibility of the husband. If he decides to engage in a second job — namely, farming — that is also his responsibility. To the extent that farming activities let a husband more successfully fulfill his role as provider, his wife is ideally supportive, regardless of her own personal preferences about farm work. Especially for women who grew up on farms and hoped to leave that life far behind, the husband's decision to add a farm represents a frustrating return to some negative aspects of childhood. At the same time, since the farm is not really her domain, most wives do not feel their resistance to farming should have veto power. To claim equality in this decision making may open the door to a reconsideration of inequality in other domains. Though no women articulated this openly, their acceptance of the husband's dominance in the decision whether or not to farm reflects this broader acceptance of the nature of marriage.

The current farm crisis makes reality far different from this ideal. Farm expenses cut into the husband's salary in bad years, thereby depriving the family of some discretionary income. Though tax benefits may be generated and certainly the long-term investment in farm land provides a nestegg for retirement and for children to inherit, many women chafe under the short-term financial drain that farming represents. In cases where the farm is not a financial drain, it has the potential to be one, and that risk is a psychological burden that some women resent. Others resist the toll it takes on their husbands. These areas of psychological and financial stress are legitimate areas of women's concern. Wives' pressure on their husbands to get out of farming has accelerated as the crisis continues.

It is important to recognize that another group of women love the farm and the life it brings. They share in the spiritual satisfaction of connection to nature and life and in the sense of accomplishment in producing food and adding to the family's income. These women may have a subtly different conception of marriage in which the wife's role is less separate, less complementary and more based on a shared responsibility for the family. Alternatively, they may simply have a greater personal preference for farming. It might be expected that these wives do considerably more farm work, but that is not the case. Nor are they likely to have different family backgrounds. It may be that they had more positive experiences of farm life as children, but such experiences were not simply a result of being better off economically or growing up on larger farms.

A husband's decision to add a farm onto a full-time job represents a loss of companionship for some women. They demand more "time for the family" and husbands recognize these demands but do not seem to share the value on companionship to the extent of articulating those concerns themselves. Other wives accept that farm life involves long hours and do not expect to share many leisure activities with their husbands. These changing expectations for companionship and couples-oriented leisure are described by Rubin (1976) as new strains in marriage among blue-collar Californians as well. There, too, these values emerged first among wives, and husbands were sometimes puzzled by them. In this regard, multiple job-holding families in Dodge County and the differential assessment of the value of farming reflect changing societal conceptions of marriage, leisure, companionship, and intimacy across occupations.

Responses to the Current Crisis

As drought years press relentlessly on the South and the farm economy makes no dramatic rebounds, part-time farmers have been forced to reassess their decisions. As would be predicted by the above analysis, financial considerations have been primary. Compared with five years before, farmers interviewed in 1987 had chosen to cut back or get out of farming rather than lose money or continue barely to break even. Over half of the Dodge County sample has decided to get out of crop and livestock production altogether or to cut back drastically. A few of these cases have experienced job relocation or health problems, but most have changed their farm operations independently of other considerations. Another quarter has made some less major reductions in the farm operation, leaving only a quarter with their farms unchanged or expanding.

This decision to reduce farming activities does not reject the lifestyle aspects, however. Though recreation may have changed, farmers are rarely selling their land or leaving their rural residence. Their homes and property are intact; cropland is being rented out, allowed to lie fallow, or enrolled in the conservation reserve program. Hundreds of acres in the county have been planted to timber for pulpwood production, and some part-time farmers have benefitted from "the Pinetree Program." For those who continue farming with low profits, all the lifestyle, achievement, recreation, and family benefits continue. Many expect to expand production again once they retire. The primacy of the off-farm job is reinforced, and many people feel confirmed that they made the right career decision.

Conclusion

Far from being unfortunate victims of structural change, most of the multiple job-holding families in Dodge County enjoy a concentration of job and farm resources that provide a relatively comfortable standard of living. Though they work long hours and give up some gratifications to join off-farm and farm work, these families obtain in return a wide range of benefits. Financial and lifestyle aspects of this choice interact to provide a compelling combination, especially when contrasted with other possible second jobs or hobbies. The recent reductions in farm operations, however, support the farmers' own statements that the economic goals of farming are central and the commitment to off-farm jobs is primary.

A broad group of studies has illuminated dimensions of multiple job-holding in various U.S. states and counties and in Canada, but more in-depth work is needed to clarify hidden assumptions and biases. The Dodge County research has suggested that most part-time farmers may not be transitional, either in or out of full-time farming, but may instead have made a career decision early in adult life to depend on off-farm work. Parents' attitudes may have supported that choice, and both parents and children may share strong aspirations for a more affluent life. This desire for a certain level of household consumption takes precedence over loyalty to a farm background. Having decided to rely on jobs to support the household, these families respond to a range of familial and personal pressures to add a farm to that career. One important component sometimes overlooked in that choice is the availability of family land.

Though the farm is highly valued as a rural residence by both men and women, the Dodge County study suggests that there is often considerable gender role specialization with regard to the farm. Husbands and wives do not share equally in a commitment to the farm or an enthusiasm for the farm's activities and challenges. Even where women love farming and support the multiple job-holding decision, their reasons for doing so reflect a somewhat different agenda of concerns. As found by so many researchers, there is great variety among part-time farmers, and a sizeable minority dissents from each of these generalizations. In addition, these dimensions of motivation may vary from place to place. Only with studies in a variety of commodity systems, ethnic groups, and regions will the full reality of multiple job-holding become clear.

In expressing their reasons for choosing this life, these Georgia men and women reveal their own attempts to find answers to the contemporary dilemmas that are widespread in our society. Their choices reveal some of the profound changes that have occurred in modern culture—as well as some of the continuities. The character of our work lives, our sense of control, accomplishment and satisfaction, are brought home by the antidotes needed for balance and health. Changes in marital expectations and husband and wife roles create new rules for negotiating the achievement of family aspirations. These aspirations themselves reflect new expectations for upward mobility, income, and standard of living. In addition, the search for a satisfying spiritual dimension to life and a tangible connection to nature and traditional religious beliefs are also revealed by part-time farmers. Understanding these motivations to combine jobs and farming draws us to analyze the most fundamental aspects of industrial life in the late twentieth century.

References

Albrecht, D. E., and S. H. Murdock. 1984. "Toward a human ecological perspective on part-time farming." *Rural Sociology* 49(No. 3):389–411.

Allen, R. H., et al. 1937. *Part-time Farming in the Southeast.* WPA Division of Social Research, Research Monograph 9. Washington, D.C.: U.S. Government Printing Office.

Barlett, Peggy F. 1984. "Microdynamics of debt, drought, and default in South Georgia." *American Journal of Agricultural Economics* 66(No. 5):836–43.

_____. 1986. "Part-time farming: saving the farm or saving the lifestyle?" *Rural Sociology* 51(No. 3):289–313.

_____. 1987. "The crisis in family farming: Who will survive?," in *Farm Work and Fieldwork: Anthropological Studies of North American Agriculture,* ed. Michael Chibnik, 29–57. Ithaca, N.Y.: Cornell University Press.

Bokemeier, Janet, and C. Milton Coughenour. 1980. "Men and women in four types of farm families: Work and attitudes." Ithaca, N.Y.: Paper presented at the Rural Sociological Society annual meeting.

Bokemeier, Janet, and Lorraine Garkovich. 1987. "Assessing the influence of farm women's self-identity on task allocation and decision making." *Rural Sociology* 52(No. 1):13–36.

Bollman, Ray D. 1981. *Part-Time Farmers and Their Adjustments to Pluriactivity.* Ljubljana, Yugoslavia: Slovene Academy of Science and Arts.

Bollman, Ray D., and Marilyn Kapitany. 1981. "Summary of notes on classification and adjustments by part-time farmers in Canada." Ljubljana, Yugoslavia: Background paper for Conference on Part-Time Farmers and Their Adjustments to Pluriactivity.

Bossen, Laurel Herbenar. 1984. *The Redivision of Labor.* Albany, N.Y.: SUNY Press.

Brooks, Nora L., Thomas A. Stucker, and Jennifer A. Bailey. 1986. "Income and well-being of farmers and the farm financial crisis." *Rural Sociology* 51(No. 4):391–405.

Buttel, Frederick H. 1982. "The political economy of part-time farming." *Geojournal* 6(No. 4):293–300.

_____. 1983. "Beyond the family farm," in *Technology and Social Change in Rural Areas,* ed. Gene F. Summers, 87–107. Boulder, Colo.: Westview Press.

Buttel, Frederick H., and G. W. Gillespie, Jr. 1984. "The sexual division of farm household labor: An exploratory study of the structure of on-farm and off-farm labor allocation among farm men and women." *Rural Sociology* 49(No. 2):183–209.

Buttel, Frederick H., Bruce F. Hall, Oscar W. Larson III, and Jack Kloppenburg. 1982. "Manpower implications of part-time farming in New York State." Unpublished Report for U.S. Department of Labor. Ithaca, N.Y.: Cornell University.

Cawley, Mary. 1983. "Part-time farming in rural development: Evidence from Western Ireland." *Sociologia Ruralis* 23(No. 1):63–75.

Coughenour, C. Milton. 1984. "Farmers and farm workers: Perspectives on occupational change and complexity," in *Research in Rural Sociology and Development,* ed. H. Schwarzweller, 1–35. Greenwich, Conn.: JAI Press.

Coughenour, C. Milton, and A. Gabbard. 1977. *Part-Time Farmers in Kentucky in the Early 1970's: The Development of Dual Careers.* Lexington, Ky.: Department of Sociology, College of Agriculture, Agricultural Experiment Station, RS-54, University of Kentucky.

Coughenour, C. Milton, and Louis Swanson. 1983. "Work statuses and occupations of men and women in farm families and the structure of farms." *Rural Sociology* 48(No. 1):24–43.

Craig, Russell, Virginia Lambert, and Keith M. Moore. 1983. "Domestic labor on family farms: The sexual division of labor and reproduction." Lexington, Ky: Paper presented at the Rural Sociological Society annual meeting.

Fink, Deborah. 1986a. "Constructing rural culture: Family and land in Iowa." *Agriculture and Human Values* 3(No. 4):43–53.

_____. 1986b. *Open Country, Iowa: Rural Women, Tradition, and Change.* Albany, N.Y.: SUNY Press.

Fuguitt, G. V. 1961. "A typology of the part-time farmer." *Rural Sociology* 26(No. 1):39–48.

Fuguitt, G. V., Anthony M. Fuller, H. Fuller, R. Gasson, and G. Jones. 1977. *Part-Time Farming: Its Nature and Implications.* Ashford, Kent, England: Wye College.

Fuller, Anthony M. 1976. "The problems of part-time farming conceptualized," in *Part-Time Farming: Proceedings of the First Rural Geography Symposium,* ed. Anthony M. Fuller and J. A. Mage, Norwich, England: GeoAbstracts, Ltd.

_____. 1983. "Part-time farming and the farm family: A note for future research." *Sociologia Ruralis* 23(No. 1):5–10.

Garrett, Patricia, Michael D. Schulman, and Damayanthi Herath. 1984. "Division of labor and decision-making among smallholders: A male/female comparison." College Station, Tex: Paper presented at the Rural Sociological Society annual meeting.

Gladwin, Christina H. 1985. "Values and goals of Florida farm women: Do they help the family farm survive?" *Agriculture and Human Values* 2(No. 1):40–47.

Gladwin, Christina H., and Robert Zabawa. 1987. "Transformations of full-time family farms in the U.S.: Can they survive?" in *Household Economies and Their Transformations*, ed., Morgan Maclachlan, 212–27. Philadelphia: University Press of America.

Harrison, A. *The farms of Buckinghamshire.* 1966. Department of Agricultural Economics Miscellaneous Studies No. 40. Reading, England: University of Reading.

Huffman, Wallace. 1977. "Interaction between farm and non-farm labor markets." *American Journal of Agricultural Economics* 59(No. 5):1054–61.

Kada, Ryohei. 1980. *Part-Time Farming: Off-Farm Employment and Farm Adjustments in the United States and Japan.* Tokyo, Japan: Center for Academic Publications.

Mage, J. A. 1976. "A typology of part-time farming," in *Part-Time Farming: Proceedings of the First Rural Geography Symposium*, ed. Anthony M. Fuller and J. A. Mage, 6–37. Norwich, England: GeoAbstracts, Ltd.

Molnar, Joseph J., and Steven L. Smith. 1983. *Part-Time Farming in Alabama: Characteristics and Consequences.* Alabama Agricultural Experiment Station, Circular 268. Auburn, Ala.: Auburn University.

Paarlberg, Don. 1980. *Farm and Food Policy: Issues of the 1980s.* Lincoln: University of Nebraska Press.

Pearson, Jessica. 1979. "Note on female farmers." *Rural Sociology* 44(No. 1):189–200.

Rawski, Evelyn Sakakida. 1972. *Agricultural Change and the Peasant Economy of South China.* Cambridge: Harvard University Press.

Rosenfeld, Rachel A. 1985. *Farm Women: Work, Farm, and Family in the United States.*Chapel Hill: University of North Carolina Press.

Rubin, Lillian. 1976. *Worlds of Pain.* New York: Harper and Row.

Rupena-Osolnik, Mara. 1983. "The role of farm women in rural pluriactivity: Experience from Yugoslavia." *Sociologia Ruralis* 23(No. 1):89–94.

Sachs, Carolyn E. 1983. *The Invisible Farmers: Women in Agricultural Production.* Totowa, N.J.: Rowmun and Allanheld.

Salant, P. 1984. *Farm Households and the Off-Farm Sector: Results from Mississippi and Tennessee.* Agricultural Economics Research Report No. 143. Washington, D.C: U.S. Department of Agriculture.

Saupe, W., and P. Salant. 1985. "Combining farm and off-farm employment as a farm management strategy." Department of Agricultural Economics, University of Wisconsin-Madison, *Managing the Farm* 18(No. 7):1–12.

Sharp, Charlotte, Douglas Gwynn, and Orville E. Thompson. 1986. "Farm size and the role of women." *The Rural Sociologist* 6(No. 4):259–64.

Tigges, Leann M., and Rachel A. Rosenfeld. 1987. "Independent farming:

Correlates and consequences for women and men." *Rural Sociology* 52(No. 3):345–64.

U.S. Department of Commerce. 1983. *Census of Agriculture, 1982.* Washington, D.C.: Bureau of the Census.

Van Es, J. C., F. C. Fliegel, C. Erickson, H. Backus, and E. Harper. 1982. *Choosing the Best of Two Worlds: Small, Part-Time Farms in Illinois.* Agricultural Economics Research Report 185. Urbana: College of Agriculture, University of Illinois.

Wilkening, Eugene, and Jess Gilbert. 1987. "Family farming in the United States," in *Family Farming in Europe and America,* ed. Boguslaw Galeski and Eugene Wilkening, 271–301. Boulder, Colo.: Westview Press.

Wimberley, Ronald C. 1983. "The emergence of part-time farming as a social form of agriculture." *Research in Sociology of Work: Peripheral Worker* 2:325–56.

Zabawa, Robert. 1987. "Macro-micro linkages and structural transformation." *American Anthropologist* 89(No. 2):366–82.

CHAPTER 4

Multiple Job-holding in Perspective: A Discussion

PAUL W. BARKLEY

However they are defined, the phenomena known as part-time farming or multiple job-holding in agriculture are conceptual, intellectual, and empirical quagmires. They seem to have gained currency because observers of U.S. agriculture have suddenly learned that farm families earn a larger proportion of their incomes from nonfarm sources than they do from the sale of farm products or through the largesse of government farm programs. This apparently does not feel right, so a problem has been declared. Alternatively, the actual count of part-timers is increasing, signalling, perhaps, that agriculture does not provide sufficient income and must be subsidized if farm families are to survive. The second view is more promising, but it leads to inquiries about reallocation of resources (including labor) and the restructuring of agriculture — a theme that most research economists find somewhat evasive and uncomfortable. The authors of each of these papers recognize these (and other) common problems, then move ahead to provide some instructions on strengths and weaknesses and some information about who part-timers are and how they behave.

In many regards, the three papers in this volume by Ahearn and Lee (Chapter 1), Fuller (Chapter 2), and Barlett (Chapter 3) seem to be cut from the same cloth. The Ahearn and Lee paper asks a simple question: Why are we spending time talking about this amorphous and disconcerting group of farms or farmers? Peggy Barlett answers, "Because they — especially the farmers — are interesting and curious." Tony Fuller answers by saying that he isn't quite sure: Fuller climbs mountains because they are there. But

71

there are some good points to be made in examining both the part-time/ multiple job issue and these three papers.

The problem of part-timing arises because we as a society chose to follow Francis Walker's notion that a farm is a place of employment and that every farm must have a farmer to go with it. Humans and land are tied together in an apparently immutable fashion. This may have been a reasonable approximation of reality in the 1880s when Walker and Henry George publicly debated the issue of what is a farm and who is a farmer. However, the intervening century has not treated the Walker conviction very well. Farms do not need solitary farmers and many families can have legal and undisputed claims upon the decision-making process required to operate a single piece of land. This being so, there may be one full-time farmer and several part-time farmers on one collection of land resources that is called a farm. Similarly, there may be one manager-overseer who makes the production decisions on a dozen land parcels while also managing four apartment houses and running 500 head of livestock on a nearby national forest. Each of the dozen land parcels may have a full-time, salaried, resident operator. Who is the farmer and what meaning does part-timing have in this context? These possibilities are mentioned but not fully developed by Ahearn and Lee. The conventional one farm/one family notion forms the backbone of the three papers. The fact that all the authors took this path is regrettable since many of the interesting and critical questions that surround the future of agriculture stem from multiple ownership, part-timing, and a more distinct separation of land and labor. While there is room for criticism here, it must be admitted that the data system that emanated from the Francis Walker/Henry George debates almost insists that, in the absence of extensive primary data sets, research be conducted in this fashion: a farm means that somewhere there is a family to go with it.

There are other points of agreement: the authors agree that part-timing has always gone on in agriculture, and that, indeed, it may be the natural condition for farming in North America. They agree that it occurs more frequently in areas where there are off-farm opportunities for farmer and/ or spouse. There is little disagreement over social causes (or explanations) for part-timing. The family is grown; mother is not fully occupied with child rearing, so she takes an off-farm job to satisfy her own career interest or to supplement family income during the expensive years while the children are in college. So what is it that the papers tell us?

The Ahearn and Lee paper is a *tour de force*. Although long and sometimes a bit obscure, the paper uses essentially all available data and the considerable experience of its authors to move through the history and reach toward the future of part-time farming. They reveal their frustrations early when they say that "one root of our [judgmental concern over part-timing] is our tradition of the idealized family farm as one of moderate size, where Ma, Pa and the kids own the land they farm and do most of the work and where most of the income comes from the farm. This was the perceived norm, and other situations were seen as deviations from the norm, i.e., as something less than ideal." This frustration comes back time and again as the authors grapple with the perception that deviating from an older norm is tantamount to creating a problem. If there is a problem, it certainly is not found in the simple fact that part-time farming exists.

In the end, after working with definitions and numbers, Ahearn and Lee conclude that there may be some problems associated with families who control agricultural resources but who have surplus labor that can be converted to cash only in the nonfarm labor market. They also worry about the obverse: the nonfarm family that has full-time employment and high income outside of agriculture but also has some control over agricultural resources–the brother who left the farm but who still owns a 50-percent undivided interest in the old family property. Is he a part-time farmer or not? Where should he be counted? How should researchers regard him? All legitimate questions that must go unanswered at the present time.

Ahearn and Lee make their strongest contribution as their paper comes to a close. They present a smaller number of hypothetical cases derived from the genre of question that is often asked in beginning courses in general economics: If a man marries his housekeeper, what happens to the GNP? The present collection of such puzzles reinforces the need for explicit definitions and higher purposes for further research related to part-time farming. If deliberated in a systematic fashion, these hypothetical cases cannot help but bring more incisiveness and precision to the next round of questions and hypotheses related to part-time farming and multiple job-holding in agriculture.

The Fuller paper carries essentially the same title as the Ahearn and Lee paper, but it is designed to bring a Canadian perspective to the question. The Canadian perspective is almost identical to the U.S. perspective. Fuller worries over definitions, purposes, and content. In contrast to Ahearn and Lee, Fuller makes the point that part-timing is the way agriculture has always been conducted and that the great burst of full-timing from 1940 to 1960 may have blinded us to this fact and created a false sense of urgency around the theme.

Fuller also emphasizes the role of the labor market in helping with farm families' decisions to go part-time, and suggests that the ultimate choice may be made for economic, social, or structural reasons. Fuller's major contribution, however, is the suggestion that a dynamic surrounds the part-time activity, compelling some to move into part-timing as they enter agriculture, some to move into part-timing as they prepare to exit farming, and some who adopt a survival strategy and move to part-timing as a way to subsidize their continuing in agricultural endeavors. He omits those who are fully employed and adequately reimbursed, but who move into farming for hobby or social reasons—the airline pilot who buys 20 acres to grow strawberries or just to be able to have horses for the children. Regardless of who is included in or excluded from the dynamic, Fuller wants to learn the triggering mechanism and the threshold values that cause people to do things that they do. I am in sympathy with this desire.

The Barlett paper comes close to satisfying Fuller's wish. Peggy Barlett has questioned scores of part-timers in an attempt to learn why they are doing it, how they got into it, and how it affects their lives. Hers is a superb, although geographically limited, empirical study.

Like most empirical studies, the Barlett paper leaves open as many themes as it closes. It tells us that approximately half of the part-time farmers in one county in Georgia find low returns the most objectionable feature of part-timing. It tells us nothing of what the part-timers themselves or what some policy instrument might do to correct this perceived problem. Nor does it tell us what distinguishes the half that object to low returns from the half that do not. Is it always income? We must know if policy instruments are to be directed at this set of part-timers.

In all, the papers have strengths and weaknesses. In general they are very instructive about what is known at each of two levels of discourse: the broad, secondary data level (Ahearn and Lee, Fuller), and the primary data/individual farm level (Barlett).

The great problem with the three papers is the orientation toward microquestions, microsituations, and microbehavior. Even the Ahearn and Lee and the Fuller papers, while dealing with aggregate data, most often reveal these data in terms of what is happening on average individual farms. There is no attempt to mention or even to ponder the question of what happens in an aggregated society when all of agriculture is conducted by part-time farmers and 90 percent of all farm family income comes from employment off the farm. The effects may not be inconsequential.

Social scientists, especially economists, have always based recommendations and conclusions on what is happening at the margin. "The margin" is a broad term that encompasses many characteristics and qualities: the margin of profit, the margin of social acceptance, and the like. One of the margins faced by an individual or family is in the labor market. If the farm operator can earn more in nonfarm labor than in farm labor, it is wise for the farmer to accept nonfarm employment. If the nonfarm opportunity requires a significant amount of the farmer's time, it may be necessary for the farmer to switch from labor-intensive agriculture to labor-extensive agriculture—from vegetable production to pasture production. A large number of such switches in a given area could change significantly the composition of farm output and the infrastructural needs of the remaining agricultural industry. Should this possibility be addressed in a set of papers that deals with the future prospects of part-time farming and multiple job-holding? In this era of instability in agriculture it probably should since shifts around this margin of transference will have important farm and nonfarm consequences.

The question can be broadened. Where is this margin of transference for most (or for certain types of) farm families? What wage will entice how many people into nonfarm situations? Is the process reversible or should it be? Here is a complex theme (or set of themes) that is hinted at in these papers, but we need hard evidence because the mixing of agriculture and nonagriculture has aggregate as well as individual consequences. And those consequences include or touch on such diverse problems as land use, family income, stability in output, firm-household relationships, the continuity of agriculture, and the labor market.

Coming back to the beginning, it must be said that the definitions used in these papers do not make it easy to dismiss the questions of part-time farming with a flippant "who cares?" It is fortunate that the authors took the pains to point out some of the conceptual and real-world problems that go along with part-time farming or multiple job-holding in agriculture. The information that they provide is an indispensable step in asking the next round of questions regarding the consequences of part-timing on various aspects of society.

PART II

Theoretical Issues

CHAPTER 5

Agricultural Household Models: Survey and Critique

WALLACE E. HUFFMAN

Agriculture in North America is highly integrated with the other sectors of the economy through markets for farm inputs, farm products, consumer goods, and labor. During the early 1950s, and to a lesser extent during the early 1980s, farm household incomes were depressed relative to nonfarm household incomes. The reasons were primarily that the supply curve for agricultural products had been shifting faster due to rapid technical change than the demand curve and real wage rates had been rising in the nonfarm sector, especially during the 1940s and 1950s. For labor to be fully employed and farm labor to earn its opportunity return compared with the nonfarm sector, net transfers of labor (and other resources) out of agriculture were necessary. The geographical dispersion of agriculture as an industry and its rural location away from most but not all industries increases the costs of obtaining information about nonfarm jobs and reduces the probability of household mobility. Although there has been a dramatic reduction in the number of farms and farm population since 1950 in the United States (and Canada), which has reduced the labor employed in agriculture, another major source of resource adjustment has been increased dual employment of farm household members — work on their own farm and work at off-farm jobs. Some refer to this phenomena as part-time farming.

The author wishes to thank Ray Bollman, Statistics Canada, for assisting with the construction of Tables 5.2 and 5.4. Financial assistance from a Ford Foundation–Aspen Institute grant is gratefully acknowledged.

79

The primary focus of this chapter is to enhance understanding of the part-time farming phenomena in North America and determination of farm household incomes. The chapter proceeds by (1) highlighting some of the significant long-term changes in farm household incomes and in off-farm work of farm household members; (2) presenting a conceptual economic model that serves as a framework for viewing agricultural household decisions on farm production, consumption, and labor supply and for viewing farm household income determination; and (3) reviewing the econometric evidence on these topics. The first three sections of the chapter take up each of these issues in turn, and the final section presents some implications.

The discussion of agriculture in this paper focuses on both the United States and Canada. The agricultural industries of these countries have many similarities. Almost all farms are private family enterprises; agriculture is highly developed and relatively capital intensive; off-farm work has become relatively important in both of them; and resources are mobile between farm and nonfarm sectors, when time is given for adjustments to take place.

Long-term Trends

At the end of World War II, the income position of the farm population in North America (United States and Canada) deteriorated relative to the incomes of the nonfarm population; but after the mid-1950s, their relative position improved steadily until 1981. Since 1981, the relative position of the farm family incomes have deteriorated again. In the United States, average per capita disposable income of the farm relative to the nonfarm population was 55.1 percent in 1950, and it declined during the early 1950s to about 45.7 percent in 1956. From the mid-1950s to 1981, the relative income position of the farm population improved steadily, although not in every year. In 1980, average per capita disposable income of the farm population was 78 percent of the income of the nonfarm population. In 1983, the ratio of per capita farm to nonfarm incomes had decreased to 76 percent. Although the ratios are different, the trends in relative income positions of the Canadian farm and nonfarm populations are similar to the United States.

During the period 1950–70, a massive net movement of people out of agriculture occurred in North America. In the United States, the result was a sharp reduction in the farm share of total population from 15 percent (15.8 million) in 1950 to 5 percent (6.9 million) in 1970, or an 83 percent decline in the absolute size of the farm population over a 20-year period. During this same period, the total number of U.S. farms decreased 68 percent, from 5.382 million to 2.730 million, and the share of all farm operators reporting any off-farm work increased 15 percentage points (Table 5.1).[1] In Canada, the pattern was similar. The share of the farm population in the total population decreased from 19.7 percent (2.76 million) in 1951 to 6.6 percent (1.4 million) in 1971, and this represented a 68-percent decline of the farm population. The total number of Canadian farms decreased by 53 percent over this period, from 623,000 to 366,000, and the share reporting off-farm work increased 6 percentage points (Table 5.2). In both the United States and Canada, the size of the farm population and number of farms changed relatively little between 1970 and 1978, but since 1978, the decline has continued (Tables 5.1 and 5.2). Off-farm participation rates of farmers have continued their upward trend.

The transfer of labor out of agriculture has occurred in three major ways. First, families may sever farm sector ties by quitting farming and retiring or taking a nonfarm job. Second, as children become adults, they may leave agriculture and take nonfarm jobs, but their parents remain in farming until they retire. Third, families may stay on their farms, but some family members may take part-time or full-time employment at nonfarm jobs, while others continue full-time farm work. Or some members may reduce their hours of farm work, take nonfarm jobs and become dual job-holders. The relative attractiveness of these alternatives depends on the age of the farm operator, spouse, and children; the size of family; the size of the farm; the location of nonfarm job opportunities; the amount and type of skills of the individuals; and the cost of commuting or moving to nonfarm jobs. All have been important sources of adjustment in North America.

Nonfarm income

The welfare of farm families, even those that operate large farms, is not determined solely by the income from their farms. In the United States, the share of the personal income of the farm population derived from nonfarm sources increased from 27 percent in 1950 to slightly more than 50 percent in 1968. Since 1968, the nonfarm income of U.S. farm operator

---

1. The number and share of farm households that report off-farm wage income is clearly conditioned by the definition of a farm. The U.S. Department of Agriculture and Census of Agriculture have chosen a farm definition that is not very restrictive; i.e., a place that has annual sales of farm products in excess of $50 before 1974 and in excess of $1,000 after 1974. Under this definition, we would expect a significant amount of off-farm work.

Table 5.1. U.S. farms and farm operators reporting off-farm work, by census region

Region/number or percent	1949	1959	1969	1978	1982	Percent change[a]			
						1949–59	1959–69	1969–78	1978–82
United States									
No. of farms (1,000)	5,382	3,708	2,730	2,479	2,204	−31.1	−26.4	−9.70	−11.7
Percent reporting any off-farm work	38.8	44.9	54.3	55.1	53.9	−20.4	−10.9	−8.30	−13.9
Percent reporting ≥ 100 days	23.3	29.9	39.9	44.4	43.7	−10.7	−1.5	1.00	−13.4
Northeast									
No. of farms (1,000)	400	255	152	149	132	−31.1	−26.4	−0.02	−12.2
Percent reporting any off-farm work	47.1	47.7	31.0	64.2	51.5	−35.5	−35.0	70.90	−34.1
Percent reporting ≥ 100 days	34.4	35.6	24.2	54.8	42.5	−34.2	−32.0	79.90	−37.7
North Central									
No. of farms (1,000)	1,868	1,460	1,152	1,103	978	−21.8	−21.1	−4.40	−12.0
Percent reporting any off-farm work	34.6	33.6	50.5	46.6	45.3	−24.1	18.5	−12.40	−14.8
Percent reporting ≥ 100 days	18.5	24.1	34.4	35.1	34.5	1.7	12.6	−2.40	−13.8
South									
No. of farms (1,000)	2,652	1,645	1,161	1,015	815	−38.0	−29.4	−13.40	−22.0
Percent reporting any off-farm work	39.3	47.5	58.2	59.6	63.9	−25.0	−13.5	−11.10	−14.9
Percent reporting ≥ 100 days	23.7	32.9	45.0	50.4	54.4	−14.0	−3.5	−2.00	−14.4
West									
No. of farms (1,000)	462	348	265	286	280	−25.4	−24.1	−8.10	−2.4
Percent reporting any off-farm work	46.2	48.9	55.1	57.4	55.7	−22.1	−12.2	11.90	−13.9
Percent reporting ≥ 100 days	30.7	35.6	41.7	46.7	45.2	−15.2	−8.2	−19.20	−13.4

Source: U.S. Department of Commerce, Census of Agriculture, 1950, 1959, 1969, 1978, 1982.
[a]Percent change in number of farms in each class.

Table 5.2. Canadian farms and farm operators reporting off-farm work by geographical region

Region/number or percent	1951	1961	1971	1981	Percent change[a]		
					1951–61	1961–71	1971–81
Canada							
No. of farms (1,000)	643.9	480.9	366.1	267.8	–29.2	–27.3	–14.0
Percent reporting any off-farm work	28.8	32.0	35.1	39.1	–18.6	–18.0	–4.2
Atlantic Region							
No. of farms (1,000)	63.7	33.4	17.1	12.9	–64.5	–67.1	–27.7
Percent reporting any off-farm work	49.5	47.6	41.5	43.5	–73.6	–75.6	–22.9
Quebec							
No. of farms (1,000)	134.3	95.8	61.3	48.1	–33.8	–44.7	–24.1
Percent reporting any off-farm work	33.9	38.8	33.4	32.1	–20.3	–59.5	–28.3
Ontario							
No. of farms (1,000)	149.9	121.3	94.7	82.4	–21.2	–24.8	–13.9
Percent reporting any off-farm work	26.5	35.1	42.8	44.2	6.8	5.0	–10.7
Prairie Province							
No. of farms (1,000)	269.6	210.4	174.7	104.3	–24.8	–18.6	–51.6
Percent reporting any off-farm work	21.4	23.5	29.7	35.8	–15.7	3.4	8.1
British Columbia							
No. of farms (1,000)	26.4	19.9	18.4	20.0	–28.1	–8.0	–8.4
Percent reporting any off-farm work	40.8	48.5	50.7	51.2	–11.0	–3.5	9.4

Source: Statistics Canada, Census of Canada, Agriculture, 1951, 1961, 1971, 1981.
[a]Percent change in number of farms in each category.

families has exceeded their net farm income in every year, except for 1973 and 1975 when farm output prices were relatively high (U.S. Department of Agriculture 1984, and 1986; Carlin and Ghelfi 1979).

Before 1978, more than 70 percent of this nonfarm income was derived from off-farm wage and salary income—primarily nonfarm during the 1970s (U.S. Department of Agriculture 1986). However, since 1978, income from nonfarm businesses and professions has become a significantly more important source of U.S. farm household income. In 1978, only 9 percent of nonfarm income of farm households was derived from nonfarm business and professional incomes, but the trend has been upward since then, and in 1985, the share was 25 percent. While this shift was occurring, the share of nonfarm income derived from off-farm wage and salary income (nonfarm and farm sources) decreased to 54 percent. The net result has been that the share of income derived from other sources, e.g., interest, dividends, welfare, etc., has remained unchanged during the period 1978-85.

In Canada, the ratio of farm households' off-farm wage and salary income and self-employment income to their net farm income has increased from 36 percent in 1958 to 74 percent in 1971 (Bollman 1979, p. 60). After 1971, off-farm labor income of Canadian farm households has exceeded their net farm income in every year. Thus, in North America, income from off-farm labor has become a very important component of income for households that also operate farms.

What are the characteristics of farms where off-farm work occurs? Although off-farm work of North American farm operators occurs most frequently among those that have relatively small gross farm sales, it is also significant for operators of larger farms. For the United States, 65 percent of the ones who have gross sales of less than $20,000 (in 1982 prices) reported some off-farm work during 1969. Forty percent reported working 100 days or more (Table 5.3). Thirty-seven percent of farm operators of

Table 5.3. Participation rates of all U.S. farm operators in off-farm work by farm sales class (1982 prices)

	1969			1982		
	Percent reporting off-farm work[a]		Share of all farms	Percent reporting off-farm work[a]		Share of all farms
Sales class	1–99 days	≥ 100 days	%	1–99 days	≥ 100 days	%
All farms[b]	54.3	39.9	100.0	53.0	43.0	100.0
Less than $20,000	64.8	52.6	65.2	66.4	58.4	60.5
$20,000–39,999	37.1	17.8	14.5	46.4	33.6	11.1
$40,000 or more	17.1	10.8	20.2	26.9	13.9	28.3

Source: U.S. Department of Commerce, Census of Agriculture, 1969, 1982, Vol. II.
[a]One or more days of off-farm work for pay during the calendar year.
[b]All farms with sales of at least $50 except for abnormal type (i.e., government sector farms, experimental and research farms, and Indian reservations).

farms that had gross sales of $20,000–$40,000 reported working one or more days off their farm and 18 percent worked 100 days or more. Among farm operators who had gross sales of $40,000 or larger, 17 percent reported some off-farm work during 1969 and 11 percent reported working 100 days or more. The frequency by farm size with which off-farm work is reported by U.S. farm operators in 1982 is similar to 1969, except for farmers in the $20,000–$40,000 gross farm sales class. The latter group reports significantly higher off-farm participation rates in 1982 than in 1969.

For Canadian farm operators, 48 percent of the ones who had gross sales of less than $10,000 (at the 1975 price level) reported some off-farm work in 1970. The off-farm participation rate was 26 percent for those who operated farms having $10,000–$49,999 gross sales in 1970 and 17 percent for those who operated farms having $50,000 or larger gross sales in 1970 (Table 5.4). The off-farm participation rate was lower in 1975 than in 1970 for farms that had sales of $10,000 and over. In 1980, the off-farm participation rates for farms in all size classes is larger, but the pattern of off-farm work participation across farm-size classes is similar to earlier years.

Table 5.4. Participation rate of Canadian farm operators in off-farm work by real gross sales size class of farm

Sales class (constant 1975 prices)	1971		1976		1981	
	Percent reporting any off-farm work	Share all farms %	Percent reporting any off-farm work	Share all farms %	Percent reporting any off-farm work	Share all farms %
All farms	35.4	100.0	33.9	100.0	38.7	100.0
Less than $10,000	47.9	46.4	50.2	45.4	55.8	41.5
$10,000–49,999	26.3	44.9	22.9	41.7	31.3	38.6
$50,000 or more	16.8	9.2	11.9	12.9	17.7	19.9
Total number of farms	129,239	363,334	114,546	337,782	123,071	317,758

Source: Statistics Canada, Census of Agriculture Indexed Agricultural Sales 1961–1981.

Note: Abnormal farms are excluded; all other farms with at least $250 of agricultural sales are included.

Off-farm participation rates differ across farms having different major commodity specializations. The U.S. census data present frequencies of off-farm work for commercial farms, which excludes the farms with small sales and part-time farm operators. (See footnote to Table 5.5 for a list of farm types.) In 1950, the operators of commercial farms that specialized in fruit and tree nut production had significantly larger off-farm participation rates than operators of other types of farms and of all commercial farm operators. The operators of commercial dairy, cash grain, and livestock (excluding dairy and poultry) had off-farm participation rates that were similar to the average of all commercial farms (Table 5.5). Over time, the frequency of off-farm work of operators of dairy farms has declined relative to the average for all commercial farms. In 1982, only 21 percent of the operators of commercial dairy farms reported any off-farm work; this compares with 53 percent for all operators of commercial farms. Although operators of commercial cash grain farms had a 3-percent larger average off-farm participation rate in 1969 than all commercial farmers, their average in 1982 was 8 percentage points below the average for all commercial farms. In 1969, the operators of commercial livestock farms (excludes dairy and poultry farms) had a significantly larger average off-farm participation rate than operators of all commercial farms. In 1982, operators of this type had the largest average off-farm participation rate for any of the 11 farm types: 61 percent for any off-farm work and 52 percent for working 100 days or more per year. The operators of commercial fruit and tree nut farms maintained much larger than average off-farm participation rates in all years. Their rates were not significantly lower in 1982 than for livestock (excluding dairy and poultry) farms.

In Canada, farms specializing in fruit and vegetable production had the largest off-farm work participation rates in all census years after 1960 (Bollman 1979, p. 73). In 1960 and 1965, the operators of Canadian dairy farms had off-farm participation rates that did not differ very much from the average rate of all Canadian farm operators. However, after 1970, operators of dairy farms had an off-farm participation rate that was significantly lower than for all Canadian farm operators and one of the lowest for any farm type. Thus, roughly similar differences in off-farm participation rates by type of farm exist for Canadian farmers as for U.S. farmers.

Off-farm participation rates also differ regionally in the United States and Canada. For the United States, the country is divided into four regions: Northeast, North Central, South, and West (Figure 5.1). The off-farm participation rates were the largest in the Northeast and West in 1949, lower in the South, and lowest in the North Central region, where a large share of the top-grade farmland and good climate are located.

Over time, the off-farm participation rate of farm operators in the South has risen relative to that of farm operators in other regions. Consequently, in 1982, the operators in the South had the largest average off-farm participation rates. In 1982, the operators located in the North Central region continued to have the lowest average participation rate among the four regions. Among the five census years, the off-farm participation rate of farmers in the South was largest in 1982. For other regions, the largest average rate occurred before 1982 — for the Northeast and West in 1978 and for the North Central region in 1969 (Table 5.1).

Table 5.5. Off-farm participation rates of U.S. farm operators (of commercial farms) for selected types of farms

Farm type[a]	1950		1969		1982	
	1–99 days[b] (%)	≥100 days[b] (%)	1–99 days (%)	≥100 days (%)	1–99 days (%)	≥100 days (%)
All types	26.7	9.1	43.2	27.3	53.0	43.0
Dairy	27.2	10.2	29.1	14.6	20.8	10.7
Cash grain	29.8	9.8	47.0	26.7	47.5	34.8
Livestock, ex-dairy, and poultry	25.0	9.5	46.3	31.3	60.8	52.3
Fruit and tree nuts	35.8	21.5	51.9	40.1	60.4	51.2

Source: U.S. Department of Commerce, *Census of Agriculture,* 1950, 1969, 1982, Vol. II.

[a]The type of farm classification represents a description based upon major source of income from farm sales. To be classified as a particular type, a farm must have sales of a particular product or group of products amounting in value to 50 percent or more of the total value of all farm products sold during the year: cash grain (corn, sorghum, small grains, soybeans for beans, cowpeas for peas, dry field and seed beans, and peas); livestock, ex-dairy, and poultry (cattle, calves, hogs, sheep, goats, wool, and mohair); fruit and tree nuts (berries, other small fruits, tree fruits, grapes, nuts, and coffee); and dairy (milk, cream); also a farm is classified as dairy type if dairy products account for ≥ 30 percent of total value of products sold, milk cows represent ≥ 50 percent, and value of dairy products sold plus value of cattle and calves sold are ≥ 50 percent of total value of farm sales. Other types: tobacco, cotton, other field crops, vegetable, poultry, general, and miscellaneous.

[b]Days of off-farm work for pay during the calendar year.

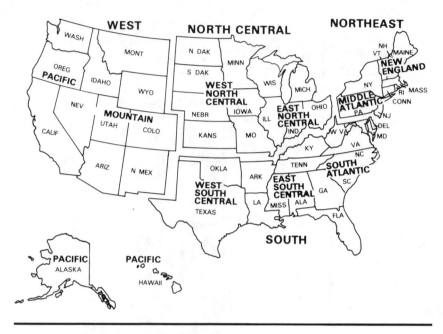

Figure 5.1. Regions of the United States. (*U.S. Department of Commerce*)

In Canada, the off-farm participation rate of farmers has historically been the largest in the Atlantic region and province of British Columbia (40–50 percent). It has been lowest in the Prairie Provinces (21–30 percent). Farm operators in provinces of Quebec and Ontario had intermediate rates of off-farm participation (25–40 percent) (Figure 5.2 and Table 5.2). Much of the difference in off-farm participation rates between farmers of Quebec and Ontario can be explained by the larger share of dairy farms in Quebec. Although the number of farms has decreased in all geographical regions over time, the absolute number of farms reporting off-farm work increased for the Prairie Provinces between 1961–71 and 1971–81 and for British Columbia, 1971–81.

Evidence on the off-farm participation rates of wives, whose husbands are farm operators, is scarce. However, in the data for the United States during the 1970s and 1980s, the off-farm participation rate of wives was 4–9 percentage points lower than for husbands (Table 5.6). The labor force participation rate of U.S. women who have a farm residence has been rising similar to the labor force participation rate of all U.S. women (Huffman 1977). Thus, my assessment is that the off-farm participation rate of farm wives in the United States was about 60 percent of the rate for farm opera-

Figure 5.2. Regions of Canada. (*Statistics Canada*)

tors in 1959 (or about 25 percent). Since then, the off-farm participation rate for wives has increased at a slightly faster rate than for husbands. Otherwise, changes in the two rates have been similar.

Integration of farm and nonfarm labor markets

In the early days, communications in North America were poor—low frequency of telephones, no televisions—and travel was slow. In North America most households did not own a car before 1930, roads were poor, and no public transportation existed in rural areas. At this time, workers had to live close to job sites. Improved communications, rural (and urban) roads, and rising average income levels of rural households have changed all of this. Almost all rural households now have at least one telephone, television, and automobile, and many have more than one.

The rural and urban roads have been improved. Currently there are about 2.9 million miles (4.7 million km.) of public U.S. rural (state, county, and township) roads, and 85–90 percent of them are all-weather roads, having good gravel, asphalt or paved surfaces (Pisarski 1987, pp. 2–3). Given there are about 1.54 million square miles (4 million sq. km.) of land in all U.S. farms, there is an average of 2 miles (1 km.) of public rural roads per square mile (km.) of farmland. There are an additional 0.9 million

Table 5.6. Indicators of the importance of off-farm wage and salary income to U.S. husband-wife farm households

Year/region	Participation rates in off-farm work (%)		Percent with off-farm wage and salary income	Off-farm wage income as percent of household income	Net farm income as percent of household income	Average annual total income (1982 prices)
	Husbands	Wives				
			1978			
United States[a]	45.7	36.6	68.7	46.1	29.7	26,314
Northeast[a]	52.3	44.1	75.6	60.3	20.4	26,470
North Central	38.9	33.6	65.7	41.5	35.9	26,548
South	52.6	38.4	69.9	53.5	20.5	25,363
West	46.1	39.3	73.9	43.3	30.8	27,372
			1982			
United States[a]	43.6	39.9	67.7	49.3	21.3	21,281
Northeast[a]	54.4	37.1	79.0	55.9	17.8	23,134
North Central	42.5	42.6	68.0	46.8	24.1	21,503
South	43.7	36.8	65.1	53.4	17.8	21,474
West	42.8	40.4	69.8	48.4	19.7	20,156

Source: U.S. Bureau of the Census, *Current Population Survey Tapes*, March of respective year.
[a]The New England states (Maine, Vermont, New Hampshire, Connecticut, and Rhode Island) are excluded.

miles of public urban roads and 99 percent of them have hard surfaces. Improved rural and other roads and improved automobiles, including gas mileage, have reduced the time and direct cost of transportation in North America. They have made it possible for people in the United States (and Canada) to live greater distances from their work. Decisions on residence need not be closely tied to job-site locations. Also, working women who have children at home or with baby sitters can be reached easily by telephone if their children become ill. These improved communication and transportation systems have enhanced the integration of farm and nonfarm labor markets and made off-farm work of farm household members feasible in North America.

Universal public elementary and secondary schooling for rural children (boys and girls) and increasing average years of schooling completed by rural youth have aided the adjustments between rural and urban labor markets in North America. Job opportunities and wage rates in the nonfarm labor markets are closely related to years of formal schooling completed, holding work experience or age constant (Smith and Welch 1977; Smith 1984).

In 1950, the rate at which farm male youth (18–24 years of age) had completed high school in the United States was about 20 percentage points lower than for nonfarm youth (U.S. Department of Commerce 1953). By 1985, high school completion rates for farm and nonfarm male youth were essentially equal (76 percent) (U.S. Department of Commerce 1983a).[2] The frequency with which farm youth complete college, however, continues to be lower than for nonfarm youth (U.S. Department of Commerce 1983a).

Schooling completion levels of farmers and their wives have increased since 1950. The evidence is for adult (25 years of age and older) males and females in the population (U.S. Department of Commerce 1953, 1983a). In 1950, the average number of years of schooling completed by farm adult males was 7.4 years. For farm adult females the average was 8.1 years. This compares with an average of 9.5 years of schooling completed for nonfarm adult males and 10.0 years for nonfarm adult females. In 1980, the average years of schooling completed by farm adult males was 11.0 years and for females was 11.4 years.[3] The average for nonfarm adult males was 12.0

---

2. Some male youth complete high school at an age older than 18 so that high school completion rates are larger than 75 percent for individuals who are, for example, 20–24 years of age. Information on the latter group is not given in the *Census of Population*.

3. The adult rural farm population does not correspond perfectly with the population of farm operators. One reason is that not all farm operators live in rural areas. The percentage of U.S. males reporting occupations of farmers and farm managers and living *off* farm increased from 4 percent in 1950 to 20 percent in 1970. Also, some individuals who comprise the adult rural farm population are not farm operators nor are their spouses.

years in 1980 and for nonfarm adult females was 11.6 years. Thus, although average schooling completion levels for the farm and nonfarm adult populations (and for males and females) were not the same in 1980, the differences that existed in 1950 were reduced significantly.

The Agricultural Household Model: A Conceptual Framework

The agricultural household model is one that combines the agricultural producer, consumer, and labor-supply decisions of agricultural households into a single conceptual framework. This model is quite versatile because it can be formulated for households that function in extremely different economic environments (Singh, Squire, and Strauss 1986, Chapters 1 and 2). One version fits subsistence farm households where the labor of their members and available land are used to produce all of the goods that the household consumes. In this case, no output or family labor is sold, nor are consumption goods, hired labor, or farm inputs purchased in the market. Another version will accommodate farm households of commercial agriculture where some consumption goods and farm inputs are purchased in the market, most (or all) of farm outputs are sold, and some family labor is sold to the external market. This latter version of the model provides a framework for viewing farm household decisions in North America. It provides insights into the driving forces behind farm household consumption, farm production, labor supply, and household income determination in a behavioral sense.

The model

The decision units are single family farm households. Household members' welfare is assumed to be summarized in a single hybrid, household-utility function. The hybrid function results from substituting a household-production function into a standard ordinal household-utility function (Pollak and Wachter 1975). Household utility is assumed to depend on the inputs of home time of the husband and wife (T_h), which are indexed separately, and of goods purchased for direct or indirect consumption (Y_h):

$$U = U(T_h, Y_h; H_h, Z_h), \ \partial U/\partial \Omega > 0, \ \partial^2 U/\partial \Omega^2 < 0, \ \Omega = T_h, Y_h, H_h (5.1)$$

Thus, T_h and Y_h are assumed to be objects of current choice. However, household utility also depends on human capital variables that are currently fixed but affect the efficiency of household production $(\mathbf{H}_h)$, e.g., schooling and experience of adults, and other household and area characteristics $(\mathbf{Z}_h)$, e.g., climate, number of children in the household, commuting distance to shopping, recreation, and schooling centers.

The level of utility attainable by the farm household is constrained by the human time endowment (and skills) of its members, by net household cash income, and by the production function for farm output. First, consider the human time constraint. The human time of two adults, the husband and wife, is distinguished. In North America, the husband-wife family is the nucleus of 88 percent of the farm households (U.S. Department of Commerce 1983b). The gender distinction exists because endowed and acquired skills of adult males and females are different. Although farm youth generally work on their parent's farm during the summer months, they are engaged on an annual basis primarily in human capital production through formal schooling. Because schooling decisions of rural youth are beyond the focus of this paper, the human time allocation decisions of children in farm households are not considered here.

Because husband's and wife's time are heterogeneous, they are indexed separately (i.e., they cannot be added together in one human time constraint). Each of them receives an endowment of time each year which the household can allocate to work on their own farm (called farm work), to work off their farm (called off-farm work), and to home time.[4] Home time is a residual category that includes mainly household work and leisure (but could be expanded to include craft activities and community service activities). An individual's annual hours of off-farm work (or farm work) may be zero. The allocation of husband's and wife's annual human time endowment is summarized as the vector equation

$$\mathbf{T} = \mathbf{T}_f + \mathbf{T}_m + \mathbf{T}_h, \mathbf{T}_m \geq 0 \tag{5.2}$$

where $\mathbf{T}$ is annual time endowment, $\mathbf{T}_f$ is annual farm work hours, $\mathbf{T}_m$ is annual off-farm work hours, and $\mathbf{T}_h$ is annual home hours.

The farm household may receive annual income from the net return on the farming operation, off-farm work, and nonfarm assets. These receipts are spent on goods for direct or indirect household consumption. (Savings and investments are ignored here as means of simplifying the model.) The farm household is assumed to be competitive in farm output and input markets (i.e., individually they do not affect the prices that they pay for

---

4. In the model that is presented, off-farm work is assumed to be wage and salary jobs. The model could be changed to one where off-farm work is at a self-employed business.

inputs or receive for outputs). The budget constraint on household cash income is

$$P_f Y_f - W_f X_f + \mathbf{W}_m' \mathbf{T}_m + V_h = P_h Y_h \tag{5.3}$$

where $P_f Y_f - W_f X_f$ is net farm income (Y_f is the annual quantity of farm output produced and sold, X_f is the quantity of purchased farm inputs, and W_f is the price of purchased farm inputs). $\mathbf{W}_m' \mathbf{T}_m$ is (net) income from off-farm work. $\mathbf{W}_m'$ is the wage rate for off-farm work net of direct cost of commuting, $\mathbf{W}_m' = \mathbf{W}_m - C_m(M)$, where $\mathbf{W}_m$ is the gross wage, and commuting cost $C(M)$ per hour worked is assumed to be a function of commuting distance (M). Farm households generally have some nonfarm assets, e.g., stocks, bonds, savings, etc., and annual income from these assets is represented by V_h. Net farm household cash income is spent as $P_h Y_h$ or on consumption goods (or inputs for household production).

The off-farm labor demand or wage offer equations facing husbands and wives are assumed to depend on their marketable human capital ($\mathbf{H}_m$), local labor market characteristics ($\mathbf{L}_m$) and job characteristics ($\mathbf{Z}_m$), but wage rates are assumed to be independent of their hours worked during the current year. The latter assumption may be a reasonable approximation, and it simplifies the resulting empirical model. The market labor demand functions are summarized in vector form as

$$\mathbf{W}_m = W_m(\mathbf{H}_m, \mathbf{L}_m, \mathbf{Z}_m) \tag{5.4}$$

The expectation is that increasing marketable human skills, e.g., formal schooling, vocational training, and experience, shift the wage offer or labor demand curve faced by an individual upward. Local labor market conditions affect wage offers when workers and firms are immobile. Land rental and ownership opportunities are expected to be a source of reduced labor mobility in North American rural labor markets.

Although most North American farms produce and sell several outputs, the analysis proceeds here assuming that one (aggregate) output (Y_f) is produced using variable inputs of husband's and wife's farm time ($\mathbf{T}_f$) and purchased inputs (X_f), including farmland services and labor hired from other households. Farm labor supplied from outside this farm household is assumed to be heterogeneous because of (1) different skills and (2) different supervisory requirements to prevent shirking. The efficiency of farm production is assumed to depend on the human capital of the husband and wife ($\mathbf{H}_f$), e.g., formal schooling, prior farming experience, public agricultural research and extension, and other exogenous farm-specific characteristics ($\mathbf{Z}_f$), i.e., length of growing season, annual precipitation, and soil characteristics. The technology of farm production is represented by the following concave production function:

$$Y_f = F(\mathbf{T}_f, X_f; \mathbf{H}_f, \mathbf{Z}_f), \; \partial Y_f/\partial T_f > 0, \; \partial Y_f/\partial X_f > 0 \tag{5.5}$$

The production function (5.5) is substituted into the cash income constraint (5.4) to obtain a farm technology–constrained measure of household net cash income.

$$P_f F(\mathbf{T}_f, X_f; \mathbf{H}_f, \mathbf{Z}_f) - W_f X_f + \mathbf{W}'_m \mathbf{T}_m + V_h = P_h Y_h \tag{5.6}$$

The decision problem facing the household is now to simultaneously choose the quantity of consumption goods to purchase, the hours of husband's and wife's farm work and off-farm work, and the quantity of purchased farm inputs so as to maximize household welfare. This can be restated formally as to maximize the new function ϕ:

$$\begin{aligned}
\phi(X_f,&\mathbf{T}_f,\mathbf{T}_m,\mathbf{T}_h,Y_h; \; \mathbf{T},M,\mathbf{H}_m,\mathbf{Z}_m,\mathbf{L}_m,\mathbf{H}_f,\mathbf{Z}_f,\mathbf{H}_h,\mathbf{Z}_h,P_f,\mathbf{W}_m,W_f,V_h,P_h) \\
&= U(\mathbf{T}_h,Y_h; \; \mathbf{H}_h,\mathbf{Z}_h) + \lambda[P_f F(\mathbf{T}_f,X_f; \; \mathbf{H}_f,\mathbf{Z}_f) - W_f X_f \\
&\quad + (\mathbf{W}_m - C_m)\,\mathbf{T}_m + V_h - P_h Y_h] + \gamma[\mathbf{T} - \mathbf{T}_f - \mathbf{T}_m - \mathbf{T}_h] \tag{5.7}
\end{aligned}$$

The Kuhn-Tucker conditions for an interior solution except for a boundary solution on off-farm work $(\mathbf{T}_m \geq 0)$ are

$$\lambda[P_f F_{X_f} - W_f] = 0 \tag{5.8}$$

$$\lambda \mathbf{P}_f \mathbf{F}_{T_f} - \gamma = 0 \tag{5.9}$$

$$\lambda \mathbf{W}'_m - \gamma \leq 0, \; \mathbf{T}_m \geq 0, \; \mathbf{T}_m \, (\lambda \mathbf{W}'_m - \lambda) = 0 \tag{5.10}$$

$$\mathbf{U}_{T_h} - \gamma = 0 \tag{5.11}$$

$$U_{Y_h} - \lambda P_h = 0 \tag{5.12}$$

$$\mathbf{T} - \mathbf{T}_f - \mathbf{T}_m - \mathbf{T}_h = 0 \tag{5.13}$$

$$P_f F\,(\mathbf{T}_f,X_f; \; \mathbf{H}_f,\mathbf{Z}_f) - W_f X_f + \mathbf{W}'_m \mathbf{T}_m + V_h - P_h Y_h = 0 \tag{5.14}$$

where λ and γ are Lagrange multipliers for marginal utility of income and human time, U_j and F_j are partial derivatives of the functions U and F, and $\mathbf{W}'_m = \mathbf{W}_m - C_m$.

Equations (5.9)–(5.11) give conditions that must be met for optimal

96   II : THEORETICAL ISSUES

time allocation by a husband and wife. Both members are assumed to
always have optimal positive annual hours of farm work and home time,
i.e., equation (5.9) and (5.11) are equalities. Equation (5.10) provides the
optimality condition for off-farm work. If $\lambda W_m' - \gamma$ or $W_m' - \gamma/\lambda < 0$,
then the marginal value of an individual's home time or farm work exceed
his/her off-farm wage offer, net of commuting cost, and optimal hours of
off-farm work are zero, i.e., $T_m^* = 0$. If $\lambda W_m' - \gamma$ or $W_m' - \gamma/\lambda = 0$, then
an individual's off-farm wage, net of commuting cost, equals the marginal
value of his/her home time or farm work, and optimal hours of off-farm
work may be positive. Furthermore, when farm and off-farm work requires
specialized skills (e.g., formal or on-the-job training) and households are
risk neutral, individuals tend to specialize in one major type of work activity (Becker 1981).

When the farm household is at an interior solution for all choices, the
decisions on farm input quantities (or how much farm output to produce)
can be separated from household consumption decisions. The reason is that
all output and input prices are determined in the external market. This gives
what has become known in the agricultural household literature as a recursive decision model (Singh, Squire, and Strauss 1986, Chapter 1). Equations
(5.8) and (5.9) can be solved jointly to obtain demand functions for husband's and wife's farm labor and purchased farm inputs (note, $\gamma/\lambda = W_m'$):

$$T_f^* = D_{T_f}^* (W_m', W_f, P_f, H_f, Z_f), \; \partial T_f^*/\partial W_m' < 0 \tag{5.15}$$

$$X_f^* = d_{X_f} (W_m', W_f, P_f, H_f, Z_f), \; \partial X_f^*/\partial W_f < 0 \tag{5.16}$$

Knowing optimal input usage, the supply function for farm output is obtained by substituting equations (5.15) and (5.16) into the production function (5.5):

$$Y_f^* = s_{Y_f} (W_m', W_f, P_f, H_f, Z_f), \; \partial Y_f^*/\partial P_f > 0 \tag{5.17}$$

In this case, equations (5.16)–(5.17) provide the information to restate cash
income of equation (5.6) or (5.14) as maximum net household cash income:

$$I_h^* = P_f s_{Y_f} (W_m', W_f, P_f, H_f, Z_f) - W_f X_f^* + W_m' T_m + V_h \tag{5.18}$$

Second, equations (5.10)–(5.12) and (5.18) can be solved jointly to obtain
demand functions for husband's and wife's home time and purchased consumption goods (note $\gamma/\lambda = W_m'$):

$$T_h^* = d_{T_h} (W_m', P_h, I_h^*, H_h, Z_h, T) \tag{5.19}$$

$$X_h^* = d_{X_h} (\mathbf{W}_m', P_h, I_h^*, \mathbf{H}_h, \mathbf{Z}_h, \mathbf{T}) \tag{5.20}$$

Now the off-farm labor-supply function is obtained by substituting equations (5.15) and (5.19) into the time constraint, equation (5.2):

$$\begin{aligned}
\mathbf{T}_m^* = T - \mathbf{T}_f^* - \mathbf{T}_h^* &= s_{T_m} (\mathbf{W}_m', W_f, P_f, P_h, I_h^*, \mathbf{H}_f, \mathbf{Z}_f, \mathbf{H}_h, \mathbf{Z}_h, \mathbf{T}) \\
&= s_{T_m} (\mathbf{W}_m', W_f, P_f, P_h, V_h, \mathbf{H}_f, \mathbf{Z}_f, \mathbf{H}_h, \mathbf{Z}_h, \mathbf{T})
\end{aligned} \tag{5.21}$$

Thus, the supply functions for husband's and wife's off-farm work contain all of the exogenous parameters in the constrained optimization statement, equation (5.7). The off-farm work decisions are quite complex because they require that the household weigh a large number of different pieces of information.

A reduced-form functional statement of total household net cash income is obtained by substituting equation (5.21) into equation (5.18) and rearranging terms:

$$I_h^* \equiv I_h^* (W_f, P_f, P_h, V_h, \mathbf{H}_h, \mathbf{Z}_h, \mathbf{H}_f, \mathbf{Z}_f, \mathbf{H}_m, \mathbf{Z}_m, \mathbf{L}_m, M, \mathbf{T}) \tag{5.22}$$

All of the variables that are exogenous to production, consumption, and labor supply decisions of these farm households are included in equation (5.22).

When optimal hours of off-farm work are zero for the husband or wife, the household's decision process is not recursive. The marginal value of the husband's/wife's time is endogenous to their consumption and farm production decisions. This means that decisions on variable farm inputs (or optimal farm output) and on household consumption must be made jointly. Equations (5.8)–(5.14) must be solved simultaneously. When neither the husband nor wife works off-farm, the household demand functions are

$$\mathbf{T}_f^* = d_{T_f}^* (W_f, P_f, P_h, V_h, \mathbf{H}_h, \mathbf{Z}_h, \mathbf{H}_f, \mathbf{Z}_f, \mathbf{T}) \tag{5.23}$$

$$X_f^* = d_{X_f}^* (W_f, P_f, P_h, V_h, \mathbf{H}_h, \mathbf{Z}_h, \mathbf{H}_f, \mathbf{Z}_f, \mathbf{T}) \tag{5.24}$$

$$\mathbf{T}_h^* = d_{T_h}^* (W_f, P_f, P_h, V_h, \mathbf{H}_h, \mathbf{Z}_h, \mathbf{H}_f, \mathbf{Z}_f, \mathbf{T}) \tag{5.25}$$

$$\gamma_h^* = d_{X_h} (W_f, P_f, P_h, V_h, \mathbf{H}_h, \mathbf{Z}_h, \mathbf{H}_f, \mathbf{Z}_f, \mathbf{T}) \tag{5.26}$$

Furthermore, substituting equations (5.23) and (5.24) into the production function (5.4), the supply function for agricultural output is now

$$Y_f^* = s_{Y_f} (W_f, P_f, P_h, V_h, \mathbf{H}_h, \mathbf{Z}_h, \mathbf{H}_f, \mathbf{Z}_f, \mathbf{T}) \tag{5.27}$$

and substituting equations (5.24) and (5.27) into the income received part of equation (5.6) and rearranging, a reduced-form functional statement for total household net cash income is obtained:

$$I_h^{*'} \equiv I_h^{*'} \ (W_f, P_f, P_h, V_h, \mathbf{H}_h, \mathbf{Z}_h, \mathbf{H}_f, \mathbf{Z}_f, \mathbf{T}) \tag{5.28}$$

There is still a possibility that the husband or wife (not both) works off-farm. The decisions are not recursive, but for the individual that works for a wage, the off-farm wage or its determinants are included in equations (5.23)–(5.28).

The above model could be modified to take account of saving and investment decisions of agricultural households and to include governmental policy parameters, e.g., marginal tax rates and governmental farm programs.

The agricultural household model is rich in implications about the exogenous variables that drive the production, consumption, and labor-supply decisions of farm households in commercial agriculture. It does not provide much information about the expected signs that coefficients of the exogenous variables are expected to have in econometric investigations, except for a few own-price elasticities for farm input demand and output supply (Singh, Squire, and Strauss 1986, Chapter 1; Huffman 1973; Lange 1979).

Estimation

The agricultural household model has implications for estimation of the coefficients of agricultural household supply-and-demand functions. First, when household production decisions are separable (recursive) from household consumption and labor-supply decisions, two separate systems of equations can be estimated. One set is an empirical representation of agricultural production decisions, equations (5.15)–(5.17), and the other set is the household demand and off-farm labor-supply equations (5.19)–(5.21). In fact, estimation of these two sets of equations need not be pursued in the same study. Alternatively, when household decisions are not separable (nonrecursive), then empirical representations of production, consumption, and labor-supply equations should be estimated as one system, i.e., equations (5.23)–(5.26). With both separable and nonseparable agricultural household decisions, one or more sets of equations will generally be estimated. Efficiency of parameter estimation can be increased by imposing relevant (based upon economic theory) cross-equation restrictions on the coefficients and taking account of likely cross-equation correlation of disturbances in the empirical specification of behavioral equations.

Because of the researcher's interest and smaller data requirements, researchers sometimes focus on a single structural or reduced-form equation in the agricultural household model, e.g., the off-farm labor-supply equation of farm operators. Reduced-form equations, which contain only one endogenous variable and several exogenous variables, should be used, rather than structural equations, where there are two or more endogenous variables, when the equation is to be estimated by ordinary least squares.

In focusing on off-farm work decisions, an equation for the probability of an individual participating in off-farm work is frequently interesting. In the agricultural household model, rational individuals are assumed to participate in off-farm work when their reservation wage (for farm and home uses of time) is less than the off-farm wage rate offered in the market. The wage offer or off-farm labor demand function is equation (5.4). The reservation wage is defined as the marginal value of an individual's time when he/she allocates all of his/her time to farm and home time (and zero hours to off-farm work). An equation for this relationship is obtained by taking equation (5.21), setting $T_m^* = 0$, and solving for $W_m' = W_m^R$:

$$W_{mj}^R = R_j (W_f, P_f, P_h, V_h, H_f, Z_f, H_h, Z_h, T) \tag{5.29}$$

where j refers to the jth individual.

Define D_j equal to 1 if $W_j^R < W_{mj}'$ and equal to 0 if $W_j^R \geq W_{mj}'$. Then

$$
\begin{aligned}
Pr (D_j = 1) &= Pr (W_j^R < W_m') \\
&= \ell(W_f, P_f, P_h, V_h, H_f, Z_f, H_h, Z_h, H_m, L_m, Z_m, M, T) \tag{5.30}
\end{aligned}
$$

where $Pr (.) \equiv$ probability for an event occurring. Thus, the probability of an individual participating in off-farm work depends on all the exogenous variables that enter his/her reservation wage and off-farm wage equations. Variables that raise the reservation wage reduce the probability of off-farm work, and variables that raise the off-farm wage offer increase the probability of off-farm work. For variables that raise both the reservation wage and wage offer, the net effect on the probability of off-farm work is a priori uncertain.[5] Estimates of these participation equations provide information about the marginal effects of exogenous variables on the probability of an individual participating in off-farm work.

The model derived in this section of the paper has been fitted to data for aggregate and farm level data of the United States and Canada. Some of the important results are summarized in the following section.

---

5. For a given farm household, the decisions for a husband and wife to participate in off-farm work are unlikely to be independent. In this case, it is necessary to consider the joint probability of the husband and/or wife participating in off-farm work. This is a straightforward extension.

Empirical Results

Econometric studies published after 1975 form the body of empirical research that has applied the agricultural household model to U.S. and Canadian agriculture. The first studies used national, state, or county aggregate data; later studies have used farm-level data. The early studies imposed the separability or recursive structural assumption and estimated either equations for farm production decisions or farm household consumption and labor-supply decisions. One study has actually tested for separability or recursiveness using aggregate data for Canada and rejected this assumption. Several of the later studies have proceeded under the nonseparability or nonrecursive decision making assumption.

In this section, a small amount of space is first allocated to reviewing estimates of sets of farm output supply and input demand equations for U.S. and Canadian agriculture that are from a recursive system. Most of the space is allocated to a discussion of off-farm labor demand, off-farm labor supply, and off-farm work participation equations. Finally some new evidence of the contribution of exogenous household, farm, and labor-market variables to U.S. farm household incomes is presented and evaluated.

Production

Weaver (1983), Shumway (1983), Antle (1984), and Huffman and Evenson (1989) have presented multiple-equation econometric estimates of one or more agricultural supply equations and several input-demand functions where cross-equation restrictions, suggested by economic theory, and cross-equation correlation of disturbances are taken into account in the estimation. Antle defines one aggregate output, but the other studies had three to five outputs. They generally distinguished 4–6 variable inputs (farm labor, machinery services, agricultural chemicals, and fuel) and a few fixed or environmental variables. All of these studies have obtained own-price supply elasticities for outputs that are positive, showing that supply curves slope upward, and own-price input-demand elasticities that are negative, showing that demand curves for inputs slope downward.

The demand for farm labor is of special interest. Huffman and Evenson (1989), using state average per farm data for 42 U.S. states from the 1950–74 agricultural censuses, obtained an estimate of the wage elasticity of demand for farm (operator plus hired) labor of -0.51. Furthermore, their results showed that farm labor and machinery services are substitutes, and a 10 percent decrease in the price of farm machinery services causes a

0.6 percent leftward shift in the demand for farm labor. Shumway's results for Texas field crops, using annual aggregate data for 1959–80, provide similar estimates for the wage elasticity of demand for farm labor and for the effect of a change in the price of capital services on farm labor demand. Weaver's estimates for North and South Dakota, using annual aggregate data for 1950–70, were somewhat different. His wage elasticities were larger, -0.8 for North Dakota and -1.0 for South Dakota, and his estimate of the effect of a change in the price of capital services on the demand for farm labor was considerably larger (1.3 to 1.6). In these studies, an increase in output prices shifts the demand for farm labor to the right.

Lopez (1984) presents one of the first attempts to address econometrically the appropriateness of the recursive structure of agricultural household decisions. He used Canadian census division data for 1971 to test whether or not the nonrecursive model is preferred to the recursive one. The model contains three consumption goods, aggregate farm output, and four variable inputs. In this model, he rejected the hypothesis of recursive structure, and showed that the price elasticities were substantially different for the nonrecursive and recursive structures. His estimates of the elasticity of demand for (hired) farm labor due to changes in the wage rate, price of farm capital, and farm output are similar to estimates obtained for the United States.

Off-farm work

Empirical evidence from five econometric studies of off-farm work in the United States and Canada were reviewed. All of them except one (Huffman 1980) assumed that farm household decisions are not separable or nonrecursive. Only one study, Lopez (1984), estimated a complete system of equations associated with farm production, consumption, and labor-supply decisions. The other studies estimated equations associated with only off-farm work. Three different aspects of off-farm work are examined: off-farm labor demand (or wage offer) functions, off-farm participation functions, and off-farm labor-supply functions. The nature of these studies and selected parameter estimates are summarized in Tables 5.7 and 5.8.

The empirical specifications of the off-farm labor demand functions that have been estimated by Sumner (1982), Huffman and Lange (1989), and Jensen and Salant (1986) are all in the spirit of equation (5.4). The $\log_e$ of the hourly off-farm wage rate received by farm operators who work off-farm was regressed on their age (or experience), age squared (or experience squared), and a few labor market characteristics. The results summarized in Table 5.7, Part A, show that an additional year of formal schooling in-

Table 5.7. Summary of econometric estimates of off-farm labor demand functions and probability of participation in off-farm work, United States and Canada

Author	Location	Data type	Dependent variable	Operator's schooling	Spouse's schooling	Operator's age	Age^2	Nonfarm asset income	Miles to nearest city	Miles^2
						Parameters				
A. Off-farm labor demand (wage) functions										
Sumner	U.S. (Ill.)	1971 farm level	Log$_e$ (hourly wage)	0.038[a]		0.0067	−0.00010		−.0019[a]	.0014[b]
Huffman/ Lange	U.S. (Iowa)	1977 farm level	Log$_e$ (hourly wage)	0.0558[a]		0.0343[ac]	−0.0007			
Jensen/ Salant	U.S. (Miss., Tenn.)	1981 farm level	Log$_e$ (hourly wage)	0.042[a]		0.054[a]	−0.0006[a]			
B. Off-farm work participation										
						Marginal effect on probability of off-farm work				
Huffman	U.S. (Iowa, N.C., Okla.)	1964 census ct. aggre. avg.	Log$_e$ (odds of off-farm work)	+[a]	+[a]	+	−	+		
Sumner	U.S. (Ill.)	1971 farm level	Probit (1,0)	+		+[a]	−[a]	−[a]	+	−[ab]
Huffman/ Lange	U.S. (Iowa)	1977 farm level	Probit (1,0)	+[a]	−	−	−	−	−[a]	+[a]
Jensen/ Salant	U.S. (Miss., Tenn.)	1981 farm level	Probit (1,0)	+[a]	−	+[a]	−[a]	−[a]		
Bollman	Canada	1971 census 1971 census	Probit (1,0)	+[a]	+[a]	−[a]		−[a]		

[a]Computed from a coefficient that is significantly different from zero at 5 percent level.
[b]The variable is actually miles to nearest town.
[c]The variable is derived experience = Age − years of schooling − 6.

Table 5.8. Summary of econometric estimates of off-farm labor supply parameters for farm operators, United States and Canada

Author	Location	Data type	Units of labor	Elasticity of off-farm work			Change in off-farm work per unit change of	
				Operator's wage	Spouse's wage	Farm output price	Operator's schooling	Spouse's schooling
Huffman	U.S. (Iowa, N.C, Okla.)	1964 census county aggregate average	Annual days	0.34[a]	−0.06	−0.430[ab]	73.50[a]	9.00
Sumner	U.S. (Ill.)	1971 farm level	Annual hours	0.40[a]			1.85	−45.90[a]
Lopez	Canada	1971 census division aggregate average	Annual days	0.18[ac]		−0.849[a]	24.88[a]	
Huffman/Lange	U.S. (Iowa)	1977 farm level	Annual hours	0.03[a]	0.07[a]		7.50[a]	7.00[a]
Jensen/Salant	U.S. (Miss., Tenn.)	1981 farm level	Annual hours	0.21[a]			−47.30[a]	−13.12

[a]Computed from a coefficient that is significantly different from zero at 5 percent level.
[b]Predicted farm output rather than output price.
[c]Days of off-farm work of all farm household members are aggregated together. The wage is for the aggregate.

creases the off-farm wage by 4–5.5 percent. An additional year of age (or work experience) also has a positive but diminishing effect on the wage. The percentage increment first increases with an increment to age (experience); at some age the maximum effect of age (experience) is reached; and for additional increments to age (experience), the wage is reduced. This inverted U shape is a typical $\log_e$ (wage)-age relationship. Thus, the evidence is that human capital variables — farmers' schooling and work experience — are important determinants of the wage that farmers receive when they work off-farm.

Off-farm work decisions include participation, which is a dichotomous decision, and an hours component. The off-farm participation equations estimated using farm-level data are in the spirit of equation (5.30). The probability of off-farm work is related to a set of household, farm, and labor market variables that are considered to be exogenous to current farm household decisions. The one aggregate study by Huffman (1980) used as the dependent variable an aggregate measure of participation over individual decisions. The measure is $\log_e$ of the odds in favor of off-farm work. The odds were defined as the share of the farm operators in an area who worked off-farm divided by the share of farm operators in the same area who did not work off-farm.

In Table 5.7, Part B, the empirical results for off-farm participation that are reported give the sign of coefficients, rather than the coefficient, of the indicated variable. The results from the five studies, four for the United States and one for Canada, show that farmers who have higher schooling levels have a larger probability of off-farm work than other farmers. On the other hand, an additional year of schooling of the farmer's wife tends to reduce the probability of him working off-farm. In the four farm level studies, additional nonfarm asset income reduces the probability of off-farm work. The probability of off-farm work is also reduced for farm operators who live a greater distance from the nearest city, but the negative marginal effect of distance becomes smaller as farm operators live a greater distance from a city. The studies do not present a consistent story about the effects of operator's age on the probability of off-farm work. Two of the farm level studies (Sumner 1982; Jensen and Salant 1986) found that the probability increases with age, suggesting that off-farm work aids exit from farming. Studies by Bollman (1979) and by Huffman and Lange (1989) found that age has a negative marginal effect, which suggests that off-farm work is used to supplement household incomes during entry into farming. In conclusion, farmers' schooling, nonfarm asset income, and distance to nearest city are key variables for determining or explaining the probability that farmers participate in off-farm work in North America.

Annual hours (or days) of off-farm work measure the intensity of off-farm work. The empirical specification of the off-farm labor-supply functions estimated in the five studies and summarized in Table 5.8 was in the spirit of equation (5.21). The reactions of annual off-farm hours (days) that are summarized in Table 5.8 are adjusted so that they represent the unconditional or expected average reaction of all farm operators, not just the ones that participate in off-farm work. The elasticities given in Table 5.8 are estimates of the percentage change of operator's hours (days) of off-farm work due to a 1-percent change in his off-farm wage, his spouse's off-farm wage, and price of farm output, respectively.

The estimates of operators' wage elasticity of off-farm labor supply are positive, showing that they respond positively to higher wage rates, other things equal. For the farm-level samples, the estimate obtained by Huffman and Lange (1989) was quite small (0.06), but the estimates obtained by Jensen and Salant (1986) and by Sumner (1982) were larger (0.21 to 0.40). For the aggregate data, Huffman (1980) obtained a wage elasticity of 0.34, which was similar to the ones obtained by Jensen and Salant (1986) and by Sumner (1982). Lopez (1984) aggregated the days of off-farm work of all farm household members together, so his elasticity is of a different nature. He obtained, however, a wage elasticity of 0.18, which seems to be consistent with the other estimates.

Lopez (1984) was the only researcher to include the farm output price as a variable explaining off-farm work. He obtained a farm output price elasticity of off-farm work of -0.18. Huffman (1980) included predicted farm output, rather than the farm output price, and obtained an elasticity of -0.43. These effects suggest that annual hours of off-farm work are highly responsive to agricultural profitability.

Four of the five studies showed a positive effect of additional farmer's schooling on off-farm work. The sizes of the marginal effects, even for the positive ones, have a wide range (two hours to 74 days annually per year of schooling). The evidence on the reaction of operator's off-farm work to an increment in his wife's schooling is mixed. Two studies obtained estimates that were positive, two obtained estimates that were negative, and Lopez's study did not include wife's schooling.

On the whole, these studies have had considerable success in explaining annual hours or days of off-farm work of farmers in North America.

Farm household income

Incomes of farm households are a result of conscious decisions made by their members and to luck. The U.S. Census Bureau surveys about 1,500 farm households as part of a much larger survey of the population each year to obtain information on household income and labor force participation. Since 1976, the state of residence of each of these farm households has been identified. This is important because agricultural input and output prices and local labor market data are collected regularly on a state level basis. These data can be combined with the CPS farm household data to provide a set of household, farm, and local labor market variables that are in the spirit of equations (5.22) and (5.28). We have chosen to use data for the income years of 1978, 1979, 1981, and 1982 to examine econometrically the determinants of farm household income. The first two years are ones when the general level of unemployment was low in the United States and net farm incomes were relatively large. The latter two years are ones where a major business recession was occurring and net farm incomes were relatively small. Table 5.6 provides a summary of the off-farm participation rate of husbands and wives in this sample and on the relative importance of off-farm wage and salary income and of net farm income to CPS farm household income.

The econometric estimates of the coefficients obtained from fitting the reduced-form farm household income equation to the four cross sections of farm households pooled over the four years are reported in Table 5.9. Household income, household asset income, the state average wage rate in manufacturing, and prices of farm outputs and inputs are deflated by the Consumer Price Index so that they are in real terms. Also, the algebraic specification of the equation is one where the dependent variable, total annual farm household income from all sources, and all of the exogenous prices and asset income are in natural logarithmic units. Two estimates of the income equation are reported. The first one includes a broad set of variables that might reasonably be expected to explain farm household income. In the second equation, variables that seemed likely to have an endogenous component with decisions affecting household cash income (i.e., number of children less than age 6 and ages 6–18) and nonfarm asset income, and that have coefficients that are not significantly different from zero in the first equation (i.e., rate of growth of employment, change in percent of jobs in the service occupations), are excluded.[6]

The equation in the second column of Table 5.9 seems "best," and the discussion focuses on it. Household income has a strong age component. Age is associated with work (farm, nonfarm, and household) experience and with the timing of a number of life-cycle decisions, e.g., marriage, family size, farm size, and planning for retirement. The results show that a one-year increase in husband's age causes a positive but diminishing

---

6. The area of farmland of each farm business is assumed to be one of the joint production, consumption, and labor supply decisions made by farm households. Thus, acres of farmland is not an exogenous variable.

Table 5.9. An econometric explanation of real total farm household income, United States, 1978, 1979, 1981, and 1982 ($N = 5,586$)

Variables	Log_e (household income)		Variable means
Husband's age	−0.023	0.028	50.5
	(10.3)[a]	(13.18)	
(Husband's age)^2	−0.00025	−0.00026	
	(11.8)	(12.5)	
Husband's yrs. schooling	0.016	0.021	11.3
	(9.6)	(9.7)	
Wife's yrs. schooling	0.015	0.018	11.8
	(6.4)	(7.2)	
Dummy (nonwhite = 1)	−0.0029	−0.045	0.03
	(0.1)	(1.5)	
Log_e (state avg. mfg. wage in 1967 prices), lagged 2 yrs.	0.10	0.129	3.03
	(1.84)	(2.3)	
Unemployment rate (state avg.)	0.006	0.008	6.67
	(1.5)	(1.9)	
Deviation of state unemployment rate from normal rate, lagged 1 yr.	−0.013	−0.010	−0.268
	(1.8)	(1.3)	
Log_e (expected state crop price index in 1967 prices), lagged 1 yr.	0.15	0.134	0.48
	(2.7)	(2.3)	
Log_e (expected state livestock price index in 1967 prices), lagged 1 yr.	−0.217	−0.253	0.54
	(3.7)	(4.1)	
Log_e (state wage for hired farm labor in 1967 prices)	0.239	0.241	0.50
	(3.2)	(3.1)	
Log_e (state price index of other farm inputs in 1967 prices)	0.174	0.256	0.54
	(1.2)	(1.8)	
Normal annual state precipitation (in./yr.)	0.0066	0.0059	35.7
	(3.1)	(2.7)	
Normal annual state growing-degree days	0.000063	0.000072	3,336
	(4.2)	(4.6)	
Precipitation × growing-degree days	−0.0000013	−0.0000013	
	(2.7)	(2.7)	
Dummy (North Central = 1)	−0.020	−0.006	0.455
	(0.7)	(0.2)	
Dummy (South = 1)	−0.021	−0.007	0.378
	(0.7)	(0.2)	
Dummy (West = 1)	−0.013	−0.008	0.118
	(0.4)	(0.2)	
Number of children < 6 yrs. of age	−0.058		0.27
	(6.1)		
Number of children age 6 to 18	−0.0005		0.69
	(0.1)		
Log_e (nonfarm asset income + $5,000)[b]	0.501		
	(23.5)		
Rate of growth of employment in state between t and $t-2$	−0.005		0.036
	(0.0)		
Change in percent of a state's jobs in service occupations over past 2 yrs.	−0.001		0.91
	(0.3)		
	−0.085	−0.085	
Time trend	11.9	(11.6)	
	4.612	8.567	
Intercept	(20.9)	(64.3)	
R^2	0.278	0.204	

Note: Income is in 1967 prices, and $20,000 was added to get rid of negative values. The farm households from the states of Maine, New Hampshire, Vermont, Massachusetts, Rhode Island, and Connecticut are excluded. The mean is $15,443.

[a]Absolute values of t-ratios are in parentheses.
[b]Income in 1967 prices, with $5,000 added to get rid of negative values.

marginal percentage increase in household income. At mean age, the marginal effect is 0.2 percent. An increase of husband's and wife's schooling is expected to increase off-farm wage offers, change off-farm and farm work hours, and enhance farm productivity. The results show that an additional year of husband's schooling increases household income on average 2.1 percent and of wife's schooling 1.8 percent. Household income for nonwhite households tends to be slightly lower than for white households (about 4.5 percent).

Three variables represent local nonfarm labor market conditions. Farm households that reside in states where the average wage in manufacturing is higher also have larger household incomes (elasticity of 0.13). Also, households that reside in states where the unemployment rate is higher have larger household incomes, but when the unemployment rate is larger than normal, farm household income is reduced. These latter two results mean that farm household incomes are affected by the general business cycle.

Eight variables represent conditions associated with expected profitability of farming. A higher expected price for crop products increases household income (elasticity of 0.13), but higher expected livestock-product prices reduces it (elasticity of −0.25). The negative effect of livestock prices seems to reflect inventory adjustments. Farmers tend to build breeding herds and to have smaller livestock sales when future livestock prices are expected to be high. The positive effect (elasticity of 0.24) of the hired farm wage rate on farm household income is evidence that this wage has positive family labor-supply effects that offset negative farm labor demand effects. This result was not expected because labor hired is considered to be an imperfect substitute for family labor. We do not have a good explanation for the positive coefficient of other farm input prices.

The climatic effects are strong statistically and economically important. An additional 3.6 inches of annual precipitation increases farm household income by 0.56 percent at the sample mean. An additional 334 growing-degree-days increases household income by 0.85 percent. Furthermore, at the sample mean, additional annual precipitation and a longer growing season are substitutes. The marginal change in income caused by additional rainfall (growing-degree-days) is reduced as the number of growing-degree-days (precipitation) increases.

Regional differences in farm household incomes are not statistically significant. However, the coefficient of the time trend is significant, and it shows that farm household incomes were declining in real terms at an average rate of 8.5 percent per year over the sample period 1978–82.

In conclusion, the agricultural household model has provided a framework that helped us gain insights about the contribution of a number of different variables to U.S. farm household incomes. Human capital and local labor market variables, including business-cycle effects; agricultural climatic conditions; and prices of farm outputs and inputs all contribute to the explanation of U.S. farm household incomes. See Emerson (1986) for a review of other approaches and Huffman (1988) for a discussion of related issues.

Implications

Part of the resource adjustment out of agriculture in North America since 1950 has been the increased off-farm work participation of farm household members. For the households that have small farm sales, off-farm income is the primary source of household cash income, except for households containing retired individuals. Negative net farm income is the price of a rural lifestyle that many of them desire to consume. Before 1981, many of these households also expected to capture significant real capital gains on farmland appreciation. The increased importance of off-farm work has meant that the size of the rural population in North America is larger than it would be otherwise. A higher density of the rural population has some advantages for the provision of quality public services to rural people. It also means that urban areas are slightly less congested than they would be if more of the rural people moved to the cities.

The increased integration of farm and nonfarm labor markets, associated with rising off-farm work of farm household members, has increased the short-run elasticity of the supply of labor to agriculture. When this fact is combined with the increasing share of farm production costs that are due to purchased inputs that are highly elastic in supply, it is clear that errors in setting U.S. government farm commodity support prices too high can and have been very costly to U.S. taxpayers. Recent attempts to take large quantities of U.S. farmland out of production for the next 10 years seem somewhat misguided, since farmland is only one input in agricultural production.

References

Antle, John. 1984. "The structure of U.S. agricultural technology, 1910-78." *American Journal of Agricultural Economics* 66:414–21.

Becker, Gary S. 1981. *A Treatise on the Family.* Cambridge, Mass.: Harvard University Press.

Bollman, Ray D. 1979. *Off-Farm Work by Farmers*. Ottawa, Canada: Statistics Canada.

Carlin, Thomas A., and L. M. Ghelfi. 1979. "Off-farm employment and the farm sector," in *Structure Issues of American Agriculture*, 270–73. Agricultural Economics Report No. 438. Washington, D.C.: Statistics and Cooperative Service, U.S. Department of Agriculture.

Emerson, Robert. 1986. "Human capital and incomes of rural households," in *Human Resources Research, 1887–1987*, ed. Ruth E. Deacon and Wallace E. Huffman, 235–49. Ames: College of Home Economics, Iowa State University.

Huffman, Wallace E. 1973. "Household behavior: Hours of work." College of Business Faculty Working Paper No. 22. Stillwater: Oklahoma State University.

————. 1977. "Interactions between farm and nonfarm labor markets." *American Journal of Agricultural Economics* 59:1054–61.

————. 1980. "Farm and off-farm work decisions: The role of human capital." *Review of Economics and Statistics* 62:14–23.

————. 1988. "Human capital for agriculture," in *Agriculture and Rural Areas Approaching the Twenty-first Century: Challenges for Agricultural Economics*, ed. R. J. Hildreth, Kathryn L. Lipton, Kenneth C. Clayton, and Carl C. O'Connor, 499–517. Ames: Iowa State University Press.

Huffman, Wallace E., and M. D. Lange. 1989. "Off-farm work decisions of husbands and wives: Joint decision making." *Review of Economics and Statistics* 71:471–80.

Huffman, Wallace E., and R. E. Evenson. 1989. "Supply and demand functions for multiproduct U.S. cash grain farms: Biases caused by research and other policies." *American Journal Agricultural Economics* 71:761–73.

Jensen, Helen H., and P. Salant. 1986. *Fringe Benefits in Operator Off-Farm Labor Supply: Evidence from Mississippi and Tennessee*. Staff Report AGES 860403. Washington, D.C.: Economic Research Service, U.S. Department of Agriculture.

Lange, Mark D. 1979. "An economic analysis of time allocation and capital labor ratios in household production of farm families in Iowa." Ph.D. dissertation, Iowa State University.

Lopez, Ramon E. 1984. "Estimating labor supply and production decisions of self-employed farm producers." *European Economic Review* 24:61–82.

Pisarski, Alan E. 1987. *The Nation's Public Works: Report on Highways, Streets, Roads and Bridges*. Washington, D.C.: National Council on Public Works Improvements.

Pollak, Robert, and M. L. Wachter. 1975. "The relevance of the household production function and its implications for the allocation of time." *Journal of Political Economy* 83:255–78.

Shumway, C. Richard. 1983. "Supply, demand, and technology in a multiproduct industry: Texas field crops." *American Journal of Agricultural Economics* 65:748–70.

Singh, I., L. Squire, and J. Strauss, eds. 1986. *Agricultural Household Models: Extensions, Applications, and Policy*. Baltimore: Johns Hopkins University Press, for the World Bank.

Smith, James P. 1984. "Race and human capital." *American Economic Review* 74:685–98.

Smith, James P., and F. Welch. 1977. "Black-white wage ratios: 1960–70." *American Economic Review* 67:323–39.

Statistics Canada. 1952. *1951 Census of Canada, Agriculture.* Ottawa: Statistics Canada.

————. 1962. *1961 Census of Canada, Agriculture.* Ottawa: Statistics Canada.

————. 1972. *1971 Census of Canada, Agriculture.* Ottawa: Statistics Canada.

————. 1982. *1981 Census of Canada, Agriculture.* Ottawa: Statistics Canada.

————. 1983. *Census of Agriculture Indexed Agricultural Sales 1961– 1981.* Ottawa: Statistics Canada.

Sumner, Daniel A. 1982. "The off-farm labor supply of farmers." *American Journal of Agricultural Economics* 64:499–509.

U.S. Bureau of the Census. Various years. *Current Population Survey Tapes.* (Unpublished computer tapes.) Washington, D.C.: Bureau of the Census.

U.S. Department of Agriculture. 1984. *Economic Indicators of the Farm Sector: Farm Sector Review, 1982.* Washington, D.C.: U.S. Government Printing Office.

————. 1986. *Economic Indicators of the Farm Sector: Farm Sector Review, 1984.* Washington, D.C.: U.S. Government Printing Office.

U.S. Department of Commerce. 1952. *Census of Agriculture, 1950.* Vol 2. Washington: D.C.: Bureau of the Census.

————. 1953. *Census of Population, 1950.* Vol. 4, Special Report, Part 5, Chapter B, Education. Washington, D.C.: U.S. Government Printing Office.

————. 1973. *Census of Agriculture, 1969.* Vol. 2. Washington, D.C.: Bureau of the Census.

————. 1983a. *Census of Agriculture, 1982.* Vol. 2. Washington, D.C.: Bureau of the Census.

————. 1983b. *Census of Population, 1980.* Vol. 1, Chapter C, *General Social and Economic Characteristics.* Washington, D.C.: U.S. Government Printing Office.

Weaver, Robert D. 1983. "Multiple input, multiple output production choices and technology in the U.S. wheat region." *American Journal of Agricultural Economics* 65:45–56.

CHAPTER 6

Efficiency Aspects of Part-time Farming

RAY D. BOLLMAN

Part-time farming is a stable and persistent feature of the Canadian agricultural structure. The proportion of census-farm operators[1] with some days of off-farm work has been stable at about one-third over the 1941 to 1986 period (Figure 6.1). There has been little discussion of the economist's turf: the efficiency considerations of this phenomenon. The objective of this chapter is to discuss the efficiency aspects of part-time farming.

The term *part-time farming* will be used throughout this chapter, partly because of tradition, partly because it is shorter than the term *multiple job-holding farming families,* and partly because this chapter starts by analyzing part-time farming as traditionally defined. I understand and support the initiative to understand the structure of agriculture by asking "what are families with farming activities doing?" Such a perspective does not constrain us to one operator, one farm. It also avoids (almost) the question of "what is a farm?" and it avoids the designation of a farm or

Helpful discussions with Ted Horbulyk and Daniel Sumner are gratefully acknowledged.

1. In the 1981 and 1986 Canadian censuses of agriculture, a census-farm was defined as an agricultural holding with $250 or more gross farm sales. In the 1961 to 1976 period, data were collected for holdings with gross sales of $50 or more. The 1941 and 1951 censuses operated under slightly different definitions with the same objective of including all agricultural holdings. However, in 1951, holdings with one to three acres *and* under $250 sales were not included which is part of the reason that the proportion of operators with "some days of off-farm work" is slightly lower in 1951 (Figure 6.1).

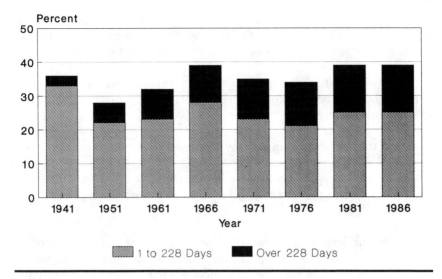

Figure 6.1. Percent of operators working off-farm, Canada. (*Statistics Canada*)

farmer or farming family as full-time or part-time. It focuses attention on the family as the unit for measuring and analyzing economic welfare and it provides, in my view, the key to understanding the structure of agriculture (as measured by traditional measures such as the size distribution of farms). The chapter is concluded by considering the total family income of part-time farming families or, if you prefer, multiple job-holding farming families.

Conceptual Issues

One of the thrusts of my earlier study on part-time farming (Bollman 1979a, 1979b) was that part-time farming was consistent (or could be consistent) with an efficient allocation of resources. This suggests that the efficiency aspect of part-time farming is (largely) an empirical question. However, at this point, one must pause to ponder, What Is the Question?

1. Is the question merely one of *technical efficiency?* Are we concerned solely or primarily with increasing the level of farm output given the input mix? That is, are we mainly interested in reaching the frontier of the farm production function?

2. Alternatively, are we concerned with whether farm resources are allocated optimally? This is the *allocative efficiency* question of whether one is at the optimal position on the farm production function.

If we proceed to the second question, we must address the issue of how to price labor for the operator and other unpaid family members. Two cases arise from the analysis:

1. If the operator (or other family member) in fact participates in off-farm work, one can use the observed price.
2. If the operator (or other family member) does not work off-farm, one must revert to the (shadow) price of leisure to obtain a price for the individual's labor.

Thus, the issue of how to price the labor of the operator (or other family member) is embedded in the discussion of the allocation of family resources. The form of the utility function and the trade-offs of the family between leisure and consumption are important issues. If "scenery"[2] is an important component of what the particular family is producing and consuming on their farm, this impacts directly on the measurement of output when we address technical efficiency in the very first question.

Are we looking for answers for farm extension workers when they advise part-time farmers on how to increase their *farm* incomes? The macro version of this question relates to the (perceived) mandate of ministries of agriculture to supply cheap food to the electorate. One way policymakers pursue the latter objective is to prevent resources from going elsewhere. If the land is paved, no food is produced. (Note that the discussion in this paragraph applies largely, albeit not solely, to discussions of technical efficiency.)

Alternatively, are we addressing questions in the broader context of economic and rural development? For example, are we looking for answers for extension workers when they advise part-time farmers on how to increase their *total* income from all sources? Or, on a larger scale, are we addressing the question for rural economic development agencies of how best to allocate human and physical capital to raise community incomes? (Note that the discussion in this paragraph applies largely, although again not solely, to discussions of allocative efficiency.)

Even more broadly, are we addressing questions of economic and so-

---

2. Scenery may be viewed here as a basket of goods including "fresh air," "open space," "good place to raise kids," "being one's own boss," and income in kind, plus other "psychic income" and home-produced benefits.

cial welfare? Specifically, should we not recognize the value of household production? For families with farming activities, off-farm work activities, *and* within-household productive activities, the value of household production would appear to be a major factor. Consequently, the efficient allocation of family human resources among farming activities, off-farm employment activities, *and* within-household production activities would appear to be an important consideration for part-time farming families.

If we observe part-time farmers to be inefficient (however defined), which is the chicken and which is the egg? Which came first, the inefficiency or the part-time farming? Do inefficient farmers adjust part of their labor to off-farm work because they recognize their farming activity to be inefficient? In this sense, part-time farming may be part of the solution, not part of the problem. This is one interpretation of "resource" in the discussion by Fuller and Mage (1976). In this context, we can make two observations:

1. Farmers with lower levels of commodity output, given the level of inputs, appear to have greater probability of exit from farming.[3] In this case, the movement out of farming appears to be at least partly due to the initial inefficiency of the farming activity.

2. Some farmers increase their days of off-farm work *and* increase their farm size in terms of gross farm sales (Bollman and Kapitany 1981). In this case, part-time farming appears *not* to constrain, and may in fact enhance, the expansion of the farm unit.

The Contribution of Part-time Farmers to Aggregate Output

Part-time farmer inefficiency would not seem to be a major issue if, in fact, the share of agricultural resources controlled by part-time farmers was insignificant. In Canada, over the period 1971 to 1986, operators with "some days of off-farm work" contributed only about 20 percent of aggregate sales (Table 6.1). If the part-time farming definition is more strict, say over 96 days of work off-farm, then only about 10 percent of aggregate sales are contributed by part-time farmers.

It is recognized that one possible reason for a small share of output contributed by part-time farmers may be due to their inefficiency! Part-

---

3. This conclusion is based on preliminary regressions from longitudinal 1966 to 1981 Census of Agriculture Match data for Canada.

Table 6.1. Distribution of census-farm operators and gross sales by number of off-farm work days, Canada

| | Number of operator days of off-farm work | | | | | | | | | |
Year	None	1–96	97–228	>228	Total	None	1–96	97–228	>228	Total
	Number of operators					Percent of total operators				
1941	472,443	188,042	49,035	23,312	732,832	64	26	7	3	100
1951	450,999	80,182	55,376	36,534	623,091	72	13	9	6	100
1961	327,228	57,319	55,033	41,323	480,903	68	12	11	9	100
1966	264,799	71,128	48,515	46,080	430,522	62	17	11	11	100
1971	236,841	45,641	41,534	42,112	366,128	65	12	11	12	100
1976	223,953	31,066	39,896	43,663	338,578	66	9	12	13	100
1981	195,225	35,677	43,256	44,203	318,361	61	11	14	14	100
1986	177,445	32,094	42,013	41,537	293,089	61	11	14	14	100
	Aggregate gross sales ($000,000)					Percent of aggregate gross sales				
1966	2,466	475	194	156	3,291	75	14	6	5	100
1971	2,872	409	205	158	3,644	79	11	6	4	100
1976	8,098	834	583	445	9,961	81	8	6	4	100
1981	12,304	1,594	849	780	15,526	79	10	5	5	100
1986	16,783	1,787	1,244	971	20,785	81	9	6	5	100

Source: Statistics Canada, Census of Agriculture, years cited above.

time farmers do control a larger share of the major inputs relative to their share of output (Table 6.2). They certainly control more land—but some of this may be scenery output.

Table 6.2. Proportion of output and resources on census-farms by operator days of off-farm work, Canada, 1986

	Number of operator days of off-farm work				
	None	1–96	97–228	>228	Total
Number of operators	175,265	31,980	41,865	41,375	290,485
Percent of operators	60.3	11.0	14.4	14.2	100.0
Aggregate sales ($000,000)	15,461	1,765	1,228	937	19,392
Percent of sales	79.7	9.1	6.3	4.8	100.0
Aggregate acres (000,000)	114	18	15	9	156
Percent of acres	73.0	11.5	9.6	6.0	100.0
Aggregate farm capital ($000,000)	75,011	10,839	10,169	8,441	104,460
Percent of farm capital	71.8	10.4	9.7	8.1	100.0
Aggregate machinery capital ($000,000)	14,735	2,153	1,868	1,355	20,111
Percent of machinery capital	73.3	10.7	9.3	6.7	100.0

Source: Statistics Canada, Census of Agriculture, 1986.

Suppose we observe, with every "census snapshot", that part-time farmers control more resources than they control outputs, and thus appear inefficient at a point in time in terms of agricultural commodity output per unit of agricultural input. Should we conclude that part-time farming is inefficient or should we merely state that "interference is temporary; do not adjust your set?" That is, part-time farming may be a phase or window through which one-third of the Canadian farm structure is always passing, either entering or leaving full-time farming. I have not addressed this perspective in this chapter. The longitudinal 1966 to 1986 Census of Agriculture Match would seem capable of shedding considerable light on this question. Previous research has provided the following observations:

1. Entry and exit rates for part-time farmers are larger than for full-time farmers.

2. Few part-time farmers "graduate" to full-time farming, but at the same time, many new full-time farmers have been part-time farmers.

3. Few full-time farmers use part-time farming as a mechanism to leave farming (Bollman and Steeves 1982; Bollman and Kapitany 1981; Kapitany and Bollman 1983).

Literature Relating to Efficiency Aspects of Part-time Farming

The consideration of "efficiency of what" can be asked as, "What are we maximizing?" If it is the efficiency of food production per se, then we would investigate the production and profits of the farm enterprise. However, if it is the welfare of the family that is to be maximized, one alternative is to investigate the utility of the family. One example of an investigation of this alternative is the study by Musser, Martin, and Wise (1975). They find a utility maximization hypothesis explains observed beef cow-calf herds that were larger than would be supported with a profit-maximization hypothesis. This example focuses the question. When investigating the efficiency aspects of part-time farms (or full-time farms for that matter), do we investigate the efficiency of food production in terms of profit maximization or cost minimization *or* do we investigate the welfare of the farm family in terms of utility maximization?

Stigler (1976) addresses two issues of discussions of "efficiency": (1) differing motivations among human agents and (2) investment in knowledge to learn about alternative technologies (i.e., different or "better" production function frontiers). Stigler (pp. 213–14) observes:

> in every motivational case, the question is: What is output? Surely no person ever seeks to maximize the output of any one thing; even the single proprietor, unassisted by hired labor, does not seek to maximize the output of corn; he seeks to maximize utility, and surely other products including leisure and health as well as corn enter into his utility function. When more of one goal is achieved at the cost of less of another goal, the increase in output due to (say) increased effort is not an increase in "efficiency"; it is a change in output . . . inefficiency attributed to motivational factors characterizes as inefficiency . . . the existence and pursuit of other desired outputs. . . . This tunnel vision of output seems entirely unrewarding; it imposes one person's goal upon other persons who have never accepted that goal.

He discusses (Stigler 1976, p. 215) the issue of production function frontiers and the choice of technology: "The problem of determining which technologies will be used by each firm (and, for that matter, each person). . . . The choice is fundamentally a matter of investment in knowledge." His example is directly applicable to our purpose:

> We observe two farmers with reasonably homogeneous land and equipment, who nevertheless obtain substantially different amounts of corn. We measure this corn output over some period of time to reduce the effects of stochastic

variation (i.e., unenumerated inputs such as weather). The observed variation is due, perhaps, to differences in knowledge, including the knowledge of technology or the knowledge of how far to carry the application of each productive factor. The farmers will differ in the cost of learning new things or the expected returns from new knowledge—one may be planning to leave agriculture shortly—so they "rationally" devote different amounts of resources to acquiring knowledge. Or one is simply more intelligent than the other, and learns more quickly or thinks more precisely (for example, makes fewer mistakes in arithmetic).

The effects of these variations in output are all attributed to specific inputs, and in the present case chiefly to the differences in entrepreneurial capacity. In neoclassical economics, the producer is always at a production frontier, but his frontier may be above or below that of other producers. The procedure allocates the foregone product to some factor, so in turn the owner of that factor will be incited to allocate it correctly.

Tauer (1987) wonders in what sense inefficiency is real or perceived. Is perceived technical inefficiency really allocative inefficiency? Alternatively, allocative inefficiency may be perceived, "because of failure of the observer to measure all relevant inputs, or to correctly perceive what is being optimized or to account for all the constraints on the optimization process, etc. (Tauer, p. 2)." Tauer also argues that measured technical inefficiency may result from aggregating inputs that may, in themselves, be allocatively inefficient.

The study by Chong, Osburn, and Price (1987) illustrates some of the dilemmas of discussions concerning the "efficiency aspects of part-time farming." They define a land-use intensity variable and conclude, "A strong and negative interrelationship was found between off-farm employment and land use intensity" (p. 230).[4]

Their study raises two issues:

1. They often refer to land-use intensity as efficiency and thus variables that lower land-use intensity are lowering efficiency.
2. The objective of maximizing food production in Korea via maximizing land-use intensity may be a real policy objective, regardless of the within-household arguments on efficiency.

Barnum and Squire (1979) model the consumption and production decisions of agricultural households as being separately and independently determined. They argue that this is appropriate for their study area in

---

4. In this case, the "land equivalent ratio" was used, which is a weighted sum of the average yields of the crop for the farm.

Malaysia because (almost) all families either work off-farm or hire labor. Because the family is participating in the off-farm labor market, the family is assumed to maximize profits in farm production subject to the market wage rate *and* the family is assumed to maximize utility in the choice between consumption and leisure subject to the market wage rate. Is this assumption appropriate for analyzing consumption and production decisions of census-farm operator households in Canada?

Lopez (1984, 1986) empirically tests a nonrecursive model and finds it provides a better fit to the data as compared to a recursive model. This implies that household consumption and production decisions are not independent. Thus, both the size of the farm and the allocation of resources within the farm are determined by family-specific variables. Lopez notes that this result holds even when the operator (or other family member) participates in some off-farm work, if differing utility levels are attained for a given amount of time in farm versus off-farm work, or if the cost of commuting to an off-farm job is recognized. (For a graphical summary of the latter case, see Bollman 1979b.) Lopez's data are census division observations which are a mix of (1) observations appropriate for a recursive model (i.e., operators who work off-farm or hire labor, or both), and (2) observations appropriate for a nonrecursive model (i.e., operators who do not work off-farm and do not hire labor). It seems to me that Lopez's results are really saying that the nonrecursive component is an important share of the total set of observations. For example, in Canada in 1986 one-third of the aggregate gross sales are from farms (representing one-third of all farms) with no hired labor *and* the operator does not participate in the off-farm labor market (Table 6.3). This is the group of farms for which a recursive model is clearly inappropriate.

Singh, Squire, and Strauss (1986, p. 89) discuss in detail the implications of recursive versus nonrecursive models for analyzing agricultural household behavior: "a sufficient condition for recursiveness is that all markets exist for commodities that are both produced and consumed, with the household being price-taker in each one, and that such commodities are homogeneous." So-called recursive models allow one to model the farm production decisions independently of the household consumption decisions, even though they take place at the same time. What are the implications of the recursiveness issue for considerations of the efficiency aspects of part-time farming? If one assumes family labor and paid labor are perfect substitutes, then a recursive model is appropriate.

In my view, such an assumption is inappropriate in North America. Since part-time farming families do participate in the off-farm labor market, the off-farm wage can be used as the "price" or opportunity cost of family labor in farm work. The implications for efficiency analysis arise in

Table 6.3. Participation of census-farm operators under age 60 in off-farm work and hired farm labor markets, Canada, 1986

	No hired non-family labor	Some hired non-family labor	All census-farms
No. operator days off-farm			
Number of operators	75,095	46,450	121,550
Percent of operators	33.3	20.6	53.8
Aggregate gross sales ($000,000)	5,487	7,656	13,144
Percent of gross sales	32.7	45.6	78.3
Average gross sales ($)	73,064	164,832	108,133
Some operator days off-farm			
Number of operators	77,860	26,395	104,255
Percent of operators	34.5	11.7	46.2
Aggregate gross sales ($000,000)	1,937	1,703	3,640
Percent of gross sales	11.5	10.1	21.7
Average gross sales ($)	24,881	64,511	34,915
All farm operators			
Number of operators	152,950	72,845	225,800
Percent of operators	67.7	32.3	100.0
Aggregate gross sales ($000,000)	7,424	9,359	16,783
Percent of gross sales	44.2	55.8	100.0
Average gross sales ($)	48,538	128,478	74,328

Source: Statistics Canada, *Census of Agriculture*, 1986.

cases of full-time farming families. If family and hired labor are not substitutes, and since no family member works off the farm, the "shadow wage" of family labor is determined endogenously with the utility function considerations of the trade-off between leisure and consumption goods. In this case, the production and consumption decisions are not separable, and the agricultural household model is not recursive. Only if the shadow wage of family labor is correctly modeled will the input mix between family labor and other inputs appear to be "allocatively efficient."

Josephson and Watt (1987, pp. 25–26) asked new farm entrants about the importance of off-farm work in getting established in farming.

In a majority of cases (64%), either the new entrant or spouse worked off the farm. . . . 29% felt that they could not have been able to start farming without the off-farm job. . . . Most respondents recognized that off-farm work interfered with their ability to operate the farm at least to some extent. While 70% said it only "partially" interfered, 6% did not qualify the extent of interference. The remaining 24% said it did not interfere at all. When asked whether they would quit off-farm work once they had become established farmers, 29% said no, 59% said maybe and 12% said yes. These results indicate a significant dependence upon off-farm work to provide income for new entrants and a definite unwillingness to give it up, even after the dependence may diminish.

Freshwater (1982) determined that part-time farmers in Saskatchewan were 7 percent less efficient than full-time farmers but that all farmers were only 46 percent as efficient as the most efficient farmers. The determination of a lower level of agricultural output per unit of agricultural input for part-time farmers was made after the actual hours of the operator's on-farm labor was taken into account. Technical efficiency was lower for part-time farmers, even after other factors such as farm size, operator's education, and operator's age were included to explain the difference between maximum expected output and observed output.

Some Empirical Observations

If we take a historical perspective of the discussion of the efficiency aspects of part-time farming, we would note that decades ago farm families in North America were not fully occupied in plant and animal husbandry. Part of the time of household members was involved in machinery repair, production of motive power (e.g., horses), production of fuel (e.g., hay and oats) plus within-household food processing (e.g., cheese and butter). Over time, it has become more efficient to produce these items in specialized locations off the farm. The participation of farm family households in such activities now appears as off-farm work by farm family members. One major source of off-farm employment for farmers in western Canada during the oil price booms of the 1970s was working in the oil fields. To the extent that the increase in off-farm work by farm family members has been associated with the shift of certain production activities to more efficient off-farm locations, a measured increase in off-farm work represents an efficient allocation of farm family labor.

Efficiency aspects of the farm

OUTPUT PER ACRE.   Output per acre is sometimes used as a partial productivity indicator of technical efficiency. The question is, do part-time farms show a different level of output per acre compared to full-time farmers? Regardless of the size of farm in terms of total farm acres, the sales per acre of part-time farmers are lower than the sales per acre of full-time farmers (Table 6.4 and Figure 6.2).

Observations in Figure 6.2 are ranked from the smallest farms to the largest farms in terms of acres per census-farm. In 1986, the median farm size (i.e., 50th percentile) was almost 240 acres. Note from the third row of Table 6.4, which is labelled "cumulative percent" of farms, that 47 percent

Table 6.4. Gross sales per acre by total farm acres and operator days worked off-farm, Canada, 1986

| | Total farm acres | | | | | | | | | | | | |
	Under 3	3 to 9	10 to 69	70 to 239	240 to 399	400 to 559	560 to 759	760 to 1,119	1,120 to 1,599	1,600 to 2,239	2,240 to 2,879	2,880 and over	Total
All census-farms													
Number of census-farms	4,690	9,800	35,205	86,520	42,610	25,085	21,775	26,160	18,535	10,595	4,330	5,190	290,480
Percent of total	2	3	12	30	15	9	7	9	6	4	1	2	100
Cumulative percent[a]	2	5	17	47	62	70	78	87	93	97	98	100	
Average sales per acre	28,032	9,254	1,696	314	208	156	118	93	81	75	68	64	1,135
Std. dev. of sales per acre	95,472	27,122	8,232	889	353	317	284	183	214	114	70	151	13,968
Sales/acre plus 1 std. dev.	123,504	36,376	9,928	1,204	561	473	402	276	295	189	138	215	15,103
Sales/acre minus 1 std. dev.	−67,440	−17,868	−6,537	−575	−145	−162	−167	−90	−132	−39	−2	−88	−12,833
Operators with no days of off-farm work													
Number of census-farms	2,310	4,355	15,255	43,960	26,795	16,290	14,580	18,495	13,940	8,370	3,500	4,410	175,265
Percent of total	1	2	9	25	15	9	8	11	8	5	2	3	100
Cumulative percent[a]	1	4	13	38	53	62	70	81	89	94	96	98	100
Average sales per acre	42,401	16,099	2,925	443	264	190	139	104	88	79	71	66	1,426
Std. dev. of sales per acre	126,711	36,868	11,650	1,122	399	354	338	198	243	124	74	161	16,923
Sales/acre plus 1 std. dev.	169,112	52,966	14,575	1,565	663	544	477	302	331	203	145	227	18,350
Sales/acre minus 1 std. dev.	−84,311	−20,769	−8,725	−679	−135	−165	−199	−94	−155	−45	−3	−95	−15,497
Operators with some days of off-farm work													
Number of census-farms	2,380	5,445	19,945	39,560	15,815	8,790	7,195	7,660	4,590	2,225	825	785	115,220
Percent of total	2	5	17	34	14	8	6	7	4	2	1	1	100
Cumulative percent[a]	2	7	24	58	72	80	86	93	97	99	99	100	100
Average sales per acre	14,087	3,784	755	162	112	93	75	67	61	58	54	50	692
Std. dev. of sales per acre	44,576	13,039	3,709	439	227	220	102	137	71	60	45	77	7,479
Sales/acre plus 1 std. dev.	58,663	16,822	4,465	601	339	312	177	203	131	118	99	127	8,171
Sales/acre minus 1 std. dev.	−30,489	−9,255	−2,954	−277	−115	−127	−27	−70	−10	−2	9	−27	−6,787

Source: Statistics Canada, *Census of Agriculture,* 1986.
[a]May not add up to 100% due to rounding.

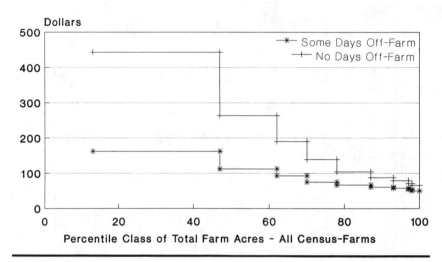

Figure 6.2. Gross sales per acre by operator days off-farm, Canada, 1986. (*Statistics Canada*)

of 1986 census-farms had less than 240 acres. For farms in the 47th to 62nd percentile class (240 to 399 acres), operators with no days of off-farm work reported $264 sales per acre and operators with some days of off-farm work reported $112 sales per acre.

CASH COSTS PER DOLLAR OF SALES. A usual textbook discussion of efficiency involves a discussion of average costs per unit of output. The question is, are the average cash costs of part-time farmers higher or lower than the average cash costs for full-time farmers? The average cash costs per dollar of sales for part-time farmers are higher than for full-time farmers across all farm sizes (Table 6.5 and Figure 6.3).

Observations in Figure 6.3 are ranked from the smallest farms to the largest farms in terms of gross sales per census-farm. In 1986, the median gross sales (i.e., 50th percentile) was $30,277. For farms in 50th to 59th percentile class (gross sales of $30,277 to 46,999), operators with no days of off-farm work reported cash costs of $0.78 per dollar of sales and operators with some days of off-farm work reported cash costs of $0.93 per dollar of sales.

GROSS SALES PER DAY OF OPERATOR WORK ON-FARM. The discussion above does not recognize any opportunity cost for the operator's labor. One might expect cash costs per dollar of sales to be higher for operators with off-farm

Table 6.5. Cash cost per dollar of sales by size of gross farm sales and operator days worked off-farm, Canada, 1986

	Percentile class of gross farm sales												
	1–9	10–19	20–29	30–39	40–49	50–59	60–69	70–79	80–89	90–94	95–98	99+	Total
	Gross Farm Sales												
	Under $2,167	$2,167 to 5,387	$5,388 to 10,560	$10,561 to 18,999	$19,000 to 30,276	$30,277 to 46,999	$47,000 to 68,640	$68,641 to 99,799	$99,800 to 157,081	$157,082 to 235,380	$235,381 to 562,549	$562,550 and over	Total
All census-farms													
Number of census-farms	29,150	29,160	29,140	28,845	29,420	29,020	29,250	29,125	29,085	14,465	11,370	2,440	290,480
Percent of total	10	10	10	10	10	10	10	10	10	5	4	1	100
Cumulative percent	10	20	30	40	50	60	70	80	90	95	99	100	
Average cost per $ of sales[a]	7.76	2.33	1.51	1.14	0.95	0.84	0.78	0.74	0.74	0.75	0.78	0.82	1.76
Std. dev. of cost per $ sales	17.67	2.85	1.37	0.86	0.59	0.43	0.35	0.29	0.25	0.23	0.22	0.23	6.06
Cost plus 1 std. dev.	25.42	5.18	2.89	2.00	1.53	1.27	1.13	1.03	0.99	0.98	1.00	1.05	7.82
Cost minus 1 std. dev.	−9.91	−.52	0.14	0.27	0.36	0.40	0.43	0.46	0.48	0.52	0.56	0.59	−4.30
Operators with no days of off-farm work													
Number of census-farms	11,260	11,385	12,000	13,575	16,530	18,520	21,010	22,750	23,930	12,200	9,910	2,205	175,265
Percent of total	6	6	7	8	9	11	12	13	14	7	6	1	100
Cumulative percent	6	13	20	28	37	48	59	72	86	93	99	100	
Average cost per $ of sales	7.76	2.22	1.44	1.05	0.88	0.78	0.74	0.72	0.72	0.74	0.77	0.82	1.38
Std. dev. of cost per $ sales	21.68	3.52	1.56	0.92	0.60	0.42	0.34	0.28	0.25	0.23	0.22	0.23	5.85
Cost plus 1 std. dev.	29.44	5.75	3.00	1.97	1.48	1.21	1.08	1.00	0.97	0.97	0.99	1.05	7.23
Cost minus 1 std. dev.	−13.92	−1.30	−.12	0.13	0.28	0.36	0.40	0.44	0.47	0.51	0.55	0.59	−4.48
Operators with some days of off-farm work													
Number of census-farms	17,890	17,775	17,140	15,270	12,895	10,500	8,245	6,380	5,160	2,265	1,460	240	115,215
Percent of total	16	15	15	13	11	9	7	6	4	2	1	0	100
Cumulative percent	16	31	46	59	70	79	87	92	97	99	100	100	
Average cost per $ of sales	7.76	2.40	1.56	1.22	1.03	0.93	0.87	0.83	0.81	0.80	0.81	0.84	2.34
Std. dev. of cost per $ sales	14.58	2.31	1.22	0.81	0.56	0.43	0.36	0.30	0.26	0.24	0.22	0.22	6.32
Cost plus 1 std. dev.	22.34	4.71	2.79	2.03	1.58	1.36	1.23	1.13	1.06	1.04	1.03	1.06	8.66
Cost minus 1 std. dev.	−6.83	0.09	0.34	0.41	0.47	0.50	0.51	0.53	0.55	0.56	0.60	0.62	−3.97

Source: Statistics Canada, *Census of Agriculture*, 1986.
[a]"Costs" are all cash costs except wages paid to family members.

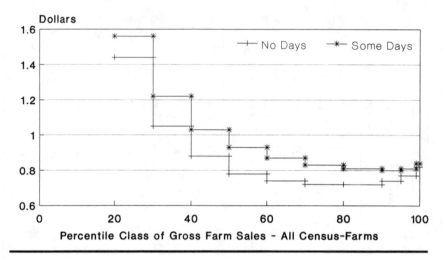

Figure 6.3. Cash cost per $ of sales by operator days off-farm, Canada, 1986. (*Statistics Canada*)

work as they substitute other inputs, including hired labor, for their own labor. If other inputs were perfect substitutes, we might expect output per day of operator's on-farm work to be flat as operators reduced their days of on-farm work.[5]

Interestingly, as operator labor is withdrawn from the farm, the gross sales per operator on-farm day falls. Operators working full-time on the farm reported sales of about $240 per day whereas operators reporting 100 through 325 days of work on the farm reported about $150 sales per day (Table 6.6 and Figures 6.4 and 6.5).

The observations in Figure 6.5 have been scaled by the percentile class of operators ranked by size class of operator days worked on-farm. For example, 20 percent of all census-farm operators work less than 150 days on their farm.[6] The operators in the 16th to 20th percentile of days of on-farm work (125 to 149 days on-farm) reported $140 sales per day worked on-farm. As can be seen from Figure 6.5, over 60 percent of all census-farm operators worked full-time on their farms.

NET CASH FARM INCOME PER DAY OF OPERATOR WORK ON-FARM. Similar to the analysis presented above, we present the net cash farm income per day

---

5. Days of operator's on-farm labor is calculated as 366 − "days of work off-farm." The figure 366 is chosen to accommodate operators who report 365 days of off-farm work!

6. See the third line in Table 6.6 labelled "cumulative percent."

Table 6.6. Gross sales and net cash farm income per day of operator work on-farm (by operator days worked on-farm), Canada, 1986

Days worked On-farm	Census-farm operators			Average sales per operator day on-farm		Average net cash farm income per operator day on-farm	
	Number	Percent	Cum. percent	Mean	St. dev.	Mean	St. dev.
1	5,590	2	2	34,070	167,587	2,704	55,717
2–24	1,210	0	2	3,819	10,919	119	5,065
25–49	1,275	0	3	819	8,003	29	2,927
50–74	4,665	2	4	392	996	−16	351
75–99	4,560	2	6	248	575	−14	222
100–124	16,215	6	12	177	483	−15	168
125–149	11,570	4	16	140	304	−12	118
150–174	13,430	5	20	143	383	−8	112
175–199	5,680	2	22	150	290	−1	110
200–224	6,255	2	24	146	292	1	102
225–249	6,495	2	26	149	313	7	103
250–274	6,975	2	29	154	286	13	113
275–299	6,870	2	31	154	251	14	82
300–324	7,625	3	34	151	213	17	77
325–349	9,345	3	37	183	262	26	91
350 and over	182,730	63	100	238	583	38	155

Source: Statistics Canada, Census of Agriculture, 1986.

Note: Operator days of on-farm work are calculated as 366 minus days of off-farm work. Thus individuals with one day of on-farm work reported 365 days of off-farm work and the reported average sales per operator day is the average gross sales for the year. Net cash farm income is calculated as gross sales minus cash expenses excluding wages paid to family members. Operator days of on-farm work are calculated as 366 minus days of off-farm work. Thus individuals with one day of on-farm work reported 365 days of off-farm work and the reported average net cash farm income per operator day is the average for the year.

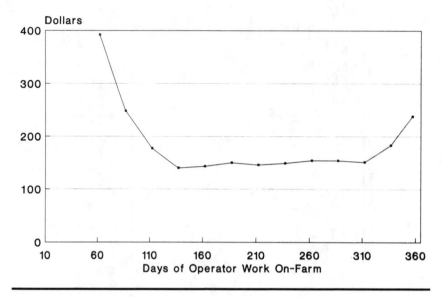

Figure 6.4. Sales per operator day on-farm, Canada, 1986. (*Statistics Canada*)

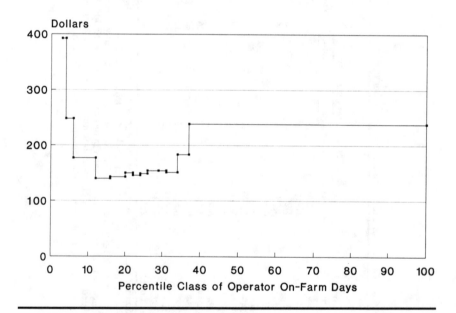

Figure 6.5. Sales per percentile class of operator days on-farm, Canada, 1986. (*Statistics Canada*)

of operator work on-farm.[7] The pattern is similar. As operator labor is withdrawn from the farm, the net cash farm income per operator on-farm day falls. Operators working full-time on the farm reported net cash farm income of about $50 per day (Table 6.6 and Figures 6.6 and 6.7). Operators working 50 to 200 days on the farm reported negative net cash farm income.

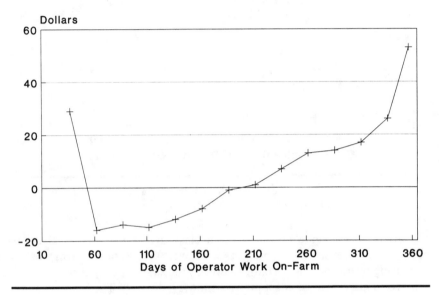

Figure 6.6. Net cash farm income per operator day on-farm, Canada, 1986. (*Statistics Canada*)

Stigler (1958) proposed a "survivor technique." He hypothesized that by looking at a distribution of firms over time, we could determine which groups of firms were efficient and which groups were inefficient by observing which groups increased their share of aggregate output and which groups were found to decline in their share of aggregate output. French (1977, p. 132) reviewed numerous studies that used the survivor technique and suggested the hypothesis had not, in general, provided helpful results. Here we disaggregate census-farms into four classes of operators days of off-farm work (see Table 6.1) and we compare the share of operators and

---

7. Net cash farm income is gross farm sales minus cash expenses, except wages paid to family members.

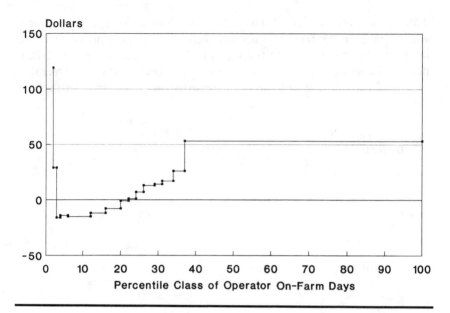

Figure 6.7. Net cash farm income per operator day on-farm, Canada, 1986. (*Statistics Canada*)

the share of aggregate output in each class over time. We see that the proportion of census-farm operators with over 97 days of off-farm work is increasing over time (Figure 6.8). However, the share of output provided by this group has remained constant over time (Figure 6.9). The constant share of output coming from a larger share of operators suggests this group is less efficient in producing agricultural output. However, the fact that the share of operators with over 96 days of work off-farm is increasing suggests that it may be a desirable status — something other than agricultural output may be the drawing card.

Efficiency aspects of the farmer and farm family

The above discussion focuses on the output and the cost per unit of output for the farm enterprise. We now consider efficiency aspects of (1) the allocation of the farm operator's labor between farm and off-farm work, and (2) the allocation of the family's labor between farm and off-farm work. We propose to observe the total income of the operator (or the family) as the earnings mix of the operator (or the family) varies from complete dependence on net farm income to complete dependence on off-farm earnings.

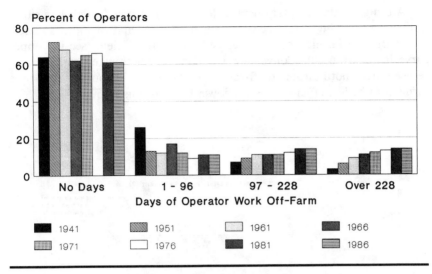

Figure 6.8. Census-farm operators by off-farm work days,
Canada. (*Statistics Canada*)

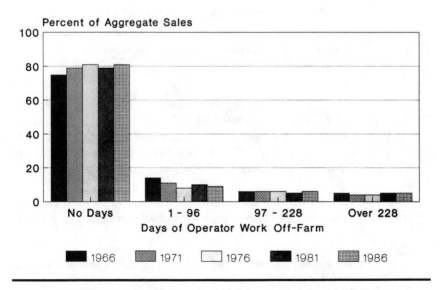

Figure 6.9. Aggregate sales by off-farm work days, Canada.
(*Statistics Canada*)

We suggest that if total operator (or family) income is higher in situations where earnings are received from both farm and off-farm sources, then part-time farming could be considered more efficient (see the upper curve in Figure 6.10). Conversely, if income is lower when earnings are received from both farm and off-farm sources, we could consider part-time farming to be less efficient (see the lower curve in Figure 6.10).[8]

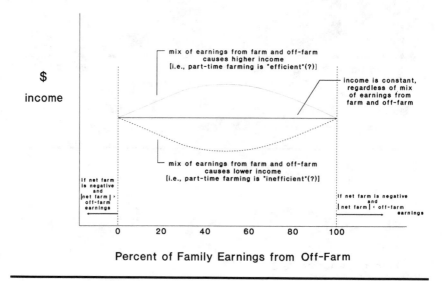

Percent of Family Earnings from Off-Farm

Figure 6.10. Alternative income patterns by degree of mix of family earnings from farm and off-farm.

Note from Figure 6.10 that we have allowed for the case of a negative "percent of total earnings contributed by off-farm earnings".[9] This situation will exist when net farm income is negative *and* the absolute value of net farm income is greater than off-farm earnings. This situation applies to about 1 percent of the operators (Table 6.7) and about 2 percent of the families (Table 6.8).

We have also allowed for the case where the percent of total earnings contributed by off-farm earnings is positive *and* greater than 100 percent.

---

8. Again, no consideration is given to scenery or the nonpecuniary benefits of a farm plus off-farm mix of earnings.

9. Off-farm earnings include wages and salaries plus net nonfarm self-employment income. Total earnings are off-farm earnings plus net farm income.

Table 6.7. Income of census-farm operator and operator's family by percent of operator earnings from off-farm employment, Canada, 1980

	Under −100%	−100% to −51%	−50% to <0%	No off-farm operator earnings	1% to 19%	20% to 39%	40% to 59%	60% to 79%	80% to 99%	No reported net farm income	101% to 149%	150% to 199%	200% and over	Total
Number of operators	1,480	510	1,425	148,145	7,265	6,810	7,730	12,040	20,965	46,945	19,170	3,145	3,770	279,385
Percent of total	1	0	1	53	3	2	3	4	8	17	7	1	1	100
Cumulative percent[a]	1	1	1	54	57	59	62	66	74	91	98	99	99	
Average operator income														
Net farm income	−12,860	−15,576	−18,428	11,294	21,511	13,831	10,019	6,463	2,298	0	−3,140	−6,942	−10,568	6,986
Off-farm employment income	9,364	6,660	2,487	7	2,045	5,860	10,319	15,756	22,988	18,151	24,285	17,199	15,937	8,088
Earnings (farm + off-farm)	−3,496	−8,916	−15,941	11,301	23,556	19,691	20,338	22,219	25,286	18,151	21,145	10,257	5,369	15,074
Total income (all sources)	−871	−5,601	−12,771	14,659	26,169	21,971	22,792	24,505	27,681	20,620	23,147	12,311	7,954	17,970
Average family income														
Net farm income	−13,419	−16,203	−19,930	12,461	22,672	14,647	10,635	7,001	2,573	282	−3,186	−7,088	−10,756	7,744
Off-farm employment income	16,827	13,815	8,176	4,793	6,979	11,340	16,180	22,196	29,802	25,910	31,456	24,611	22,842	13,893
Earnings (farm + off-farm)	3,408	−2,388	−11,754	17,254	29,651	25,987	26,815	29,197	32,375	26,192	28,270	17,523	12,086	21,637
Total income (all sources)	7,988	3,937	−6,497	22,395	33,592	29,685	30,685	32,714	36,055	30,165	31,477	20,892	16,034	26,131

Source: Statistics Canada, *1981 Agriculture-Population Linkage.*
aMay not add up to 100% due to rounding.

Table 6.8. Income of census-farm operator and operator's family by percent of family earnings from off-farm employment, Canada, 1980

					Percent of family earnings from off-farm employment									
	Under −100%	−100% to −51%	−50% to <0%	No family off-farm earnings	1% to 19%	20% to 39%	40% to 59%	60% to 79%	80% to 99%	No reported net farm income	101% to 149%	150% to 199%	200% and over	Total
Number of operator families	1,950	845	2,680	74,010	23,905	20,610	19,625	21,895	33,585	195	72,785	3,270	4,025	279,385
Percent of total	1	0	1	26	9	7	7	8	12	0	26	1	1	100
Cumulative percent[a]	1	1	2	28	37	44	51	59	71	71	97	99	99	
Average operator income														
Net farm income	−13,346	−18,028	−28,504	11,024	25,375	16,425	11,151	6,986	2,442	131	−1,075	−7,434	−10,661	6,986
Off-farm employment income	5,194	2,774	935	7	417	1,479	3,793	8,314	16,436	37,509	17,823	13,200	11,824	8,088
Earnings (farm + off-farm)	−8,152	−15,254	−27,569	11,031	25,792	17,904	14,944	15,300	18,878	37,640	16,748	5,766	1,163	15,074
Total income (all sources)	−5,178	−11,342	−23,682	14,717	28,704	20,488	17,277	17,536	21,409	40,961	19,399	8,204	4,313	17,970
Average family income														
Net farm income	−14,481	−18,939	−31,853	12,350	28,045	17,886	12,251	7,687	2,666	25	−1,156	−8,188	−11,781	7,744
Off-farm employment income	11,011	7,940	3,168	15	2,742	7,473	12,269	18,421	27,421	47,369	26,276	20,272	17,617	13,893
Earnings (farm + off-farm)	−3,470	−10,999	−28,685	12,365	30,787	25,359	24,520	26,108	30,087	47,394	25,120	12,084	5,836	21,637
Total income (all sources)	1,264	−3,907	−22,716	17,891	35,026	29,338	28,373	29,863	34,251	54,103	29,260	15,992	10,604	26,131

Source: Statistics Canada, 1981 Agriculture-Population Linkage.
[a]May not add up to 100% due to rounding.

This situation will exist when net farm income is negative *and* the absolute value of net farm income is less than off-farm earnings. This situation applies to about 9 percent of the operators and 28 percent of the families. Observations are scaled by percentile (or cumulative percent) ranking of operators (Figure 6.11) or families (Figure 6.12) according to the percent of operator (or family) total earnings from off-farm earnings. Note that 53 percent of operators and 26 percent of families reported no off-farm earnings.

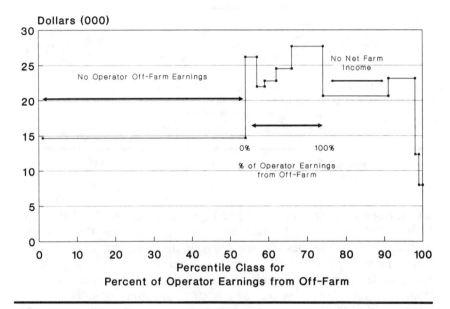

Figure 6.11. Average operator total income from all sources, Canada, 1980. (*Statistics Canada*)

It was proposed above that we might conclude part-time farming is efficient if total income were *higher* with a mix of farm and off-farm earnings. Alternatively, we might conclude that part-time farming is inefficient if total income were *lower* with a mix of farm and off-farm earnings.[10] The results indicate support for both interpretations! (See Table 6.7 and Figure

---

10. This hypothesis assumes that reported incomes are not (seriously) distorted due to the influence of tax laws. In Canada, if the farm has a "reasonable expectation of profit" but the tax-filer's major source of income is not farming, then the tax-filer is allowed to write off up to a $5,000 farm loss against nonfarm income.

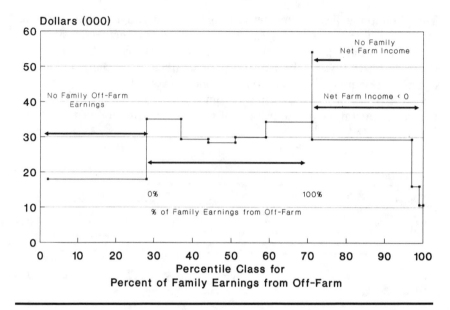

Figure 6.12. Average family total income, Canada, 1980.
(*Statistics Canada*)

6.11 for operators and Table 6.8 and Figure 6.12 for families.) Part-time farmers and part-time farm families have higher incomes than (1) farm operators or farm families who rely solely on the farm, and (2) farm operators or farm families who rely solely on off-farm work. This suggests that part-time farming represents an efficient allocation of operator or family labor resources. However, the income curve is lower for operators and families with a 50:50 mix of earnings from farm and off-farm sources. This suggests that it is inefficient to try to equally balance farming and off-farm activity. If one or the other is relatively small, the total income of the operator or the family is higher.

One comment on the role of public policy

The few analysts in Canada who have considered the impact of public policies on part-time farmers view public policy either as exhibiting benign neglect with respect to part-time farming or as being biased against the part-time farmer. Thus, to the extent a bias exists, it is perceived to be against the part-time farmer. To what extent has such a policy stance constrained the sector to be largely a sector of full-time farmers? Uhlin (1985, p. 168) observed that in Sweden, "agricultural policy has endeavoured to create family farms with minimum farm sizes that would give the farm family full employment . . . [this] has meant the creation of indivisibilities (labour input)." If part-time farmers are equally efficient, to what extent does the present policy stance cause inefficiency in the sector?

Conclusion

The concept of efficiency implies a measure of output per unit of input. For part-time farming families, the fundamental question seems to be, What is the output? Are the marketed farm products the only output? Is scenery or, more generally, the part-time farming way-of-life, an output in itself?

The following questions are appropriate to the efficiency of multiple job-holding farm families: (1) Under what conditions may part-time farmers be efficient producers of food? and (2) Are part-time farmers to be encouraged or discouraged on efficiency grounds?

Regarding the first question, I must unfortunately answer with a question, Is this the right question? My data indicate that part-time farmers use more cash inputs to produce a dollar of agricultural commodity outputs. Should part-time farmers be judged in terms of their production of agricultural commodities? Are part-time farmers producing only food? Why are we considering only the food produced by (part-time) farmers?

Regarding the second question, I respond again with questions. Whether or not part-time farming should be encouraged would seem to depend upon the questions, Efficiency of producing what? and Whom would we be encouraging? My data suggest that part-time farmers and part-time farming families have higher incomes than full-time farmers or full-time farming families. Also, my data suggest that part-time farmers and part-time farming families have higher incomes than farmers or farming families who work full-time off the farm. This suggests part-time farming might be encouraged since part-time farmers (and farming families) show higher incomes. However, who are we or whom would we be encouraging? Would the body politic view the outcome differently if the families that were encouraged to move into part-time farming were (1) smaller-scale lower income farm families, or (2) higher income nonfarm families searching for the (perceived) amenities of the rural lifestyle.

As Stigler (1976) suggests, investigations of the reasons why individuals choose a certain allocation of resources would appear to be more enlightening than investigations of the distance individuals are measured to be away from a possible output/input maximum.

References

Barnum, Howard N., and Lyn Squire. 1979. *A Model of An Agricultural Household: Theory and Evidence.* Staff Occasional Paper No. 27. Baltimore: Johns Hopkins University Press, for the World Bank.

Bollman, Ray D. 1979a. *Off-Farm Work by Farmers.* Catalogue No. 99–756. Ottawa: Statistics Canada.

_____. 1979b. "Off-farm work by farmers: An application of the kinked demand curve for labour." *Canadian Journal of Agricultural Economics* 27:37–60.

Bollman, Ray D., and Allan D. Steeves. 1982. "The stocks and flows of Canadian census-farm operators over the period 1966–1976." *Canadian Review of Sociology and Anthropology* 19:576–90.

Bollman, Ray D., and Marilyn Kapitany. 1981. "Notes on classification of and adjustment by part-time farmers in Canada." Ljubljana, Yugoslavia: Background paper prepared for the Seminar on Mixed Households (Part-time Farmers), June 22–24.

Chong, H. Suh, Donald D. Osburn, and Edward C. Price. 1987. "Farm production and off-farm employment in areas of rapid rural industrialization," in *Agriculture and Economic Instability,* ed. Margot Bellamy and Bruce Greenshields, 228–31. Aldershot, England: Gower for the International Association of Agricultural Economists.

French, Ben C. 1977. "The analysis of productive efficiency in agricultural marketing: models, methods, and progress," in *A Survey of Agricultural Economics Literature: Traditional Fields of Agricultural Economics,* ed. Lee R. Martin, 84–169. Minneapolis: University of Minnesota Press, for the American Agricultural Economics Association.

Freshwater, David. 1982. "Are part-time farmers efficient?: An analysis of technical efficiency in Saskatchewan agriculture." Winnipeg: Department of Agricultural Economics and Farm Management, University of Manitoba.

Fuller, Anthony M., and Julius A. Mage, eds. 1976. *Part-time Farming: Problem or Resource in Rural Development.* Norwich, England: GeoAbstracts Limited, for the University of Guelph.

Josephson, R. M., and J. B. Watt. 1987. "Financial arrangements of new farm entrants in the early 1980's." *Canadian Farm Economics* 21:22–27.

Kapitany, M., and Ray D. Bollman. 1983. "Entry, exit and structural change in agriculture: Summary results from the 1966 to 1981 census of agriculture match," in *Proceedings of the Business and Economics Section of the American Statistical Association,* 100–109. Washington, D.C.: American Statistical Association.

Lopez, Ramon E. 1984. "Estimating labor supply and production decisions of self-employed farm producers." *European Economic Review* 24:61–82.

_____. 1986. "Structural models of the farm household that allow for interdependent utility and profit-maximization decisions," in *Agricultural Household Models: Extensions, Applications and Policy,* ed. Inderjit Singh, Lyn Squire, and John Strauss, 306–25. Baltimore: Johns Hopkins University Press, for the World Bank.

Musser, Wesley, N., Neil R. Martin, Jr., and James O. Wise. 1975. "The beef cow-calf enterprise in the Georgia piedmont: A case study in conspicuous production." *Southern Journal of Agricultural Economics* July: 89–95.

Singh, Inderjit, Lyn Squire, and John Strauss, eds. 1986. *Agricultural Household Models: Extensions, Applications and Policy.* Baltimore: Johns Hopkins University Press, for the World Bank.

Statistics Canada. Various years. *Census of Agriculture.* Ottawa: Statistics Canada.

_____. *1981 Agriculture-Population Linkage.* (Unpublished tabulations.) Ottawa: Statistics Canada.

Stigler, George J. 1958. "The economics of scale." *Journal of Law and Economics* 1:54–71.

_____. 1976. "The xistence of x-efficiency." *American Economic Review* 66:213–16.

Tauer, Loren W. 1987. "A note on measuring technical efficiency." Staff Paper 87–12. Ithaca, N.Y.: Department of Agricultural Economics, Cornell University.

Uhlin, Hans-Erik. 1985. *Concepts and Measurement of Technical and Structural Change in Swedish Agriculture.* Uppsala, Sweden: Department of Economics and Statistics, Swedish University of Agricultural Sciences.

CHAPTER 7

Modelling On-farm Enterprise Adjustments

THOMAS A. CARLIN
SUSAN BENTLEY

Modeling farm and producer behavior is extremely complex and . . . empirical results can be greatly influenced through unintentionally biased assumptions and the exclusion of important behavioral details and constraints.

BAUM AND RICHARDSON 1983

Modelling Farm Decisions for Policy Analysis

It is likely that multiple job-holding always existed among farm families, but the incidence of multiple job-holding has increased substantially since World War II. In our opinion, multiple job-holding is one of the major structural changes that has occurred in the farm sector, yet it receives relatively little attention among mainline agricultural economists, for reasons we will discuss later. The topic receives greater attention among sociologists and other social scientists. The topic seldom emerges during discussions among public interest groups interested in influencing farm policy.

What Model?

Modelling farm enterprises is a complex and extensive topic. The literature is replete with articles on modelling. Heady and others' pioneering work, commencing in the 1950s, adapted linear programming to problems of farm organization and production, and initiated an impressive model building period in the agricultural economics profession that has proceeded almost uninterrupted for two generations. Today's farm firm models have an impressive array of components. It is beyond the intent of this chapter to review the inventory of existing farm-level models in any detail or to assess various techniques for modelling on-farm behavior. Rather, the focus here will be on issues an analyst would need to address before commencing the model-building process. The diversity of models available will be illustrated by describing a generic farm-level model. This generic model provides a focal point for the discussion.

Our generic model begins with a starting state, some assumed quantity of land, capital, and labor initially available for use in farm production (Figure 7.1). A core component of the model is an optimization routine for selecting alternative enterprises subject to constraints, generally solved using some mathematical programing algorithm. The model may also contain a whole farm accounting module, a tax module, a farm program/policy

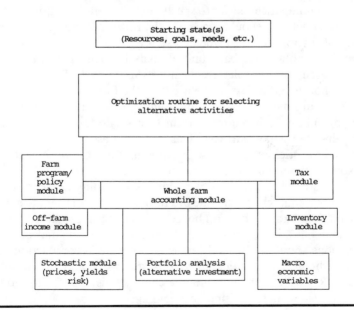

Figure 7.1. Generic farm level model.

module, and perhaps a module that introduces stochastic prices or yields. Some contain an off-farm income component, but this component tends to be passive within the model. That is, off-farm income is carried as a component of the accounting routine and levels and growth in off-farm income tend to be exogenously determined. Regardless of the model specification, they tend to have one feature in common. The "modeler," the person using or building the model, determines the starting state, the options to be considered, and the constraints that are placed on the system. Off-farm work is rarely considered. Is it rarely considered because of gaps in theory, lack of data, or shortsightedness on the part of the modeler?

What Are the Problems?

Several points seem relevant to uncovering some of the problems in modelling on-farm adjustments to multiple job-holding.

Context for decision making

In our view, the selection of the observational unit dictates the context under which goals are established and decisions made. Goals are a key ingredient enabling the modeler to specify the objective function used in the farm-level model. We should recognize the historic debate at least among agricultural economists as to whether we use the business establishment or the farm household as the basic unit of analysis. When the farm establishment is chosen, the modeler frequently assumes that all other decisions within the household adjust to the needs of the farm. This may not be the case. We get around the observational unit problem in our national data systems by simply assigning each farm to a single family (in the case of partnerships, the senior partner). This statistical assumption conveniently helps avoid the sticky problem of partitioning farm establishment income and resources among more than one household.

When addressing questions of multiple job-holding in the farm sector, we come down squarely on the side of Huffman (1980) in that the appropriate observational unit is the farm household. The farm production function can be viewed as a component of the household utility maximization process. Decisions about on-farm adjustments are made in conjunction with or even subordinate to decisions about off-farm work and household consumption. Regardless of the technique chosen, this is a key to modelling on-farm adjustments to multiple job-holding.

Economists would tend to view the farm production function as part of the household income constraint to utility maximization as Huffman has demonstrated in Chapter 5 of this book. Sociologists would argue that this is one of a broader set of possibilities. For example, farming could also be considered a consumption item; the part-time farm may provide a hobby or a rural residence. Other part-time farm families, while considering farm income a primary goal, may also regard farming as an investment (to provide a nest egg, for example), a future retirement activity, a form of recreation, or a chance to be their own boss (Barlett 1986). Thus, maximizing current income from resources available for farming may not be the primary objective of the household.

In our view, the theoretical work adapting the basic labor/leisure model to the question of allocating household time between farm and off-farm work is well underway and provides the appropriate context for applied research on multiple job-holding (Huffman 1980; Bollman 1979; Jensen and Salant 1986; Streeter and Saupe 1986). Recent work by Jensen and Salant (1986) incorporating fringe benefits from off-farm work into the model and by Streeter and Saupe (1986) incorporating nonpecuniary benefits from farming have been useful extensions. Most of this theoretical work utilized a single farm production function or assumed the farm produced a single commodity.

Are there theoretical paradigms?

Are there theoretical paradigms available that can be used to tease out answers to questions about on-farm adjustments to multiple job-holding? First, one must recognize our biases. We have spent most of our professional careers doing applied research and staff analysis as employees of a federal government agency. We are less interested in expanding theoretical paradigms per se than in using them to answer a variety of public policy questions. Our proposition is that there are paradigms available that can give useful insights into the question of on-farm adjustments of multiple job-holding. The problem is less with theory than it is with the modeler's view of the decision-making environment as seen by the farm household. The first prerequisite is for the modeler to recognize and accept the notion that farming is perhaps one of a broader array of income/consumption opportunities available to household members and that a decision to work off-farm is not out of scope or somehow morally wrong. Often modelers accept, almost unconsciously, the assumption that farming is and should be the primary activity of the family and that all other decisions are subservient to it.

The product-product model in microeconomics seems to us to be a useful paradigm for understanding on-farm adjustments to off-farm work.

Certainly the model is flexible enough to incorporate off-farm employment into the decision-making framework. Focusing on labor as the primary resource constraint with off-farm employment assumed to be a wage job, off-farm work is most likely either supplementary or competitive with on-farm activities. There were a number of studies conducted in the late 1950s and 1960s which substantiated the supplementary nature of the relationship between farming and off-farm work (Salant and Munoz 1981). Researchers were interested in the on-farm adjustments to farm operators taking off-farm jobs in areas which today we would characterize as being dominated by "marginal farming." Because there was substantial underemployment of operators (and other family members, for that matter) on the farm, off-farm work could be undertaken without altering the farming operation. Another variant of this phenomenon was what a former colleague of ours referred to as "go-getters." These were farm operators (assumed to be male, of course) who would take their wives to work in the morning and go get them at night. This illustrates an additional complexity in modelling house-hold decisions. Who should work off-farm and how much? There has also been research which has pointed to the competitive relationship between farming and off-farm work. For example, Scott and Chen's modelling of the effects of off-farm employment on farm operations suggested that "small" farmers decreased labor-intensive livestock enterprises and contin-ued with crop production as they increased their off-farm employment (Sa-lant and Munoz 1981).

Multiple job-holding could be considered in the conventional product-product model, either simultaneously or sequentially. That is, off-farm work could be treated as one of several alternative enterprises (using capital and/or labor) to be included within the model or off-farm work could constrain the farm level decision model in particular ways. Few micro-models that we have reviewed incorporate either option, although the po-tential exists to do so.

Options dilemma

Perhaps one reason for the lack of specificity of off-farm work in micromodels is the scarcity of information about the options farm family members have. This involves at least three areas: options for off-farm em-ployment, who does what in the household, and what can be done on the farm. Stated differently, do we know about the types and characteristics of off-farm jobs held by or available to farm family members? Given this, do we know how the off-farm job "plays out" in the overall household decision framework? Finally, can we identify the potential farm enterprises available for inclusion in the model?

There is substantial information about the industries and occupations of rural workers. This gives some information about the option set available to farm household members. Past survey information about the types of jobs held by farm family members suggests that the distribution is not too different from that for the total population. Much less is known about how off-farm work and farming activities interact within the farm household. Few data sets are designed to provide detailed information about off-farm work while at the same time providing necessary information about the farm business. Some exceptions are the Economic Research Service Family Farm Surveys conducted in Mississippi-Tennessee and in Wisconsin discussed by Saupe and Gould in Chapter 10 of this book. The last national data set that obtained some detailed data on off-farm jobs was the 1979 Farm Finance Survey conducted by the Bureau of Census. Most members of farm households who work off-farm work at wage or salary jobs. Working hours tend to be specified by the employer thus they are likely to be "lumpy." This in turn likely requires substantial specificity within the model.

Most households in the United States, including farm households, are composed of families; a family is defined as two or more persons related by blood, marriage, or adoption living in a single dwelling unit. While there has been increased interest in the role of farm women on farms, both in terms of their labor input and their role in decision making (Wilkening and Bharadwaj 1967; Jones and Rosenfeld 1981), little is known about the roles of other (nonoperator) farm household members in the farm enterprise. Identifying who provides labor on the farm and who is capable of managing the enterprise would enable researchers to assess the substitutability of labor both in terms of productivity and decision making. On many part-time farms, off-farm work by a household member may have no impact on farm production; on others, young adults or grandparents may be able to replace other adults who decide to work off-farm. The issue of labor substitution can get even more complex if one wishes to relax the single household assumption. Multiple household farming is one area where both theorists and statisticians fear to tread.

Identifying alternative crop and livestock enterprises for inclusion in a farm model may be a less difficult task. Most primary and secondary data that we have looked at suggests that farm households engaged in multiple job-holding choose from the same menu of crops and livestock enterprises as do full-time farm households. Within that menu, however, multiple job-holders tend to choose the less labor-intensive enterprises. Most colleges of agriculture do a fairly good job of providing production information about major crops and livestock produced in their respective state. Some of the assumptions underlying the enterprise budgets may need to be revisited.

For example, there may be differences in the complement of machinery and equipment between the two types. Discussions about enterprise selection at conferences eventually turn to the question of specialty crops. It is not unusual to hear presentations about the possibilities for rabbit or quail production, pick your own vegetable and fruit crops, etc. While specialty crops may well be among the option set, there are important questions about demand, processing, and marketing which need to be addressed before such activities can legitimately be included in any model.

Who cares?

Some ideas about potential end users of research on on-farm adjustments to multiple job-holding will also likely shape how the models are specified. Agricultural economics is an applied profession where we attempt to use theory and data to solve practical problems. Models are then built to help answer the primary question. The models can often be used to address additional issues that were not the initial genesis of the model. Thinking about end users is, in part, an exercise involving identifying the problem to be researched.

One could probably produce a substantial list of potential users of information about on-farm adjustments to multiple job-holding. A substantial share of the public interest groups concerned with farming tends to focus on specific farm commodities (e.g., dairy, rice, wheat, etc.). Most of us are aware of the substantial concentration of farm production. Regardless of the commodity, save tobacco and one or two others, the bulk of the production occurs on a few relatively large commercial farms (Reimund, Brooks, and Velde 1986). Because there is a negative correlation between multiple job-holding (at least on the part of the operator) and size of farm (as measured by gross sales), the economics of agriculture is more likely to drive the decision making of households producing the bulk of food and fiber commodities. Adding multiple job-holding considerations to these models may not enhance the model results all that much. That is, understanding how large firms might adjust to alternative policies provides considerable and generally sufficient information about potential behavior of the farm sector. Consequently, interest in multiple job-holding among this group is likely to be limited. We have, however, identified three groups of potential clientele which either are or probably should be interested in the topic.

A first group of users would be those interested in the human resource side of farming. In general, the policy agenda among this user group is to increase the well-being of the respective target population. This policy interest has been expressed using labels such as "small farm," "limited resource farms," or "low income farms." Such groups are potential or should be potential users of research on multiple job-holding in that multiple job-holding provides a realistic option for the use of human resources of farm families. It is our general observation that most proponents of this school generally give only lip service to off-farm employment and tend to focus primarily on farm options to increase family well-being. This "farm first" approach reflects the strong farm fundamentalist values held by the group. However, such values can lead to policy prescriptions which are unrealistic when applied to real-life situations.

A second user group would be those interested in the changing structure of U.S. agriculture. Such persons are generally interested in the organization, ownership, and control of resources employed in producing food and fiber. Here, multiple job-holding is of interest because of its implications for how the sector is organized. For example, there has been considerable discussion over the years of the emerging dual farm structure in the United States; a relatively small number of farms produce the bulk of our food and fiber, while the majority produce very little. Within specified areas of the country, multiple job-holding may also change the structure of local agriculture. Research information on multiple job-holding as it affects resources engaged in farming would be useful to this group also.

The third user group is those interested in rural community development. We would argue that there is important interaction between the evolving structure of the nonfarm and farm sectors in rural communities. In some sections of the United States, the incidence of multiple job-holding is high; the agriculture sector in those communities has taken on a certain character which is unlikely to change much in the foreseeable future. Other areas where agriculture is still dominated by full-time farming and where agriculture is a significant component of the economy are facing difficult long-run structural questions. There has been interesting and pioneering research on the question of how rural communities develop around alternative farming structures. In our opinion, given the diverse economic transformation of rural America over the last 20 years, it is probably time to examine the implications of how changes in the local nonfarm economy might affect farming. Research about on-farm adjustments to multiple job-holding will be useful in assessing how the local farming sector might adjust to expanded nonfarm employment opportunities.

Conclusions

Is the reason that multiple job-holding has not been considered in farm-level models because of gaps in theory, lack of data, or because the options are overlooked by the modeler? We conclude that the primary problems are with the modeler and the data. While the theory can certainly be developed further, existing paradigms prove sufficient to allow researchers to analyze on-farm adjustments to multiple job-holding. After all, the models only consider those options the modeler wishes to have considered. As for data, while existing farm data systems typically do not contain detailed labor data for household members, there is information available to assist the modeler to understand the options available for off-farm employment. Thus, even here, we don't have to wait.

References

Barlett, Peggy F. 1986. "Part-time farming: Saving the farm or saving the lifestyle?" *Rural Sociology* 51:289–313.

Baum, Kenneth H., and James W. Richardson. 1983. "FLIPCOM: Farm-level continuous optimization models for integrated policy analysis," in *Modeling Farm Decisions for Policy Analysis,* ed. Kenneth H. Baum and Lyle P. Schertz, 211–34. Boulder: Westview Press.

Bollman, Ray D. 1979. "Off-farm work by farmers: An application of the kinked demand curve for labour." *Canadian Journal of Agricultural Economics* 27:37–60.

Huffman, Wallace E. 1980. "Farm and off-farm work decisions: The role of human capital." *Review of Economics and Statistics* 62:14–18.

Jensen, Helen H., and Priscilla Salant. 1986. *Fringe Benefits in Operator Off-farm Labor Supply: Evidence From Mississippi and Tennessee.* Staff Report AGES 860403. Washington, D.C.: Economic Research Service, U.S. Department of Agriculture.

Jones, Calvin, and Rachel A. Rosenfeld. 1981. *American Farm Women: Findings from a National Survey.* Report No. 130. Chicago: National Opinion Research Center.

Reimund, Donn A., Nora L. Brooks, and Paul D. Velde. 1986. *The U.S. Farm Sector in the Mid-1980's.* Agricultural Economics Report No. 548. Washington, D.C.: Economic Research Service, U.S. Department of Agriculture.

Salant, Priscilla, and Robert D. Munoz. 1981. *Rural Industrialization and Its Impact on the Agricultural Community: A Review of the Literature.* Staff Report AGES 810316. Washington, D.C.: Economic Research Service, U.S. Department of Agriculture.

Streeter, Deborah H., and William E. Saupe. 1986. "Nonmonetary considerations in farm operator labor allocations." A. E. Res. 86–28. Ithaca, N.Y.: Department of Agricultural Economics, Cornell University.

Wilkening, Eugene A., and Lakshmi K. Bharadwaj. 1967. "Dimensions of aspirations, work roles, and decision-making among farm husbands and wives in Wisconsin." *Journal of Marriage and the Family* 29:703–11.

CHAPTER 8

Useful Directions for Research on Multiple Job-holding among Farm Families

DANIEL A. SUMNER

Significant progress was made over the last 20 years in developing an understanding of the economics of multiple job-holding among farm families. Although some important research appeared earlier, in the late 1970s and early 1980s a series of papers and Ph.D. dissertations appeared which used basic tools of labor economics and econometrics to examine the cross-sectional patterns of off-farm participation, hours of work, and wages (see Huffman [Chapter 5] and Lass, Findeis, and Hallberg [Chapter 14] in this volume for a list). While useful, the research to date has left a number of major holes and provide a number of further research opportunities.

This recent research was generally motivated by a growing recognition of the importance of off-farm work as a typical pattern among farm families. As Huffman documents in Chapter 5, working off the farm has long been a common practice in North America, but the proportion of farmers choosing this pattern grew during the 1960s and early 1970s. Off-farm work is also a common practice in almost all other developed and less-developed countries, including those in Europe, Latin America, and Asia (see Kada 1980; Pereira and Sumner 1988; and Sumner 1981 for examples and citations).

Whereas the demand for research on off-farm work was generated by observations and empirical puzzles, the supply of research was facilitated

---

The views expressed in this paper are solely those of the author and may not reflect those of the Council of Economic Advisers or the U.S. government.

by advances in labor economics and associated econometrics. Most of the recent papers that attempt to explain or account for off-farm work patterns (including those in this volume) have made direct use of models and econometric approaches developed for use on analytically similar labor economics issues outside of agriculture.

A major hole in the off-farm work literature is an explanation of the time-series pattern of multiple job-holding among farmers. It is ironic, though not uncommon, that a time-series puzzle has seemed to stimulate mostly cross-sectional research. This seems to be another case of looking for the keys under the lamp post because the light is better.

This chapter will consider the questions, issues, and puzzles that indicate useful future developments in the economics of multiple job-holding among farm families. It will also consider research in labor economics and related econometrics that may provide useful tools or insights. The chapter will focus mostly on efforts to explain multiple job-holding rather than research on the consequences of multiple job-holding. That is, multiple job-holding is treated (mostly) as the endogenous variable to be explained rather than as one of the variables used to account for patterns of resource use, income distribution, or other aspects of the economics of agriculture. Obviously, the allocation of labor of farm families is part of a larger system of supply equations and demand equations. It is useful, however, to take the more limited topic to keep this review more focused. The fine chapter by Bollman (Chapter 6) in this volume considers a part of what is left out here.

As is standard in the literature, the term "farmers" here refers to the self-employed operator of a farm rather than a hired farm employee. Farm families include the operator, spouse, and children. In this context, a farm operated as a partnership may have more than one farmer and farm family. The multiple job-holding of hired farm employees is discussed in some of the papers in Emerson (1984).

Multiple Job-holding and Standard Labor-supply Models

Multiple job-holding is an exception rather than the rule in employment patterns. Stinson (1986) documents that only 5 percent of the U.S. labor force holds more than one job simultaneously. (There may be considerable undercount in these data due to seasonality when compared to how multiple job-holding is measured in the off-farm work literature.) In recent years, about 50 percent of U.S. farmers work off the farm either full-time or part-time, as Huffman documents (Chapter 5). This high proportion constitutes the first and major fact to be explained by research on multiple job-holding among farm families. The more specific empirical questions are: Why is the proportion so high? Why has it grown over time? and How and why does it vary by locale, farm type, local characteristics, and individual farm family characteristics?

The observation of a high degree of off-farm work is only a puzzling fact as compared to the pattern of multiple job-holding in other occupations or in the past. However, very little research has been done on explaining the patterns of multiple job-holding across occupations (see, however, Shishko and Rostker 1976). Casual observation suggests that some other occupations also have relatively high proportions of multiple job-holding. These observations are confirmed in Stinson (1986). For example, many school teachers work at other jobs in the summer. Many college teachers are also self-employed as consultants and many craftsmen work as self-employed providers of home repair services.

Economists' simple models of labor markets make no particular distinction between having one employer or several. Therefore, multiple job-holding does not require any elaboration of the basic model of labor supply and leisure demand. In fact, this model is uninformative about the number of jobs a worker holds. The standard labor-supply model assumes that a worker's wage depends on human capital and is independent of hours of work. However, once we extend the basic model to include costs of maintaining employment or traveling between jobs, or productivity increase for working more than some minimum hours of work at one job, then holding only a single job is optimal unless there are offsetting forces. Further, even a small amount of job specific human capital would cause a worker to choose the single job offering the best wage and potential wage growth. In a model that includes these features, multiple job-holding becomes a puzzle to be explained.

The single job implication is usually not explicit in labor-supply models. Therefore when multiple job-holding among farm families is considered, the elaboration of the basic model may also not be particularly explicit. In applications to off-farm work, the now standard approach is to assume that the marginal wage at off-farm jobs is independent of hours of work but that the marginal value product (MVP) of time spent working on the farm is downward sloping. If the farm MVP falls below this marginal wage before it reaches the marginal value of time spent at nonemployment activities, then the farm family member takes a job off the farm. That is, the standard model is elaborated to include a farm wage that depends on hours of farm work, and so multiple job-holding may be optimal in the more complicated model (Sumner 1982).

Nonfarm Labor Economics and Multiple Job-holding

Insights into off-farm work can be obtained by treating it as a part of the larger question of the overall industry, occupation, gender, or time-series pattern of multiple job-holding in the economy. For example, in the farm case we find a large proportion of farmers who work off the farm full-time (more than 200 days), as well as many who work off the farm only a small amount. Working off the farm an intermediate amount is less common. It seems that farming may conveniently be either a part-time job itself or a full-time occupation that allows farmers to work part-time at other jobs.

Farming is typically a self-employment occupation and, as such, may provide more flexibility than many other jobs. Nonagricultural self-employment seems to have increased recently from less than 10 percent for males and 5 percent for females to over 11 percent for males and about 7 percent of the labor force for females (Blau 1987; Becker 1984). The connection between self-employment and multiple job-holding in the nonfarm economy is relatively unexplored territory. We do know that about one-third of nonfarm multiple job-holders were self-employed, usually in the second job (Stinson 1986). Including agriculture with other occupations would help to indicate if time-series or cross-section patterns found in the farm samples were explained by the same factors that explain the patterns of multiple job-holding in the nonfarm economy. Agricultural economists have a tendency to treat farm economics issues as having unique agricultural explanations but, of course, this may not be the case.

In 1949 about 39 percent of the approximately 5.4 million farmers worked off the farm. This proportion *rose* to about 45 percent in 1959, and to about 54 percent of 2.7 million farmers by 1969. It remained there in recent years, as the number of farmers fell to 2.2 million by 1982. However, stated somewhat differently, the proportion of nonfarm employees who also farmed (as either primary or secondary occupations) *fell* from about 4.2 percent in 1949 to about 2.8 percent in 1959 and to about 2.0 percent in 1969. It continued downward in the 1970s, reaching about 1.2 percent in 1982. Thus, viewed from the perspective of the nonfarm labor market, farm moonlighting has *fallen* dramatically in the postwar period.

The key modelling issue this perspective raises is that the choice to farm be treated as endogenous. We may be missing a significant part of the story if we model off-farm work as a choice that is made after the decision to farm has been settled. Not only are we likely to miss explanations for the patterns observed in the data, but we will also bias our estimates of explanatory variables in hours of off-farm work or earnings functions.

To be a multiple job-holder in farming, one must enter both the farm and nonfarm employment markets. It is now standard practice to account for self-selection in off-farm work in estimation of off-farm work wage and hours equations. (This is discussed further in the next section.) However, it may also be important to account for self-selection of farm work by non-farm workers. In particular, we would expect that the parameters of the farm earnings function may be sensitive to the choice to farm. For example, I may have chosen not to farm because my potential earnings in farming were unusually low, given my observable characteristics.

The needed development is to approach the multiple job-holding of farm families question with a sample that includes both farmers and nonfarm workers. A model of the choice to farm would be a part of the system of equations. Multiple job-holders in farming would be recognized to be avoiding both the corner solution of full-time farming and the corner solution of full-time nonfarm work.

This research program would also help us estimate the influence of self-selection into farming on the effects exogenous human capital and other variables have on endogenous farm characteristics. For example, we generally find that more schooling is associated with larger farm size (Sumner and Leiby 1987). But this finding may, at least in part, be a function of the self-selection process. The reasoning is as follows: Earnings are higher in nonfarm occupations for those with more schooling. Therefore, the opportunity cost of choosing to farm is higher for those with more schooling. Unless they operate a farm large enough to return a standard of living comparable to their nonfarm alternatives, they are less likely to be found in the sample of farmers. Because of this selection effect, we could attribute higher earnings of more highly educated farmers to the productivity of schooling in farming whereas, in fact, estimation of the parameter is plagued by sample selection bias. This same sort of problem arises in many other contexts including on-farm resource allocation and efficiency aspects of part-time farming.

Choice-based Sampling

Combining analysis of the decision to farm together with analysis of multiple job-holding raises troublesome data issues. Even large random samples of families have relatively few farmers and, obviously, even fewer multiple job-holding farmers. One approach is to attempt to use the Current Population Surveys (CPS), but huge samples must be used to include a significant number of farmers.

One alternative is to use the CPS and randomly overselect farmers and multiple job-holders in the creation of a working file. Recent developments in the statistical analysis of such choice-based samples makes consistent estimation with such data feasible. Manski and Lerman (1977) developed estimators, and recent econometric evaluation is in Amemiya and Vuong (1987).

The application of selection bias and choice-based sampling in the estimation-of-earnings functions of lawyers in Goddeeris (1988) contains a number of interesting ideas for application to multiple job-holding of farm families. His work drew on two separate surveys which asked similar questions. In the farm family application, the idea would be to survey farm families in a way that would allow the results to be combined with another standard data set such as the Michigan Panel Study of Income Dynamics or the National Longitudinal Survey.

A More Careful Analysis of Selection Bias

The understanding of potential sample-selection problems and the relevant econometric modelling and estimation techniques represent advances in labor economics and econometrics in the 1970s that were then quickly applied to off-farm work of farm families. In the off-farm work context the major issue is that our sample knowledge of the potential off-farm wage of farmers comes necessarily only from those who have wage observations. Further, we have reason to expect that this self-selected subsample may face different wage opportunities than those who have chosen not to work off the farm. In estimating the wage function it is important to appropriately account for the nonrandom nature of the sample.

This suggests that we use our economic and econometric model of the choice to participate off the farm to adjust the wage estimation (and labor supply) for the conditional nature of the observations. The simplest procedure, attributed to Heckman (1979), is the calculation of a selection-bias correction factor from a first-step estimation of the participation equation. The correction factor is then introduced as an additional explanatory variable in the wage and hours of work equations (see Sumner 1982 for one application). This procedure has become standard in estimation of off-farm work models.

In general the Heckman approach and related alternatives depend on having information on factors that affect participation but do not directly affect the wage rate opportunities or hours of off-farm work. Identification may be attainable in the off-farm work case because some exogenous farm or family characteristics affect the potential payoff from farm work, whereas they do not directly affect the wage rate available for off-farm work. For example, farm output prices, input prices, weather, or the presence of mature children in the household would be likely to affect the value of time spent working on the farm but not a wage offer off the farm.

The importance of the sample-selection issue is well established in labor economics whenever a sample may be split into two relatively large subgroups for which an endogenous participation decision is applicable. Applications have included the labor supply and wages of married women, the rate of return to college education, the union/nonunion wage differential and the wages and hours of off-farm work of farmers.

The literature of the last 10 years has provided several alternate approaches to the sample-selection issue and further has demonstrated the sensitivity of estimates to the approach taken. This general lack of robustness raises major problems in application and interpretation that have not been generally appreciated in the literature on off-farm work. In particular, Heckman's two-stage estimator based on a probit specification in the participation equation has been shown to be inefficient in a general context and sensitive to the normality assumptions underlying the first stage probit equation. (See analysis and discussion in Heckman and MaCurdy 1980; Nelson 1984; Mroz 1987.) There is now considerable evidence that inappropriate correction for selection effects can significantly bias estimates. Applications of these methods to off-farm work should be approached much more carefully than has been current practice.

Complications in the Wage Equation

One of the standard assumptions in labor economics is that the wage rate offered to a worker is independent of the hours of work. Further simplifications include ignoring overtime rates, ignoring the impact of taxes that may shift the relevant earnings equations, ignoring lumpiness due to fringe benefits, ignoring fixed costs of working (Cogan 1981), and ignoring regulations or union contracts that may encourage employers to impose restrictions on hours of work.

All of these factors suggest that the budget constraint related to time allocation may be nonlinear and, in particular, that it may have kinks or jumps and areas of nonconvexity (Hausman 1985). Such complications affect both the appropriate modelling and the econometric analysis of time allocation. A recursive model, in which the wage equation is estimated and then used in the hours of work equation or in the structural participation equation, is not appropriate in this case. Instead, the economics dictate a fully simultaneous econometric model in which net marginal and average wage depend on hours of work and labor-supply depends on the wage. Such an approach demands careful attention to identification because it is naturally difficult to find exclusion restrictions. That is, most factors that affect wages directly may also affect hours of work or farm earnings. Recent applied labor-supply studies such as Gustman and Steinmeier (1986) deal with a number of these issues. In particular in their work on the labor supply of the elderly, Gustman and Steinmeier also consider a population for which part-time employment is important and find that wage rates are sensitive to hours of work.

Intertemporal Substitution and Panel Data

Among the initial hypotheses proposed to explain off-farm work was the suggestion that farm family members may work off the farm when the returns to farm labor are temporarily low. As the marginal value product of farm work varies, it may periodically fall below the wage rate available at off-farm work. These periods may occur each year during a slack season or they may occur occasionally during years of low yields or low prices. This hypothesis may account for seasonal off-farm work among crop farmers and the low participation in off-farm work among dairy farmers or family farmers.

The theoretical model of intermittent off-farm work must have a time dimension that is lacking in the simple, static, one-period model common in the literature. The appropriate multi-period model incorporates intertemporal substitution both on the farm and in the utility function. Time in one period is an imperfect substitute for time in subsequent periods. It may also be appropriate to consider the impact on wage opportunities of seasonal or temporary work. Such a model implies that expectations about all future periods affect current allocations.

In the general labor-supply literature the major reference on these issues is to MaCurdy (1981), where he proposes a fixed-effects model for use with panel data (see also MaCurdy 1983). Fixed effects have been applied to wage functions and farm-specific human capital by Sumner and Frazao (1989) in an LDC context. Altonji (1986) also contains useful references and a discussion of the impacts of alternative specifications.

In order to estimate these models it is important to have data that include multiple time periods and some variation in exogenous temporal changes in returns to farming relative to off-farm work. Panel data allow one to consider explicitly how individual behavior may vary over time. They also allow the use of fixed effects as controls for individual heterogeneity when a full set of exogenous explanatory variables may not be available. Tests between fixed effects and alternative random-effects models are discussed in Wu (1973) and Hausman (1978).

More complex time-series error structures are discussed in the panel-data context by MaCurdy (1982). The analysis of cross-section time series issues in the context of panel data or repeated cross sections is treated in detail in Heckman and Robb (1985) and other papers in the Heckman and Singer (1985) volume. The use of repeated random cross sections can allow some of the same benefits as panel data and may not be subject to some of the potential problems.

Life Cycle and Other Related Issues

Variation in labor supply over the life cycle was treated in detail by MaCurdy (1981) using panel data. His influential model has not yet been applied to time allocation among farmers. The application by Nakamura and Nakamura (1985) to dynamic labor supply of women is more similar to the issue of multiple job-holding among farm families.

Treating labor supply in a life-cycle context makes clear the problem with treating past work experience as exogenous in a current wage or hours of work equation. This problem is especially acute for occupation-specific human capital. Using past off-farm experience in the wage equation as an exogenous explanatory variable has been standard practice. However, if unobserved and persistent individual characteristics are associated with higher wages, they would also be associated with increased past labor supply. Therefore, the experience effect in the wage equation would be biased upwards and a similar bias would occur in hours of work and structural participation. Mroz (1987) has stressed the importance of this bias in the estimation of labor supply and wage equations for married women.

A common hypothesis in the past has been that a significant portion of off-farm work by farmers was a transition either into or out of farming. There has been little serious modelling of the adjustment costs, borrowing constraints, or specific human capital required to make such hypotheses more specific. It is important to develop models of these phenomena and to measure variation over time in transitional versus long-term off-farm work. A farmer planning a permanent full-time move to nonfarm work may take some off-farm employment in order to build his human capital and raise future wage rates. In this case, current off-farm work is determined, in part, by expected future employment. Testing the importance of off-farm job experience for the nonfarm wage rate is a key issue in indicating the potential strength of this hypothesis. Sumner and Frazao (1989) apply such reasoning to LDC data.

Conclusion

The economics of multiple job-holding among farm families is a natural merging of the applied theory of the firm and the economics of household behavior and labor supply. The uniquely agricultural aspects of the problem are related mostly to the farm's demand for labor and managerial effort. The farm and the household can be separated conceptually only by simplifying assumptions that may obscure important issues. For example, in the study of tax changes and agriculture some analysts have ignored income earned from nonfarm activities of the household. This leaves out a majority of the taxable income for most farm families and will clearly miss a considerable part of the adjustments families make in response to tax changes. In discussions of farm size distributions some have suggested that family farms are only those that get most of their income from farming. Such a classification excludes many farms of significant size in years for which net farm income is low. It may also leave out many full-time farms when one spouse has a career off the farm (Sumner 1986).

Most farm families have considerable stake in the nonfarm labor market. This observation is important in understanding the traditional economics of agriculture. However, we should not make too much of this fact because most agricultural output in the United States is produced by farmers that are primarily farmers. Traditional farm programs, for example, are oriented toward output of a few farm commodities, and especially commodities for which part-time farming is less common. Thus, we may not expect substantial aggregate effect on the overall supply reactions to farm programs from variations in numbers of part-time farms or in off-farm work. The potential for easy labor-supply adjustment by farms should increase farm output supply elasticities but we should not expect a large effect.

On the other hand, in terms of numbers of people with some stake in farm programs, multiple job-holding among farm families is of major importance. For most of these people, farm program changes will affect their farming operation but will have far less impact on overall family income or wealth. An interesting and useful topic is to consider the impact of market-oriented farm policies, including decoupled income transfers, on multiple job-holding among farm families. The effects will be varied and subtle. It is certainly not obvious to me whether off-farm labor supply is increased or reduced by the current array of farm programs.

Turning the questions around to ask how multiple job-holding affects the consequences of farm programs is of equal interest. It is certainly the case that the better we model the farm sector, including time allocation of farm families, the more accurate will be our understanding of the impact of policy.

My major objective in this chapter has been to present a long enough list of needed developments for research on off-farm work that we could be assured of a full research agenda. The sketch provided above certainly suggests plenty of work.

References

Altonji, Joseph. 1986. "Intertemporal substitution in labor supply: Evidence from micro data." *Journal of Political Economy* 94:S116–S215.

Amemiya, Takeshi, and Quang H. Vuong. 1987. "A comparison of two consistent estimators in the choice-based sampling qualitative response model." *Econometrica* 55:699–702.

Becker, Eugene H. 1984. "Self-employed workers: An update to 1983." *Monthly Labor Review* 107:14–18.

Blau, David M. 1987. "A time-series analysis of self-employment in the United States." *Journal of Political Economy* 95:445–67.

Cogan, John. 1981. "Fixed costs and labor supply." *Econometrica* 49:945–64.

Emerson, Robert, ed. 1984. *Seasonal Agricultural Labor Markets in the United States*. Ames: Iowa State University Press.

Goddeeris, J. H. 1988. "Compensating differentials and self-selection: An application to lawyers." *Journal of Political Economy* 96:411–27.

Gustman, Alan L., and Thomas L. Steinmeier. 1986. "A structural retirement model." *Econometrica* 54:555–84.

Hausman, Jerry A. 1978. "Specification tests in econometrics." *Econometrica* 46:1251–71.

_____. 1985. "The econometrics of nonlinear budget sets." *Econometrica* 53:1255–82.

Heckman, James J. 1979. "Sample selection bias as a specification error." *Econometrica* 47:153–61.

Heckman, James J., and Richard Robb. 1985. "Alternative methods for evaluating the impact of interventions," in *Econometric Analysis of Longitudinal Labor Market Data*, ed. James J. Heckman and Burton Singer, 156–245. Cambridge: Cambridge University Press.

Heckman, James J., and Thomas E. MaCurdy. 1980. "A life-cycle model of female labour supply." *Rev. Econ. Studies* 47:47–74.

Heckman, James J., and Burton Singer, eds. 1985. *Econometric Analysis of Longitudinal Labor Market Data.* Cambridge: Cambridge University Press.

Kada, Ryohei. 1980. *Part-time Family Farming: Off-Farm Employment and Farm Adjustments in the United States and Japan.* Tokyo: Center for Academic Publications.

MaCurdy, Thomas E. 1981. "An empirical model of labor supply in a life-cycle setting." *Journal of Political Economy* 89:1059–85.

———. 1982. "The use of time series processes to model the error structure of earnings in a longitudinal data analysis." *Journal of Econometrics* 18:83–114.

———. 1983. "A simple scheme for estimating an intertemporal model of labor supply and consumption in the presence of taxes and uncertainty." *International Economic Review* 24:265–89.

Manski, Charles F., and Steven R. Lerman. 1977. "The estimation of choice probabilities from choice based samples." *Econometrica* 45:1877–88.

Mroz, Thomas A. 1987. "The sensitivity of an empirical model of married women's hours of work to economic and statistical assumptions." *Econometrica* 55:765–801.

Nakamura, A., and M. Nakamura. 1985. "Dynamic models of the labor force behavior of married women which can be estimated using limited amounts of past information." *Journal of Econometrics* 27:273–98.

Nelson, F. D. 1984. "Efficiency of the two-steps estimator for models with endogenous sample selection." *Journal of Econometrics* 24:181–86.

Pereira, Montegomery P., and Daniel A. Sumner. 1988. "Land and labor market participation in rural India." Unpublished paper. Raleigh: Department of Economics, North Carolina State University.

Shishko, R., and B. Rostker. 1976. "The economics of multiple job-holding." *American Economic Review* 66:298–308.

Stinson, John F. 1986. "Moonlighting by women jumped to record highs." *Monthly Labor Review* 109:22–25.

Sumner, Daniel A. 1981. "Wage functions and occupational selection in a rural less developed country setting." *Review of Economics and Statistics* 43:513–19.

———. 1982. "The off-farm labor supply of farmers." *American Journal of Agricultural Economics* 64:499–509.

———. 1986. *Structural Consequences of Agricultural Commodity Programs.* Washington, D.C.: American Enterprise Institute.

Sumner, Daniel A., and Elizabeth Frazao. 1989. "Wage rates in a poor rural area with emphasis on the impact of farm and non-farm experience." *Economic Development and Cultural Change* 37:709–18.

Sumner, Daniel A., and James D. Leiby. 1987. "An econometric analysis of the effects of human capital on size and growth among dairy farms." *American Journal of Agricultural Economics* 69:465–70.

Wu, De-Min. 1973. "Alternative tests of independence between stochastic regressors and disturbances." *Econometrica* 41:733–50.

PART III

Results of Farm Household Surveys

CHAPTER 9

Evolving Dimensions of Dual Employment of Illinois Farm Families

R. G. F. SPITZE
R. K. MAHONEY

Multiple job-holding has been important to the agricultural sector of this nation for as long as relevant data are available (Black 1953, pp. 232–3). Its importance to total economic growth has increased as the economy has become more industrialized and urbanized. Similarly, it grew in importance to farming and the rural community as technology was injected into agricultural production processes. As this occurs, farm labor and management are confronted continually with the necessity to adjust resource use in response to the squeeze between the inelastic demand for their product and rising labor and capital opportunity costs. Part of the adjustment takes the form of migration of labor and capital resources out of agriculture and part emerges as dual employment.

Dual employment, involving members of farm families working part- or full-time off the farm, occurs in all regions, but is differentially affected by the functioning of the varied labor markets. If alternative employment opportunities are readily accessible within commuting distance of the farm, dual employment can serve as the adjustment. In the absence of such opportunities, out-migration may be necessary. The push for such adjustments from the farm labor-supply side is affected by the nature of farming while the pull from the labor demand side is affected by the nature of the farm service sector and of the general industrial economy. These economic forces vary by state and region (Ahearn 1986; Findeis 1985).

The purpose of this chapter is to report on the findings from analyses

163

of a primary survey of a representative sample of all farm families in Illinois for 1985. It was designed as a follow-up of a similar study for 1971, almost fifteen years earlier (Hanson 1972; Mahoney 1987). Illinois offers a unique setting for a study of dual employment because it is both a substantial commercial crops-livestock farming state and a highly urbanized, diversified manufacturing state. Furthermore, the latter is dispersed sufficiently so that standard metropolitan areas exist throughout the state, except for the southern most region.

Dual Employment in the National Setting

Off-farm employment as a continuing phenomenon has been the subject of many research reports for decades. In general, as economic development has impacted the U.S. economy and its agricultural sector, dual employment has risen, both in absolute terms and as a proportion of total farm family income. Current data about these trends were often confounded by disturbances in farm income flows and by inflation-deflation trends. Again in general, off-farm income has been more stable and hence dependable than farm income in the total income flow to farm families (Friedman 1957; Sumner 1982). An understanding of these general national trends is important as background for the results discovered in the Illinois study.

In Table 9.1, trends in terms of compound annual rates of change for

Table 9.1. United States farm family income, farm population, and unemployment levels, rates of change, 1960–85

Period	Net farm income per farm (constant $)	Off-farm income per farm (constant $)	Total family income per farm (constant $)	Number of farms	Average unemployment rate average
			Percent		
1960–65	4.2	10.5	7.2	−3.3	5.4
1965–70	0.9	4.6	2.9	−2.6	3.8
1970–75	7.8	2.7	4.9	−3.1	6.0
1975–80[a]	−7.8	0.9	−3.3	−0.7	6.7
1980–85[a]	2.5	0.1	1.1	−1.3	8.2

Sources: U.S. Department of Agriculture, Economic Indicators of the Farm Sector, National Financial Summary, 1986; Economic Report of the President, Transmitted to the Congress, February, 1988.

Note: Compound annual rates of change for period indicated, except for unemployment rates presented as averages; constant 1982 dollars derived using GNP deflator from Economic Report of the President 1988.

[a]Data for all 1980 income rates were the average of years 1979–81, used because of the unusual drop in farm income for that one year.

U.S. farm and off-farm income per farm in constant dollars are presented, along with two labor market factors, number of farms and unemployment levels in the national economy. Although the farm income trend in current dollar terms has been highly variable and generally positive, much of the increase, particularly in the 1970s, was due to inflation. When deflated, increases in net farm income per farm slowed from 0.9 percent and 7.8 percent per year in the late 1960s and early 1970s to −7.8 percent in the late 1970s, before beginning to rebound again in this decade.

However, the rate of increase in off-farm income in constant dollars has slowed substantially throughout the twenty-five year period to essentially no growth in the first half of this decade. Although the jump in net farm income in the early 1970s probably slowed the decline in farm numbers and may have similarly relieved the farm family of the necessity to reach out for off-farm income augmentation, the explanation for the demise of the growth of off-farm earnings seems more likely related to the general worsening economic conditions (R. G. F. Spitze 1987).

Generally, unemployment levels nationwide have risen from a low of 3.8 percent in the late 1960s to 8.2 percent in the first half of the 1980s. Multiple job-holding appears to be substantially driven by the employment opportunities offered in the economy and is likely to be particularly important at the margins of lower skill levels and job security where farm labor operates. These trends raise the serious question of whether farm families can depend in the future upon their off-farm jobs to serve as both a supplementing and stabilizing income source as they did during the dramatic adjustments associated with the farm technological revolution of the post–World War II period.

The impacts of these overall employment, income, and farm adjustment levels can be even more pronounced in a region where manufacturing, such as farm machinery, automobile, heavy equipment, and electrical goods, dominates. Thus, it will be instructive to determine the dual employment developments in Illinois over the past fifteen years.

Description of Illinois Studies

Sample primary mail surveys to represent all Illinois farm families were completed for the years 1971 and 1985. Purposes of both studies were to ascertain the level and source of farm and off-farm income for all members of the farm families, to determine farm and personal characteristics of the respondents, and to identify the determinants of off-farm earnings. The studies were similarly designed, implemented, and interpreted, to include in the analysis comparisons and changes during the intervening period.

Survey and sampling methods used in the 1985 study closely paralleled those of the 1971 study. Data for the studies were obtained from a random sample of 3.2 percent of Illinois farmers (4,000 in 1971 and 3,000 in 1985) drawn by the Illinois State Crop and Livestock Reporting Service. The sample was drawn from listings of all farm operators in the state as defined by the Census of Agriculture. The samples were proportional to the geographic distribution of all farm operators in Illinois. To maximize both the utility and validity of these primary data, several important procedural choices had to be made. With limitations on resources and an appreciation for the value of statewide analysis, carefully designed mail surveys were chosen. Interviews or telephone surveys would probably have generated higher response rates than mail surveys, but the cost would have been much higher. Telephone surveys would also have limited the data collected.

Since the respondents must understand the purposes for a satisfactory mail survey, an introductory letter concerning the nature of the study was sent to all county extension advisors, and an explanatory cover letter was sent to the sample farmers. A self-addressed, stamped return envelope was also included.

In 1971, a pretest of 200 farmers randomly selected in six counties in east-central Illinois was completed and analyzed prior to the primary data collection. In 1985, two pretests were completed of approximately 100 farmers each, prior to the primary data collection. As a result of the pretest experience in 1971, one reminder card was sent to the entire sample. In 1985, a second mailing consisting of a cover letter and survey was sent to nonrespondents. For all pretests, a follow-up contact by telephone was made to determine the reasons for not responding and to obtain selected characteristics from the questionnaire particularly sensitive to possible bias in the data to be collected. In 1985, nonrespondents were also asked about their farming status, age, and education. In 1971, several respondents were then personally interviewed to secure additional assistance in questionnaire design and survey procedure.

Standard (z) distribution tests were computed for differences between respondents and nonrespondents in the pretest in the percentages reporting off-farm work and the average acreage per farm. No significant differences between the respondents and nonrespondents in these respects appeared for either study. The results from the pretests supported the conclusion that these statewide surveys could be implemented without important bias in the data sought.

Following the steps outlined above, the final questionnaire was processed and mailed to the master samples of all Illinois farmers. In 1971, approximately 40 percent of the 4,000 questionnaires were returned. From these returned questionnaires, 1,400 farmers (35 percent of the total sample) were selected to provide the observations for this study. In 1985, the final response rate was 39.2 percent or 896 usable surveys. In both studies, some questionnaires were omitted because of incompleteness or inaccuracies, or because the respondent was not the actual operator of the farm. However, none of these reasons seemed to be associated with selectivity factors that might bias the data critical to the studies. In 1985, the sample size was adjusted to reflect the relatively large number of nonactive operators in the sample, and completed surveys from the second pretest were included in the final analysis. The characteristics of the 1971 sample were comparable to those of all Illinois farmers included in the 1969 Census of Agriculture according to geographic distribution, farm size by acreage, age distribution, and economic class of farm as measured by gross farm sales.

Comparative Average Farm Family Income and Sources

Table 9.2 presents comparative data from the 1971 and 1985 surveys for off-farm income by source and family member, as well as net farm income.[1] Some important characteristics appear: (1) although Illinois farms are generally commercial and specialized, off-farm income to farm families still exceeded income from farm sources in both periods; (2) the relative importance of off-farm income remained essentially unchanged (52 percent in 1971 versus 53 percent in 1985) which exactly mirrors changes for those specific years at the national level (56 percent in 1971 versus 57 percent in 1985), albeit the latter being at slightly higher levels, expected when compared to that of a commercial farming state; (3) the absolute levels of off-farm income in real terms increased significantly, $14,277 in 1971 to $16,097 in 1985, again very similar to the national levels of $14,800 in 1971 to $16,700 in 1985, this increase all occurring in the decade of the 1970s; (4) off-farm wage and salary income was the largest component of total off-farm income but declined during the period, 68 percent in 1971 to 55 percent in 1985, probably reflecting the deteriorating employment conditions; (5) within the wage and salary component, the earnings of the spouse grew in importance both in absolute and proportionate terms, $2,566 or 18 percent in 1971 versus $3,082 or 19 percent in 1985,[2] again probably reflecting

---

1. Throughout this paper, all reported data for 1971 are from Hanson and Spitze 1976; 1985 data are from Mahoney 1987.

2. Spouses' off-farm earnings accounted for 34.8 percent of all off-farm wage and salary earnings in 1985 compared with 26.6 percent in 1971.

Table 9.2. Comparison of average farm household income in Illinois from all sources

	1971 (N = 1,400)		1985 (N = 896)	
	Percent[a]	Income (1985 $)[b]	Percent[a]	Income (1985 $)
Off-farm wage and salary income				
Operator	46.7	6,667	33.1	5,330
Spouse	18.0	2,566	19.1	3,082
Other household members	2.8	403	2.8	456
Total wage and salary	67.5	9,636	55.0	8,868
Net nonfarm business income	8.2	1,170	6.8	1,090
Custom farm work	4.1	591	4.3	687
Interest income	6.8	969	14.3	2,300
Dividends	4.4	629	2.3	364
Rental income				
Nonfarm	...	...		364
Farm	...	...		554
Total rental income	2.8	403	5.7	918
Royalties	0.2	25	0.5	78
Trusts and estates	2.5	352	3.6	573
Pensions and retirement benefits	2.7	390	5.4	864
Nonagricultural govt. payments	...	...	0.6	103
Miscellaneous	0.8	113	1.5	252
Total off-farm household income	100.0	14,277	100.0	16,097
Net farm income		13,296		14,637
Total farm household income		27,573		30,734
Proportion of income from farm sources		.4822		.4774

[a]1971 income translated into 1985 dollars using GNP deflator.
[b]Percent of total off-farm income for year indicated.

relatively poorer employment prospects for the industrial skills of the operator compared to better prospects in service employment by spouses, and their better education and smaller families; (6) interest and rental income, although still small, grew in importance, likely reflecting the rise in real interest levels; (7) pensions and retirement income similarly rose, probably due to the importance of social security benefits; and finally (8) net farm income slightly increased, $13,296 in 1971 to $14,673 in 1985, and was at a slightly higher level than national net farm income averages, $11,700 in 1971 to $12,800 in 1985. The latter observation was expected given the commercial status of Illinois farming.

Off-farm Employment and Occupations

Operators

Overall, 40.6 percent of the farm operators surveyed reported off-farm employment in 1985 compared with 45 percent of the surveyed farm operators in 1971. The decline was likely due to the labor demand conditions in

Illinois for occupations traditionally employing farm operators, as well as to an increase in farm size and enterprise intensity. When asked, most operators reported jobs terminating and increased farm labor needs as the reasons for discontinuing off-farm employment or changing off-farm jobs.

Table 9.3 presents the occupations reported by farm operators and spouses in 1985 and 1971 as well as the average salaries reported for each occupation in 1985. In 1985, farm operators reported less employment in trade occupations, public service jobs, and factory jobs than in 1971. These declines are likely due to the effects of the loss of manufacturing jobs—in turn also reflecting the impact in Illinois of the farm crisis—and the reduction in public programs. When the farm economy is weak, farm site construction falls, as well as machinery purchases, etc., hurting farmers employed in trade industries and farm input agribusinesses. Cutbacks and reorganizations in this industry has resulted in fewer available jobs as well as increasing competition for existing jobs.

Table 9.4 presents a comparison between the perceived availability of jobs among respondents in 1971 and 1985. Jobs were considered significantly less available in 1985 than in 1971. In 1971, 48 percent of farm operators indicated that off-farm jobs paying a reasonable wage or salary were difficult to find or unavailable compared with over 67 percent of farm operators responding in 1985.

Table 9.3. Off-farm occupations and earnings reported in Illinois by farm operators and spouses, 1971 and 1985

	Operators			Spouses		
Occupation	Distribution[a] (%)		Earnings in 1985 ($)	Distribution[a] (%)		Earnings in 1985 ($)
Farm-related sales	10.3	(5.0)	$6,254	0.9	(NA)	$3,867
Nonfarm-related sales	4.7	(4.0)	14,816	5.1	(10.0)	3,787
Farm-related business person	9.7	(4.0)	11,135	2.4	(NA)	4.125
Nonfarm-related business employee	6.5	(4.0)	16,246	5.4	(4.0)	6,147
Farm-related business employee	8.2	(10.0)	9,310	2.4	(NA)	9,318
Teacher	2.9	(NA)	25,380	16.0	(17.0)	11,428
Office worker	3.5	(NA)	21,417	28.6	(27.0)	8,541
Medical services	0.6	(NA)	10,000	12.2	(15.0)	10,460
Food services	0.6	(NA)	14,025	6.0	(8.0)	4,024
Public service employee	11.1	(21.0)	12,978	7.4	(NA)	6,949
Trade occupation	12.6	(34.0)	15,107	2.4	(NA)	8,750
Factory employee	9.4	(17.0)	22,514	3.2	(9.0)	13,373
Transportation	8.8	(NA)	10,797	1.2	(NA)	2,825
Other	11.1	(1.0)	11,435	6.8	(10.0)	3,002

[a]1971 figures presented in parentheses.
NA = not available.

Table 9.4. Comparison by job availability for farm operators in Illinois

Availability	1971 (%)	1985 (%)
Easily available	6.0	3.7
Fairly available	21.0	11.6
Sometimes available	25.0	17.2
Rather difficult to find	41.0	52.1
Not available	7.0	15.4
Total	100.0	100.0

In Table 9.5, primary and secondary reasons for working off the farm are reported from participants in the study who were employed off the farm. For operators, farm reasons, such as additional investments or debt reduction, were the primary reasons, but were also frequently given as secondary reasons. Operators chose family reasons, such as education for the children and additional family needs, as the second most important reason for off-farm work. Many operators choosing other reasons indicated that off-farm employment was their primary occupation.

Spouses

In 1985, 46.1 percent of farm spouses reported off-farm employment compared to only 29 percent in 1971.[3] Several factors likely account for this increase including increases in education, smaller families, growth in the service sector, the changing perceptions of women working, increased career desires by many women, and increasing financial stress in the farm business.

The off-farm occupations reported by farm spouses in 1971 and 1985 were presented in Table 9.3. Survey categories differed between 1971 and 1985; thus the comparisons are not precise. A large decrease was reported for spouses employed in factories and retail sales, while employment in business occupations increased. Employment in teaching, office work, medical, and food services remained fairly constant, with these fields continuing to employ the largest numbers of farm spouses. These occupations allow relative ease of exit and entry for women who, for family reasons, tend to be more mobile in the job market than men (Sander 1986).

As revealed in Table 9.5, the 1985 study found that family considerations were of primary importance to farm spouses when making employ-

---

3. Farm spouses were either husbands or wives. However, 98.5 percent of the respondent spouses were women. Therefore, it is assumed that spouse employment decisions and earnings are essentially those of women.

Table 9.5. Reasons for working off the farm, 1985

Reason for off-farm work	Operators		Spouses	
	Primary	Secondary	Primary	Secondary
		Number		
Additional income for farm	116	66	49	54
Reduce farm debts	51	95	41	68
Education for children	13	68	30	53
Home improvements	5	51	25	48
Additional family expenses	62	73	101	78
Retirement/old age security	13	66	7	46
Utilize labor not used on farm	13	58	1	19
Acquire off-farm experience in order to leave farming	1	10	0	7
Provide income needed to move off the farm	1	6	5	8
Change in routine	2	22	13	29
Fringe benefits	1	50	4	49
Enjoy working off-farm	7	34	14	41
Do not know	3	1	0	2
Other	41[a]	8	22	4

Note: Respondents were asked to choose one primary reason and as many secondary reasons as applicable.
[a]Most selecting "other" indicated that their off-farm job was their primary occupation.

ment decisions. Comparisons between 1971 and 1985 of the number of dependent children reported are presented in Table 9.6. In 1985, farm households reported fewer dependent children than farm households in 1971. This decrease is likely due to increased off-farm opportunities for farm spouses and to changing priorities. As the value of time in the labor market for women increases, children become more expensive and fewer are desired. Farm spouses reported family reasons and more money as the primary reasons for changing or discontinuing off-farm employment. Also, spouses were more likely than operators to work off-farm for a change in routine or because they enjoyed off-farm work. This suggests that many farm spouses have a personal preference for off-farm work. The value of time can be influenced by pecuniary and nonpecuniary factors.

Table 9.6. Comparison by number of dependent children reported by Illinois farm families

Number of children	1971 (%)	1985 (%)
0	42.7	47.0
1–2	31.7	36.4
3–4	19.6	15.1
5 or more	6.0	1.5
Total	100.0	100.0

Off-farm Employment and Personal Factors

Age

Table 9.7 presents income and off-farm employment findings in relation to age.[4] Earnings show an inverted U-shape pattern, initially increasing and then declining. The increase is likely due to higher productivity gained through experience, while the decrease in later years is likely attributable to a decline in overall labor hours and an increased demand for leisure asso-

---

4. Analysis of variance, or t-tests, were used to measure the statistical significance of differences between means in cross-classification tables. The t-values are reported for off-farm participation and off-farm wage and salary earnings in Tables 9.7, 9.9, 9.10, 9.11, and 9.12.

Table 9.7. Income and off-farm employment by age of Illinois operator, 1985

				Age			
		<35	35–44	45–54	55–64	65+	t
Total off-farm income	($)	12,134	17,548	18,328	16,946	13,732	...
Net cash farm income	($)	14,595	17,343	22,955	20,487	13,235	...
Total household income	($)	26,729	34,891	41,283	37,433	26,967	
Proportion of household income from farm sources	(%)	54.6	49.7	55.6	54.7	49.1	...
Distribution of farm operators	(%)	16.0	20.9	21.5	28.3	13.3	...
Distribution of farm spouses	(%)	18.4	23.7	24.6	24.6	8.7	...
Proportion of operators working off-farm	(%)	47.1	53.4	40.9	37.0	16.7	2.80*
Proportion of spouses working off-farm	(%)	53.4	58.9	52.5	31.9	3.6	4.00**
Wage earnings by operators working off-farm	($)	11,711	16,897	16,370	12,319	11,542	2.09**
Wage earnings by spouses working off-farm	($)	8,315	7,529	10,442	5,488	2,139	1.58**

*Significant at the .025 level.
**Significant at the .01 level.

ciated with older ages. Both farm and off-farm income was highest for farm households whose operator is 45–54 years old. Many of these operators are at their productive peak for both on and off-farm employment, benefiting from experience and good health. The proportion of operators working off-farm also increased initially then declined (Huffman 1976). Operators at ages 35–44 reported the highest frequency of off-farm work.

For spouses, the high levels of off-farm labor market participation during the primary child-bearing years (less than 44) were unexpected. However, this measured labor market participation, not time spent in work. In other words, many under the age of 45 may be working part-time, while others are committed to off-farm work and make accommodating household adjustments. Even when women work full-time outside the home and earn as much or more than their husbands, they still undertake most household and child care tasks (G. D. Spitze 1986). The initial decline in earnings of spouses with off-farm employment suggests more part-time employment. The earnings increase for spouses age 45–54 may reflect more full-time employment as well as returns for experience. The decline for older spouses also reflects a probable decline in overall work hours and an increased demand for leisure.

Education

In Table 9.8 levels of education for operators and spouses were compared for 1971 and 1985. Operators and spouses in 1985 were considerably more educated than their counterparts in 1971. Higher education enhances productivity, thus the value of time both on and off-farm (Schultz 1981).

The income and off-farm employment findings presented in Table 9.9 indicate that as operators became more educated, there was a statistically significant increase in participation in off-farm employment. Surprisingly, the off-farm earnings for those working off-farm are quite large for those

Table 9.8. Comparison of Illinois farm operators and spouses by education

	Operators		Spouses	
	1971	1985	1971	1985
		Percent		
Grade school	25.0	9.1	24.6	4.9
Some high school	11.0	8.1	8.8	5.8
High school	47.0	45.7	47.0	51.4
Some college	11.0	21.8	12.5	21.7
College degree	6.0	11.7	7.1	12.4
Graduate degree	...	3.6	...	3.8
Total	100.0	100.0	100.0	100.0

Table 9.9. Income and off-farm employment by education, Illinois, 1985

				Levels of Education				
		Grade school	Some high school	High school	Some college	College degree	Graduate degree	t
Total off-farm income[a]	($)	8,422	16,624	15,462	17,077	20,872	24,138	...
Net cash farm income[a]	($)	13,071	18,241	19,671	15,386	23,568	12,737	...
Total household income[a]	($)	21,493	34,865	35,133	32,463	44,440	36,875	...
Proportion of total household income from farm sources[a]	(%)	60.8	52.3	56.0	47.4	53.0	34.5	...
Distribution of farm operators	(%)	9.1	8.1	45.7	21.8	11.7	3.6	...
Distribution of farm spouses	(%)	4.9	5.8	51.4	21.7	12.4	3.8	...
Proportion of operators working off-farm	(%)	18.5	31.8	41.1	48.6	43.0	55.2	1.52**
Proportion of spouses working off-farm	(%)	22.6	32.4	40.8	52.9	59.6	85.7	2.33*
Wage earnings by operators working off-farm	($)	18,453	14,711	11,580	14,275	18,918	23,456	.59
Wage earnings by spouses working off-farm	($)	5,014	4,106	7,197	8,834	8,369	16,024	1.34

[a]Classified by level of education of farm operator.
*Significant at the .05 level.
**Significant at the .10 level.

with only a grade-school education, declining through high school, then increasing steadily. This high level of earnings for the less educated was attributed to experience, since many of these operators tended to be older operators, likely to have many years of off-farm experience.

For spouses, the increase in off-farm employment was statistically significant across education levels. Spouses reported in 1985 that participation in off-farm employment consistently increased as education increased. The earnings for spouses working off-farm also tended to increase with education; yet their off-farm earnings lagged behind those of the operator, suggesting more part-time work by spouses as well as limited high-paying job opportunities in rural areas for farm women.

Off-farm Employment and Farm Factors

Farm sales

Table 9.10 shows that off-farm earnings tended to decline as farm sales increased, while farm and total household income increased. Not only did farm operators generally participate less in the off-farm labor markets as farm sales increased but the off-farm earnings for those working off-farm also declined, suggesting more part-time employment.

Participation in off-farm employment by farm spouses displayed an inconsistent pattern, suggesting that spouse off-farm labor market participation was related less to farm production factors than to other factors such as education, job availability, and family considerations.

Debt-to-asset ratio

Table 9.11 presents the income and off-farm employment factors by debt-to-asset ratios. The proportion of both operators and spouses working off-farm tended to increase as the debt-to-asset ratio increased, although off-farm earnings for those working off the farm fluctuate across these ratios. These findings suggest that many Illinois farms were indeed seeking relief from farm financial obligations through off-farm employment, but off-farm earnings were influenced by education, experience, time available for off-farm work, and job availability.

Farm type

Table 9.12 presents the income and off-farm employment findings by farm type. General crop farms were defined as farms with crops only, and

Table 9.10. Income and off-farm employment by farm sales, Illinois, 1985

Classes by farm sales		Less than 2,500	2,500–4,999	5,000–9,999	10,000–19,999	20,000–39,999	40,000–99,999	100,000–249,999	250,000–499,999	500,000 and over	t
Total off-farm income	($)	25,455	24,872	24,119	25,706	20,633	16,510	12,341	17,363	10,569	...
Net cash farm income	($)	−366	−245	858	3,189	7,543	14,063	29,290	38,285	57,048	...
Total household income	($)	25,079	24,627	24,977	28,895	28,176	30,573	41,631	55,648	67,617	...
Proportion of household income from farm sources	(%)	0.0	0.0	3.5	11.0	26.8	46.0	70.4	68.8	84.4	...
Distribution of farms	(%)	3.8	3.4	4.0	8.1	14.6	29.8	27.8	6.0	2.5	...
Proportion of operators working off-farm	(%)	69.0	81.8	62.1	67.3	57.3	41.7	23.6	21.4	0.0	3.26*
Proportion of spouses working off-farm	(%)	54.6	80.0	47.6	47.8	52.3	49.7	39.3	54.8	22.2	1.70**
Wage earnings by operators working off-farm	($)	26,370	22,711	18,613	22,524	16,659	11,028	7,387	7,235	0.0	1.60**
Wage earnings by spouses working off-farm	($)	7,569	7,718	7,773	8,876	6,993	8,773	8,529	10,608	12,049	1.41**

*Significant at the .05 level.
**Significant at the .10 level.

176

Table 9.11. Income and off-farm employment by debt-to-asset ratio, Illinois, 1985

| | | Debt-to-asset ratio | | | | | | |
		0	.01–.24	.25–.49	.50–.74	.75–.99	1.00 or more	t
Total off-farm income	($)	17,526	19,874	13,191	16,675	17,391	18,916	...
Net cash farm income	($)	15,868	21,631	27,219	10,736	6,916	20,070	...
Total household income	($)	33,394	41,505	40,410	27,411	24,307	38,986	...
Proportion of household income from farm source	(%)	47.5	52.1	67.4	39.2	28.5	51.5	...
Distribution of farms	(%)	26.0	25.1	19.8	16.3	7.8	5.0	...
Proportion of operators working off-farm	(%)	36.1	46.9	34.1	40.9	62.8	51.5	3.06*
Proportion of spouses working off-farm	(%)	34.1	47.6	48.7	53.3	65.3	56.7	1.81**
Wage earnings of operators working off-farm	($)	15,085	14,896	12,041	15,787	10,622	16,860	1.84**
Wage earnings of spouses working off-farm	($)	7,181	7,782	8,423	10,063	9,187	8,989	1.58**

*Significant at the .025 level.
**Significant at the .10 level.

Table 9.12. Income and off-farm employment by farm type, Illinois, 1985

| | | Farm type | | | | | |
		General crop	Crop/live-stock	Cattle	Hog	Dairy	t
Total off-farm income	($)	18,272	16,779	12,592	13,160	7,659	...
Net cash farm income	($)	19,551	13,792	19,295	24,688	17,416	...
Total household income	($)	37,823	30,571	31,887	37,848	25,075	...
Proportion of household income from farming	(%)	51.7	45.1	60.5	65.2	69.5	...
Distribution of farms	(%)	60.5	5.1	11.4	12.3	10.7	...
Proportion of operators working off-farm	(%)	49.1	31.3	21.4	22.5	16.2	2.66*
Proportion of spouses working off-farm	(%)	48.2	48.2	39.3	45.3	36.5	1.19
Wage earnings of operators working off-farm	($)	12,847	20,066	1,804	2,065	10,207	1.35
Wage earnings of spouses working off-farm	($)	9,116	8,587	5,002	3,030	6,205	1.54**

*Significant at the .05 level.
**Significant at the .10 level.

no livestock. Crop-livestock farms were primarily crop farms with some livestock, but fewer than 100 cattle and/or 200 hogs. Similarly, cattle farms had at least 100 head of cattle (beef-cow or feeder), while hog farms had at least 200 hogs. Dairy farms were defined as those reporting any dairy cattle.

Off-farm income declined as farms became more labor intensive with the addition of various livestock enterprises. The participation in off-farm labor markets also declined for operators as farm enterprises became more labor demanding. However, spouse off-farm participation appears unaffected by farm type. Yet, the earnings for those spouses working off-farm is less on livestock farms than for those from crop farms, suggesting more part-time work due to farm labor needs.

Summary and Implications

Multiple job-holding among farm families has prevailed since American agriculture commenced rapid commercialization. As the agricultural sector faces the continual injection of technology, a highly competitive sector, and an inelastic product market, its human factors must constantly adjust by shifting resources completely out of agriculture or pursuing at least part-time off-farm employment. These adjustments are affected by the income prospects from the occupation of farming on one side, and on the other, the employment opportunities offered beyond the farm. Even though off-farm income of farm families has been generally increasing in absolute terms and as a proportion of total family income in the United States, inflation has clouded the picture.

Trends since 1960 are as follows: (1) net farm income per farm highly variable, (2) off-farm income per farm in constant dollars declining, (3) total farm family income variable but moderated by more stable off-farm income, (4) number of farms and farm population persistently declining, and (5) unemployment rate rising. It would appear likely that the latter greatly influences the off-farm income flows. These trends can be found mirrored in the dual employment experiences of farm families in highly commercial farming and industrial states.

These trends were substantiated by primary studies of Illinois farm family income, the results of which are reported in this chapter. A follow-up study using primary farm sample data was completed for 1985 in Illinois, that paralleled in design a study in 1971, about fifteen years earlier. Comparative findings include

1. off-farm income in such a commercialized farming, industrial state as Illinois still exceeded farm income, but remained relatively unchanged between these periods;

2. off-farm wage and salary income for that period declined for farm operators, but increased for spouses, reflecting generally deteriorating skilled employment opportunities, as borne out in the jobs and job availability reported by respondents;

3. proportions of farm operators working off the farm similarly declined while that of spouses increased;

4. dominant reasons for working off the farm for operators were related to farm objectives, while spouses reported family needs;

5. earnings related to the operator's age revealed an inverted U pattern, initially increasing and then declining;

6. spouses reported more off-farm jobs (not the same as time at jobs) during child-bearing years, probably again emphasizing the perceived needs for family support;

7. higher education was reflected in higher off-farm labor market participation for both operators and spouses; and

8. off-farm earnings tended to be inversely related to size of operation, directly related to level of indebtedness, and inversely related to importance of livestock enterprises.

These findings, both national and for Illinois, clearly point to the critical importance of high employment levels, strong educational opportunities, and facilitation of transfer and flexibility in farm human-resources use. These conditions are prerequisites for supporting the continued adjustments confronting farm families as they strive to maintain relative income positions in a growing economy.

References

Ahearn, Mary. 1986. *Financial Well-being of Farm Operators and Their Households.* Agricultural Economic Report No. 563. Washington, D.C.: Economic Research Service, U.S. Department of Agriculture.

Black, John D. 1953. *Introduction to Economics for Agriculture.* New York: MacMillan Co.

Findeis, Jill. 1985. "The growing importance of off-farm income." *Farm Economics.* University Park: Pennsylvania State University and Cooperative Extension Service, U.S. Department of Agriculture.

Friedman, Milton. 1957. *A Theory on the Consumption Function*. Princeton: Princeton University Press.

Hanson, Ronald J. 1972. *An Economic Analysis of Off-Farm Income as a Factor in the Improvement of the Low Farm Income Farmers in Illinois*. Ph.D. dissertation. Urbana: University of Illinois.

Hanson, Ronald J., and R. G. F. Spitze. 1976. *An Analysis of Off-Farm Income in the Improvement of Illinois Farm Family Income*. University of Illinois Agricultural Experiment Station AERR139. Urbana: University of Illinois.

Huffman, W. E. 1976. "The production value of human time in U.S. agriculture." *American Journal of Agricultural Economics* 58(No. 4):672–83.

Mahoney, Rosemary K. 1987. *An Analysis of Off-Farm Income to Illinois Farm Households*. M.S. thesis. Urbana: University of Illinois.

Sander, William. 1986. "Farm women, work, and fertility." *Quarterly Journal of Economics* 100(August):653–57.

Schultz, Theodore W. 1981. *Investing in People: the Economics of Population Quality*. Berkeley: University of California Press.

Spitze, Glenna D. 1986. "The division of task responsibility in U.S. households: Longitudinal adjustments to change." *Social Forces* 64(No. 3):689–701.

Spitze, R. G. F. 1987. "The evolution and implications of the U.S. Food Security Act of 1985." *Agricultural Economics*. Pp. 175–90.

Sumner, Daniel A. 1982. "The off-farm labor supply of farmers." *American Journal of Agricultural Economics* 64(No. 3):499–509.

U.S. Council of Economic Advisers, Office of the President. 1988. *Economic Report of the President, Transmitted to the Congress, February, 1988*. Washington, D.C.: U.S. Government Printing Office.

U.S. Department of Agriculture. 1986. *Economic Indicators of the Farm Sector, National Financial Summary, 1986*. Washington, D.C.: U.S. Government Printing Office.

CHAPTER 10

Multiple Job-holding among Farm Families: Results from the Wisconsin Family Farm Surveys

WILLIAM SAUPE

BRIAN W. GOULD

Regional surveys, such as the 1983 and 1987 Wisconsin family farm surveys, can be used (1) to complement national descriptive studies, (2) to facilitate modelling and testing hypotheses, and (3) to document economic and social conditions for local users.

In the first session of this symposium, national vantage points were used to develop the historical perspective and to consider future prospects for multiple job-holding among farm families in the United States and Canada. National data were also used to describe farm enterprise adjustments made in response to multiple job-holding. Regional studies cannot provide such a national data base or a national overview. However, because the research effort is concentrated in a relatively small geographic area, a regional survey may be able to obtain detailed data that are more specific to regional issues than a national survey. Regional surveys may thus be valuable for analyses that augment the detail in national studies, or that provide regional support or contrast to national results.

In the second session of this symposium the theoretical bases of multiple job-holding and the effects of off-farm work on farm efficiency were explored. Providing the specific data needed for testing such analytical models or hypotheses is a second use of regional studies. In a regional survey, precisely defined data can be collected for use in multivariate analyses that test hypotheses about off-farm labor allocations, e.g., explaining the probability of off-farm work, the hours worked off farm, the wage rates received, or the simultaneous nature of off-farm work decisions by farm operators and spouses. The units of observation can be households or individuals, for example, instead of counties, and the use of proxy variables can be reduced compared to using secondary data.

Third, regional studies are useful for describing economic and social conditions in the limited geographical area from which the samples were drawn, and perhaps for other similar areas. The data serve as benchmarks for public policymakers, program managers, Extension faculty, those involved with community economic development, and others concerned with the topics covered and the geographical area. For such users, multivariate analyses may help substantiate the cross-tabulations and other descriptive statistics often used with lay audiences.

Genesis of the Wisconsin Family Farm Surveys

An example of the usefulness of regional surveys in analysis of off-farm labor force participation can be found in the 1983 and 1987 Wisconsin family farm surveys. These surveys are recent products of a decade of collaboration in a research program among scientists in the Economic Research Service, U.S. Department of Agriculture (ERS,USDA) and agricultural economists at the University of Wisconsin-Madison.[1]

The relevance of this research program was enhanced because it was preceded by two studies to determine what information was needed about farm families to facilitate efficient public policies and programs regarding farm family well-being. Finding major gaps in the existing data series, the research program initiated primary data collection by first developing a questionnaire that would fill those gaps. After field testing and revision, the instrument was first used in 1980 with case studies of 169 farm households that were participants in a Cooperative Extension Service program for low equity, recent farm entrants in central and western Wisconsin. In

---

1. ERS, USDA support and collaboration have been with Thomas Carlin, Kenneth Deavers, Priscilla Salant, and Susan Bentley. Financial support for conducting the 1983 and 1987 Wisconsin Family Farm Surveys was received from the Economic Research Service of the U.S. Department of Agriculture and the Research Division of the College of Agricultural and Life Sciences in the University of Wisconsin-Madison. In addition, salary support was received from the Cooperative Extension Service and the College of Agricultural and Life Sciences, University of Wisconsin-Madison. The Ford Foundation, through the Aspen Institute, also supported the 1987 follow-up survey. We acknowledge with thanks the assistance of Susan Bentley in much of the analysis reported here.

effect a large scale pretest, this study facilitated further revision and clarification in the questionnaire.

The empirical findings of that first study were also useful in Wisconsin as they showed that, contrary to conventional thinking, dairy farm families could be involved in multiple job-holding without causing the demise of the dairy enterprise. The findings also showed that (1) in the midst of an American agricultural boom these farmers on average had annual financial obligations for family living, principal payments, and capital replacement that exceeded their annual income from all sources by about $15,000; (2) that the prices of farm land and dairy cattle had been bid to levels well above that justified by their income generating ability; and (3) that farmers who entered farming by renting land (instead of the traditional procedure of buying a farm) fared better financially than those buying land (Saupe et al. 1986).

The ERS, USDA then used the questionnaire in a 1981 study of a random sample of 1,069 farm households in 29 counties in northern Mississippi and southwestern Tennessee. Several descriptive studies pertaining to multiple job-holding were made by Salant (1982, 1983, 1984) and Hoover and Crecink (1981) based on this 1981 survey. Following the approach suggested by Huffman (1976a, 1976b, 1980), Bollman (1979), and Sumner (1982), Streeter (1984) also used these data to develop an agricultural production function to obtain the on-farm labor returns to each farm operator, which was then included among the explanatory variables to estimate a labor-supply function for their hours of off-farm work. Nonpecuniary considerations in the labor allocation of farm operators were also examined by Streeter and Saupe (1986), using the Mississippi and Tennessee farm survey data.

The 1983 and 1987 Wisconsin Family Farm Surveys

Given the development and use of the surveys in the Mississippi and Tennessee environment, the questionnaire was then applied to the southwestern region of Wisconsin. The 1983 family farm survey in southwestern Wisconsin provided data from a random sample of 529 farm families for several descriptive and analytical studies. The study area included the eight counties of Buffalo, Crawford, Jackson, LaCrosse, Monroe, Richland, Trempealeau, and Vernon, with a total of 12,240 farms in 1982. The data were for calendar year 1982, with asset, debt, and net worth information as of January 1, 1983. The data were used to examine off-farm employment (Saupe and Salant 1985; Salant 1985, 1986), linkages between farm households and community economic development (Shaffer, Salant, and Saupe 1986), and the financial viability of family farms (Salant and Saupe 1986a, 1986b; Salant, Smale, and Saupe 1986; Smale, Saupe, and Salant 1986). Information was also obtained describing the health status of farm families (Jensen and Saupe 1987), the use of soil conserving practices (Belknap and Saupe 1988a), farmers' business plans for the future, farm families in poverty, and other farm household and business characteristics (Salant and Saupe 1984; Salant, Saupe, and Belknap 1985).

The survey year 1982 marked the last of the "good economic times" for Wisconsin farmers, and unexpected financial reversals began emerging shortly thereafter. While there was a great deal of anecdotal information about what happened to farm families since 1982, it seemed important that the in-depth 1982 data base be supplemented to document those changes. In early 1987 the identical 529 farm operators that had been surveyed four years earlier were contacted and interviewed when possible. Based on their status early in 1987, the operators were sorted into three groups, i.e., those that (1) had died since the 1983 survey ($n = 23$), (2) had left farming since the survey ($n = 106$), or (3) continued to be farm operators in 1987 ($n = 400$), as shown in Figure 10.1.

Regarding generalizations from the surveys to the study area, it should be noted that (1) the 529 farm operators interviewed in 1983 constituted a random sample of all farmers in the study area at that time, (2) the 106 operators that left farming are a random sample of all farmers in the study area who left farming by 1987, and (3) the 400 continuing farmers are a random sample of all farmers who were farming in 1982 and continued to farm in 1987. However, without data on the farm entrants during the 1983–87 period we cannot generalize to the 1987 total farm population in the study area.[2] Finally, the 106 farmers that left farming during that period (about 20 percent of the 1983 farmers) represent the gross movement of farm operators out of farming; to determine the net decrease, data on the farm operator entrants during the 1983–87 period would be needed.

The focus of the 1987 *Wisconsin Family Farm Survey* was on the farm operator and the household of the operator, not on the farm business as the unit of observation. For the continuing farmers, the group of most interest here, a questionnaire similar to that used in 1983 was used to obtain information about labor allocation on and off the farm, farm household characteristics, farm assets, sources and amounts of farm credit, farm and non-farm income, and farming practices. Information concerning how the farm

---

2. As indicated in Figure 10.1, recent farming entrants will be identified and described in a study begun in July 1989. This will complete the sample needed for a proposed continuation in 1991 of this longitudinal study of all farm families.

SOUTHWESTERN WISCONSIN LONGITUDINAL
FAMILY FARM SURVEYS

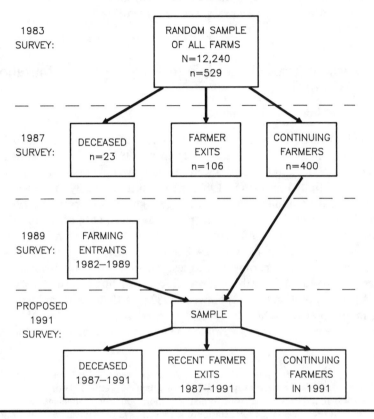

Figure 10.1 Longitudinal survey plan and distribution of respondents. (*Unpublished Wisconsin family farm surveys*)

household had responded to the change in the farm financial climate observed over the 1982–86 period was also obtained.

For those farm operators that had left farming, the questionnaire was modified to obtain information regarding how the family had adjusted since leaving farming. Specifically, information was obtained about the employment status of adult family members, levels of wage and passive income, levels of debt including any remaining farm-related debt, reasons for leaving farming, and the transition process used to leave farming.

The 1987 interviews were made on the farm, or place of residence in the case of persons who had left farming, by trained and experienced professional enumerators. Interviews averaged about 90 minutes in length. After the interviews were completed there was an extensive data entry and screening process before analyses were initiated.

Characteristics of Multiple Job-holding Farm Households in Wisconsin

Level of household income

As illustrated in Figure 10.1, three-fourths of the farm operators in the 1983 survey continued to operate a farm in 1987. Of the 400 continuing farm operators, 342 (86 percent) were reinterviewed.[3] For these farm operators who continued to farm in 1987, the mean total family income from all sources (in 1982 dollars) did not change significantly between 1982 and 1986. However, net income from farming was lower, with off-farm jobs and passive income from nonfarm investments and transfers making up the difference.[4] Differences between 1982 and 1986 are statistically significant for the three largest income categories, but not for total income or for wages paid to family members for work on their home farm.

As shown by Figure 10.2, between 1982 and 1986 net farm income as a percent of total household income decreased from 55 to 43 percent.[5] In contrast, the role of off-farm employment as a source of income increased

---

3. The means for the 14 percent who were nonrespondents in 1987 were compared with the 1987 respondents for several key variables, using their respective 1983 data. A significant difference was found only for years of formal education, with nonrespondents averaging two years less than respondents. Our conclusion was that the 342 respondents were not different from a random sample of continuing farmers in the study area.

4. The distribution of income by source was as follows:

	1982	1986	
		1982 $	Nominal $
Net cash farm operating income	$15,741	$12,058	$13,503
Home farm wage transfers	1,814	1,869	2,093
Off-farm employment income	7,507	9,304	10,418
Nonfarm transfers & investment income	3,502	4,600	5,151
Total household income	$28,564	$27,831	$31,165

"Home farm wage transfers" are payments made to household members (e.g., spouse, children) from the farm business for work done on their own farm. Payments of this kind are included as a farm business expense in calculating net cash farm operating income.

5. If home farm wage transfers are included in a measure of "farm-related income," then the decrease would have been from 61 to 50 percent.

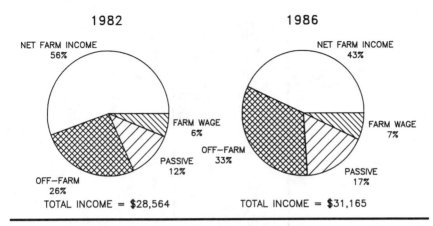

Figure 10.2. Distribution of household income by source, southwestern Wisconsin. (*Unpublished Wisconsin family farm surveys*)

from 26 to 33 percent. The importance of off-farm income to the continuing farm households can be further examined by partitioning them into two groups: (1) those households that had no adult member working off-farm, and (2) those where at least one member worked off-farm. The distribution of sources of household income for these two groups is presented in Table 10.1 for 1982 and 1986. For those households where there was some off-farm work, the proportion of total income originating from the farm was about 35 percent in both years. For those households with no off-farm work, over 78 percent of household income originated from net farm income in 1982 and 67 percent in 1986. This farm income is vulnerable to shocks from nature, input and product price changes, and adjustments in federal farm programs (Jesse et al. 1988.)[6]

Experience from the 1983 survey indicates that these averages hide great diversity in income, with some families doing reasonably well, and many others near or below federal poverty standards. From the 1986 data, the poverty threshold income according to the federal poverty criteria was calculated for each household. The federal poverty threshold varies by the

---

6. James Johnson and Kenneth Erickson, Agriculture and Rural Economy Division, Economic Research Service, U.S. Department of Agriculture, provided access to other data for Wisconsin that emphasize this point. During the five years 1982–86, average per farm income from farming fluctuated in a range from about $6,040 to $17,870, while that from nonfarm sources was consistently trending upward, from $11,100 to $14,300. This is discussed in more detail in Jesse et al. (1988).

Table 10.1. Distribution of total household income by off-farm work status (1982 dollars)

Source of income	1982				1986			
	No off-farm work	Percent	Off-farm work	Percent	No off-farm work	Percent	Off-farm work	Percent
Net farm income	$22,048	78.5	$10,756	37.2	$17,403	66.9	$9,941	34.8
Home farm wages	1,840	6.6	1,793	6.2	2,058	7.9	1,794	6.2
Off-farm employment	...	...	13,441	46.4	...	...	12,988	45.5
Passive income	4,193	14.9	2,955	10.2	6,557	25.2	3,825	13.4
Total income[a]	$28,081	100.0	$28,945	100.0	$26,019	100.0	$28,547	100.0

Source: Wisconsin Family Farm Survey, 1983, 1987.

[a]The undeflated 1986 levels of total income were $29,137 for households which did not have a household member working off-farm versus $31,968 for those that did.

number of family members, the number of children under the age of 18 years, and the age of the household "head" in one- and two-person households. The poverty measure allows for a comparison of equivalent levels of well-being across individuals and time. Using the observed household income levels and comparing them with the poverty income criteria, it was found that in 1986 16 percent of the continuing farm households were at or below the poverty level. Ten percent more were above the poverty level by 50 percent or less. The remainder of the survey households had income levels greater than 150 percent of the poverty level of income.

Employment income and wage rates

The increase in mean off-farm earned income between 1982 and 1986 for the survey households occurred because a larger percentage of farm operators, spouses, and other adults worked off the farm, because they worked more hours on average, and because of higher wage rates. As shown in Figure 10.3, 29 percent of farm operators worked off-farm in 1982. This increased to slightly more than 31 percent in 1986. For farm spouses, the increase was from 38 percent in 1982 to 46 percent in 1986.

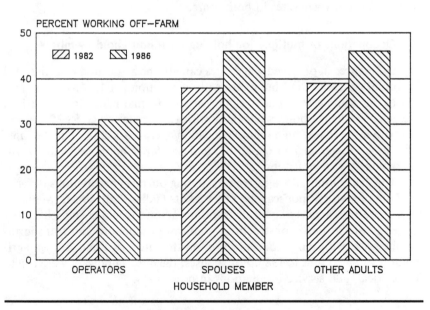

Figure 10.3. Proportion of farm family members working off-farm, southwestern Wisconsin. (*Unpublished Wisconsin family farm surveys*)

Table 10.2 indicates that the attributes of off-farm labor market participation differ substantially between farm operators and spouses. In both years, approximately one-fourth of the farm operators working off-farm were self-employed in nonfarm business enterprises. This compares with 10 percent or less of farm spouses. The extent of off-farm labor market commitment varied between operators and spouses. There appears to be a bimodal distribution of the number of farm operators that worked off-farm in terms of the number of hours worked, i.e., in 1982, 43 percent of those working worked less than 800 hours and 43 percent worked full-time (i.e., 1,600 hours or more). In 1986, these proportions increased to 46 and 45 percent, respectively. In contrast to this pattern, there was a relatively even distribution among all three categories for farm spouses in both years.

In general, persons with full-time off-farm employment received higher wage rates than part-time workers.[7] Farm operators working less than 800 hours in 1986 averaged $7.24 per hour, compared with $13.22 for those working full-time. Spouses working fewer than 800 hours averaged $5.76, compared with $7.43 for those working over 1,600 hours per year. All but one of the farm operators in these groups were male and all but one of the spouses were female. Without controlling for any other factor that affects wage rates, operator (male) wage rates were about three dollars higher than spouse (female) wage rates in both years.

Occupations of multiple job-holding farm household members

Differences in observed wage rates can also be associated with the level of formal education and indirectly with occupation. In 1986, farm operators in our sample with under eight years of formal education earned an average of $6.95 per hour, while those with 12 years averaged $8.29. Operators with more than a high school education averaged $13.06. For the same year, spouses averaged $3.68, $5.83, and $8.15 per hour, respectively, for the same levels of education.

The distribution of wage workers among off-farm occupations differed for farm operators, spouses, and other adults (Table 10.3). For farm operators, there was a fairly equal distribution among teaching, agriculturally related nonfarm jobs, construction, nonfarm production, and transportation in 1982, with more concentration on the latter two and less on agriculturally related jobs in 1986. For spouses, the most important were teaching, clerical, and service occupations in both years.

---

7. While not completely consistent in Table 10.2, in unpublished multivariate analyses with these data the wage rates (and the receipt of fringe benefits) have been correlated with hours worked for both operators and spouses.

Table 10.2. Distribution of operator and spouse wages by hours worked off-farm

Number of hours worked	1982						1986					
	Operator			Spouse			Operator			Spouse		
	Number	Percent	Wage	Number	Percent	Wage	Number	Percent	Wage	Number	Percent	Wage
Wage work (hours)												
1–799	31	42.5	$7.69	38	36.2	$5.85	38	46.3	$7.24	39	29.5	$5.76
800–1599	11	15.0	11.24	30	28.6	6.89	7	8.5	7.24	44	33.3	7.03
1600 or more	31	42.5	10.53	37	35.2	5.94	37	45.2	13.22	49	37.2	7.43
Sub-total	73	100.0	$9.43	105	100.0	$6.18	82	100.0	$9.94	132	100.0	$6.80
None	242	...	...	191	...	...	235	...	...	163	...	...
Self-employed	27	...	...	10	...	...	25	...	...	6	...	...
Total	342	...	...	306	...	...	342	...	...	301	...	...

Source: Wisconsin Family Farm Survey, 1983, 1987.

Table 10.3. Distribution of off-farm wage earners among occupations

Occupation[a]	Continuing farmers 1982				Continuing farmers 1986				Wisconsin wage earners		
	Operator	Spouse	Other	Total	Operator	Spouse	Other	Total	Male	Female	Total
	Percent										
Public administration	9.6	1.0	...	1.5	6.1	...	...	2.1	0.4	0.2	0.3
Other administration	4.1	3.8	1.0	2.8	6.1	4.5	2.5	5.1	10.4	5.2	8.1
Teachers	13.7	15.2	2.9	10.2	11.0	14.4	2.5	13.1	3.2	6.9	4.8
Health-related	...	10.5	1.0	4.2	...	8.3	1.7	5.1	1.4	9.5	4.9
Sales occupations	2.7	2.9	6.7	4.2	3.7	8.3	15.8	6.5	6.6	9.9	8.0
Clerical	6.8	26.7	10.5	15.5	6.1	28.8	5.8	20.1	5.7	28.1	15.3
Service occupations	1.4	20.0	26.7	17.7	2.4	21.2	18.3	14.0	8.7	15.4	11.5
Agricultural-related	11.0	...	23.8	11.7	7.3	0.8	10.8	3.3	2.8	1.4	2.2
Construction and mechanics	12.3	...	3.8	4.6	13.5	...	6.7	5.1	17.8	2.1	11.0
Production-related	13.7	8.6	9.5	10.2	18.3	9.8	22.5	13.1	26.2	13.0	20.5
Transportation	15.1	2.9	3.8	6.4	23.2	0.3	3.3	10.3	6.8	0.8	4.2
Other occupations	9.6	8.6	10.5	9.5	2.4	1.5	10.0	1.9	10.0	7.5	9.2
	100.0	100.0	100.0	100.0	100.0	100.0	100.0	100.0	100.0	100.0	100.0
	Number										
Number of off-farm workers	73	105	105	...	82	132	120	...	...	...	...

Source: Wisconsin Family Farm Survey, 1983, 1987 (for continuing farmers); 1980 Census of Population (for Wisconsin wage earners).
[a]These occupations are for wage and salary workers only. Self-employed persons are not included.

The distribution of all (rural and urban) Wisconsin wage earners among occupations is presented in the last three columns in Table 10.3, as reported in the 1980 Census of Population. Comparison of all Wisconsin male wage earners with the 1982 and 1986 sample farm operators shows that more of the latter were involved with public administration (mostly as local government officials on a part-time basis), as teachers, and as workers in nonfarm agriculturally related occupations. Given the rural nature of the study region, it was not surprising that a lower proportion of farm operators worked in production-related positions compared to male workers in the state as a whole. Farm spouses from the sample were more concentrated in teaching and service occupations than their statewide female counterparts, equally concentrated in clerical work, but less so in nonfarm production occupations (see Table 10.3).

Distribution of hours worked by farm type

The structure of farming as described by farm type, farm size, and farm financial position are also associated with the multiple job-holding of farm household members. In Table 10.4, the 342 continuing farm operators are partitioned according to farm type following the Census of Agriculture system. Seventy percent of the farms were categorized as dairy farms, 9 percent as cash grain farms and 11 percent as other farm types. Given the time commitment associated with operating a dairy farm, it was not surprising that relatively fewer dairy farm operators and spouses worked off-farm. The 39 dairy farm operators that worked off-farm comprised 16 percent of total dairy farmers, while 41 percent of all other operators worked off-farm. About 39 percent of the spouses worked off their dairy farms, compared with 55 percent for spouses of non-dairy farms. In addition, the dairy farm operators and spouses that did work off-farm, on average worked fewer hours off-farm.

Differences in the allocation of time among farm production, off-farm work, and home production between the farm operator and spouse are also suggested in the bottom panel of Table 10.4. For all operators who worked off-farm, the off-farm hours (1,177 hours) were approximately the same as those worked by spouses (1,221 hours). However, those operators allocated an additional 2,256 hours to work on the farm, compared to 658 by the spouses. Spouses, more than farm operators, seem to allocate time to a third demand, i.e., home production. Data on home production was not collected in this study, but this differential gives an indication of the allocation of time for home production by these spouses.

It is reasonable that farm operators and spouses that did not work off-farm worked significantly more hours on the farm than those who com-

Table 10.4. Mean hours worked on and off-farm by off-farm work status and farm type, Wisconsin farm operators and spouses, 1986

Farm type	Operator		Spouse	
	Worked off-farm	No off-farm work	Worked off-farm	No off-farm work
Dairy	(N = 39)	(N = 199)	(N = 84)	(N = 129)
Farm hours	3284**	3882	863**	1529
Off-farm hours	758	...	1146	...
Total hours	4042	3882	2009**	1529
Cash grain	(N = 13)	(N = 17)	(N = 13)	(N = 11)
Farm hours	1061**	2312	302	113
Off-farm hours	1564	...	1336	...
Total hours	2625	2312	1638**	113
Other farm types	(N = 30)	(N = 44)	(N = 35)	(N = 29)
Farm hours	1437*	2054	301*	750
Off-farm hours	1555	...	1356	...
Total hours	2992**	2054	1657**	750
All farms	(N = 82)	(N = 260)	(N = 132)	(N = 169)
Farm hours	2256**	3470	658**	1303
Off-farm hours	1177	...	1221	...
Total hours	3433	3470	1879**	1303

Source: Wisconsin Family Farm Survey, 1987.
Note: Significance of t-tests of the mean farm hours worked for those operators and spouses who worked off-farm versus those who did not are denoted in the table. T-tests of differences in off-farm hours between farm types were also conducted (i.e., comparisons going down the columns), and it was found that dairy farm operators who worked off-farm had significantly less off-farm hours than did nondairy operators.
*Significant at the .05 level.
**Significant at the .01 level.

bined farm and off-farm work. Regarding total hours worked, however, farm operators worked essentially the same total hours whether they were multiple job-holders or not (3,433 hours versus 3,470 hours). Spouses who combined farm with off-farm work averaged more total hours, 1,879 hours compared with 1,303 hours for spouses who did not.

Distribution of hours worked by farm size

In Table 10.5, the surveyed farms are divided according to size as measured by the number of operated acres. Fourteen percent of the farms had 100 acres or less, 34 percent operated between 101 and 250 acres, 27 percent operated between 251 and 400 acres, and 25 percent had more than 400 acres. The proportion of farm operators who worked off-farm decreased from 38 percent of the operators of the smallest farms (18 of 48 operators) to 16 percent for the largest farms (14 of 86 operators). Regard-

Table 10.5. Mean hours worked on and off-farm by off-farm work status and farm size, Wisconsin farm operators and spouses, 1986

	Operator		Spouse	
Farm size	Worked off-farm	No off-farm work	Worked off-farm	No off-farm work
1–100 acres	(N = 18)	(N = 30)	(N = 24)	(N = 21)
Farm hours	1296*	2175	303*	831
Off-farm hours	1758	...	1255	...
Total hours	3054**	2175	1558**	831
101–250 acres	(N = 37)	(N = 78)	(N = 49)	(N = 50)
Farm hours	2265**	3184	771	1050
Off-farm hours	1103	...	1336	...
Total hours	3368	3184	2107**	1050
251–400 acres	(N = 13)	(N = 80)	(N = 29)	(N = 54)
Farm hours	2767**	3757	718*	1379
Off-farm hours	824	...	1264	...
Total hours	3591	3757	1982**	1379
401 or more acres	(N = 14)	(N = 72)	(N = 30)	(N = 44)
Farm hours	2992**	3999	702*	1722
Off-farm hours	956	...	962	...
Total hours	3948	3999	1664	1722

Source: Wisconsin Family Farm Survey, 1987.
Note: The table indicates results of t-tests of the mean farm hours worked for those operators and spouses who worked off-farm versus those who did not. T-tests of differences in off-farm hours between farm size categories were also conducted (i.e., comparisons going down the columns), and it was found that farm operators who worked off-farm and operated less than 100 acres had significantly more off-farm hours versus other operators who worked off-farm.
*Significant at the .05 level.
**Significant at the .01 level.

less of farm size, farm operators who worked off-farm worked significantly fewer farm hours compared to those who did not. The larger the farm size, the greater the number of farm hours worked by the operator, regardless of off-farm work status. In addition, there is a general pattern of fewer off-farm work hours the larger the farm size.

There was no significant difference in total work hours of farm operators by size of farm, except for the operators of the smallest farms. This implies that, for the larger sized farms, there is an allocation of a fixed work time budget between off-farm and farm-related work time. The relationship between farm size and hours worked off-farm by the spouses was not as clear cut as for the farm operators. For those who worked off-farm, the mean on-farm hours was relatively constant except for the smallest farm group. For spouses that did not work off-farm there was a general increase in the number of hours worked on-farm, from 831 hours for the smallest sized farms to over 1722 hours in the largest farm size category. In contrast to the trend observed for farm operators, the total farm plus off-farm work time of spouses with off-farm work was greater than for those that did not work off-farm, except for the largest sized farms.

Distribution of hours worked by financial status

In this perspective on farm structure, financial status is measured as the ratio of total debt to total value of assets. As shown in Table 10.6, three-quarters of the operators had debt-to-asset ratios of .40 or less. There were 94 survey farmers with no debt, which was 27 percent of the total. Their mean age was 62 years, significantly older than the 47 years of the rest of the farmers. Their spouses on average were 58 years old, compared with 44 years for the remainder. This age difference, as well as financial status, probably affected the percentage of these older persons who worked off-farm. The incidence of off-farm work for the debt free group was 20 percent of the operators (versus 25 percent for the remainder) and 27 percent of the spouses (versus 50 percent). However, for those who did work

Table 10.6. Mean hours worked on and off-farm by off-farm work status and financial condition, Wisconsin farm operators and spouses, 1986

	Operator		Spouse	
Debt-asset ratio	Worked off-farm	No off-farm work	Worked off-farm	No off-farm work
No debt	(N = 19)	(N = 75)	(N = 20)	(N = 55)
Farm hours	1583**	2838	197**	938
Off-farm hours	1217	. . .	1164	. . .
Total hours	2800	2838	1361	938
.01 to .40	(N = 41)	(N = 120)	(N = 71)	(N = 74)
Farm hours	2264**	3732	625**	1508
Off-farm hours	1277	. . .	1282	. . .
Total hours	3541	3732	1907	1508
.41 to .70	(N = 10)	(N = 37)	(N = 23)	(N = 21)
Farm hours	2905	3456	899	1319
Off-farm hours	730	. . .	970	. . .
Total hours	3635	3456	1869	1319
.71 or more	(N = 12)	(N = 28)	(N = 18)	(N = 19)
Farm hours	2754**	4054	997	1544
Off-farm hours	1147	. . .	1363	. . .
Total hours	3901	4054	2360	1544

Source: Wisconsin Family Farm Survey, 1987.
Note: The table indicates results of t-tests of the mean farm hours worked for those operators and spouses who worked off-farm versus those who did not.
*Significant at the .05 level.
**Significant at the .01 level.

off-farm, the hours worked were little different from the younger persons. In terms of the relationship of hours worked off-farm to the debt-to asset ratio, no pattern among the farm operators or spouses is revealed in Table 10.6. In addition, the total hours worked (on-farm plus off-farm) by part-time farmers was not different from the full-time farm operators within each debt-to-asset group.

Analyses of Multiple Job-holding from Wisconsin Farm Survey Data

Multivariate analyses of the data from the 1983 and 1987 Wisconsin Family Farm Surveys give additional insight into multiple job-holding by farm household members. McCarthy and Salant (1986) analyzed the decision of married farm women to allocate labor to off-farm employment, using the 1983 survey data. Their model of the labor allocation decision was estimated in the following four steps: (1) the likelihood of off-farm labor market participation, (2) the level of the off-farm market wage rate, (3) the likelihood of receiving fringe benefits in the off-farm employment, and (4) the estimated hours of off-farm work. They found that being employed or looking for off-farm work by married farm women was associated positively with years of formal education and having received nonfarm vocational training, and negatively with living on a dairy farm and the level of net farm income. The estimated off-farm wage rate was also positively associated with years of formal education, as was the probability of receiving health insurance as a fringe benefit. The latter was also positively associated with holding a public administration job and negatively related to having a health problem that limited work at some time during the year. Finally, hours of work in the off-farm job was positively associated with the wage rate, and negatively with having preschool children in the home, and having a disabling health problem.

Belknap and Saupe (1988b) used the 1983 *Wisconsin Family Farm Survey* data to analyze the simultaneous decisions by farm operators and spouses in allocating their labor between farm and off-farm work. They first estimated a farm "production function" based on gross farm sales, to estimate the marginal returns to operator and spouse labor on the farm. Next, potential off-farm wages for operator and spouse were estimated following the Heckman procedure for testing and correcting for sample selection bias. Finally, the four estimates of returns to labor (on and off the farm, for both operator and spouse) were combined with other explanatory variables in a multinomial logit equation that calculated the probabilities of four possible outcomes, as follows: neither operator or spouse works off the farm, both work off the farm, the operator only works off the farm, or the spouse only works off the farm.

From the farm production function, Belknap and Saupe found the marginal returns to farm labor to be $5.68 per hour for the operators and $5.49 per hour for spouses when evaluated at the mean, compared with $9.14 and $5.00 per hour, respectively, for off-farm work. Estimated wage rates were positively influenced by having completed more than a high school education and years of prior off-farm work, in the case of the operator, and by years of prior off-farm work and the distance commuted in the case of the spouse. Being a dairy farmer was negatively related to wage rate in the case of the operator.

The probability of the farm operator working off-farm was positively related to the number of persons in the household, but negatively related to the presence of preschool children, the size of the farm measured by gross sales, the passive income received from nonfarm assets, and the proportion of farm sales that came from a dairy enterprise. The probability of the spouse working off-farm was positively associated with her years of formal education, having received nonfarm vocational training, and receiving health insurance as a fringe benefit of off-farm work. It was negatively related to the weeks she was disabled during the year, the presence of preschool children, and by the total tractor horsepower available on the farm.

Belknap and Saupe found that the probability of both the operator and spouse working off-farm was positively associated with the spouse having received nonfarm vocational training, the presence of teenagers in the household, and paying a relatively high rate of interest on farm loans; it was negatively associated with being a dairy farm, having relatively large quantity of tractor horsepower on the farm, and receiving relatively large amounts of passive income from nonfarm assets. A high return to operator labor relative to the spouse labor both in farm work and off-farm work, increased the probability that only the operator would work off the farm.

Gould and Saupe (1988) examined the lack of symmetry in the reasons why female farm spouses entered and the reasons they exited the off-farm labor market. They formulated a series of models based on the Heckman's sample-selection model of labor supply to examine the dynamics of labor force participation, using the 1983 and 1987 Wisconsin family farm surveys. They first estimated the probability of a farm spouse working off the farm, finding such participation positively associated with years of formal education and the subject having received nonfarm vocational training within the last four years. Participation was negatively associated with the level of farm income, the presence of children under six years of age, and the unemployment rate in the county of residence. Residing on a dairy farm was negatively related to the probability of off-farm work, unless the farmer was a relatively recent entrant, in which case it was positive.

The off-farm wage rate was next estimated for spouses, and was found to be positively associated with years of formal education, previous off-farm work experience, and presence of small children in the home, and negatively with the unemployment rate in the county of residence. Age displayed an increasing and then decreasing relationship with wage rate.

The probability of entry into the off-farm labor market by 1986 for a spouse that was not so employed in 1982 was positively associated with estimated wage rate, the increase in estimated wage rate since 1982, years of previous off-farm work experience, and recent participation in nonfarm job training (if over 38 years of age). Probability of entry was negatively associated with the recent birth of a child, per capita family income, and being relatively recent farm entrants.

The probability that a farm spouse who had been working off-farm in 1982 and was not in 1986 was positively related to having worked relatively few hours in 1982, giving birth to a child since 1982, and being older. It was negatively related to level of off-farm wage, increase in off-farm wage between 1982 and 1986, and the number of continuous years of off-farm employment.

The Gould and Saupe results support the notion of state dependence of farm spouses' off-farm labor supply. That is, not only is it important for policymakers to understand future values of those variables likely to affect off-farm work activity, but also it is important to understand the implications of previous levels of income, labor market experience, and wages on the exit and entry process. From the probit models of exit and entry, wage and income elasticities were calculated for both the exit and entry process. In terms of entering the off-farm wage market, an elastic own-wage elasticity of 1.3 was found. In contrast, the exit wage elasticity was negative and less than unity (e.g., -0.71).

Concluding Comments

Because of their timing, the longitudinal Wisconsin family farm surveys are an important resource for measuring status and change in many aspects of farm family well-being, with implications that reach well beyond their southwestern Wisconsin site. Their detailed information on the allocation of time by farm adults between farm and off-farm work make them well-suited for study of many multiple job-holding issues. The surveys will continue to be useful in providing descriptive detail not available in national surveys, as a source of well-defined variables for hypothesis testing and modelling, and for describing farm family circumstances for local users in the study area.

References

Belknap, John, and William Saupe. 1988a. "Farm family resources and the adoption of no-plow tillage in Southwestern Wisconsin." *North Central Journal of Agricultural Economics* 10(No. 1):13–23.

————. (1988b). "Simultaneous farm labor allocation decisions." Staff Paper. Madison: Department of Agricultural Economics, University of Wisconsin.

Bollman, Ray D. 1979. "Off-farm work by farmers: An application of the kinked demand curve for labour." *Canadian Journal of Agricultural Economics* 27:37–60.

Gould, Brian W., and William Saupe. 1988. "A longitudinal analysis of non-farm labor market entry and exit of married farm women in Wisconsin." Staff Paper No. 286. Madison: Department of Agricultural Economics, University of Wisconsin.

Hoover, Herbert, and John Crecink. 1981. *Part Time Farming—Its Role and Prospects in the Clay-Hills Area of Mississippi.* Mississippi Agricultural Experiment Station, Bulletin 627.

Huffman, Wallace E. 1976a. *A Cross-Sectional Analysis of Nonfarm Work of Farm Family Members.* Report No. DLMA 91-19-75-18-1. Springfield, Virginia: National Technical Information Service.

————. 1976b. "The productive time of farm wives: Iowa, North Carolina, and Oklahoma." *American Journal of Agricultural Economics* 58:836–841.

————. 1980. "Farm and off-farm work decisions: The role of human capital." *Review of Economics and Statistics* 62:14–18.

Jensen, Helen H., and William Saupe. 1987. "Determinants of health insurance coverage for farm family households: A Midwestern study." *North Central Journal of Agricultural Economics* 9(No. 1):145–55.

Jesse, Edward W., et al. 1988. "Status of Wisconsin farming—1988." Madison: Department of Agricultural Economics, College of Agricultural and Life Sciences, and the Cooperative Extension Service, University of Wisconsin.

McCarthy, Mary R., and Priscilla Salant. 1986. "The off-farm labor supply of married farm women: evidence from Wisconsin." Staff Paper No. 257. Madison: Department of Agricultural Economics, University of Wisconsin.

Salant, Priscilla. 1982. "Family farms in Mississippi-Tennessee Sand Clay Hills: survey highlights." Staff Report No. AGES 820412. Washington, D.C.: Economic Research Service, U.S. Department of Agriculture.

————. 1983. "Farm women: Contribution to farm and family." Department of Agricultural Economics Research Report No. 140. Mississippi Agriculture and

Forestry Station in cooperation with U.S. Department of Agriculture.

_____. 1984. "Farm households and the off-farm sector: Results from Mississippi and Tennessee." Department of Agricultural Economics Research Report No. 143. Mississippi Agriculture and Forestry Experiment Station in cooperation with U.S. Department of Agriculture.

_____. 1985. "Farmwomen's work off the farm." *Rural Development Perspectives* 1(No. 2):25–27. Washington, D.C.: U.S. Department of Agriculture.

_____. 1986. "Off-farm employment: One solution to the farm crisis?" *Community Economics Newsletter* No. 111. University of Wisconsin-Madison and Cooperative Extension.

Salant, Priscilla, and William Saupe. 1984. "Wisconsin family farm survey finds enormous diversity." *Rural Development News* 9(No. 2)7–8.

_____. 1986a. "Farm household viability: Policy implications from the Wisconsin family farm survey." *Economic Issues* No. 97. University of Wisconsin-Madison.

_____. 1986b. "Financial viability of farm families." *Rural Development Perspectives* 3(No. 1):34–37. Washington, D.C.: Economic Research Service, U.S. Department of Agriculture.

Salant, Priscilla, Melinda Smale, and William Saupe. 1986. "Farm viability: Results from the USDA farm households surveys." Rural Development Research Report. Washington, D.C.: Economic Research Service, U.S. Department of Agriculture.

Salant, Priscilla, William Saupe, and John Belknap. 1985. "Highlights of the 1983 Wisconsin family farm survey." Research Report R3294. Madison: College of Agriculture and Life Sciences, University of Wisconsin.

Saupe, William, and Priscilla Salant. 1985. "Combining farm and off-farm employment as a farm management strategy." *Managing the Farm* 9(No. 17). Madison: University of Wisconsin and the Cooperative Extension Service.

Saupe, William, Larry Fitzmaurice, Maynard Nelson, and John Gruidl. 1986. "Extension service small farm program: A comparison of three strategies for farm entry and survival, 1979–1982." Report A3364. Madison: University of Wisconsin-Extension.

Shaffer, Ron, Priscilla Salant, and William Saupe. 1986. "Understanding the synergistic link between rural communities and farming," in *New Dimensions in Rural Policy,* studies prepared for the use of the Subcommittee on Agriculture and Transportation of the Joint Economic Committee, Congress of the United States, Washington, D.C. S. Prt. 99–153:308–21.

Smale, Melinda, William Saupe, and Priscilla Salant. 1986. "Farm family characteristics and the viability of farm households in Wisconsin and Mississippi-Tennessee." *Agricultural Economics Research* 38:2:11–27. Washington, D.C.: Economic Research Service, U.S. Department of Agriculture.

Streeter, Deborah H. 1984. "A supply function for off-farm work by farm operators in Mississippi and Tennessee." Ph.D. dissertation, Department of Agricultural Economics, University of Wisconsin.

Streeter, Deborah H., and William Saupe. 1986. "Nonmonetary considerations in farm labor allocations." *A.E. Res. 86–28*. Ithaca: Department of Agricultural Economics, Cornell University.

Sumner, Daniel A. 1982. "The off-farm labor supply of farmers." *American Journal of Agricultural Economics* 64:499–509. U.S. Department *Wisconsin*.

U.S. Department of Commerce, Bureau of the Census. *1980 Census of Population*. Vol. 1, Chapter C, Part 51. Wisconsin. PC80-1-C51. August 1983. (Page 74, Table 61. "Selected Social and Economic Characteristics by Race: 1980 and 1970.") Washington, D.C.: U.S. Government Printing Office.

Wisconsin Family Farm Survey. 1983, 1987, 1989. Unpublished. Madison: Department of Agricultural Economics, University of Wisconsin.

CHAPTER 11

Off-farm Employment Participation in Louisiana: An Analysis of Survey Results

TESFA G. GEBREMEDHIN

Agriculture in Louisiana, as in any other state in the country, is a highly diversified industry in continual change. The general trend in Louisiana production agriculture is toward fewer but larger farms, a long-term trend shared by all states. The trend toward greater concentration in the agricultural industry has been of considerable interest to agricultural researchers and public policymakers (Heady and Sonka 1974). Much of the interest is centered around (1) the alarming rate at which the number of small to medium-size farms has been declining over time, (2) the disproportionate percentage of total agricultural production now generated by a relatively small percentage of farms in the large-size category, and (3) the rising percentage of farm family income derived from off-farm sources (Ghebremedhin 1988).

An important observation is that agriculture is moving toward a bimodal system, with increasing numbers of large farms at one end of the spectrum and increasing numbers of part-time small-scale farms at the other end. One result of this trend is the possible emergence of large commercial farms in traditionally strong agricultural areas and part-time farm operations near certain employment centers. The traditional family farms or medium-size farms with gross annual farm earnings in the range of $40,000 to $250,000 are experiencing the greatest decline in numbers as they either scale up to become large commercial farms or reduce the volume of business to become smaller, part-time farms with greater dependence on off-farm earnings (Schertz et al. 1979; Kohl, Shabman, and Stoevener 1987).

The structural changes in production agriculture have serious implications for resource use and enterprise combinations; the development and effectiveness of desirable public policy; population distribution, labor mobility, local economic viability, and social growth; the general well-being of farm families in rural communities; and the future survival of small-scale farms as viable economic units and as a way of life. According to the 1982 Census of Agriculture, the survival of small-scale farms implies a greater number of farm families, a large number of agricultural enterprises, potential contribution of farm income and the filling of local market niches, more viable communities contributing to the quality of life, provision of a competitive yardstick against which prices and quality of commercial farm products can be judged, and a substantial demand for public and private goods and services that may have been overlooked over the years (Marshall 1976; Hallberg, Findeis, and Lass 1987).

The shifting structure of production agriculture characterized by technological change and economic growth has created problems for farmers, forcing them either to get large, get out of farming, or get off-farm work to survive (Gladwin and Zabawa 1985). The opportunity for the farm population to migrate to urban centers for better economic opportunities has facilitated the consolidation of land into larger but fewer farms over time. Many workers from agriculture who were either farmers or farm employees have been displaced. Higher urban wages and salaries, more attractive jobs, and better educational opportunities and other social services in contrast to relatively lower farm wages, limited employment opportunities, and low or negative income in agriculture, have combined to produce a large migration of the farm population, particularly the working-age group, from many rural communities to urban centers. With better training, educated workers have migrated to urban centers, leaving rural areas in a spiral of diminishing attractiveness to employers and diminishing opportunities for residents. Rural counties and communities whose economies rely heavily on farming and farming-related businesses are having trouble maintaining many social services and have been forced to cut back on these services as erratic farmland values and declining numbers of taxpayers threaten local tax revenues, often when such services are most in demand for the rural communities (Mazie 1986; Ghebremedhin 1988).

Off-farm employment has been an integral part of the emerging structure of production agriculture. The shift toward more off-farm work by farm families has been one of the most dramatic changes which has taken place in production agriculture in Louisiana. In the past, the farm business was an important component and main source of family income. Any income from off-farm sources had been considered of minor importance to the well-being of the farm family. Even though family income has improved to a large extent over the years, lack of adequate income from farming has continued to be a major problem on many small-scale farms because family requirements have also increased more rapidly. Judged against conventional desires, current farm incomes seem less adequate than ever before. Because of this inadequacy, small-scale farm families in particular, are becoming increasingly dependent on off-farm employment as a means of survival. Off-farm income has become a growing component of total household income and the basis of family living (Ghebremedhin and Armaud-Golden 1987).

The relationship between off-farm employment and the farm business is particularly important for small-scale farm families whose off-farm employment supports their households during periods of low or negative net farm income. The latter situations include a wide range of circumstances from older and retired families who are living primarily on savings, social security, veteran payments, and other income sources to younger families struggling with very limited agricultural resources. Off-farm employment is a phenomenon commonly thought to be limited to families who run relatively small-scale farms. Financial pressure and family requirements have forced many operators of small-scale, medium-size and large farms to expand their farm operations and/or increase their off-farm income. Currently, some farm operators of large size units have also depended on off-farm employment as a supplementary source of income. However, families operating small-scale farms usually have depended more on off-farm employment than those operating large farms. Consequently, farming has become a secondary occupation to some other off-farm source of income for the majority of small-scale farm families (Ghebremedhin and Armaud-Golden 1987).

Survey Methods and Discussion

The parishes surrounding the Baton Rouge metropolitan center were surveyed for the study. These rural communities are characterized by a high concentration of small-scale farm operations and have agriculture as the principal economic base. There are relatively high concentrations of low-income rural farm families whose major source of income is off-farm employment. The survey data on the demographic and economic characteristics of farm families were ascertained by personal interviews through structured questionnaires from randomly selected farm families in the rural communities of the study area. The various characteristics include family size, educational status, race, sex, age distributions, farm size, farm ownership, farm and nonfarm income, total family income, days worked off-farm, mileage travelled to nonfarm jobs or businesses, farm and off-farm work experience, conventional sources and kinds of off-farm jobs most accessible to farm families seeking off-farm employment, the rate of pay received for off-farm jobs, and the barriers encountered in seeking off-farm jobs. Extension agents, employees of the Farmers Home Administration, vocational agricultural teachers, the Livestock and Crop Reporting Service, and individual farmers supplied a list of farmers to be considered in the study. A total of 142 questionnaires were collected from 74 white and 68 black farm households. All the farm operators in the survey were males assisted by their female spouses and children in their farm operations. A total of 136 households and at least one family member who had some type of off-farm work or business. In 78 households which consisted of 33 white and 45 black farm households, both the operators and spouses had off-farm jobs. A total of 123 operators and 91 spouses of the total farm household surveyed worked off the farm (Table 11.1). Most of the black operators, compared with the white, were older and had less education (Table 11.2). They also had larger family sizes and stayed in farming for a longer period of time. Average farm income for black farm operators was $8,846, compared with $26,406 for the white farm operator (Table 11.3). Average farm size owned by black farm operators was 20 acres compared with 77 acres owned by the white farm operators (Table 11.4). Over 70 percent of the land rented was under sharecropping agreements, particularly common with black farm operators. About 90 percent of the black farm operators reported gross farm product sales of less than $10,000 per year.

By examining the breakdown of off-farm income for the total farm households surveyed, it was estimated that approximately 68 percent of the

Table 11.1.   Persons working off-farm by race and sex, Louisiana

	Operator	Spouse	Total
White	56	45	101
Black	67	46	113
Total	123	91	214

Table 11.2.   Average age and years of education by race and sex, Louisiana

	Age	Education
White		
Operator	39	13 +
Spouse	36	13 +
Black		
Operator	52	11 −
Spouse	48	12 +

Table 11.3. Average farm, off-farm, and household dollar income by race, Louisiana

	White	Black	Average
Average farm income	26,406	8,846	17,626
Average off-farm income	23,943	26,789	25,366
Average household income	50,349	35,635	42,992

Table 11.4. Average land owned and rented and years in farming by race, Louisiana

	White	Black	Average
Average land owned (acres)	77	20	48.5
Average land rented (acres)	278	76	177.0
Average years in farming	14	27	20.5

total household income received was from nonfarm income sources, of which 42 percent was earned by farm operators and 26 percent by the spouses. As indicated in Table 11.5, average off-farm income for the white family household was $23,943, of which 70 percent ($16,847) was contributed by the farm operator who worked an average of 212 days per year and 30 percent ($7,096) by the spouse who worked 204 days off-farm. Average off-farm income for the black family household was $26,789, of which 66 percent ($17,682) was earned by the farm operator who worked an average of 243 days per year and 34 percent ($9,107) by the spouse who worked 200 days off-farm. Farm operators more frequently worked off-farm than did spouses. The survey results indicated that the differential in off-farm income between farm operators and spouses might be due to a gap in occupational skill levels and geographic mobility to off-farm jobs. The survey also indicated that the blacks worked more days and had more years of experience in off-farm work than the whites. A black farm operator had an average of 15 years of experience in off-farm work compared with 11 years for the white farm operator. A black spouse had an average of 13 years of off-farm work experience compared with 7 years for the white spouse. In view of these results, the black households depended more on off-farm income than on farm income for their livelihood as compared with the white households.

Table 11.5. Average off-farm dollar income and annual days worked off-farm by race and sex, Louisiana

	Dollars			Days		
	Operator	Spouse	Total	Operator	Spouse	Average
All	17,264	8,102	25,366	228	206	217
White	16,847	7,096	23,943	212	204	208
Black	17,682	9,107	26,789	243	208	226

The farm families and residents of low-income rural areas, though able and willing to work, could not find jobs. Finding a job in rural communities and small towns is perceived by many to be difficult for a variety of reasons. The most serious factors hindering the farm operators and their spouses from securing gainful employment in their communities and surrounding areas were limited job opportunities. The main reason is that the number of nonagricultural jobs in the rural areas has not increased enough to absorb the large number of low-skilled workers displaced by structural changes in agriculture. The second most frequently cited problem was lack of adequate information about off-farm jobs in the rural areas. Perhaps not knowing the right persons and right places for job information was a serious problem. Many rural people believed that personal ties to family members, relatives, friends, or local influentials were instrumental in getting hired. Blacks and less educated low-income farm families especially appeared to suffer from social isolation which they felt barred them from obtaining decent jobs in their communities. Blacks also thought racial discrimination seriously limited their ability to obtain jobs. The third problem was that many farm families believed that lack of marketable skills kept them from finding gainful employment. Consequently, there has been a growing number of displaced farmworkers with limited employable skills for absorption into the nonagricultural job market, or often more importantly, limited job search skills and confidence to find off-farm employment for the skills they do have.

Statistical Results and Analysis

An ordinary least squares (OLS) regression method was applied to evaluate the relative importance of some social and economic characteristics that contributed to the explanation of off-farm employment participation in the rural communities of Louisiana. The basic statistical linear regression function selected was

$$Y = \beta_0 + \sum_{i=1}^{13} \beta_i X_i \qquad\qquad i = 1, 2, 3, \ldots, 13$$

where

Y = Total family off-farm income which is the combination of off-farm income of the operator and spouse (dollars)

X_1 = Age of operator (years)

X_2 = Age of spouse (years)
X_3 = Education of operator (years)
X_4 = Education of spouse (years)
X_5 = Distance travelled by operator to off-farm job (miles)
X_6 = Number of hours worked per year by operator (hours)
X_7 = Experience of operator in off-farm work (years)
X_8 = Distance travelled by spouse to off-farm work (miles)
X_9 = Number of hours worked per year by spouse (hours)
X_{10} = Experience of spouse in off-farm work (years)
X_{11} = Size of farm operated (acres)
X_{12} = Total family members in household
X_{13} = Gross farm income (dollars)

The statistical associations between total off-farm income and the socioeconomic variables are hypothesized to be $\beta_i > 0$.

The results of the linear regression model are presented in Table 11.6. Eight of the explanatory variables significantly affect total off-farm income of farm families. The coefficients representing age of operator (X_1), educa-

Table 11.6. Regression coefficients and related statistics of factors affecting total off-farm income of selected Louisiana farm families

Independent variable	Mean	Parameter estimate	t-ratio	$Pr > \lvert t \rvert$
Constant		−43062.93	−1.91	0.0667**
X_1 = Age of operator	45.38	1397.03	2.63	0.0142*
X_2 = Age of spouse	41.48	−1305.40	−2.57	0.0164**
X_3 = Education of operator (yrs)	12.80	7694.64	4.14	0.0003*
X_4 = Education of spouse (yrs)	12.75	−2598.33	−1.74	0.0960***
X_5 = Distance travelled to off-farm job (operator)	18.84	170.95	2.39	0.0245**
X_6 = Number of hours worked off-farm by operator	1916.80	10.32	2.42	0.0227**
X_7 = Experience in off-farm job (operator years)	16.03	−118.53	−1.02	0.3159
X_8 = Distance travelled to off-farm job (spouse)	10.33	−104.65	−0.61	0.5463
X_9 = Number of hours worked off-farm by spouse	1644.80	8.21	2.16	0.0040*
X_{10} = Experience in off-farm job (spouse years)	11.75	654.15	2.62	0.0146**
X_{11} = Size of farm operated (acres)	144.25	1.14	0.15	0.8824
X_{12} = Total family members	4.10	327.28	0.29	0.7740
X_{13} = Gross farm income	$14974.00	0.11	0.72	0.4768

Note: $R^2 = 0.70$; $F = 4.63$; $Pr > F = 0.0004$; mean of total off-farm income = 22142.53.
*Significant at the .01 level for one-tailed test.
**Significant at the .05 level for one-tailed test.
***Significant at the .10 level for one-tailed test.

tion of operator (X_3), distance travelled to off-farm work by operator (X_5), hours worked off-farm by operator (X_6) and spouse (X_9), and years of experience of spouse in off-farm work (X_{10}) were all found to have positive influences on off-farm employment participation and were significant at a probability level of 5 percent.

The age (X_2) and education (X_4) coefficients for the spouse were negative but significant. Off-farm income was expected to be directly related to the age of the spouse (X_2) based on the assumption that older spouses have more off-farm work experience, and therefore will receive higher salaries and wages. The negative sign may be explained by the fact that off-farm work generally available in the area requires physical strength. For this reason, the employers can be expected to prefer young female workers rather than experienced older workers with declining strength.

Education of spouse (X_4) was expected to have a positive influence on off-farm employment participation. This is because education increases the earning capacity of farm women and may qualify them for certain skilled jobs in rural areas. The possible interpretation of the negative sign may be that an increase in education increases the productivity of the spouse in the household or on the farm more than it increases productivity in off-farm employment. The nature of off-farm jobs available in rural communities does not require high levels of formal education and therefore, these jobs pay relatively lower wages and salaries.

The coefficients on size of farm operated (X_{11}), number of family members in the household (X_{12}), and gross farm income (X_{13}) were positive as expected but not significant. The coefficients on years of experience of operator in off-farm work (X_7) and distance travelled to off-farm work by spouse (X_8) were negative and not significant. The nonsignificant and negative coefficient for experience of operator in off-farm work (X_7) indicates that years of experience in off-farm jobs may not be essential in the study area. The nonsignificant and negative coefficient for distance travelled by spouse (X_8) to off-farm work may indicate that there is not much variation in the distance travelled to the job by spouses in the rural communities.

Concluding Remarks

The shifting structure of production agriculture has resulted in more off-farm employment among farm families and it is doubtful that greater reliance on off-farm income is a temporary phenomenon. While farming remains to many a way of life, it frequently is no longer the only means of economic livelihood for farm families. In fact, farming has become a secondary occupation to some other employment and source of income for the majority of farm families. On the average, in all small-scale farm groupings, off-farm employment contributes more net cash income than does farming to total family income. In general, off-farm income tends to be more stable and less variable from year to year than farm income and creates a more even flow of income over time. For many small-scale farms, off-farm income acts as a safety net ensuring family survivability in the farm and rural communities. As a result, most small-scale farm families seek jobs away from their farms for at least a short time to earn supplementary family income. The farm families increasingly combine farm work with full- or part-time off-farm employment. Some small farm families hold full-time jobs in the cities and do their farming at night and on weekends, and in many cases one or more household members are required to work off the farm in order to escape poverty and to continue living in the community of their choice. However, a wide variety of off-farm jobs were held by the respondents in the rural areas and small towns and the majority were low-skilled and low-paying. The off-farm jobs were in secondary labor markets and paid low wages commensurate with the residents' basic educational skills and work experience. With Louisiana now posting the highest unemployment rates in the country, opportunities for future off-farm employment are reduced. It will probably be more difficult and critical for small-scale farm families in general and minority farm families in particular, to maintain economic viability and survivability.

References

Ghebremedhin, Tesfa G. 1988. "Assessing the impacts of technology on Southern agriculture and rural communities." New Orleans: Paper presented at the Southern Agricultural Economics Association annual meeting.

Ghebremedhin, Tesfa G., and Tammy Armaud-Golden. 1987. *An Economic Analysis of Off-Farm Employment in the Rural Economy of Louisiana.* Research Report. Baton Rouge: Department of Agricultural Economics, Southern University.

Gladwin, Christina H., and Robert Zabawa. 1985. "After structural change: Are part-time or full-time farmers better off?" Gainesville: Food and Resource Economics Department, Institute of Food and Agricultural Sciences, University of Florida.

Hallberg, M. C., J. L. Findeis, and Daniel Lass. 1987. "Part-time farming in Pennsylvania and Massachusetts: Survey results." *A.E. & R.S. 194.* University Park: Department of Agricultural Economics and Rural Sociology, Agricultural Experiment Station, Pennsylvania State University.

Heady, Earl O., and Steven T. Sonka. 1974. "Farm size, rural community income and consumer welfare." *Americal Journal of Agricultural Economics* 56(No. 3):534–42.

Kohl, David M., Leonard A. Shabman and Herbert H. Stoevener. 1987. "Agricultural transition: Its implication for agricultural economics Extension in the Southeast." *Southern Journal of Agricultural Economics* 19(No. 1):35–42.

Marshall, Ray. 1976. *Small Farmers in Arkansas.* Austin: Center for the Study of Human Resources, University of Texas.

Mazie, Sara Mills, ed. 1986. "The farm crisis of the 1980's." *Rural Development Perspectives* 2(No. 3):8–9.

Schertz, L. P., et al. 1979. *Another Revolution In U.S. Farming.* Washington, D.C.: U.S. Department of Agriculture.

U.S. Department of Commerce. 1984. *1982 Census of Agriculture,* Vol. 1, Area Report (Louisiana). Washington, D.C.: Bureau of the Census.

CHAPTER 12

Multiple Job-holding among Farm Families and the Increase in Women's Farming

CHRISTINA H. GLADWIN

Perhaps because 86 percent of all U.S. farms are now part-time farms, leaving only 300,000 full-time farms left in the United States (Cochrane 1986), the interest in multiple job-holding among North American farm families has recently increased, as noted by the papers in this volume. Wozniak and Scholl (1988) point out, however, that interest in farm operators' employment off the farm first surfaced in the mid-1960s, when the majority of the farm family's income began to originate from off-farm sources. That interest grew in the early 1980s, when the farming role of farm women was suddenly discovered on film (*County, The River, Places in the Heart*) as well as in research (Downie and Gladwin 1981; Huffman 1976; Rosenfeld 1985; Sachs 1983; Scholl 1982).

Although much has been written since, most of the literature on U.S. farm women is still "fugitive," as noted by Friedland (1987). More importantly, it is still a matter of debate whether farm women are really doing more of the farming than they did in the past—say 50 years ago, as I have argued in previous papers (Gladwin 1985b, 1985c). Other authors have counterargued that farm women are now farming less (Fink 1987), or have not found much if any evidence of women's farming in the location of their own research (Barlett 1988).

The author was assisted by research associates Dr. Masuma Downie in Baker County, Janet Weston in Gilchrist County, Susanne Wilson in Brevard County, Donna Sorenson in Jefferson County, Peggy Rowe in Levy County, and Marilyn Carroll in Hillsborough County, but takes sole responsibility for the contents herein.

The purpose of this paper is to reexamine this question and to relate it to the evidence of multiple job-holding among farm families in Florida. In particular, I ask if the increase in women's farming that researchers and I observe in Florida is specific only to part-time farms. What happens on full-time farms and in agribusinesses? Are women playing an active farming role in the full-time farming/agribusiness sector of south and central Florida? Or are women in Florida active only in the part-time farming sector that is centered in north-central Florida, where previous research was conducted? A related question that must also be asked is whether survey data from north and south Florida is sufficient evidence to answer this question.

Before these questions can be answered, it is useful to review previous evidence of multiple job-holding on part-time farms in north Florida (Gladwin 1982, 1983, 1985a, 1985b). Based on 1980–81 field work in two north Florida counties, Baker and Gilchrist, this research showed that

1. women worked long hours (an average of 78 hours per week versus 62 hours per week by their men) as seen in Table 12.1, and their farm work hours of 22 hours per week, exclusive of garden work, were twice the national average of the 1930s of 11 hours per week (Vanek 1974);

Table 12.1. Average hours per week of farm work, off-farm work, housework, and garden work of men and women, Baker and Gilchrist Counties ($N = 48$)

	Men	Women
Average hours/week of farm work	34.7	21.80
Average hours/week of off-farm work	20.2	17.40
Sub-total	54.9	39.20
Average hours/week of housework	1.9	26.52
Year-round total	56.8	65.72
Average hours/week of spring-summer garden work[a]	5.1	12.35
Garden-season total	61.9	78.07

Source: Gladwin, 1985b, 1985c.
[a]Applied only in the 8 to 10 weeks of the spring-summer gardening season.

2. the off-farm earnings of the farm husband was the number one income source of the farm family for 42 percent of the north Florida sample (Table 12.2), before farm income (36 percent) and the wife's off-farm income (8 percent);

3. multiple roles and job-holding was the norm in north Florida, with both farm husband and wife juggling farm work, off-farm work, house-

work, and garden work; but this juggling act took various forms such that no one clear pattern emerged from these data (Table 12.3);

4. the farm wife's decision of whether to be a full-time farmer, part-time farmer, have full-time off-farm work, part-time off-farm work, a combination of the above, or none of the above depended on family and farm

Table 12.2. Importance of farm and off-farm income to farm women

	Ranking (%)	
Income source	Number 1	Number 2
Off-farm income of husband	42	12
Farm income	36	46
Off-farm income of wife	8	20
Retirement pension and social security	12	6
Savings	2	10
No other income source	. . .	6

Source: Gladwin, 1983.

Table 12.3. Farm families with different combinations of husband's and wife's farm and off-farm work (N = 48)

Wife is a full-time farmer (N = 11)	
Both husband and wife are full-time farmers (FTF)	4
and husband has full-time off-farm work (FOFW)	1
and wife has part-time off-farm work (POFW)	1
Wife is FTF	
and husband has FOFW and is a part-time farmer (PTF)	3
and husband is PTF and ill	2
Wife is a part-time farmer (N = 24)	
Both husband and wife are PTF	
and both have FOFW	4
and husband has FOFW	1
and husband has POFW	3
and wife has FOFW and husband has POFW	1
and wife has POFW and husband has FOFW	5
Wife is a PTF	
and has FOFW, and husband is FTF and has POFW	1
and has POFW, and husband is FTF	3
and has POFW, and husband is FTF and has POFW	1
and husband is FTF	3
and has POFW and husband is ill	1
and husband is deceased	1
Wife does not farm but works off-farm (N = 10)	
Both husband and wife have FOFW	3
and husband is PTF	1
Wife has FOFW	
and husband is FTF	3
and husband is FTF and has POFW	1
Wife has POFW and husband is retired or ill	2
Wife does not farm or work off-farm (N = 3)	
and husband is PTF	1
and husband is PTF and has FOFW	2

characteristics more than on a woman's personal characteristics or previous job training and experience. However, all of these variables are involved on a path to a particular outcome as shown in the decision tree in Figure 12.1; the model, which uses an expert systems approach to elicit women's decision rules in the tree, predicts 90 percent of women's farmwork versus off-farm work decisions (Gladwin 1982).

Based on this evidence, I concluded that women on part-time farms in north Florida are now doing *more* of the farming (Gladwin 1985b). They are stepping in and substituting for their husbands, more of whom must now work off the farm at a high-paying job to subsidize the farm operation and keep the family's living standard at an acceptable level. Because rural men's wages are higher than rural women's in Florida, more women are becoming part-time and full-time farmers in line with their "pitching in and helping" attitudes, aimed at keeping the farm going and the family together (Gladwin 1985c). Their ideology is not feminist; they identify with members of their families and their struggles and, in times of farm crisis, defend their class interests. Flora (1981) suggests that because they are clearly in charge of reproduction and ideological reproduction in the family, farm women tend to reject questions of women's rights.

National Evidence of the Increase of Women Farming

Do available national data support the hypothesis that women are now doing more of the farming? Unfortunately, women farmers have been so invisible in the past (Sachs 1983) that some of the national data have been contradictory until recently. For example, the U.S. Census of Agriculture undercounts farm wives as operators by allowing only one family member to be listed as "the main operator." Since most couples list the husband as operator, the census finds only 5.4 percent of farm operators to be women (Kalbacher 1985). By contrast, when the 1980 National Farm Woman Survey conducted by the U.S. Department of Agriculture asked 2,500 women by phone if they considered themselves to be "a main operator," 55 percent answered yes (Jones and Rosenfeld 1981).

Although the hours-of-work data from north Florida in Table 12.1 suggest that farm women are farming more now, it is impossible to distinguish regional variation from change over time with these data. Fortunately, data from the 1984 Ford Tractor mail-out survey of 3,300 North American farm women fill the gap, because these data are directly comparable with the 1980 USDA survey of 2,500 U.S. farm women. In the rows of Table 12.4 are listed the tasks on a farm that a woman may perform on a

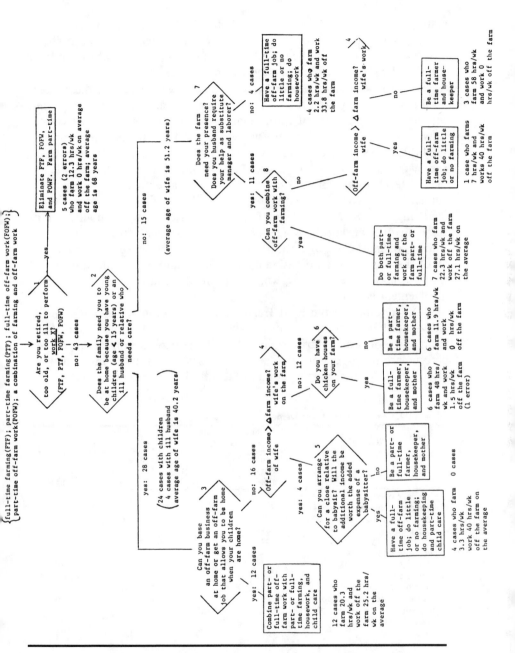

Figure 12.1. The decision of a farm wife to farm full- or part-time or work off the farm.

regular basis (column 1), an occasional basis (column 2), or never. (Because "never" is a residual category, the percentage of women who never perform the task is omitted from the table.) Table 12.4 reports the results from both the 1980 USDA survey and the 1984 Ford Tractor results.

Table 12.4 shows that farm women *regularly* take care of the garden, do the bookkeeping and financial work, act as chauffeur and "gofer," and supervise and take care of farm animals. A comparison of the survey results, moreover, shows that *more* women regularly performed these tasks in 1984 than in 1980. These results are significant at the .01 significance level, except for gardening, which is significantly different from 1980 to 1984 at the .05 level. In addition, both surveys show that occasionally women supervised farm work of hired labor and family members, harvested crops, made major purchases of equipment, and did field work without machinery. Only one-third of the women, however, occasionally did the plowing or discing, or marketing of farm products. In 1984 *more* women were doing all of these tasks on an occasional basis, and again, the results are significant at the .01 level. Clearly, women are involved in farm work, and that involvement is increasing.

Other results of the Ford Tractor survey show, in agreement with the USDA study, that 54 percent of the women consider themselves one of the main operators on the farm, while only 3 percent are sole operators, and 43 percent are not operators. Women's increased involvement in farm tasks also leads to greater participation in farm decision making.

Table 12.4. Farm women's involvement in farm tasks

	1980 USDA Survey (N = 2,500)		1984 Ford Tractor Survey (N = 3,300)	
	Regular duty (%)	Occasionally (%)	Regular duty (%)	Occasionally (%)
Taking care of garden	74	14	76	18
Bookkeeping, maintaining records, etc.	61	17	69	21
Running farm errands	47	38	51	45
Taking care of farm animals	37	29	44	41
Supervising farm work of other family members	24	26	25	46
Harvesting crops	22	29	22	49
Making major purchases of farm equipment and supplies	14	23	14	36
Supervising work of hired labor	11	25	13	43
Doing field work without machinery	17	25	13	48
Plowing, discing, cultivating, or planting	11	26	10	37
Marketing products	15	18	12	30

Source: Gladwin, 1985b.

Why the Increase in Women's Farming?

Researchers of the sexual division of labor in preindustrial societies of the Third World, starting with Boserup (1970), generally agree that women's agricultural contributions *decline* with agricultural intensification. The inverse of the Boserup hypothesis can also be used to explain the present *increase* in women's farming on labor-scarce part-time farms of industrial societies. According to this hypothesis, women's participation in agricultural production should increase, as agriculture becomes less capitalized and more labor-*extensive*, on part-time family farms in industrial societies.

Although estimates vary, recent data attest to the increase in the number and size of part-time family farms. Historically, this increase occurred in the 1950s through 1970s in the southeastern United States; it is now occurring, due to the farm crisis, in many states in the Midwest. Ahearn and Lee's paper (Chapter 1, this volume) shows that farming is the major occupation of the farm operator and farm income is the major family income source for only 39 percent of all farms, so that part-time farms now comprise 61 percent of farms. Other estimates of the proportion of part-time farms are as high as 86 percent; the full-time farms which produce most marketed food production (67 percent) comprise only 12 percent of all farms (Cochrane 1986).

Surprisingly, part-time farms with part-time farmers are remarkably stable and are even growing in numbers in Canada (Buttel and LaRamee 1987). These are the small part-time farms that "fiddle with farming," according to Cochrane, and earn less than $40,000 in gross sales per year; they are more persistent and were less at risk of going out of business than were larger farms in the 1980s. Why are these farms so remarkably stable? Ethnographic studies conducted in 10 north Florida counties identify the Chayanovian "survival strategies" used by part-time farmers, once they are transformed from full-time farms. These include multiple job-holding by both farm husband and wife; increasing the farming role of the farm wife and children; keeping debts low; using old equipment; producing commodities via labor-flexible, low-profit, low-risk operations (like the cow-calf operation); raising subsistence crops; and cutting back production in bad times and expanding again in good times. Use of these strategies allows the part-time farm to survive. Unfortunately their use also makes the part-time farm produce less and less of the marketed food we buy in the grocery store.

As part-time farming increases, the *extensification and feminization* of agriculture in an industrial society also occurs. Because the able-bodied male on the family farm has to get a good-paying off-farm job in order to subsidize the farm and meet an increasing debt load, he has less time to farm. He may decide to scale down the farm enterprise and switch from a labor-intensive cropping pattern (e.g., vegetables, row crops) to a labor-extensive cropping pattern (e.g., a cow-calf operation). At the same time, the farm wife—if she doesn't have a full-time off-farm job herself— may substitute for him and spend more time on production tasks, in addition to bookkeeping, child care, housework, and garden work. Florida farm women claim, "The men get it started, and we finish it." With agricultural extensification, women's participation in farming increases.

The increase in women's farming is also partly due to technological advances reducing domestic work within the home. Because of modern home appliances, time spent doing housework, usually done by women, has decreased from 50 to 26 hours per week during the last 50 years (Vanek 1974). This released time has allowed modern farm women to increase either their farm work or their off-farm work. Although some women choose to spend that time off the farm, in the north Florida sample an equal proportion of them chose to farm.

Counterhypotheses

This hypothesis, then, ties the increase in women's farming to multiple job-holding on part-time farms. Sachs (1985), however, suggests another hypothesis for the recent increase in women's farming. Her recent study of women's employment on farms and in the food processing sector suggests that U.S. women are now farming more, not only on part-time farms but also on corporate agribusiness farms. Using Census of Population data from 1950 to 1980, she shows that the percentage of farmers, farm managers, and farm workers who are women has increased from 2.7 percent (1950) to 9.7 percent (1980), 6.2 percent to 9.1 percent, and 8.9 percent to 21.5 percent, respectively. Sachs's results suggest that more women are entering agriculture simply because they have followed their tasks relating to food from the household to the marketplace, as agriculture has changed from a subsistence to commercial activity over the last 200 years. In the movement of food from farm to table, women are more likely to be employed as the food is closer to the table (Sachs 1985, p. 15). At the same time, feminist changes in ideology play a role: more women are now entering occupations and industries which were typically male, and agriculture is no exception.

Friedland (1987 p. 8), on the other hand, suggests that women will increasingly enter the agricultural labor force not only on part-time farms but also in full-time agribusinesses, because as agriculture becomes more and more business oriented ("as agribusiness further characterizes capitalist agriculture") women will accept low-paying jobs doing the most taxing tasks that men will not. Women, especially minority women, are always the lowest-paid workers doing the dirtiest and most disagreeable jobs in hierarchical organizational structures such as large agribusinesses. And "the more that producing firms get larger, the more capital investment increases, the more the mechanization," the greater will be "the feminization of the labor force."

Further Evidence from South Florida

Which of these hypotheses is more correct? Is the increase in women farming tied to the phenomenon of multiple job-holding on part-time farms? Or is it mainly due to the advance of feminism as an ideology that allows women to enter previously male occupations, or the commercialization of food-processing tasks done traditionally by women as Sachs suggests, or the increasingly agribusiness orientation of agriculture as Friedland suggests?

To see if women's farming was restricted to the part-time farming sector of north Florida, further interviews were conducted with both farm women in north Florida and agribusiness women in south Florida, where big agribusiness firms are located. Over a time period of three to five years, personal interviews of farm and agribusiness women were conducted in six counties in Florida. These counties are shown in Figure 12.2, a map which also indicates the rank of the top ten Florida counties with respect to cash receipts and population. The six counties included Jefferson and Gilchrist in north-central Florida, Hillsborough and Brevard in south-central Florida, and Collier and Hendry Counties in south Florida. A glance at the map shows that Hillsborough County is the third largest agricultural county in the state in terms of receipts, while Hendry is the sixth, Collier the tenth, and Brevard's population (but not receipts) is ranked ninth (Clouser and Beaulieu 1986).

Observation showed that south Florida women contribute to the revenues of both large and small agribusiness firms, which include citrus groves, cattle ranches, nurseries, truck farms, strawberry farms, packing sheds for fruits and vegetables, apiaries and honey-processing plants, exotic fish processing plants, fertilizer and seed supply houses, and distribution firms. Most of these women serve as "indoor farmers": they are general managers of the office, operate microcomputers, and keep the general ledger and payroll accounts of the agribusiness. While they are usually

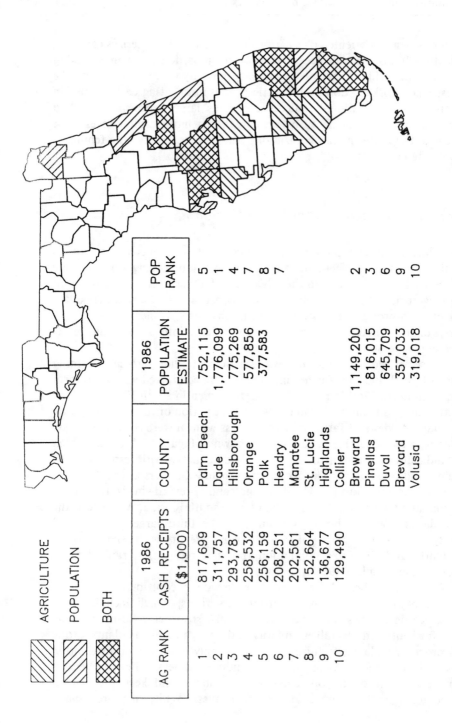

Figure 12.2. Ten top counties, value of ag cash receipts and population. (*Clouser and Beaulieu 1986*)

AG RANK	1986 CASH RECEIPTS ($1,000)	COUNTY	1986 POPULATION ESTIMATE	POP RANK
1	817,699	Palm Beach	752,115	5
2	311,757	Dade	1,776,099	1
3	293,787	Hillsborough	775,269	4
4	258,532	Orange	577,856	7
5	256,159	Polk	377,583	8
6	208,251	Hendry		7
7	202,561	Manatee		
8	152,664	St. Lucie		
9	136,677	Highlands		
10	129,490	Collier		
		Broward	1,149,200	2
		Pinellas	816,015	3
		Duval	645,709	6
		Brevard	357,033	9
		Volusia	319,018	10

AGRICULTURE

POPULATION

BOTH

daughters or wives of the production managers of the firm and are serving the family corporation which they will one day inherit, sometimes they are trained bookkeepers hired especially for the job of managing the office or operating the computer. Still other women have more direct contact with the produce of agribusinesses, as packers, sorters, and graders in packing houses, as farm workers in the fields, or as crew leaders with their own businesses. Many agribusiness women are single heads of households, supporting their children and often running their own businesses. Finally, many young agribusiness women are also "agribusiness wives" who are juggling full-time or part-time off-farm work (which may be in another agribusiness) with part-time farm/agribusiness tasks like bookkeeping, accounting, and computer programming for their own family's agribusiness.

How multiple are their roles, and how much do they work? Some of the study results are shown in Tables 12.5–7, which include results both for the entire sample of north and south Florida women in eight counties ($N =$ 213) and for the subsample of south Florida women in four counties ($N =$ 100). For brevity, time spent in housework, garden work, and child-care, although substantial, is excluded from the data reported here, and the focus is on the division of labor between farm/agribusiness work versus off-farm (nonagribusiness) work.

Results in Table 12.5 show the number and percent of women (and men) who consider themselves to be (a) full-time farmers or agribusiness persons (FTF), (b) part-time farmers/agribusiness persons (PTF), (c) full-time off-farm workers (FOFW) not in agriculture, (d) part-time off-farm

Table 12.5. Men and women who consider themselves to be full-time farmers, part-time farmers, full-time or part-time off-farm workers, or none

	North and south Florida ($N = 213$)		South Florida ($N = 100$)	
	Women	Men	Women	Men
	Number (%)			
Full-time farmers (FTF)	74[a] (5%)	107 (50%)	48 (48%)	63 (63%)
Part-time farmers (PTF)	81 (38%)	56 (26%)	29 (29%)	10 (10%)
Has full-time off-farm work (FOFW)	60 (28%)	71 (33%)	24 (24%)	24 (24%)
Has part-time off-farm work (POFW)	42 (20%)	17 (8%)	16 (16%)	5 (5%)
Has no farm or off-farm work	8 (4%)	7 (3%)	1 (1%)	0 (0%)

Note: Numbers and percentages do not add up to 100 percent because all categories are not mutually exclusive.

[a]Sample is from all eight counties, four in north Florida and four in south and central Florida.

Table 12.6.   Average hours per week of work performed on own farm or agribusiness,
              employed by farm/agribusiness, and performed off-farm, for people reporting
              some work in these categories

	North and south Florida (N = 213)		South Florida (N = 100)	
	Women	Men	Women	Men
On own family's farm or agribusiness	28.57[a] (N = 160)[b]	44.74 (N = 154)	36.90 (N = 66)	54.81 (N = 56)
Employed by farm/agribusiness	44.32 (N = 30)	62.80 (N = 10)	44.47 (N = 29)	60.44 (N = 9)
On off-farm job (no ag)	23.84 (N = 91)	29.81 (N = 91)	16.65 (N = 10)	45.36 (N = 14)
Total hours of farm/ agribusiness and off-farm work	40.79 (N = 198)	58.64 (N = 175)	41.10 (N = 96)	60.09 (N = 71)

[a]Zero hours per week of work are not counted in this table.
[b]N = number of observations used to calculate the mean.

Table 12.7.   Average hours per week of farm/agribusiness work and off-farm work

	North and south Florida (N = 213)		South Florida (N = 100)	
	Women	Men	Women	Men
Farm or agribusiness work[a]	27.70	35.30	37.25	36.13
Off-farm work (no ag)	10.19	12.73	1.67	6.35
Total, excluding housework and garden work	37.89	48.03	38.92	42.48

Note: Includes observations with zero hours per week.
[a]Self-employed on own farm/agribusiness or employed by others.

workers (POFW) not in agriculture, or (e) none of the above. Data from both north and south Florida show that more women consider themselves to be full-timers (48 percent) than part-timers (29 percent). In contrast, 50 percent of the men in the state sample are full-timers, although this is less than the 63 percent of men in south Florida who are full-timers. Hence agribusiness women in south or central Florida are more likely to be full-time farmers, and married to a full-time farmer. Off-farm work (part-time or full-time) is not as prevalent in south Florida as in north Florida. This is to be expected, given the better economic conditions of south Florida agriculture.

Hours of work data, seen in Tables 12.6 and 12.7, show that south Florida agribusiness women's hours of farm work are even longer than those of Florida farm women. Table 12.6 shows average hours per week of work on their own family's farm/agribusiness, as well as work hours employed in another's agribusiness, in an off-farm job and total hours of work, excluding housework and garden work. The estimates in Table 12.6

exclude observations of 0 hours of work; the estimates are for people reporting some work in these categories. Results show that women in both north and south Florida work 29 hours per week on their own family farm/agribusiness, whereas south Florida women work 37 hours/week on average. Hence south Florida agribusiness women work longer hours in agriculture than do farm women in north Florida. These hours are even higher for women employed in another's farm/agribusiness: they work on average 44 hours per week. The pattern is the same for men: men in south Florida work 55 hours per week on their own farm/agribusiness, while men in the whole state work 45 hours per week on average. Total hours per week are 41 hours for women in both south Florida and the whole state, and 59–60 hours for men.

Estimates in Table 12.7 include observations of 0 hours of work, and hence are lower than those in Table 12.6. Results, however, show the same pattern: south Florida women work longer hours in agribusiness activities than off the farm (or agribusiness). Here, hours of farm/agribusiness work includes work either in the family's agribusiness or another employer's agribusiness. Women in south Florida work 37 hours per week on farm/agribusiness work, and only 2 hours per week on off-farm work, for a total of 39 hours per week. By contrast, women in the whole state sample work 28 hours per week on farm/agribusiness work, 10 hours per week on off-farm work, for a total of 38 hours per week. Multiple job-holding seems to be a north Florida phenomenon. Due to the good economic conditions for agriculture in south Florida, most agribusiness women there can be full-time farmers and only have to juggle housework, child care, and garden work with their agribusiness work.

Conclusion

An amazing number of women in Florida farm on part-time farms or co-manage full-time family agribusinesses, and the increase in women's farming in Florida comes both from the part-time and corporate agribusiness sectors. Farming by women is not restricted just to the part-time farming sector, where multiple job-holding occurs. Nor is it tied solely to the phenomenon of multiple job-holding, although a greater number of women farmers may be found on part-time farms than in the agribusiness sector. Why? The majority of farms in Florida (as in the United States) are now part-time farms: estimates of the extent of part-time farming in the United States range from 61 to 86 percent of all farms. The majority of women doing the farming are thus on part-time farms now and will be on part-time farms in the future. Due to multiple job-holding of all family members, farm women have to substitute for men on more and more farming tasks, or give up the farm.

There are women heavily involved in south Florida agribusinesses, however, where the businesses are so big (sometimes with $2,000,000 in yearly gross sales) that they need full-time manager/accountants in the office, tasks which women do more frequently than men. As the business expands, the woman who did the bookkeeping on a part-time basis now becomes a full-time office manager, i.e., a full-time, albeit "indoor," farmer. These women are indispensable to the agribusiness. One cannot visit a south Florida agribusiness without encountering one or more women in the office.

With further concentration of U.S. agribusiness, moreover, one can expect the numbers of these full-time agribusiness women in the office to also decrease. This is expected to occur in the south Florida counties with the greatest projected increases in population: Hillsborough, Collier, and Hendry, for example. At the present time, women who are or will be big landowners in these counties are heavily engaged in learning the politics of zoning ordinances, so that they can sell off their land at the highest price when the time comes. They are clearly not going to stay in farming, when they can develop their land for residential or industrial purposes at ten times the profitability.

These women, women in co-managerial positions in agribusiness offices, however, do not make up the bulk of semi-skilled farm workers, processors, pickers, packers, sorters, and graders who constitute the majority of women employed in south Florida agribusinesses. As they themselves testify, "we are also women in Florida agriculture." Their numbers are bound to increase as the food processing chain gets longer and more complex, as Sachs points out, and as agribusinesses become larger and more hierarchically organized, as Friedland points out. In my judgment, however, their numbers will not exceed the numbers of women farming on part-time farms in Florida, as there are simply too many part-time farms.

I conclude that in Florida, the increase in women's farming is mainly due to multiple job-holding in the part-time farming sector, but not solely. It is happening in the full-time agribusiness sector as well, where multiple job-holding is not so prevalent, for reasons pointed out by Sachs and Friedland. In fact, this is why the increase in women's farming is so notable in Florida as compared to other states like Georgia or Iowa. Florida has, as Buttel and LaRamee (1987) have noted, the two kinds of farm/firms that have been increasing in numbers in the 1980s: part-time farms with part-time farmers as found in north Florida, and "industrial-type" farms with more than 10 hired laborers as found in south and central Florida. Because both of these high-growth enterprises are found in Florida, and because both have women doing some of the farming tasks, women on Florida farms and in agribusinesses are highly visible.

Finally, I must ask if the hypotheses above can really be tested with these micro-level data. Clearly they cannot; cross-sectional hours-of-work data do not show an increase in farming over time. They do, however, allow us to understand why the national results in Table 12.4 showed an increase in women's farming during the 1980s, by showing the substantial amount of farmwork done by women in both the part-time farming and agribusiness sectors of Florida. Further answers to the questions posed in this paper must come from time-series data from the Population Census or comparisons with archival data about Florida farm women in previous decades – or the U.S. Agricultural Census, if changed to tell us how many U.S. farms and agribusinesses have a (paid or unpaid) woman co-manager acting as one of the main operators of the family enterprise. Without such a change, policymakers are working in the dark about whether and why the U.S. family farm/agribusiness will survive in the future. With a change in the U.S. Agricultural Census, we could show that the family farm with a full-time male farmer is on the demise, while the farm with management shared between an active woman farmer and a part-time male farmer is surviving.

References

Barlett, Peggy. 1988. "Industrial agriculture," *Economic Anthropology,* ed. S. Plattner, 253–91. Stanford, Calif.: Stanford University Press.

Boserup, Ester. 1970. *Woman's Role in Economic Development.* New York: St. Martin's Press.

Buttel, Frederick, and Pierre LaRamee. 1987. "The disappearing middle: A sociological perspective." Paper prepared for the Rural Sociological Society annual meeting, Madison, Wis.

Clouser, Rodney, and Lionel Beaulieu. 1986. "Florida agriculture: Maintaining compatibility with the state's urban growth," in *Florida Agriculture in the '80s: 1986 Update, 256.* Gainesville, Fla.: Institute of Food and Agricultural Sciences.

Cochrane, Willard W. 1986. "The need to rethink agricultural policy in general and to perform some radical surgery on commodity programs in particular," in *Agricultural Change: Consequences for Southern Farms and Rural Communities,* ed. J. Molnar, 391–412. Boulder, Colo.: Westview Press.

Downie, Masuma, and Christina Gladwin. 1981. "Florida farm wives: They help the family farm survive." Gainesville: Food and Resource Economics Department, Institute of Food and Agricultural Sciences, University of Florida.

Fink, Deborah. 1987. "Farming in open country, Iowa: Women and the changing farm economy," in *Farm Work and Fieldwork,* ed. M. Chibnik, 121–44. Ithaca, N.Y.: Cornell University Press.

Flora, Cornelia Butler. 1981. "Farm women, farming systems, and agricultural structure: Suggestions for scholarship." *Rural Sociologist* 1(6):25–34.

Friedland, William H. 1987. "Women and agriculture: A state of the art assessment." Paper presented for the panel "Rural Sociology: Changing Agricultural Structure and Gender," American Sociological Association, Chicago, Ill.

Gladwin, Christina. 1982. "Off-farm work and its effect on Florida farm wives' contribution to the family farm," in *World Development and Women,* Vol. II, ed. M. Rojas, 11–E, 1–38. Blacksburg, Va.: Virginia Tech Title XII Women in International Development Office.

_____. 1983. "How Florida women help the farm and agribusiness firm survive." Gainesville: University of Florida Cooperative Extension Service Circular 613.

_____. 1985a. "Values and goals of Florida farm women: Do they help the family farm survive?" *Agriculture and Human Values* II (1):40–47.

_____. 1985b. "The increase in women's farming: A response to structural change." Florida Food and Resource Economics No. 66, Sept.–Oct., Gainesville: University of Florida.

_____. 1985c. "Changes in women's roles on the farm: A response to the intensification or capitalization of agriculture?" in *Women Creating Wealth: Transforming Economic Development,* ed. A. Spring and R. Gallin, 139–42. Washington, D.C.: Association for Women in Development.

Huffman, Wallace. 1976. "The value of productive time of farm wives: Iowa, North Carolina, and Oklahoma." *American Journal of Agricultural Economics* 58 (No. 5):836–41.

Jones, Calvin, and Rachel Ann Rosenfeld. 1981. *American Farm Women: Findings from a National Survey.* NORC Report No. 130. Chicago: National Opinion Research Center.

Kalbacher, Judith Z. 1985. *A Profile of Female Farmers in America.* Rural Development Research Report No. 45. Washington, D.C.: Economic Research Service, U.S. Department of Agriculture.

Rosenfeld, Rachel Ann. 1985. *Farm Women: Work, Farm, and Family in the United States.* Chapel Hill: University of North Carolina Press.

Sachs, Carolyn E. 1983. *The Invisible Farmers: Women in Agricultural Production.* Totowa, N.J.: Rowman and Allanheld.

_____. 1985. "Women's work and food." Paper presented at Rural Sociological Society annual meetings, Blacksburg, Va.

Scholl, Kathleen K. 1982. "Household and farm task participation of women," in *Household Production,* special issue of *Family Economics Review* (3), 1–7. Washington, D.C.: U.S. Department of Agriculture.

Vanek, Joanne. 1974. "Time Spent in Housework." *Scientific American* 23(No. 5):116–20.

Wozniak, Patricia J., and Kathleen K. Scholl. 1988. "Employment decisions: Full-time or part-time farming?" Baton Rouge: Department of Experimental Statistics, Louisiana State University.

CHAPTER 13

The Future Role of
Farm Household Surveys:
A Discussion

MARY AHEARN

The chapters in this volume by Spitze and Mahoney, Saupe and Gould, Gebremedhin, and Gladwin report on results from local area surveys conducted during the 1980s. I will first briefly comment on these four studies, but most of my comments are applicable to the broader group of recent local area data collection and analysis efforts.[1] For local area data collection and analysis to make the greatest contribution, it is important to understand where such studies have a comparative advantage. After describing their most important roles, I will then suggest some possible future goals of these data collection efforts.

Comments on the Four Local Area Studies

The paper by Christina Gladwin (Chapter 12) discusses the role of off-farm income and multiple job-holding, but the major focus is on the increased role of farm women in farm activities and on competing hypotheses to explain this trend. In the end, Gladwin acknowledges that the current empirical evidence does not permit this question to be answered unequivocally.

One of the more interesting points made by Gladwin is that when farm

---

1. There are several other studies that could have been included in a conference session on farm surveys, e.g., the work done in North Dakota and Ohio.

women are asked if they consider themselves to be one of the farm operators of the business, the majority said they did so. However, in the Census
of Agriculture, which asks for the gender of the one operator, it was found
that only 5 percent of farms are operated by women. Our major sources of
national farm data are likely tieing us to a traditional view of the major
divisions of labor in the farm business and household.

My major criticism of this paper is that many of the statements are not
identified as being those of the respondents or value-laden interpretations
of the researcher. For example, the paper states that it is unfortunate that
survival strategies of part-time farms mean they provide less of the marketed share of farm commodities. Who believes this is unfortunate? The
respondents or the researcher? In another example, it is stated that women
do a better job as business managers and accountants than men. What is
the proof of such a statement?

The papers by Spitze and Mahoney, Saupe and Gould, and Gebremedhin (Chapters 9, 10, and 11) similarly focus on the role of off-farm
employment within a local area. The studies each found that off-farm income accounted for at least 50 percent of the income of farm operator
households (although the early 1982 Wisconsin survey found less than 50
percent). They had similar findings regarding the factors explaining off-
farm labor force participation. There were differing results with regard to
the off-farm labor force participation of operators versus spouses. Such
differences are very likely due to differences in the most common types of
farming specialties and the local market area characteristics of the sampled
areas. For example, the Saupe-Gould results indicated that spouses had a
higher off-farm labor participation rate than operators. This is opposite of
what we know for the nation as a whole and is likely due to the type of
farming that dominates and the labor market in the area. It is likely that
unique local labor markets were a factor in the unexpected results found by
Gebremedhin that age and level of education were negatively related to the
off-farm income of spouses.

The Illinois studies described in the Spitze-Mahoney paper uniquely
provide data to compare from an early time period, 1971, to more current
data. One of the most significant changes during this period was the increase in labor force participation of spouses from 29 percent in 1971 to 46
percent in 1985. The sample sizes were quite large for the Illinois studies
and coverage was for the entire state. In contrast, both the Wisconsin and
Louisiana studies were limited to small areas of the state, which limited
their usefulness for drawing implications for the whole state and, certainly,
for the whole nation. The Wisconsin studies did the most complete job in
measuring farm income since individual farm income and expenses were
collected separately, allowing the researchers the flexibility to determine a

consistent accounting framework. The Saupe-Gould paper not only provided a presentation of survey results but described a rich body of research that has been underway in this general area of well-being of farm operator households in Wisconsin. A unique contribution of the Gebremedhin paper was the comparison of the role of off-farm income in white versus black farm operator households.

Traditional Sources of Data

The most common source of farm financial data at the national and state levels has traditionally been from the Economic Research Service, U.S. Department of Agriculture (ERS/USDA). The Economic Research Service has published off-farm income estimates since 1960. However, the traditional ERS data have been limited to total and average income and expense estimates. In addition, farm management record-keeping systems maintained by some state land grant universities have been valuable sources of time-series data, although they have not necessarily been representative of all farms in those states. The advantage to the farm record systems has been that individual records are available for processing within the state to address specific issues of interest which are inadequately addressed by simple totals and averages. The major focus of both the traditional data sources, ERS and the state farm record systems, has been on the farm business in contrast to the people whose financial well-being is directly affected by the success or failures of the businesses.

State-Federal Division of Labor in Data Collection

Even before the farm sector experienced the financial stress in the early part of this decade, efforts to collect farm household-level data for the United States (in USDA) and in some states (e.g., Wisconsin) had been initiated. A major goal of these efforts was to better understand the distribution of well-being variables, including the role of off-farm income. There was as much interest in measuring the characteristics of those in the sector who were well-off by any standards as there was in measuring the characteristics of those at the low end of the financial distribution. The severe decline in farmland values accelerated interest in this type of distributional information. The four area studies reviewed here are a sample from these efforts.

However, applied researchers are well aware of the very high costs associated with primary data collection and processing—currently approaching $100 per contact for personally enumerated surveys for data collection alone. For this reason, it is worth considering which issues are more appropriately handled by federal versus state projects before discussing specific recommendations for collection of farm household data.

The U.S. Department of Agriculture has a legal mandate to collect the necessary data to estimate and report on the farm sector's (farm) income and costs of production for specific commodities. The USDA's mission also includes providing annual intelligence on the well-being of farm people both at the U.S. and state levels. Because of the legally mandated estimates, limited additional resources are required to meet the goal of providing summary comparative analysis by state on the well-being of farm people.

A major advantage of federal involvement is the consistency that is brought to the research across states, which avoids across-state differences resulting from conceptual and empirical variations. Increasingly, USDA is responding to demands for more distributional analysis at the state level. For example, in addition to the traditional annually published state data, in 1988 USDA has released 26 individual state reports and 7 regional reports (for the remaining contiguous states) on the well-being of farm businesses and households. These reports include distributional information by size and type of farm.

The supply of state-level estimates by the federal government has decreased efforts at the state level to collect additional data solely for the purpose of measuring the basic financial position of farms and farm households in the state. In most cases, the federal program has collected state data of higher quality (as measured by more complete information, a larger sample size, and with higher response rates) than the data collected in the same state through state-led initiatives. However, traditional research geared toward academic audiences is a secondary priority for use of the farm business and household data collected by USDA, but often the very rich federal data base is underutilized for research purposes.

Collection of data by state analysts at the state and substate levels is most appropriate when either the federal data do not provide statistically reliable estimates for the area of interest, the variables of interest are not included in the federal data collection process, or panel data are of interest. In addition, if ease of access to primary data records is an important consideration (as it is for most research purposes), collection of data at the state level is justifiable because of the elaborate, legal access rules to individual farm records collected by USDA. (These rules are a result of privacy considerations.) Federal and local area data collection and analysis projects play different roles in analyzing rural development issues as well. Federal data are useful for combining with substate local area characteristics, such as county employment and income which are available on the Bureau of Economic Analysis' county data file, because they vary considerably across the country. Local area projects, on the other hand, are less useful for this purpose because they quite often lack the variability in local area characteristics.

However, local area projects provide an excellent opportunity to examine local area characteristics that are not available on national data bases and to then draw implications which will be useful rural development tools. The major focus of the data collection efforts described in Chapters 9 through 12 was on research. This focus is clearly where state data collection initiatives have their comparative advantage.

Future Directions for Collection and Analysis of Farm Business and Household Data

Future collection of data on farm operator households and their farm businesses is certainly necessary to enhance our understanding of the well-being, resource allocations, and adjustments of farm operator households. In conclusion, I would like to provide some recommendations for future data collection efforts to accomplish these goals:

1. Define a clear income unit. Although such a recommendation is straightforward, its application is complicated by the many farm producers and the variety of ways in which they organize the production practices, e.g., partnerships and contract production arrangements, and by the household-business linkages. The household income unit will include the farm operator since he or she is the major entrepreneur and decision maker in the agricultural production process by the current definition. The household income unit will also include members of the operator's household which make allocations of all their human and nonhuman capital in an integrated fashion. The farm operator household as a combined unit is the major recipient of the residual income from the farm business. In addition, since a definition of a farm will necessarily be part of the definition of a farm operator household, the official farm definition should be employed.

A consistent specification of the income unit for farm households is the single greatest weakness in the current federal data system. The USDA income data assumes that one farm operator household is associated with one farm business and that the farm household is the recipient of all of the residual income from the farming business. For wealth statistics, both the traditional and the new Farm Costs and Returns Survey data of USDA are limited to farm assets and debt, and the traditional data include landlord data and do not allow for separation of operator and landlord balance sheet data. The only public use data available on farm people, the Current Population Survey (CPS), is seriously flawed as representative of farm operator households because of its definition of the income unit. The CPS defines farm people as either those who reside on farms (but 20 percent of operator households do not, and others do), those whose major occupation is farming (but the majority of farm operators have a nonfarm job as their major occupation), or those who receive self-employment income (but this excludes operator households whose farms are incorporated and includes landlord households). Unfortunately, these data are often used as if they are for farm operator households, and sometimes they are even mixed and matched in describing a composite financial picture of farm operator households.

2. Understand the advantages and limitations of the definition of income that is employed. Ideally, collect gross income and expense items by categories. This will ensure that a consistent farm income definition can be used across respondents, and different definitions can be employed for different purposes. Each of the four area surveys reviewed here collected and measured farm income differently, limiting the comparability of results across states. Some of the most likely income definitions are a USDA accrual concept, a USDA cash concept, or a tax-based concept (which is consistent with the Current Population Survey concept).

3. Identify business relationships with contractors, landlords, and relatives in analyzing the well-being of farm operator households. How many farms is the household associated with? Who provides inputs, including capital assets, and who receives residual returns?

4. Separately identify the role of the spouse in the household, given the variation in results pertaining to time allocations and off-farm income earning abilities of spouses. Gladwin (Chapter 12) reported that in the short time period of 1980–84 alone, there was a statistically significant increase in farm women's contribution to farming activities.

The topic of the spouse's role in farm and off-farm activities provides a good example of the dangers in the variety of income unit definitions in our current federal data system. According to the Census of Agriculture's Farm Finance Survey which uses the farm operator household concept, farm operators (about 95 percent who are men) are more likely than their spouses to work off the farm. These data are consistent with a 1980 USDA survey of farm women. The Current Population Survey shows, in contrast, that women who reside on farms are more likely than their spouses to work off the farm. Obviously, if the CPS data for farm residents were used as representative of farm operator households, erroneous conclusions would be reached.

5. Collect number of hours worked on and off the farm (both in farm production and household production) for operator and spouse. This will allow for more complete studies of time allocation relative to marginal returns from each type of activity, for example, based on the comprehensive household production function approach.

6. Collect prices and quantities of inputs and outputs for farm production. This will allow for analysis of economic efficiency, both technical and allocative.

7. There are currently attempts to measure how farm operator households actually have adjusted during the 1980s, e.g., as described by Saupe and Gould (Chapter 10). An evaluation of the panel approach to data collection is still pending, but preliminary results are promising. Although analysis of panel data are an improvement over our standard analysis of farm operator households for policy purposes, the important policy questions will deal with the adjustments farm households are expected to undertake in response to proposed policy changes. Farm simulation with policy feedback, price changes, and off-farm supply equations are needed in our models to analyze proposed policy changes *ex ante.*

8. Collect expenditure data for households to provide an estimate of family living expenses and savings or dissavings.

9. Collect attitudes, goals, and plans for farming. It is not easy to incorporate these into our models, but they would be of use in explaining behavior where our models fail.

PART IV

Rural Labor
Markets

CHAPTER 14

Factors Affecting the Supply of Off-farm Labor: A Review of Empirical Evidence

DANIEL A. LASS

JILL L. FINDEIS

MILTON C. HALLBERG

The supply of off-farm labor by farm families has received increased attention in recent years. Given the importance of off-farm income to farm families, the attention is certainly justified. Off-farm employment by one or more family members is not only prevalent in the United States but appears to be a permanent phenomenon as well. The growth in off-farm income relative to farm income which has occurred may make farm families just as susceptible to economic conditions of the non-farm economy as they are to the profitability of farming (Findeis and Reddy 1987b).

Both theoretical and empirical models have been developed to deal with choice where corner solutions may exist. The farm family faces such a problem. The essence of the decision by the farm operator to participate in the off-farm labor markets was captured by Lee (1965). Recently, research has focused on the allocation decisions of the farm family (Huffman 1980; Furtan, Van Kooten, and Thompson 1985; Thompson 1985; Rosenfeld 1985). The allocation decisions by the family are cast within the context of utility maximization (Huffman 1980; Shishko and Rostker 1976) or the household production models of Becker (1965) and Gronau (1973). The majority of our current empirical evidence on the factors affecting off-farm employment comes from the application of these microeconomic decision models to survey data.

The prevalence and magnitudes of off-farm employment income have created research interests in the implications of these trends for the well-being of farm households (Carlin and Reinsel 1973; Ahearn, Johnson, and Strickland 1985). There is also growing recognition that off-farm employment may affect the farm organization through the creation of additional financial resources or through constraints imposed by off-farm employment. These changes may affect farm investment decisions, choice of enterprise mix, and input use. At the macroeconomic level, off-farm employment has been shown to affect the structure of agriculture (Carlin and Ghelfi 1979), the distribution of income (Findeis and Reddy 1987a), and the stability of income (Tweeten 1983). Despite low or even negative net returns, many small farms have continued to operate principally supported by off-farm income. This has been particularly true in the 1970s and 1980s (Cochrane 1987).

The objective of this chapter is to assess the current stock of empirical information about the allocation of farm family labor to off-farm employment. The factors which have been demonstrated to affect participation decisions and the supply of off-farm labor by farm men and women will be reviewed. A brief review of the theoretical model and the resulting empirical specification will be presented in the following section. The theoretical and empirical models provide a framework for the discussion of the empirical evidence. Empirical results from a number of studies of off-farm labor participation are reviewed in the third section of the chapter. Studies which have estimated labor-supply models will then be reviewed, the main focus of the chapter. Parameter estimates, where comparable, and elasticities will illustrate the current stock of knowledge about factors affecting the supply of off-farm labor. In the final section, some of the issues which require further research are discussed.

Theoretical and Empirical Models

Farm households are assumed to maximize utility by choosing levels of purchased goods (Y_1) and leisure (L).[1] We assume for simplicity that consideration of leisure for the farm operator (L_1) and the spouse (L_2) are sufficient for the maximization of household utility. In addition, a vector of exogenous environmental factors (**E**) determines the levels of utility. We

---

1. We will use the assumption of utility maximization. We could alternatively employ the household production models of Becker (1965) and Gronau (1973); however, the resulting empirical specifications are similar.

assume that both the operator and spouse have opportunities to work on-farm (F_1 and F_2) and off-farm (M_1 and M_2). The typical budget constraint is imposed on the household as well as a constraint for the total amount of time available. Farm profits and off-farm wages contribute to household income. Leisure, on-farm labor, and off-farm labor compete for the allocation of total time. The problem is then similar to the analysis of multiple job-holdings by Shishko and Rostker (1976). An important difference arises in that the wage received for farm work is not assumed constant. Given the normal regularity conditions for the production function, on-farm labor by both the operator and spouse will face diminishing marginal returns. The production function therefore imposes the final constraint on the maximization of utility by the farm household.

Following Huffman (1980) and Gronau (1973), the model is stated formally as the maximization of utility:

$$U = U(Y_1, L_1, L_2; \mathbf{E}) \tag{14.1}$$

subject to the constraints

$$P_1 Y_1 = P_q Q - RX + w_1 M_1 + w_2 M_2 + V \tag{14.2}$$

$$Q = f(X, F_1, F_2; G) \text{ and} \tag{14.3}$$

$$T_i = L_i + F_i + M_i; i = 1, 2 \tag{14.4}$$

The household chooses the levels of purchased goods, leisure, farm labor, off-farm labor, farm inputs (X), and farm output (Q) given prices (P_1, P_q), off-farm wages (w_1, w_2), other income (V), and other exogenous factors (G). An interior solution for the optimal allocation of time between leisure, on-farm work, and off-farm work is determined by solving the set of first order conditions (see Huffman 1980). However, corner solutions may exist for both the operator and spouse. The Kuhn-Tucker conditions are then appropriate and provide the following participation rules:

$$D_i = \begin{array}{l} 1 \ if \ w_i^* > 0 \\ 0 \ if \ w_i^* \leq 0 \end{array} \tag{14.5}$$

where

$$w_i^* = (w_i - P_q \frac{\partial Q}{\partial F_i}) \ \Big| \ M_i = 0 \tag{14.6}$$

is the unobserved difference between the market wage and the shadow value of farm labor for the operator ($i=1$) or spouse ($i=2$). Solving the Kuhn-Tucker conditions in terms of the exogenous factors leads to the empirical specification for the participation decision as a probability model. The binary decision to participate is generally modeled using one of the probability models (Probit or Logit).

The complete empirical specification depends upon the characteristics of the data set and the appropriate estimation methods. Given the decision to participate, the market wage rate will be observed. Market wages are typically missing for nonparticipants. Wage equations are generally estimated by Heckman's (1974) procedure to correct for the censored nature of the sample.[2] The resulting model is then used to predict wages for those who do not participate in the off-farm labor market and the Tobit procedure is applied to the entire sample of data for the time spent working off-farm. Alternatively, the Heckman procedure can be used to estimate the labor-supply function using the subsample of working individuals.

Factors Affecting Participation Decisions

Models of the participation decisions of farm men and women follow directly from the Kuhn-Tucker conditions, i.e., equations (14.5) and (14.6). Arguments of both the utility and production functions are the factors which affect the decision to participate in the off-farm labor markets. We will discuss the factors exogenous to these decisions according to the categories suggested by Leistritz et al. 1985: (1) individual characteristics, (2) family characteristics, (3) farm production characteristics, (4) financial characteristics of the farm family, and (5) locational characteristics. Discussion of the factors affecting participation decisions will be brief as they have been reviewed in detail elsewhere. (Findeis, Hallberg, and Lass 1987 provide tabular reviews of studies by author which indicate the signs and significance of each variable.) The studies which will be reviewed are presented in Table 14.1. While the list is not exhaustive, these studies provide a representative set of results for U.S. and Canadian farm families.

---

2. Empirical procedures for limited dependent variables are reviewed by Amemiya (1981) and Maddala (1986). Thompson (1985) provides a review of the theoretical issues as well as the variations in empirical results that can be expected with the alternative methods.

Table 14.1. Description of studies reviewed

Study	Data year	Geographic area
Buttel et al.	1981	New York
Furtan et al.	1980	Saskatchewan
Huffman	1964	Counties of Iowa, North Carolina and Oklahoma
Huffman and Lange	1977	Iowa
Jensen and Salant	1981	Mississippi and Tennessee
Lass et al.	1985	Massachusetts
Leistritz et al.	1985	North Dakota
Polzin and MacDonald	1964	Total U.S.
Findeis and Reddy	1978, 1984	Total U.S.
Rosenfeld	1980	Total U.S.
Sander	1980	Total U.S.
Simpson and Kapitany	1977	Saskatchewan
Streeter and Saupe	1981	Mississippi and Tennessee
Sumner	1971	Illinois
Thompson	1981	Saskatchewan

Individual characteristics

The variables typically included in off-farm participation models are the individual's age, education, and work experience. An age-squared variable has also been included to capture a life-cycle effect. For farm men, advancing age has been shown to be positively and then negatively related to the probability of off-farm work reflecting a life-cycle effect. For farm women the results have been less clear (Findeis, Hallberg, and Lass 1987). Several recent studies have found evidence of the life-cycle effect (i.e., Huffman and Lange 1989; Lass, Findeis, and Hallberg 1988), while others have found conflicting results (Rosenfeld 1985; Leistritz et al. 1985). Where the life-cycle effect is observed, participation peaks between ages 45 and 55.

The effects of increases in human capital on off-farm labor-participation decision include both direct and indirect effects and are ambiguous. The decision rule central to the off-farm participation decision is affected in two ways. Human capital enhances an individual's performance in farm operations, thereby increasing the shadow value of labor. The value of labor off the farm is similarly increased. The actual affect on the participation decision is left as an empirical issue. Education and experience are the two commonly used indicators of an individual's stock of human capital.

Empirical evidence suggests that education has a positive influence on the probability of off-farm employment participation for both farm men and women. These results suggest that the effects of human capital on off-farm wages outweigh the increase in the shadow value of labor on the farm.

The results of Simpson and Kapitany (1983) were an exception; however, their negative impact of education on participation was not statistically significant. Education has been argued to increase labor productivity both on-farm and off-farm. The lack of statistically significant impacts of education on participation may represent this confounding influence of education on relative productivities.

Experience has been shown to have the anticipated impacts on off-farm participation. On-farm experience by farm operators reduces the probability of participation while off-farm experience results in an increase. However, the empirical information is limited especially for off-farm experience. Inclusion of both age and experience variables is difficult due to strong collinearity.

Family characteristics

Characteristics of the farm family may affect participation decisions by individuals. Variables included to capture effects of family characteristics include the presence or number of dependent children and factors affecting the spouse's decision. The number and presence of children appear to be most important for farm women. Women are less likely to work off-farm if children are present. The presence of children typically increased the probability of off-farm employment by farm men; however, the impacts were generally not significant. The age of the children also appears important with preschool children having the strongest impacts. Huffman and Lange (1989) obtained significant negative impacts of preschool children on the probabilities of off-farm work by men and women.

At least one variable reflecting characteristics of the individual's spouse are included in the participation models. Consistent results have been observed for variables which measure off-farm employment by the spouse and on-farm work experience by farm men. For both men and women, off-farm participation by the spouse results in a higher probability of off-farm work. Greater farm work experience by men results in a lower probability of off-farm work by farm women. Huffman (1980) found that the wife's education had a positive effect on the husbands decision to work off-farm. Furtan, Van Kooten, and Thompson (1985) found the same positive effect for farm women but the opposite effect for farm men. Recent research investigating joint decisions by farm men and women have found evidence that participation decisions are not made jointly (Huffman and Lange, 1989; Lass, Findeis, and Hallberg 1988). We clearly have much to learn about intrafamily decisions.

Farm production and financial characteristics

Since off-farm employment is most prevalent among families operating small and modest sized farms, it is not surprising to find that the probabilities of participation for both men and women are inversely related to farm income. Farm income has been incorporated in both net and gross form. From a theoretical perspective, net farm income is more appealing (Sumner 1982). However, net farm income or profits should be estimated as an endogenous variable. Gross farm income is often argued to be an indicator of farm size or scale. Other measures of farm scale include farm output (Huffman 1980), capital value (Simpson and Kapitany 1983), and acreage operated (Leistritz et al. 1985). Measures of scale generally result in significantly lower rates of participation.

Income from other sources which secures the family's financial position also reduces the probability of off-farm employment. The studies reviewed here show that as income from sources other than off-farm employment increase, participation rates for both farm men and women decrease, with one exception. Huffman (1980) included measures of both realized and unrealized income. Realized income had an unexpected positive effect on the probability of off-farm work. A review of farm characteristics indicates that the larger the farm, the lower the probability that farm men will work off-farm. There are also labor-intensive farm enterprises that restrict participation in off-farm employment. Sumner (1982) found that increases in the percentage of swine or dairy livestock on the farm significantly reduced the probability of off-farm participation. Dairy production is the prime example of such an enterprise while beef production tends to allow greater levels of off-farm employment (Leistritz et al. 1985). We remain relatively ignorant of how the operation of the farm affects off-farm work or how off-farm employment by family members affects the operation and organization of the farm. For farm women, our knowledge is even more limited. For example, Lass, Findeis, and Hallberg (1988) found no significant enterprise effects on participation decisions by Massachusetts farm women.

Locational characteristics

This review found that little is understood about the impacts of another set of factors on the prevalence of off-farm work: the influence of location. The participation of farm family members in off-farm markets is affected not only by their willingness and ability to supply labor but also by the demand for this labor. To capture the impacts of access to and availability to employment opportunities, researchers have included various location related measures. Sander (1983) used a population density variable and

Buttel et al. (1982) included a measure to reflect urbanization. Binary variables have also been included to represent location (Leistritz et al. 1985;
Sumner 1982). Sumner found that northern and southern Illinois farmers
worked off-farm more frequently, probably due to the relatively greater
level of economic activity in those two regions. The increased probability of
working off-farm was consistent with his finding that farmers received
higher off-farm wage rates in those two regions. He found that both the
probability of participation and the off-farm wage were negatively related
to the distance to the nearest city.

Location variables have generally performed poorly. It is likely that
binary location variables measure regional differences in farming as well as
location relative to employment opportunities. The effects of job availability, access to jobs, and employment growth in communities are important
areas of research (see Findeis, Lass, and Hallberg, Chapter 15 this volume).

Factors Affecting the Supply of Off-farm Labor

We will concentrate in this section on empirical results from studies in
which final supply functions were estimated. The results from estimation of
wage equations provide additional important information and will be discussed where appropriate.

The model above illustrates that factors which determine the supply of
off-farm labor are those which affect farm production decisions and family
decisions for commodity choice and the attainment of utility. Shifts in the
transformation function (farm production technology), off-farm wage rate,
or utility function will affect the number of hours supplied to the off-farm
market. Arguments of both the utility and production functions are factors
which affect off-farm labor supply. We will again discuss the factors exogenous to these decisions according to the five categories defined above, but
first will focus on two major determinants which may be considered endogenous to the system, the off-farm wage and farm output.

Off-farm wage rates

Wages represent the market value of an individual's stock of human
capital and can be considered fixed in the short-run. However, wage equations are estimated as part of the model to provide predicted wages for
individuals who do not participate in the off-farm markets. Assuming
leisure is a normal good, the response of off-farm labor supply to an increase in the wage is ambiguous. As market wages increase, substitutions of

market labor for consumption (leisure) and farm labor occur. There are also income effects for consumption and an income effect due to the reduction of farm income as labor is substituted from farm work to market work. Thus, the signs and magnitudes for elasticities of supply are uncertain for both farm men and women.

Empirical evidence suggests that substitution effects outweigh income effects. Empirical estimates of the own-wage elasticity for farm men are presented in Table 14.2 and range from 0.32 (Streeter and Saupe 1986) to 2.05 (Thompson 1985).[3] Thompson's results demonstrate the variation in estimates obtained from different methodologies. Her estimates ranged from 0.70 for the subsample of men who worked off-farm to 2.05 for the entire sample using the Tobit model. Huffman (1980) obtained results consistent with those of Streeter and Saupe (1986), whereas Sumner (1982) found the elasticity to be near unity. Huffman and Lange (1989) found the elasticities for men to be much lower in their recent study of joint decisions by husbands and wives.

Estimates for farm women are also typically positive in sign but are more elastic (see Table 14.2). Furtan, Van Kooten, and Thompson (1985) found the elasticity for Canadian farm women to be substantially more elastic at 4.21. Thompson's (1985) estimates for the own-wage elasticity for Canadian women varied dramatically depending upon the estimation technique. The two-stage Heckman approach yielded estimates which showed an inelastic response, 0.12. The Tobit approach yielded elasticity estimates of approximately 3.3. The Tobit approach would be expected to yield a higher elasticity estimate since it utilizes the entire sample including zero values for hours worked off-farm. Huffman and Lange (1989) found the

---

3. Many of these results must be interpreted cautiously. Where the elasticity was not presented, we have used the authors' results and the sample means to calculate the elasticities.

Table 14.2. Estimated wage elasticities for off-farm labor supply models

Variable	Huffman	Furtan et al.	Thompson	Streeter and Saupe	Sumner
			Men		
Wage					
Own	0.34[a]	0.72	0.70–2.05[a]	0.32[a]	1.01[a]–1.13[a]
Spouse	−0.06	3.28	...	...	...
			Women		
Wage					
Own	...	4.21[a]	0.12–3.36[a]	...	...
Spouse	...	−0.40	...	...	...

[a]Elasticity calculated from statistically significant parameter estimate.

wage elasticity for women to be inelastic (0.038) when both the husband and wife worked off-farm. They also found that the wage elasticity was negative (-0.119) when only the wife worked off-farm.

Cross elasticities of supply with respect to the spouse's wage are also presented in Table 14.2. For men, Huffman (1980) found that the wife's off-farm labor was a substitute, although inelastic. Furtan, Van Kooten, and Thompson (1985) found an opposite and elastic effect for Canadian men. However, neither were found to be statistically different from zero. Furtan, Van Kooten, and Thompson also estimated the effect of the men's wage on the labor supply of women. Using the average hours worked off-farm to calculate the elasticity, the men's labor appears to be a substitute for women working off-farm. The estimate was inelastic (-0.40) and not significantly different from zero. Huffman and Lange (1989) found that both the husband's and wive's labor were complements for each other although inelastic. Thus, empirical evidence provides no consistent support for the hypothesis that farm men and women adjust their hours worked off-farm according to their spouse's opportunities.

Farm output

Inclusion of a measure of farm output in the labor-supply function can be defended on both theoretical and intuitive grounds. Intuitively, we expect farmers with larger farms to participate in the off-farm markets less frequently and to supply fewer hours when they do participate. Theoretically, the value of the operators labor can be derived as a shadow value (Sumner 1982). Variable profits or quasi-rents are maximized in the short run by choosing the levels of outputs and variable inputs subject to the set of fixed factors and the production technology. The operator and spouse can be considered residual claimants to the quasi-rents and receive a shadow value for their labor. Thus, output supplies, input demands, and the shadow value of labor will be determined by the set of output and input prices, the set of fixed factors, the current stock of technology, and other exogenous factors such as human capital.

Empirical studies have followed one of two approaches to modeling the impacts of farm production on off-farm labor supply. Ideally, the quasi-rent function would be estimated and the predicted values subsequently used as independent variables in the supply function. However, the data needed to estimate quasi-rents or short run profits are often unavailable or difficult to obtain in surveys. The value of total sales or production is then used as an alternative. Production functions are estimated and the predicted values used in the estimation of the supply function (Huffman 1980). A second alternative is to estimate the labor-supply function as a reduced form model. The exogenous factors that affect production (and variable profits) are used in estimation of the labor-supply function. The resulting parameter estimates suffer from the maladies common to all reduced-form coefficients. However, they provide indications of the total effect of the variable in question on the supply of off-farm labor. The effects of individual exogenous factors on the supply of off-farm labor will be discussed below.

We expect that increases in farm returns or output would reduce the supply of labor to the off-farm markets by both the operator and spouse. Greater farm output or sales may be assumed to indicate higher short run profits. If leisure is a normal good, we would expect lower participation rates and fewer hours supplied. Results of previous studies support this hypothesis. Huffman found the elasticity of off-farm labor supply to be −0.43 with respect to gross farm sales and parameter was highly significant. Streeter and Saupe (1986) also found a negative relationship between predicted sales and off-farm supply. Using their parameter estimate and the sample means of gross sales and hours worked, we calculated the elasticity of labor supply with respect to farm sales to be −0.28. Thus their result is consistent with that of Huffman (1980). Sander (1983) found that net farm income was negatively related to off-farm labor supply for both men and women. Again the results were highly significant. Polzin and MacDonald (1971) estimated labor-supply functions using county-level data for four U.S. states. They obtained inverse relationships between average value of farm products sold and the average days worked off-farm. Their results were robust across all four states and were consistently significant. Furtan, Van Kooten, and Thompson (1985) used a measure of net worth of the farm in the labor-supply equation. Net worth was also found to be negatively related to the supply of off-farm labor.

While the empirical results of different studies can not be strictly compared, we do observe a clear negative relationship between farm output and off-farm labor supply. Of the studies that support this relationship, two provide us with estimates of the elasticity of off-farm labor supply with respect to farm sales. Our "best" estimate of the elasticity would lie in the range −0.28 to −0.43. However, this conclusion is based on only two observations from two different years and geographic regions. Still, the similarity of the estimates is striking.

Individual characteristics

Human capital may be the most important individual characteristic affecting the supply of off-farm labor. Farm operators build human capital through investments in education and experience. The effects of human capital on the supply of off-farm labor include both direct and indirect effects. Human capital is assumed to affect both the farm production function and the off-farm wage. In terms of the model above, human capital represents elements of the vectors **E** and **G**. To determine the effects of a change in human capital on labor supply, we must sort out the various partial effects which make up the total effect. Assume for simplicity that the off-farm supply function for an individual can be written

$$M = m(w(h), f(X,h), h) \qquad (14.7)$$

where $m(.)$ represents the supply function for off-farm labor, h represents human capital and all other variables are as defined above. Totally differentiating (14.7), we have

$$dM = \frac{\partial m}{\partial w} \frac{\partial w}{\partial h} dh + \frac{\partial m}{\partial f} \frac{\partial f}{\partial h} dh + \frac{\partial m}{\partial f} \frac{\partial f}{\partial x} dX + \frac{\partial m}{\partial h} dh \qquad (14.8)$$

The relevant total derivative is then

$$\frac{dM}{dh} = \frac{\partial m}{\partial w} \frac{\partial w}{\partial h} + \frac{\partial m}{\partial f} \frac{\partial f}{\partial h} + \frac{\partial m}{\partial f} \frac{\partial f}{\partial x} \frac{dX}{dh} + \frac{\partial m}{\partial h} \qquad (14.9)$$

The total derivative can then be determined from estimated parameters of the wage equation, the farm production function and the off-farm labor-supply function. Previous results for the elements of human capital, education, and experience can be interpreted following this framework.

The true effect of education on hours worked should include the indirect effect via the wage rate. The education elasticity of wages and the own-wage elasticity of hours worked can be combined to estimate the elasticity of hours worked with respect to education. Education elasticities were calculated using reported parameters and sample means.[4] Our calculations yielded estimates which ranged from 0.15 (Thompson 1985) to 1.01 (Furtan, Van Kooten, and Thompson 1985) for farm men. Calculations for farm women using the results from Furtan, Van Kooten, and Thompson (1985) and Thompson (1985) were inelastic although very close to unity. Huffman and Lange (1989) also found inelastic effects. Thus the education elasticities of wages for both farm men and women appear to be inelastic.

Production functions were estimated by Huffman (1980) and Streeter

---

4. Huffman (1980) did not report the estimated wage equation. However, he did indicate the education elasticity of wages to be about 0.67.

and Saupe (1986). However, only Huffman (1980) reported the education elasticity of production. He estimated that an increase in the level of education by one year (about 10 percent) would result in an increase of 2.2 percent in production. Streeter and Saupe (1986) did not include education in the reported production function.

Huffman (1980) found a positive (an elasticity of 1.03) and significant direct effect of education on the days worked off-farm. Thompson (1985) also obtained positive and significant direct effects of education on the hours worked off-farm (elasticities of 1.29 to 1.80). Sumner (1982) concluded that the direct effect of education on hours worked was statistically zero. The implications of the positive effects are unclear. Education in the supply function may represent an exogenous factor of the utility function. Positive direct effects of education on the number of hours worked are surprising from the standpoint of a trade-off of labor for leisure.

The total effects of education on off-farm labor supply were calculated by aggregating the partial effects. For example, Huffman's (1980) education elasticity of wage was multiplied by the wage elasticity of labor to obtain the indirect effect of education on off-farm labor. We calculated the indirect effect of education on labor through production in a similar manner and added the direct effect of education on the labor-supply function. The total effect in elasticity form was 1.16 for Huffman's model. Calculations from other studies ranged from 0.45 (Sumner 1982) to 2.01 (Thompson 1985). The majority of the results indicated a positive and inelastic to slightly elastic effect of education on the supply of off-farm labor.

Gaining experience is also a means of building human capital. Empirical results for both farm men and women demonstrate positive effects of experience on the off-farm wage. Sumner (1982) measured job experience for the current job and included a dummy variable for those who also worked at another off-farm job in the past. The coefficient for current job experience had the expected positive and significant effect on wages although inelastic (0.17). A similar inelastic effect was found by Streeter and Saupe (1986); however, the estimated coefficient was not statistically significant. The parameter estimated by Sumner (1982) for the dummy variable for other jobs was positive but not statistically significant. Sumner also considered the impacts of nonfarm job training, but did not find a significant effect. Furtan, Van Kooten, and Thompson (1985) and Thompson (1985) utilized the individual's age as a proxy for experience.[5] Significant

---

5. Age was adjusted by the number of years of education and plus six years. Thompson (1985) also adjusted the women's experience measure for child bearing years using the number of years between first and last children.

inelastic results were found for men. Using the Furtan, Van Kooten, and Thompson (1985) results we estimated the elasticity to be about 0.64. Thompson (1985) included experience in quadratic form in the wage equation. Wages were found to first increase and then decrease with additional experience. The results of Huffman and Lange (1989) also support the hypothesis that experience is a depreciable form of human capital for both men and women.

Empirical evidence suggests the marginal effects of experience on the wage rate are small. Combined with the wage elasticity of off-farm supply, the total effect is inelastic. We calculated the total experience elasticity of off-farm labor supply to be 0.46, using the results of Furtan, Van Kooten, and Thompson (1985), while Sumner's (1982) model results in a more inelastic estimate of 0.17.

The effects of farm experience on the supply of off-farm labor was estimated by Furtan, Van Kooten, and Thompson (1985), Sumner (1982), and Streeter and Saupe (1986). Furtan, Van Kooten, and Thompson estimated the direct impact of years farming on the supply of off-farm labor. We calculated an elasticity of -1.26 for farm men using their results. However, they did not include age as a variable in their model. Thus, experience may be capturing the effects of advanced age on the allocation of time to off-farm work. Sumner (1982) included a dummy variable to indicate whether the individual had been farming six years prior to the survey. The estimated coefficient was negative and significantly different from zero. Sumner also found that operators with "some farm training" supplied fewer hours, although the estimated impact was not significant. Streeter and Saupe (1986) included a measure of the years of farm experience for the operator in the farm revenue function. While the estimated parameter had the expected positive sign it was not statistically significant.

Previous research has demonstrated that off-farm experience increases the time spent working off-farm. However, the results indicate that the impacts were inelastic and primarily affected the supply indirectly through the wage rate. Direct impacts of off-farm experience on labor supply have not been clearly demonstrated. Farm experience has also been demonstrated to affect the supply of off-farm labor. Farm experience affects the supply indirectly through the farm production function and directly through the labor-supply function. However, the latter effect may be spurious due to incomplete model specification.

The final individual effect included in off-farm labor-supply models is the individual's age. It is hypothesized that individuals will increase their work effort in earlier years as they accumulate assets to draw on later in life. This "life-cycle" hypothesis is supported in most all models of off-farm labor supply. Work effort is typically at a maximum in the late 40's and early 50's for both males and females. Huffman (1980) estimated the age of maximum work effort to be 53 for farm men, while Sumner (1982) estimated that work effort peaked at 47 years of age. Inclusion of age in models all but eliminates the possibility of measuring the impacts of experience within the same model due to severe collinearity between age and experience. However, the importance of experience in the supply equation can more appropriately be accounted for by the wage rate. Collinearity problems are then relevant to the participation equations where one can argue that theory supports the inclusion of both age and experience.

Farm production characteristics

Production characteristics enter the off-farm labor-supply function in one of two ways. As we discussed above, the production process can be modeled and the predicted values for output or variable profits used as explanatory variables in the supply function (Huffman 1980; Streeter and Saupe 1986). Alternatively, the supply function can be estimated as a reduced form model with the relevant factors of production included in the model (Sumner 1982). We will concentrate in this section on the reduced form models and the factors which have been demonstrated to affect the supply of off-farm labor.

Huffman (1980) estimated a production function and used the predicted values as an explanatory variable in the labor-supply function. Huffman also included the variance of the distribution of farm sales to capture the effects of farm size distribution on the supply of labor. As variation in the distribution of farm sales increases, the supply of off-farm labor should also increase. However, increases in the variance of farm returns may alternatively capture the effects of risk on labor supply. Greater levels of risk may result in the use of off-farm labor as a means of diversification to spread risk. We would again expect a positive sign for the estimated parameter. Huffman found that the variance of farm sales positively affected the supply of off-farm labor. Thus, his results are consistent with expectations in either case. Sumner (1982) also included measures to capture farm size and risk effects. Greater concentrations of corn and soybeans, swine, or dairy farm enterprises were found to first decrease and then increase the levels of labor supply. (He included these three variables in quadratic form.) However, he found that the effects were not statistically significant.

Streeter and Saupe (1986) estimated the farm revenue function and included predicted values in the labor-supply function. They also included the percentage of farm revenues from beef production directly in the off-farm labor-supply function. Their results indicate that farmers who concentrate on beef production supply significantly more hours to the off-farm labor markets. Thompson (1985) found the presence of livestock had an opposite effect on the supply of off-farm labor for Canadian farm men. The presence of livestock was estimated to decrease the supply of off-farm labor by 26 percent to 51 percent. Furtan, Van Kooten, and Thompson (1985) also found that the presence of livestock reduced off-farm supply by 41 percent. However, Thompson (1985) and Furtan, Van Kooten, and Thompson (1985) used only a dummy variable to indicate the presence of livestock and did not discriminate between dairy and beef or swine. Beef is certainly less labor intensive relative to dairy farming. While the results are in conflict, we would expect that a labor-intensive enterprise such as dairy farming inhibits off-farm labor supply by the farm family. The relative mix of farm types in the sample is an important consideration that could not be determined from the results presented by the authors.

One last caveat is appropriate. We are considering the impacts of enterprise mix on the intensity of off-farm labor supply measured as days or hours worked. The effects of enterprise mix on the time supplied may be less important than the effects on the initial participation decision. Results from estimated participation models support this hypothesis as discussed above.

The final farm characteristics of interest are measurements of the relative intensity of machinery and the value of assets. Thompson (1985) included a variable to measure the value of machinery relative to the value of land on the farm. Her results indicate a significant but inelastic response of labor supply to an increase in the value of machinery relative to land. A 10 percent increase in the ratio produced only a 1.5 percent increase in the hours of labor supplied. Furtan, Van Kooten, and Thompson (1985) included the net worth of the farm household and found a negative wealth effect on the hours supplied for both farm men and women. The impact was more than three times as strong for men than women and was significant in both equations.

Family characteristics

Family characteristics, especially the presence of children, have been shown to have important effects on the participation decisions for men and women. As Rosenfeld (1985) and Thompson (1985) have discussed, traditional families tend to place homemaking and child care responsibilities on women. Gronau (1973) suggests that women have a comparative advantage in these aspects of household production. We therefore expect that the presence and number of children will be inversely related to the hours worked by farm women. Empirical results for labor supply by women support this hypothesis. Furtan, Van Kooten, and Thompson (1985) found a significant negative effect of the number of children on the number of hours supplied by the wife. Using their results we estimate that each child reduced the hours worked by 41 percent. Thompson also found a negative impact of young children, each child reducing the hours supplied by 13 to 17 percent. Thompson included the number of children in two other age brackets. Each child between the ages of 6 to 12 reduced the hours worked by 9 to 31 percent. Older children had little effect on the hours worked. Sander (1983) found that the total number of children reduced the number of hours worked by women. He found a significant reduction for women under 45 years of age, probably reflecting the presence of younger children for these women.

The effects of children on the labor supply by men are uncertain. Children may require child care time by the husband. Alternatively, there may be further pressure for additional income for larger families. Empirical results support the hypothesis that more children represent greater financial demands. Huffman (1980) found that the number of children less than 5 years of age significantly increased the number of days spent working off the farm. Each child was estimated to increase the days worked by about 66 percent. Other researchers included children in the supply function in terms of total numbers. Furtan, Van Kooten, and Thompson (1985) found that each child increased hours worked by 11 percent. Sumner (1982) found that there was a positive effect of total children although the estimate was not significantly different from zero. He found that each child increased the hours worked by only about 2 percent. Thompson (1985) included only children between the ages 13 to 18 in her supply function for men. She estimated that each child would reduce the hours worked by as much as 7 percent; however, the coefficient was not statistically significant. We might expect the opposite effect since older children can often substitute for on-farm labor. Children were not included in the models of Sander (1983) or Streeter and Saupe (1986) for the husbands supply.

The time spent working off-farm by both men and women might be affected by the characteristics of their spouse. Since both men and women may supply labor to the off-farm markets, the inclusion and importance of the spouses' characteristics give evidence of joint and simultaneous labor allocation decisions. Both Huffman (1980) and Sumner (1982) included the wife's education in the supply function for men. Greater educational attainment by the wife increases her probability of working off-farm and the hours worked. If the wife's off-farm labor is a substitute for that of the husband, then the wife's education should be negatively correlated with the husband's hours worked. Sumner obtained a negative and significant coefficient for the wife's education. Each year of education by the wife reduced the husband's hours worked by nearly 10 percent. Huffman (1980) found the opposite effect; however, the estimated coefficient was not statistically significant. The results of Huffman and Lange (forthcoming) demonstrate the importance of capturing the joint nature of decisions. Where both the husband and wife worked off-farm, education of the spouse had a positive effect on the hours worked for both the husband and wife.

The final characteristic which has been considered is the race of the family. Nonwhite farmers have been shown to work fewer hours by both Huffman (1980) and Streeter and Saupe (1986). Huffman (1980) estimated a direct and significant effect on the labor supply. Streeter and Saupe (1986) found that the off-farm wage rates of nonwhite farmers were lower, although not significantly. Lower wages would then result in fewer hours supplied to the off-farm markets. Both results may represent constraints on opportunities for minorities.

Financial characteristics

Financial characteristics of the farm family are included to capture the effects of exogenous non-wage income on the consumption of leisure. If leisure is a normal good, higher levels of income from non-wage sources would result in fewer hours of off-farm employment. Empirical results generally support this hypothesis. Sumner (1982), Thompson (1985), and Streeter and Saupe (1986) all obtained negative coefficients for other income variables. Sumner (1982) found the level of other income to be statistically important to the participation decision, but the estimated effect he obtained for the supply equation was not statistically significant. Streeter and Saupe (1986) included other income in their model in quadratic form. Surprisingly, their results imply that leisure becomes an inferior good as other income increases beyond $975. Ignoring their second order term, we calculated the income elasticity of off-farm labor to be −0.05 at the sample means.

Thompson (1985) used an aggregate of income other than the individual's wage income in her supply functions for farm men and women. Her measure for women, for example, included gross farm income, other non-labor income, and the husband's off-farm income. A similar measure was used in the supply function for men. The income elasticity of off-farm labor for working women was calculated to be about −0.38, using her estimated parameter. The elasticity calculated for men was also inelastic (−0.87). These elasticities represent an aggregation of the separate effects of farm output, other income and the off-farm income from the spouse. We saw above that the estimated elasticities of off-farm labor supply with respect to farm output ranged from −0.28 to −0.43. If these effects can be simply aggregated, Thompson's results are consistent with those obtained from estimating the effects separately. However, the inclusion of the spouse's off-farm income makes interpretation difficult. If time allocation decisions of the husband and wife are made jointly and simultaneously, inclusion of the spouse's off-farm income would result in biased estimates for the supply functions.

Furtan, Van Kooten, and Thompson (1985) included a measure of the net worth of the farm household in the supply functions for men and women. A significant and negative wealth effect on the hours worked was obtained. Huffman (1980) used measures of both realized and unrealized other income. He found a surprising positive and significant effect of realized income on the hours worked. Huffman found that unrealized income (appreciation on farm real estate, etc.) had the expected negative sign; however, the coefficient was not significantly different from zero. The two effects were found to be inelastic (0.102 and −0.100 respectively).

Jensen and Salant (1985) and Streeter and Saupe (1986) investigated the importance of fringe benefits to off-farm labor supply. They found that the presence of health benefits for the off-farm job provided important incentives for supply. If health benefits were provided, operators were found to work nearly 18 percent more hours (Streeter and Saupe). This may reflect the fact that operators must increase the number of hours worked at a job in order to receive health benefits. However, Jensen and Salant (1985) reported that a large percentage (55 percent) of farm operators who worked off-farm part-time received health benefits.

Locational characteristics

The final set of factors considered are locational characteristics for the farm family. These factors have generally been included in the models to capture local labor market effects. It is assumed that farmers located near urban areas have access to more active labor markets. They would be expected to work off-farm more frequently and supply more hours. Sumner (1982) included dummy variables to capture geographic location of farms in Illinois. He found that northern Illinois farmers worked significantly fewer hours off-farm. Streeter and Saupe (1986) included the distance to the off-farm job in the labor-supply function. Their results show that as distance to the job increases, the number of hours increase. If the variable is measuring access to labor markets, the sign is unexpected. However, the variable is more likely related to the fixed costs of labor supply. Cogan (1981) has shown that the effects of "time costs" on the supply of labor are ambiguous. Thus the coefficient may indicate that farmers increase the number of hours worked as the "time costs" of the job increase.

Sander (1983) included the population density of census regions in his model of off-farm labor supply. He found significantly greater supply of off-farm labor for farm men located in relatively urbanized areas. Density had no apparent effect on the supply by farm women. Polzin and Mac-Donald (1971) included two variables to measure the economic activity of the area. Using averages for the 48 contiguous states, they found that the percentage of population classified as rural-farm had a significant and negative effect on the supply of off-farm labor. They also found that the percentage of non-agricultural jobs in manufacturing was positively related to the supply of off-farm labor. Using county level data for four of the states provided similar results for population classification and manufacturing activity.

Summary and Conclusions

Previous research has demonstrated consistent results for many of the factors affecting the supply of off-farm labor. Table 14.3 provides a summary of the direct effects on the supply of off-farm labor. The off-farm wage, education, off-farm experience, and children have been shown to be positively related to the time spent working off-farm for men. In addition, results suggest that off-farm labor may be used as a form of diversification to reduce risk. Capital intensity also appears to release operators to work off-farm more hours. Location near an urban area has been shown to affect the supply of off-farm labor indirectly through higher wages. The availability of health benefits has been shown to be an important consideration in labor-supply decisions.

Several farm characteristics are inversely related to the supply of off-farm labor. The supply of labor to the off-farm markets declines with increases in gross or net farm revenues and the net worth of the farm household. Farm experience has been shown to reduce the intensity of off-farm work as has the presence of livestock on the farm. Greater levels of non-wage income reduce the hours spent working off-farm due to the income effect on the consumption of leisure.

While there have been several studies in recent years which have concentrated on the allocation of time by farm women (Rosenfeld 1985; Thompson 1985), our knowledge of the factors determining the labor supply by women remains limited. Thompson concentrated on characteristics of the family and their effects on labor supply. The presence and number of children has been shown to be one of the most important factors which reduces the supply of labor by women. The negative income effect has also

Table 14.3. Factors directly affecting off-farm labor supply: direction and estimated magnitudes of elasticities

Factor	Farm men		Farm women	
	Direction of effect	Magnitude of effect	Direction of effect	Magnitude of effect
Individual characteristics				
Wage	+	0.3 to 1.0	+	3.5 to 4.0
Education	+	0.0 to 1.0	a	a
Farm experience	−	−1.3	a	a
Farm training (DV)	−	−0.3	a	a
Age	+	} Max hours at	−	−1.5
(Age)²	−	age 47 to 53	a	a
Race (nonwhite)	−	−0.6 to −0.8	a	a
Farm characteristics				
Farm output	−	−0.3 to −0.4	a	a
Risk	+	0.34	a	a
Livestock (DV)	−	−0.3 to −0.5	a	a
Machinery/land	+	0.15	a	a
Family characteristics				
Children				
Age < 6 years	+	0.6	−	−0.15
6 to 12 years	a	a	−	−0.1 to −0.3
13 to 18 years	a	a	−	−0.04 to 0.0
Total	+	0.02 to 0.6	−	−0.4
Spouse's education	−	−1.0	−	b
Financial characteristics				
Other income	−	−0.1 to −0.8	−	−0.4
Assets	−	−0.1 to −0.7	−	−0.2
Health benefits				
with job (DV)	+	0.18	a	a
Locational characteristics				
Density	+	b	a	a
Distance to job	+	b	a	a
Distance to city	−	b	a	a

a = Not investigated.
b = Information not available.

been demonstrated for women. The supply of labor by women appears to be more elastic with respect to wages than their male counterparts. Both education and experience have also been shown to be positively related to supply. However, the effects of farm characteristics on the time spent working off-farm by women has not been adequately addressed. Few results have been obtained which address the responsiveness of off-farm labor supply to farm output and other farm production characteristics.

Streeter and Saupe (1986) have extended the typical model of labor supply to consider the nonmonetary benefits to farming. Nonpecuniary benefits can be considered within the context of an externality. The appeal of a farm lifestyle results in a disturbance of the decision rule for working off-farm. The results of Streeter and Saupe explain why many farmers may not equate the value of their time on-farm to the off-farm wage rate.

We might expect that time allocation decisions by the farm family would be made jointly. There is little support in previous research for the hypothesis that the decision to work off-farm by the husband is determined concurrently with the decision by the wife (Huffman and Lange 1989; Lass, Findeis, and Hallberg 1988). Huffman and Lange (1989) did find significant cross-wage effects in their research on joint decisions. However, relatively few studies have considered the husband and wife's labor-supply models in a joint and simultaneous framework. Such models will provide further information on the substitutions of operator and spouse labor.

Research on off-farm labor supply has focused on the microeconomic decisions of farm households. The results provide insights into the labor allocation problems faced by the farm family. However, we currently lack information on the reactions of farm families to changing economic conditions that is important for farm policy decisions. Further research should be directed toward the impacts of output and input price changes, new technologies and extension activities on the labor allocation decisions. Our current stock of knowledge allows us to predict the directions of many effects; however, the magnitudes of these impacts are uncertain. Price elasticity estimates for the farm household would provide information needed to unravel the substitution and income effects on the supply of off-farm labor. Additional research should also be directed towards the effects of risk on the supply of off-farm labor. Previous research suggests that off-farm labor may be an important hedge against risk.

References

Ahearn, Mary, Jim Johnson, and Roger Strickland. 1985. "The distribution of income and wealth of farm operator households." *American Journal of Agricultural Economics* 67:1087–94.

Amemiya, Takeshi. 1981. "Qualitative response models: A survey." *Journal of Economic Literature* 29:1483–1536.

Becker, G. S. 1965. "A theory of the allocation of time." *Economic Journal* 75:493–517.

Buttel, Frederick H., Bruce F. Hall, Oscar W. Larson III, and Jack Kloppenburg. 1982. "Manpower implications of part-time farming in New York State." Unpublished report prepared for the Employment and Training Administration, U.S. Department of Labor. Ithaca, N.Y.: Cornell University.

Carlin, Thomas A., and Edward I. Reinsel. 1973. "Combining income and wealth: An analysis of farm family 'well being'." *American Journal of Agricultural Economics* 55:38–44.

Carlin, Thomas A., and L. M. Ghelfi. 1979. "Off-farm employment and the farm structure," in *Structure Issues of American Agriculture*, 270– 73. Agricultural Economic Report No. 438. Washington, D.C.: Statistics and Cooperative Service, U.S. Department of Agriculture.

Cochrane, Willard W. 1987. "Saving the modest-sized farm or, the case for part-time farming." *Choices* Second Quarter:4–7.

Cogan, John F. 1981. "Fixed costs and labor supply." *Econometrica* 49:945–63.

Findeis, Jill L., and Venkateshwar. K. Reddy. 1987a. "Decomposition of income distribution among farm families." *Northeastern Journal of Agricultural and Resource Economics* 16:165–73.

Findeis, Jill L., and Venkateshwar K. Reddy. 1987b. "Regional aspects of off-farm income: Distributional issues and impacts." East Lansing, Mich.: Paper presented at the 1987 annual meeting of the American Agricultural Economics Association.

Findeis, Jill L., M. C. Hallberg and Daniel A. Lass. 1987. "Off-farm employment: Research and issues." Staff Paper No. 146. University Park: Department of Agricultural Economics and Rural Sociology, Pennsylvania State University.

Furtan, William H., G. C. Van Kooten, and S. J. Thompson. 1985. "The estimation of off-farm supply functions in Saskatchewan." *Journal of Agricultural Economics* 36:211–20.

Gronau, R. 1973. "The intrafamily allocation of time: The value of the housewive's time." *The American Economic Review* 63:634–51.

Heckman, J. 1974. "Shadow prices, market wages, and labor supply." *Econometrica* 42:679–94.

Huffman, Wallace E. 1980. "Farm and off-farm work decisions: The role of human capital." *Review of Economics and Statistics* 62:14–23.

Huffman, Wallace E., and Mark D. Lange. 1989. "Off-farm work decisions of husbands and wives: Joint decision making." *Review of Economics and Statistics* 71(No. 3):471–80.

Jensen, Helen, and Priscilla Salant. 1985. "The role of fringe benefits in operator off-farm labor supply." *American Journal of Agricultural Economics* 67:1095–99.

Lass, Daniel A., Jill L. Findeis, and M. C. Hallberg. 1988. "Off-farm labor participation decisions by Massachusetts farm households." Research Paper Series No. 88–2. Amherst: Department of Agricultural and Resource Economics, University of Massachusetts.

Lee, John E. 1965. "Allocating farm resources between farm and nonfarm uses." *Journal of Farm Economics* 47:83–92.

Leistritz, F. Larry, Harvey G. Vreugdenhill, Brenda L. Ekstrom, and Arlen G. Leholm. 1985. *Off-Farm Income and Employment of North Dakota Farm Families.* Agricultural Economics Misc. Report No. 88. Fargo: Agricultural Experiment Station, North Dakota State University.

Maddala, G. S. 1986. *Limited Dependent and Qualitative Variables in Econometrics.* Econometric Society Monograph No. 3. New York: Cambridge University Press.

Polzin, Paul, and Peter MacDonald. 1971. "Off-farm work: A marginal analysis." *Quarterly Journal of Economics* 85:840–45.

Rosenfeld, Rachel. 1985. *Farm Women.* Chapel Hill: University of North Carolina Press.

Sander, William. 1983. "Off-farm employment and incomes of farmers." *Oxford Agrarian Studies* 12:34–47.

Shishko, R., and B. Rostker. 1976. "The economics of multiple job holding." *The American Economic Review* 66:298–308.

Simpson, Wayne, and Marilyn Kapitany. 1983. "Off-farm work behavior of farm operators." *American Journal of Agricultural Economics* 65:801–5.

Streeter, Deborah, and William E. Saupe. 1986. "Nonmonetary considerations in farm operator labor allocations." A. E. Res. 86-28. Ithaca, N.Y.: Department of Agricultural Economics, Cornell University.

Sumner, Daniel. 1982. "The off-farm labor supply of farmers." *American Journal of Agricultural Economics* 64:499–509.

Thompson, Shelley. 1985. "A model of off-farm employment." *Forum No. 10.* West Germany: Kieler Wissenschaftsverlag.

Tweeten, Luther. 1983. "Economic instability in agriculture: The contributions of prices, government programs and exports." *American Journal of Agricultural Economics* 65:922–31.

CHAPTER 15

Effects of Location on
Off-farm Employment Decisions

JILL L. FINDEIS

DANIEL A. LASS

MILTON C. HALLBERG

Numerous studies of off-farm employment have focused on factors affecting participation in off-farm work and off-farm labor supply (e.g., Sumner 1982; Huffman 1980; Buttel et al. 1982; Thompson 1985). A comparison of these and similar studies indicates that off-farm work decisions by the principal farm operator or farm spouse are affected by the characteristics of the individual, the farm family, and the farm operation, including the farm's financial status.[1] Location of the farm relative to off-farm employment opportunities may be important as well. Previous studies have alluded to the potential effects of availability of and access to off-farm jobs. However, location variables have generally been poor indicators of off-farm labor decisions (Findeis, Hallberg, and Lass 1987).

The authors appreciate the financial support of the Northeast Regional Center for Rural Development. The Center provided funding for individual farm family surveys in Massachusetts and Pennsylvania that provided data for the empirical analysis presented in this chapter.
1. Findeis, Hallberg, and Lass 1987 survey a sample of studies of off-farm labor participation and labor supply. These include Huffman 1980; Sumner 1982; Simpson and Kapitany 1983; Reddy and Findeis 1988; Furtan, Van Kooten, and Thompson 1985; Thompson 1985; Buttel et al. 1982; Leistritz et al. 1985; Streeter and Saupe 1986; Rosenfeld 1985; and Sander 1983. Lass, Findeis, and Hallberg (Chapter 14, this volume) provide further comparisons.

The interest in location stems from the recognition that off-farm employment of farm family members depends in part on the demand for labor in local labor markets. Industries within commuting distance of farms determine both the number and types of off-farm jobs. The structure of occupations within a local labor market, wage rates, the time requirements of work, and the stability of employment opportunities are dimensions of off-farm work dependent on the industries providing employment.

Where jobs exist that match the human capital possessed by farm household members, time allocation decisions are made between leisure and work: on-farm, off-farm, and household. In the neoclassical model, these decisions are made on the basis of the marginal returns to farm work, off-farm work, and leisure, although it is recognized that inflexibilities in the time requirements of work alternatives exist that may cause actual time allocations to diverge from the optimal (Chong, Osburn, and Price 1987). It is reasonable to expect that multiple job-holding—farm and nonfarm; household and nonfarm; or household, farm, and nonfarm—will be more prevalent in locations where there is significant employment in the nonfarm sector. The existence of off-farm work opportunities means that a farming-dependent household is able to choose between alternative income sources and to diversify its income portfolio. When labor time is reallocated, the results may be less time spent in farming and/or household work.[2] If labor previously allocated to farming is reallocated off-farm, the operation of the farm—the enterprises selected and the farm inputs purchased—may adjust accordingly. On-farm investment strategies may change as well (Saxena and Findeis 1987). To what extent the organization of the farm and farm household change in response depends on whether work time is substituted for leisure, the initial redundancy of on-farm labor resources, the availability of substitute family or hired labor, and the characteristics of the off-farm job or jobs employing household members. For example, if nonfarm employment is part-time, seasonal, or full-time, year-round will have important effects on farm and household organization.

In locations where off-farm employment opportunities exist, farm families adjusting labor resources out of agriculture represent only one segment of all part-time farm families. The possibilities for combining farm and nonfarm lifestyles attract families into farming as well (Barlett 1986). Just as farm families are "pushed" and "pulled" into off-farm employment

---

2. Even if nonfarm employment has no effect on the quantity of time allocated to farm or household work, nonfarm employment may change the scheduling of farm or household work. For example, less work related to farming may be done during the traditional nonfarm work week. This may affect work schedules of farm input suppliers, implement dealers, and extension personnel delivering educational programs.

(Kada 1980; Fuguitt 1958), nonfarm families can be similarly thought of as being "pushed" and "pulled" into farming: "pulled" by the attractiveness of a farming lifestyle but "pushed" by the need to shelter income from taxes. Nonfarm families considering dual employment on-farm and off-farm consider the trade-offs between current income and long-term wealth accumulation, and attempt to choose an optimum income portfolio while balancing the time requirements of on-farm and off-farm work. Like farm families becoming employed off-farm, nonfarm families moving into part-time farming may choose different enterprises and farm inputs than traditional, full-time farmers.

In locations where nonfarm job opportunities are not accessible, where the demand for labor outside farming is low, or where local labor markets operate inefficiently, it is equally reasonable to expect that multiple job-holding will be less prevalent. The likelihood of financially distressed farm households being able to locate off-farm work is diminished.

This paper will examine whether these arguments can be supported theoretically and empirically.

Conceptual Framework

When off-farm employment opportunities exist, the allocation of time between onfarm and off-farm work is standardly depicted as in Figure 15.1 (Sumner 1982). T_f indicates the amount of time allocated to farming when the individual does not participate in off-farm work. Letting (U_0, U_1) represent the individual's preferences for alternative work-income combinations (and thus leisure), T_f is determined by the tangency (Z) between U_0 and the curve (F) representing the net returns to on-farm work.

When the individual works off-farm, the optimal allocation of time to farming is T_f^w, which is determined by the tangency (Z') of F and the line (NF) indicating earnings from nonfarm work. At this tangency, the marginal returns to on-farm and off-farm work are equal. The total amount of time spent working is determined by the tangency between the work-income preference curves and NF. In Figure 15.1 the total time spent working with multiple job-holding is $T_f^w + T_{nf}$. T_{nf} represents the time allocated to off-farm work.

In some rural labor markets farm family members may not be willing or able to work off-farm due to labor demand conditions. Recent research (Carter 1982; Korsching and Sapp 1978; Lichter and Costanzo 1987; Lichter 1987) indicates that nonmetropolitan residents suffer more underemployment than individuals residing in metropolitan areas. Residents of non-

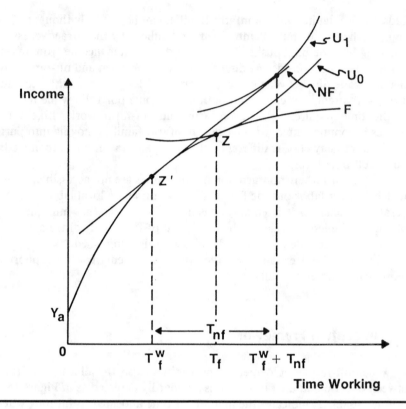

Figure 15.1. Time allocation of work time between farming
and nonfarm work. (*Adapted from Sumner 1982*)

metropolitan regions are shown to have higher rates of underemployment
than urban residents due to low income and low hours, in particular (Lichter 1987).

Underemployment due to low income reflects the lower wages paid to
rural workers, on average, relative to urban workers. The existence of the
nonfarm earnings curve (*NF*) clearly depends on the demand for labor in
the nonfarm sector. In some rural locations, off-farm employment opportunities may not exist or the marginal returns to labor in farming may
exceed the off-farm wage over the full range of time allocated to work.
Farm households in locations where off-farm wages are generally low are
less likely to participate in off-farm work, *ceteris paribus*. Long commuting
distances in very rural areas can compound this result. Although higher
transportation costs will not affect the optimal allocation of time to farm
work per day (Bollman 1979), the allocation of time between farm and off-

farm work over a year will reflect the effects of higher transportation costs and greater travel time. Bollman (p. 54) notes that "operators may be observed to have an 'available' off-farm wage greater than the marginal return to farm work due to the costs of commuting." The result is that longer commuting distances can be expected to reduce participation in off-farm work.

Underemployment due to low hours represents employed individuals that prefer to work more hours, indicating an excess supply of labor resources. This implies that farm family members participating in off-farm work may *want* to work more hours than the number of hours demanded by employers. In locations where underemployment exists, the number of hours worked off-farm will diverge from the efficient allocation, T_{nf}. More time will be spent on-farm, even though the marginal returns to on-farm work are lower.

Finally, inflexibilities in the time requirements of off-farm employment opportunities may also lead to suboptimal time allocations. The seasonal nature of the labor requirements of farming means that additional labor resources may be required during certain time periods. If the time requirements of off-farm work are institutionally rigid (or if the time requirements of farming and the jobs demanded by employers are not consistent), off-farm work may not be possible even though excess labor resources exist on-farm. One solution is to rely on other family labor or substitute hired labor, particularly for manual work. However, where labor markets do not operate efficiently, farm families may find it difficult to hire substitute labor for on-farm work or for household work, including child care. The markets for hired labor will determine if these alternatives are viable.

Changes in the Demand for Labor

When firms temporarily lay off workers or businesses permanently close down, the anticipated result will be fewer farm families dependent on off-farm employment. Jobs may be eliminated, full-time jobs may become part-time, wages may fall, and fringe benefits be reduced or dropped.

In the 1980s, this scenario has been common in many rural areas. The economic decline in some regions has been due principally to agriculture. The lack of industry diversification in many agriculturally dependent regions has meant that conditions adverse to agriculture affect farm households at the farm gate as well as through ag-related off-farm employment.

Rural areas in the 1980s have also been particularly vulnerable to fluctuations in product demand at the national level and have been negatively affected by the flight of capital to other regions or countries (Markusen 1986). Where this occurs, it is unlikely that off-farm work *can* become more prevalent. Declines in the real wage in manufacturing industries and in the service sectors in some regions (Bender 1987) make it more unlikely that labor will move out of agriculture in these economies, *ceteris paribus*. Only if on-farm returns to farm family labor decline as well will families search for off-farm work.

Alternatively, increases in labor demand lead to reductions in unemployment and underemployment. Wages can be expected to increase, resulting in more labor being "pulled" into off-farm work. In areas where demand for labor is increasing faster than labor supply, employers are more likely to employ more marginal workers and to be more flexible in terms of work hours. Where labor shortages exist, employers may be more willing to adjust the time requirements of off-farm jobs to accommodate the competing time requirements of farming, particularly if the human capital possessed by farm family members matches the skill requirements of industries.

Farm families can adjust to changes in the (off-farm) demand for labor by pursuing off-farm employment or varying current conditions of off-farm employment. When the principal farm operator works off-farm, the labor of the farm spouse may be substituted for operator labor, if the off-farm returns to the principal farm operator are higher than for the spouse. Hired labor may also be substituted. However, where the demand for (off-farm) labor is increasing, farm families may be unable to hire supplementary labor because the wage is too high. Alternative nonfarm employers in growing rural areas may be able to bid hired labor away from farming (Findeis 1987).

Where hired labor cannot be substituted, an alternative strategy is to adjust the farm operation itself to be less labor intensive. Capital may be substituted for labor. Or the size of the farm operation may be reduced. This may result in a lower return to on-farm labor (F to F') but a higher total return to labor, as shown in Figure 15.2. The result is a smaller farm operation, more time allocated to off-farm work, and a higher total income. Figure 15.2 can also be used to describe the time allocation decisions of nonfarm families that become part-time farmers. Families who purchase a farm (F') can expect to spend some time at off-farm work and some time farming. Investment in the farm (facilitated by off-farm income) may cause the farm net earnings function to increase over time. In the long run, time may be allocated only to the farm, if the farm business is shown to be profitable.

In either case, it is reasonable to expect that off-farm work should be more prevalent in expanding economies, and farm size should be on

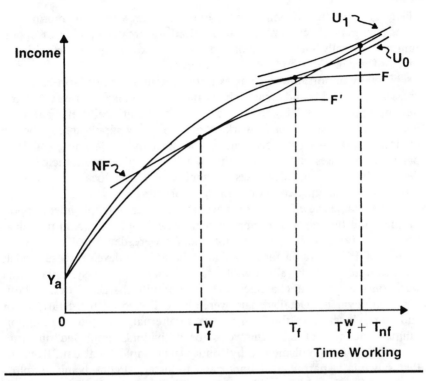

Figure 15.2. Hypothetical effects of off-farm work coupled with changes in farm size.

average smaller. With the exception of farms with high net incomes, growth of off-farm job opportunities should put downward pressure on farm size either by encouraging labor resources to move into the nonfarm labor market or by reducing the supply of hired farm labor.

These issues are addressed empirically below by examining off-farm participation decisions among Pennsylvania farm families.

Empirical Analysis

Off-farm work participation models and labor-supply models should reflect the influences of a farm's location on off-farm work decisions. Distance from off-farm employment opportunities is expected to affect the probability of participation in off-farm work and the days of work supplied. The number of employment opportunities within commuting distance also may affect employment decisions—a greater number of opportunities generally means a greater diversity of off-farm opportunities in terms of occupations and job time requirements.

Equally important are changes in the demand for nonfarm labor. Increases in labor demand create job vacancies which may induce farm families to supply more labor to off-farm work. Additionally, if wage rates increase, individuals already working off-farm may supply more labor to off-farm work. Alternatively, where labor demand is declining, off-farm participation rates and the quantity of labor supplied are anticipated to decline. Increases and decreases in employment in a local labor market reflect these changing conditions in the short run.

To examine the effects of distance, the number of employment opportunities, and the impacts of employment growth and decline on participation in off-farm work, participation models were developed based on a sample of Pennsylvania farm families. The data to develop these models were collected in 1986–87 from 989 farm families in Pennsylvania.[3] Data were collected on farm characteristics, farm family characteristics, and off-farm employment. Detailed data were also collected on hired farm labor and on the location of the farm relative to alternative employment opportunities and current off-farm work for individuals employed off-farm. These data were supplemented by county-level employment data from the Pennsylvania Department of Labor and Industry: "Pennsylvania Employment and Earnings," "Pennsylvania Total Civilian Labor Force, Unemployment and Employment, Industry Employment by Establishment, 1977–86," and "Employment and Wages of Workers Covered by the Pennsylvania Unemployment Compensation Law by County and Industry."

Separate labor participation models were estimated for principal farm operators and farm spouses. The probability that the individual works off-farm depends on the individual's reservation wage (w_o^*) relative to the market wage rate net of commuting costs (w_o^n). Participation decisions by the farm operator and farm spouse (i.e., D_o, D_s) can be expressed as follows, where $D_i = 1$ represents the decision to work off-farm and $D_i = 0$ represents the decision not to participate in off-farm work:

$$D_o = \begin{array}{l} 1 \ if \ w_o^* < w_o^n \\ 0 \ if \ w_o^* \geq w_o^n \end{array} \tag{15.1}$$

---

3. For a detailed description of these data, see Hallberg, Findeis, and Lass (1987).

and

$$D_s = \begin{array}{l} 1 \; if \; w_s^* < w_s^n \\ 0 \; if \; w_s^* \geq w_s^n \end{array} \qquad (15.2)$$

Whether the farm operator, farm spouse, or both participate in off-farm work is assumed to depend on the characteristics of (1) the individual, (2) the farm family, (3) the farm, and (4) the location of the farm relative to off-farm employment opportunities. To measure the influence of these factors on the likelihood of off-farm work, the following dichotomous dependent variable models were specified:

Principal Farm Operator:

$$Pr(D_o = 1) = f(AGE_o, \; AGESQ_o, \; EDUC_o, \; FARMEXP_o, \; CHL5_f, \\ CHL14_f, \; EMPST_s, \; DAIRY_f, \; LSTOCK_f, \; SALES_f, \\ DIST_t, \; EMP_t, \; \Delta M_t, \; \Delta S_t) \qquad (15.3)$$

Farm Spouse:

$$Pr(D_s = 1) = (AGE_s, \; AGESQ_s, \; EDUC_s, \; FARMEXP_s, \; CHL5_f, \\ CHL14_f, \; EMPST_o, \; DAIRY_f, \; LSTOCK_f, \; SALES_f, \\ DIST_t, \; EMP_t, \; \Delta M_t, \; \Delta S_t) \qquad (15.4)$$

where for the operator ($i = o$) and spouse ($i = s$):

$Pr(D_i = 1)$ = the probability that the operator/spouse participates in off-farm work

AGE_i = age of individual

$AGESQ_i$ = square of age of individual

$EDUC_i$ = education of operator/spouse in years of schooling

$FARMEXP_i$ = years spent farming by operator/spouse

$CHL5_f$ = 1 if children 5 years of age or under are present; 0 otherwise

$CHL14_f$ = number of children 14 years of age or older

$EMPST_i$ = employment status of the individual's spouse: 1 if spouse is employed off-farm; 0 otherwise

$DAIRY_f$ = 1 if principal farm enterprise is dairy production; 0 otherwise

$LSTOCK_f$ = 1 if principal farm enterprise is livestock production; 0 otherwise

SALES_f = farm size as measured by annual value of farm sales

DIST_t = distance to the nearest town

EMP_t = 1986 density of employment in county of residence (in persons employed per square mile)

ΔM_t = percent change in employment in manufacturing industries in county of residence for 1980–86

ΔS_t = percent change in employment in service industries in county of residence for 1980–86.

Equations (15.3) and (15.4) were estimated using probit techniques. The estimated coefficients are in Table 15.1. The age and age-squared variables conform in sign to expectations of a life-cycle effect, as shown by previous studies (e.g., Huffman 1980; Sumner 1982; Reddy and Findeis

Table 15.1. Estimated coefficients of off-farm participation among Pennsylvania farm operators and spouses, 1986.

Variable	Estimated coefficients[a]	
	Operator	Spouse
AGE_i	0.1823	0.1581
	(4.83)	(2.12)
AGESQ_i	−0.0022	−0.0018
	(−1.85)	(−2.23)
EDUC_i	0.0947	0.1125
	(1.78)	(2.36)
FARMEXP_i	−0.0485	−0.0373
	(−1.20)	(−0.98)
CHL5_f	0.6134	−0.5312
	(1.68)	(−7.43)
CHL14_f	0.0841	0.0017
	(3.79)	(0.32)
EMPST_i	0.3212	0.3711
	(4.48)	(3.27)
DAIRY_f	−0.6146	−0.4773
	(−3.36)	(−1.82)
LSTOCK_f	0.7120	0.4769
	(8.67)	(1.20)
SALES_f	−0.7029	−0.4003
	(−9.21)	(−2.26)
DIST_t	0.0122	−0.0044
	(0.007)	(−0.13)
EMP_t	0.0031	0.0011
	(2.79)	(1.88)
ΔM_t	0.0561	0.0091
	(2.02)	(0.65)
ΔS_t	0.0724	0.0966
	(3.18)	(3.56)
Log-likelihood	−718	−629
Correct predictions (%)	74	70

[a]T-statistics are indicated in parentheses.

1988). However, the age-squared variable was not significant for operators. Years of education also conformed to expectations of sign (i.e., positive), but the education coefficient was significant only for the farm spouse. A similar result for farm operators was reported in Sumner (1982). The presence of children under 5 years of age and the number of children 14 or older in the household were positively related to participation in off-farm work among farm operators. The positive effect of older children on farm operator participation in off-farm work may be due to a perceived need for financing college educations, or could reflect the substitution of other family labor for farm operator labor on-farm. Among farm spouses the presence of young children reduced participation but the number of older children had no effect. For both operators and spouses, the employment of one spouse off-farm had a positive effect on the off-farm participation of the other spouse. This result is consistent with Reddy and Findeis (1988).

The farm operation also affected the probability of participation. As in Sumner (1982) and Salant, Saupe, and Belknap (1984), operators of dairy farms were less likely to work off-farm than farmers with other principal enterprises. The results also indicate that farm operators on farms where livestock is the principal enterprise are more likely to work off-farm. Dairy and livestock operations do not appear to influence (either positively or negatively) participation in off-farm employment among farm spouses. Finally, the dollar value of farm sales had the anticipated effect — operators and spouses operating smaller farms as measured by annual sales had a greater likelihood of working off-farm.

The location variables performed relatively well, with the exception of the distance variable. No relationship was found between distance and off-farm work, perhaps due to the relatively large number of rural towns in Pennsylvania. Except in the northern tier counties of Pennsylvania, most of the farms surveyed were within 60 miles of a major town (or towns).

The other location-related variables (i.e., EMP_t, ΔM_t, and ΔS_t) were statistically significant for the farm operator. The density of employment in the surrounding county at the time of the survey positively influenced the probability of off-farm work. Changes in employment in manufacturing and in the service sectors also were positively related to off-farm work. Growth in manufacturing employment is associated with greater participation among farmers in the off-farm labor market. Where manufacturing employment declined over the 1980–86 period, the probability of off-farm work among area farmers was lower. Similar observations can be made for service sector employment. In addition, it should be noted that a comparison of the partial derivatives calculated from the estimated coefficients indicates that changes in service sector employment had a greater effect on off-farm employment among operators than changes in manufacturing.

For farm spouses, change in service sector employment was shown to have a statistically significant positive effect on farm spouse participation in off-farm employment. This was not surprising, given the movement of many women into the expanding service sector. What was surprising was the lack of a significant relationship between the density of county-wide employment in 1986 and off-farm work among farm spouses. Similarly, change in manufacturing employment was shown to have no discernible impact on the probability of farm spouses being employed off-farm.

Conclusions

This paper seeks to provide a discussion of the effects of location on off-farm labor participation and labor supply, and an empirical analysis of the effects of location-related variables on the likelihood of off-farm work. Previous studies have principally relied on measures of distance and population density to reflect location. These variables have not performed well.

The approach used here was to consider the effects of *changes* in employment and the level of employment, as well as distance. The employment change variables performed well, in terms of explaining labor participation. In particular, growth in service sector employment was shown to have a strong, positive impact on participation among both operators and spouses.

Future work should explore the effects of these variables in other regions as well as alternative measures of location. Such research is particularly important as a basis for better understanding the influence of rural development policies and strategies on farm family behavior and welfare.

References

Barlett, Peggy. 1986. "Part-time farming: Saving the farm or saving the lifestyle?" *Rural Sociology* 51:289–313.

Bender, Lloyd D. 1987. "The role of services in rural development policies." *Land Economics* 63(No. 1):62–71.

Bollman, Ray D. 1979. "Off-farm work by farmers: An application of the kinked demand curve for labour." *Canadian Journal of Agricultural Economics* 27:37–60.

Buttel, Frederick H., Bruce F. Hall, Oscar W. Larson III, and Jack Kloppenburg. 1982. "Manpower implications of part-time farming in New York State."

Unpublished report for the Employment and Training Administration, U.S. Department of Labor. Ithaca, N.Y.: Cornell University.

Carter, K. A. 1982. "Inadequacies of the traditional labor force framework for rural areas: A labor utilization framework applied to survey data." *Rural Sociology* 47(No. 3):459–74.

Chong, H. S., D. D. Osburn, and E. C. Price. 1987. "Farm production and off-farm employment in areas of rapid rural industrialization," in *Agriculture and Economic Instability,* ed. M. Bellamy and B. Greenshields, 228–31. I.A.A.E. Occasional Paper No. 4. Aldershot, England: Gower Publishing Co.

Findeis, J. L. 1987. "Labor and agriculture: A changing profile." *Farm Economics.* University Park: Pennsylvania State University and Cooperative Extension Service, U.S. Department of Agriculture.

Findeis, J. L., M. C. Hallberg, and D. Lass. 1987. "Off-farm employment: Research and issues." East Lansing, Mich.: Paper presented in the organized symposium "Off-farm employment and labor adjustments" at the American Agricultural Economics Association annual meeting.

Fuguitt, Glenn V. 1958. "Part-time farming and the push-pull hypothesis." *American Journal of Sociology* 23:392–97.

Furtan, William H., G. C. Van Kooten and S. J. Thompson. 1985. "The estimation of off-farm labour supply functions in Saskatchewan." *Journal of Agricultural Economics* 36:211–20.

Hallberg, M. C., J. L. Findeis, and D. Lass. 1987. "Part-time farming in Pennsylvania and Massachusetts: Survey results." *A.E. & R.S. 194.* University Park: Department of Agricultural Economics and Rural Sociology, Pennsylvania State University.

Huffman, Wallace E. 1980. "Farm and off-farm work decisions: The role of human capital." *The Review of Economics and Statistics* 62:14–23.

Kada, Ryohei. 1980. *Part-Time Family Farming: Off-Farm Employment and Farm Adjustments in the United States and Japan.* Tokyo: Center for Academic Publications.

Korsching, P. F., and S. G. Sapp. 1978. "Unemployment estimation in rural areas: A critique of official procedures and a comparison with survey data." *Rural Sociology* 43(No. 1):103–12.

Leistritz, F. Larry, Harvey G. Vreugdenhil, Brenda L. Ekstrom, and Arlen G. Leholm. 1985. *Off-Farm Income and Employment of North Dakota Farm Families.* Agricultural Economics Misc. Report No. 88, Fargo: Agricultural Experiment Station, North Dakota State University.

Lichter, D. T. 1987. "Measuring underemployment in rural areas." *Rural Development Perspectives* 3:(No. 2):11–14.

Lichter, D. T., and J. A. Costanzo. 1987. "Nonmetropolitan unemployment and labor force composition." Mimeo. University Park: Population Issues Research Center, Pennsylvania State University.

Markusen, A. 1986. "Regional responses to shifts in national and international economic forces — the U.S. experience." Paper presented to the Regional Economic Development Conference, Binghamton, N.Y.

Reddy, Venkateshwar, and J. L. Findeis. 1988. "Determinants of off-farm labor force participation: Implications for low income farmers." *North Central Journal of Agricultural Economics* 10:(No. 1):91–102.

Rosenfeld, Rachel. 1985. *Farm Women: Work, Farm and Family in the United States.* Chapel Hill: Institute for Research in Social Science Monograph Series, University of North Carolina Press.

Salant, Priscilla, William E. Saupe, and John Belknap. 1984. *Highlights of the 1983 Wisconsin Family Farm Survey.* Madison: College of Agricultural and Life Sciences, University of Wisconsin.

Sander, William. 1983. "Off-farm employment and incomes of farmers." *Oxford Agrarian Studies* 12:34–47.

Saxena, S., and J. L. Findeis. 1987. "Production and labor supply decisions of Pennsylvania farmers." Paper presented at the Vth European Congress of Agricultural Economists, Balatonszeplak, Hungary.

Simpson, Wayne, and Marilyn Kapitany. 1983. "Off-farm work behavior of farm operators." *American Journal of Agricultural Economics* 65:801–5.

Streeter, Deborah H., and William E. Saupe. 1986. "Nonmonetary considerations in farm operator labor allocations." *A.E. Res. 86-28.* Ithaca, N.Y.: Department of Agricultural Economics, Cornell University.

Sumner, Daniel. 1982. "The off-farm labor supply of farmers." *American Journal of Agricultural Economics* 64:499–509.

Thompson, Shelley. 1985. "A model of off-farm employment." *Forum No. 10.* West Germany: Kieler Wissenschaftsverlag.

CHAPTER 16

The Market for Farm Family Labor

THOMAS G. JOHNSON

Off-farm Employment in an Occupation/Residential Choice Paradigm

Among the many decisions we make as families and individuals, two stand out in terms of economic significance. First, there is our choice of occupation preference, including the level of skills we will develop, and perhaps who our employer will be. The second significant decision is our choice of residential location in a spatial context.

These choices are very closely related, of course. Our "choice set" in each of these decision areas is conditional upon our choice in the other area. If we choose an occupation first, our range of potential residential alternatives is restricted to those areas where our chosen occupation and skills command a sufficiently high rate of remuneration to attract us, and, perhaps, where our chosen employer is located. If residential location is our primary choice then our occupation choice is limited to those that are demanded within our acceptable commuting range.

Commuting patterns and demand for local public goods are subsidiary decisions in this process. Each of us has unique preferences for commuting and local public goods, that is, "goods" that can only be consumed by residing in a particular area. Local public goods include education, police service, transportation, other public services, environmental aesthetics, and proximity to family and friends. We will consider trading some remuneration to live in an area that offers more desirable public goods. Commuting, while a cost, is often a means of combining a preferred residential choice with a preferred occupational choice.

In terms of this occupation/residence choice, part-time farm families have either chosen farming as one of their occupations, or they have chosen a farm as their residence. If it were not for the spatial relationship between farms, farming, and the farm residence, these choices would not be so different from those of any other family. The fact is, however, that the choice of farming involves a very severe restriction on residential choice, while the choice of a farm residence greatly reduces a family's employment opportunities. This view of farming casts a very illuminating light on the allocation decision of potentially part-time farm families.

Off-farm labor demand

Since the demand for the off-farm labor of part-time farmers is really just the demand for nonfarm labor in farming areas, there is little one can say about the micro- or household level demand from the perspective of part-time farm families. The aggregate demand for nonfarm labor is really many demands, differentiated on the basis of (1) spatial location, (2) skills, and (3) the temporal dimension. The buyers in this market are not particularly concerned with the part-time nature of the seller except as it influences availability; that is, that the laborer provides the labor where and when it is needed, and that the laborer possesses the needed skills. From this perspective, the demand for off-farm employees is really a matter of appropriate jobs in farming areas.

Off-farm labor supply

The supply of off-farm employment, on the other hand, is the sum of the labor offered by nonfarm members of the labor force and the excess supply (after the on-farm demands are met) of farm families. In general, nonfarm laborers in this market will tend to be more supply elastic because of greater spatial mobility and temporal flexibility. The research of Lass, Findeis, and Hallberg (Chapter 14, this volume) supports this hypothesis. For this and other reasons, nonfarm laborers will tend to exert disproportional influence on the wage rate in this market.

The literature dealing with estimates of off-farm labor supply functions is quite large. As Lass, Findeis, and Hallberg (Chapter 14, this volume) indicate, the range of estimated parameters is wide. This lack of agreement is somewhat disconcerting. The differences are probably due to both the techniques employed and structural differences in supply over space and time. However, the important variables are well-known and most signs, if not magnitudes, can be accurately predicted by neoclassical theory (Findeis, Lass, and Hallberg (Chapter 15, this volume); Huffman 1980; Sumner 1982). Still, some relationships warrant closer scrutiny within the occupation/residential choice paradigm.

The neoclassical theory of household production, combined with the occupation/residential choice perspective provide an ample framework for developing hypotheses about the roles of various farm family characteristics in the allocation of labor. For example, after the effects of wage rate and on-farm productivity are accounted for, the role of education in the decision to supply off-farm employment could be ambiguous if we did not recognize the effect of education on productivity and the nature of the market into which the part-time farm family sells its labor. Many studies have shown that education increases the productivity of part-time farm families both on and off the farm. Because of the part-time farm family's decision to reside in a rural area, this greater productivity due to education will make family members more likely to take employment in the rural labor market even at below opportunity cost wage rates.

The spatial market paradigm also predicts that greater distance between residence (farm) and off-farm job will reduce the probability that a family member will take a job but increase the hours if they do. Clearly, distance represents a cost of off-farm employment that must be covered by a higher effective wage rate. This cost does not rise in proportion to the number of hours worked. Therefore, those jobs which offer low hours per day will be more frequently precluded by longer commuting distances.

Finally, the relationship between age and experience in the supply of off-farm employment must be treated carefully. The age variable itself plays many roles in the decision to supply labor to the off-farm market. One of these roles, of course, is formal and informal experience. Other roles include productivity, aspirations, family size, wealth, mobility, flexibility, and many others. If these roles are not explicitly identified in the analysis, then the estimated parameters will reflect the collective effect of all of them. In general, the overall effect of age is usually nonlinear—increasing the probability and size of off-farm employment up to some threshold age (or ages), but decreasing it thereafter. It is a serious mistake to interpret this effect solely in terms of any one of the variables listed above.

Economic and social factors affecting the off-farm labor market

The above discussion deals with the family level factors that influence the level, elasticity, and other characteristics of the demand for, and supply of, off-farm labor. The institutional and socio-economic environment in which the market is located also influences the market. In this section several testable hypotheses are suggested and discussed. Some of these are relatively obvious but are included for the sake of completeness.

First, when times are difficult in agriculture, more off-farm labor will be offered. There is evidence that the recent farm crisis encouraged many farm families to seek off-farm employment either to help sustain the farm, or to ease themselves out of farming. Furthermore, it is clear that both strategies are effective when off-farm employment opportunities exist.

Next, when times are good in the nonagricultural industries, more off-farm labor will be offered. There are both supply and demand aspects involved in this hypothesis. A strong nonagricultural economy will shift the demand for labor to the right, raising the effective returns to potential off-farm laborers and evoking a supply response. Unfortunately, in many rural areas a depressed agricultural economy leads to a depressed nonagricultural economy.

Third, the labor force participation rate among women is lower in rural areas than in urban areas but is catching up. This will continue to shift the supply of off-farm labor function to the right in most rural areas, increasing the level of off-farm employment when the opportunities exist. This could reduce or at least dampen increases in nonagricultural wage rates in these rural areas.

Fourth, the Tiebout hypothesis (Tiebout 1956) predicts that families will choose to live in communities which provide their preferred mixes of local public services and public goods. Because of the spatial nature of farming, this effect will primarily influence nonfarm families. Therefore, policies which improve the level and quality of public goods and services in specific rural areas will shift out the supply of labor, reduce wages, and reduce the level of off-farm employment. If this case occurs, one would expect to observe rates of growth in population that exceed the growth in employment and a growing number of out-commuters. Potentially offsetting this effect is the increased economic activity which often accompanies population growth, and the increased demand for land for development purposes.

The Tiebout hypothesis also predicts that public goods and services which are attractive to employers will influence the location decisions of new and relocating firms. Thus, improvements in certain public goods and services will shift out the demand for labor, raise wages, and cause a response in the supply of off-farm labor. This case will be characterized by employment growth relative to population and a growing number of in-commuters.

Risk and uncertainty also play a role in the decision to supply off-farm employment. Kraybill and Johnson (1986) show how greater risk in agricultural enterprises can be expected to shift out the supply of off-farm labor. Therefore, rural areas with more diversified and/or stable agricultural production alternatives will be associated with lower levels of off-farm employment, *ceteris paribus.*

On the other hand, more diversified economies will be more isolated from business downturns, particularly downturns in the agricultural economy. These economies will be more likely to offer employment to part-time farmers when agriculture is depressed.

Conclusions

Farmers have always combined farming enterprises with other complementary economic activities. Some were millers, other were direct marketers, and still others performed custom services for neighbors. As our economy has become more specialized and sophisticated so have the enterprise mix of full- and part-time farmers. While this has made the issue of off-farm employment more obvious, it probably has not become any more prevalent. Certainly, the gap between desired nonfarm activities and the opportunities to engage in them is at least as large as in the past.

Is it desirable for policymakers to influence this market? In many ways, strengthening this market may be the most effective means of achieving certain policy goals—even those related to agriculture. For example, a more efficient and robust rural labor market could enhance efforts to increase and stabilize farm family income, protect the family farm, maintain minimum levels of public services in rural areas, ease the transition out of farming for those who must leave, and reduce underemployment in agriculture.

What might policymakers due to strengthen rural labor markets? The following preliminary list should be considered:

1. Create jobs in rural areas, particularly those that are complementary with agricultural activity
2. Develop the entrepreneurship of rural residents in general, and farm families in particular
3. Support public education, especially innovative programs to overcome the problems of rural education
4. Support rural infrastructure improvements to encourage rural businesses and to increase the accessibility of jobs to rural residents
5. Improve the availability of job training programs to rural residents
6. Remove institutional impediments to part-time farming in our tax laws, social security, credit programs, etc.

Finally, what should the academic community be doing relative to the rural labor market? While research has revealed a great deal about the micro-level decision making of part-time farm families, much less is known about the role that part-time farms and farm families play, and could play, in the agricultural industry and in the economy and social fabric of their communities.

References

Huffman, Wallace E. 1980. "Farm and off-farm work decisions: The role of human capital." *The Review of Economics and Statistics* 62:14–23.

Kraybill, David, and Thomas G. Johnson. 1986. "Off-farm employment and its effects in the community." Staff Paper SP 86-18, Blacksburg: Virginia Polytechnic and State University.

Sumner, Daniel. 1982. "The off-farm labor supply of farmers." *American Journal of Agricultural Economics* 64:499–509.

Tiebout, Charles M. 1956. "A pure theory of local expenditures." *Journal of Political Economy* 64:416–24.

PART V

Public Programs for the Multiple Job-holding Farm Family

CHAPTER 17

Traditional Farm Commodity Programs and Multiple Job-holding

LUTHER TWEETEN

Of special interest for this chapter is how multiple job-holding (here also referred to as part-time farming) and commodity programs interact to influence farm income and structure. Are part-time farmers more or less likely than full-time farmers to participate in government commodity programs? Is the lower participation rate of small farms in commodity programs the result of more part-time farming on such farms or the result of just being small farms? Before turning to empirical findings relating multiple job-holding to farm commodity programs, a conceptual framework is outlined.

Conceptual Framework

Perceptions regarding part-time farming have shifted considerably over time. Figure 17.1(A) depicts the conventional wisdom at least as I perceived it in 1972–73 when I was at the Institute for Research on Poverty at the University of Wisconsin-Madison working on the Rural Income Maintenance (negative income tax) Experiment. The marginal value product curve for operators in farming was viewed as MVP_F, the curve for off-farm employment was viewed as MVP_N, and the farm labor-supply curve was S. Equilibrium employment of the hypothetical operator was q with q_f devoted to farming. Beyond q_f, returns were higher in nonfarm employment which was $q - q_f$.

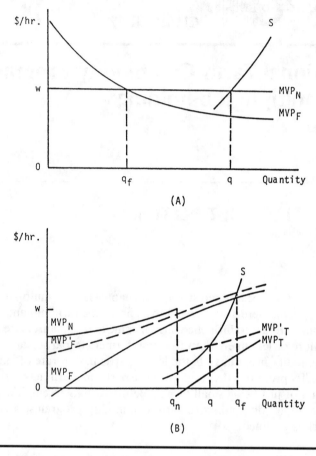

Figure 17.1. Hypothetical labor supply S, and marginal value products for farm work MVP_F, for farm work including nonmonetary value MVP'_F, and off-farm work MVP_N with multiple job-holding.

My perception changed sharply based on results of studies in east-central Oklahoma and elsewhere. The modified labor supply-demand relationship for farming is depicted in Figure 17.1(B). The marginal value product of operator labor in off-farm employment is MVP_N. It slopes upward to the right because part-time nonfarm jobs either are unavailable or pay less per hour than full-time jobs. The typical nonfarm job was 40 hours per week in east-central Oklahoma although off-farm employment of part-time operators averaged 44 hours per week (Sanford et al. 1984). The maximum available off-farm employment is designated q_n in Figure 17.1(B).

Returns to part-time operators in Oklahoma averaged $11 per hour in off-farm work and were very low, often negative, for farm work. In contrast, labor-management returns to full-time operators on commercial farms with sales of $150,000 or more per year averaged as high or higher than in off-farm employment from 1967 to 1983 based on Illinois data (Sonka, Hornbacker, and Hudson 1987). Similar conclusions are evident from Economic Research Service data (U.S. Department of Agriculture 1987). The 1986 Farm Costs and Returns Survey (U.S. Department of Agriculture 1988) indicated that farmers with annual sales in excess of $100,000 spent an average of 57 hours per week on their farming operations. In contrast, farmers with sales of under $20,000 spent less than 30 hours per week on their farming operations.

Based on the foregoing considerations, the long-term farm marginal value product in Figure 17.1(B) is MVP_F and with psychic, tax, and other benefits included is MVP'_F. MVP_F would slope downward if all nonlabor resources were fixed, but it slopes upward because of economies of size when land, labor, and capital are allowed to vary in least-cost combination. An operator with access to a full-time commercial farming operation and with supply curve S optimally allocates q_f to farm work and no time to off-farm work. Few operators can assemble the resources to realize such an opportunity, however. Help from parents or other benefactors is essential, and not many potential full-time operators can acquire it.

An operator unable to engage in farming on an economic size, full-time unit realizes highest returns by devoting q_n to a 40-hour-per-week nonfarm job. The total or highest possible marginal value product curve for such an operator is formed by adding MVP'_F horizontally to MVP_N to the right of q_n giving $MVP_N MVP'_T$. Excluding psychic benefits of farming, q_n is optimal employment — all in the nonfarm sector. However, psychic and tax benefits of farming shift the marginal value product to MVP'_T. Equilibrium is then q employment with q_n devoted to "full-time" off-farm work and $q - q_n$ devoted to the farm. The monetary return to operators of small farms is very low compared to the nonfarm wage w, but tax and psychic benefits compensate as apparent in growing numbers of part-time small farms. Pressures of meeting financial commitments have also forced full-time farmers or spouses to obtain off-farm work.

Psychic satisfactions do not pay off mortgages, hence MVP'_T does not become a viable option without off-farm income. In fact, for many part-time farmers, presence of off-farm earnings from q_n raises MVP'_T so that q exceeds q_f.

Some part-time farm operators may prefer land-intensive operations such as the production of fruits and vegetables not covered by commodity programs. But the pressures of limited time and machinery are expected to direct part-time farming operations to labor-extensive and flexible operations such as the beef cow-calf enterprise not covered by commodity programs. The high administrative overhead costs of participating in farm commodity programs constitutes a real burden per unit of output or resources on small, part-time farms. This discourages participation.

On the other hand, part-time farmers are pressed to minimize farm labor requirements by participating in commodity programs which reduce resource use and production. Whether a greater proportion of part-time operators or full-time operators participate in farm commodity programs is an empirical question to be examined subsequently.

Empirical Findings

Table 17.1 provides a broad overview of the place of commodity programs and part-time farming in farmers' income statements. Government payments are a proxy measure of commodity programs and off-farm income is a proxy measure of part-time farming. (The latter obviously is a flawed proxy for off-farm employment especially on large farms where considerable off-farm income is from dividends and interest.) The following are some observations regarding part-time farming, commodity programs, farm structure, and their interrelationship:

1. Government payments are bigger for large farms than for small farms but mid-size farms are relatively most dependent on government programs. Payments per dollar of gross farm income (or as a percent of gross as in Table 17.1) averaged 2.1 cents on large farms, 12.9 cents on farms with sales of $40,000 to $99,999, and 8.7 cents on farms with sales of less than $40,000 in 1986. In contrast to 1986, in 1965 and 1975 small farms benefited absolutely the least but relatively (per dollar of gross farm income) the most from commodity programs.

2. The contribution of direct payments and commodity programs to the viability of medium-size farms is especially apparent from government payments expressed as a percent of income from all sources in Table 17.1. Farms with sales of over $500,000 or with sales of under $40,000 received only 5–6 percent of total income from payments, while farms with sales of $40,000 to $250,000 received 32–37 percent of their total income from government payments.

3. Farms with sales of less than $40,000 averaged only $1,315 of payments in 1986 and in general received few benefits from commodity pro-

Table 17.1. Distribution of government payments and income from farm and off-farm sources by farm size for selected years, United States

Item and year	Farm size by economic sales class ($000)					
	$500 and over	$250–500	$100–250	$40–100	Less than $40	All farms
	Dollars per farm					
Government payments						
1965	...	...	...	2,480	628	734
% of gross farm income	...	...	...	(3.8)	(7.5)	(5.4)
% of all income	...	...	...	(13.2)	(9.7)	(10.0)
1975	5,182	1,684	1,094	731	171	321
% of gross farm income	(0.3)	(0.5)	(0.6)	(1.0)	(1.4)	(0.8)
% of all income	(0.8)	(1.6)	(2.2)	(3.3)	(1.5)	(1.8)
1986	35,998	26,403	18.294	10,387	1,315	5,341
% of gross farm income	(2.1)	(6.7)	(10.2)	(12.9)	(8.7)	(7.3)
% of all income	(5.4)	(19.2)	(31.9)	(36.8)	(5.8)	(13.8)
Net farm income						
1965	...	...	...	15,136	2,746	3,533
1975	599,545	99,000	41,802	17,146	1,145	8,785
1986	635,517	124,386	44,795	14,455	139	18,426
Off-farm income						
1965	...	...	...	3,680	3,757	3,792
% of all income	...	...	...	(19.5)	(57.8)	(51.8)
1975	12,182	9,184	7,198	5,076	10,254	9,481
% of all income	(2.0)	(8.5)	(14.7)	(22.8)	(90.0)	(51.9)
1986	27,057	13,319	12,602	13,780	22,534	20,212
% of all income	(4.1)	(9.7)	(22.0)	(48.0)	(99.4)	(52.3)
All income from farm and off-farm sources						
1965	...	...	...	18,816	6,503	7,325
1975	611,727	108,184	49,000	22,222	11,399	18,266
1986	662,574	137,705	57,397	28,235	22,673	38,638

Source: U.S. Department of Agriculture, 1987.
Note: All values including farm size in this and subsequent tables are in current, nominal dollars.

grams. Direct government payments averaged only 8.7 percent of gross farm income and 5.8 percent of income from all sources on these small farms in 1986. Termination of direct payments would have turned their net farm income from slightly positive to a negative $1,176 per farm. In recent years, net farm income has been small or negative on small farms, hence termination of programs would have done them little economic harm if they also would have terminated their farming activities. The conclusion is that these small farms (accounting for nearly three-fourths of all farms) are neither helped nor hurt much by commodity programs because they sell little. Much of their gross farm income is from the rental value of their dwelling and food produced and consumed on the farm.

4. Although many full-time small farms were in poverty, small farms

with off-farm income probably averaged near the U.S. median family income of $29,458 in 1986.[1] The average farm had an income well above U.S. median family income in 1986. In the absence of government commodity programs and off-farm income, most farm families would have an income well below the U.S. median.

5. The proportion of overall income of farmers from off-farm sources remained surprisingly stable at 52 percent for the years 1965, 1975, and 1986. The rise of off-farm income certainly was one of the revolutionary changes in agriculture since World War II but the revolution largely had run its course by 1965.

Off-farm income and, to a lesser extent, commodity programs played a major role in retaining people on farms in the 1980s. Despite financial stress, farm numbers dropped only 1.6 percent per year and population dropped only 2.4 percent per year in the 1980s. These rates were well below rates of decline in the 1950s and 1960s. The rates in the 1980s are near those expected from deaths and retirements alone. Net migration from farming averaged only 98,500 annually in the financial stress years 1982–86 compared to 741,000 annually in the 1950s. More people left farms each year in the 1950s than in the entire 1980s financial stress period up to 1987.

Farm numbers declined from 3.3 million in 1965 to 2.2 million in 1986. Farms with sales of over $40,000 grew in numbers from 1965 to 1980 but only the classes of farms with sales above $100,000 have grown in numbers since 1980.

To illustrate further the economic characteristics of farms, shares of farm numbers and income by economic size classes are shown in Table 17.2. Numbers of farms with sales of under $40,000 per year declined substantially as a proportion of all farms as noted in Table 17.2, but some of that decline was due to inflation moving farms to higher sales classes. The exodus from small farms has been mainly full-time operators and their families. Few such farms remain; small farms dominated by part-time farmers will display resiliency.

Output as measured by gross farm income is heavily concentrated on large farms (Table 17.2). In 1986, the 4.3 percent of all farms with sales of over $250,000 accounted for 47.3 percent of all output. The 73 percent of all farms with sales of under $40,000 accounted for 15 percent of farm "output," a figure exaggerated by including the rental value of the farm dwelling.

The share of net farm income from small farms has fallen even more sharply than the share of gross receipts. Net farm income has averaged near

---

1. Inferences may be distorted because a farm (especially a large farm) may include more than one operator family.

Table 17.2. Shares of farm numbers, government payments, and other income by economic sales class of farms

Item and year	$500 and over	$250–500	$100–250	$40–100	Less than $40	All farms
			Percent			
Farm numbers						
1965	...	...	...	3.7	95.2	100.0
1975	0.4	1.5	3.8	12.5	81.7	100.0
1986	1.3	3.0	9.5	13.3	72.9	100.0
Gross farm income						
1965	...	...	...	17.9	59.1	100.0
1975	20.6	13.2	15.8	24.2	26.2	100.0
1986	31.3	16.0	23.1	14.5	15.0	100.0
Government payments						
1965	...	...	...	12.6	81.4	100.0
1975	7.0	7.9	13.0	28.6	43.5	100.0
1986	9.0	14.7	32.5	28.9	17.9	100.0
Net farm income						
1965	...	...	...	16.0	74.0	100.0
1975	29.8	17.0	18.1	24.5	10.6	100.0
1986	45.9	20.0	23.1	10.4	0.5	100.0
Off-farm income						
1965	...	...	...	2.0	94.4	100.0
1975	0.6	1.5	2.9	4.4	88.3	100.0
1986	1.8	2.0	5.9	7.9	81.3	100.0
All income from farm and off-farm sources						
1965	...	...	...	9.6	4.5	100.0
1975	14.6	8.9	10.2	15.3	51.0	100.0
1986	22.8	10.6	14.1	9.7	42.8	100.0

Source: U.S. Department of Agriculture, 1987.

zero on small farms in recent years. These farms compensate for low farm income with off-farm income. That small farms earn more off-farm income per farm than other farms is apparent in Table 17.2 because their share of off-farm income exceeds their share of farm numbers. Government programs and off-farm income help to even the distribution of total income from all sources among economic classes of farms. Due mainly to growth of off-farm income, the distribution of income among economic classes of farms has become more even. To examine further the relationship between off-farm work and commodity programs, Table 17.3 from the 1979 Farm Finance Survey (U.S. Department of Commerce 1982) shows number of farms, off-farm income, and total net cash farm income from all sources classified by type of farm and operator's days of off-farm work. Highlights of the table are as follows:

1. Dairy and grain and soybean farms covered by commodity programs are relatively prominent among full-time farm operators whereas

Table 17.3. Number of farms, off-farm income, and total net cash income from all sources by farm type and off-farm work by operator, United States, 1979

Farm type	No off-farm work			1–199 days off-farm work			200 days or more off-farm work		
	Farms (No.)	Off-farm income ($000)	Total net cash income ($000)	Farms (No.)	Off-farm income ($000)	Total net cash income ($000)	Farms (No.)	Off-farm income ($000)	Total net cash income ($000)
Grains and soybeans	243,368	1,571,085	6,251,155	115,493	1,155,021	2,777,847	151,478	3,197,549	3,743,133
(%)[a]	(25.4)	(21.5)	(24.4)	(26.5)	(20.4)	(26.0)	(18.3)	(17.7)	(18.2)
Cotton	18,324	166,465	847,172	3,561	39,567	153,527	5,101	99,049	164,642
(%)	(1.9)	(2.3)	(3.3)	(0.8)	(0.7)	(1.4)	(0.6)	(0.5)	(0.8)
Tobacco	50,498	266,208	662,184	31,480	323,332	507,607	44,195	772,994	894,236
(%)	(5.3)	(3.6)	(2.6)	(7.2)	(5.7)	(4.7)	(5.3)	(4.3)	(4.4)
Dairy	115,321	538,255	3,901,133	27,274	193,851	744,236	12,195	220,544	421,729
(%)	(12.0)	(7.4)	(15.2)	(6.2)	(3.4)	(7.0)	(1.5)	(1.2)	(2.0)
Horticulture, fruits, and vegetables	59,609	813,422	3,428,607	29,956	571,702	1,134,013	54,619	1,512,795	1,967,518
(%)	(6.2)	(11.1)	(13.4)	(6.9)	(10.1)	(10.6)	(6.6)	(8.4)	(9.6)
Beef	245,024	2,266,068	5,201,836	116,318	1,841,517	2,566,113	325,789	7,366,897	8,099,296
(%)	(25.6)	(31.0)	(20.3)	(26.7)	(32.6)	(24.0)	(39.4)	(40.7)	(39.5)
Hog	66,075	374,096	1,345,092	30,819	309,562	486,630	83,457	1,506,382	1,605,907
(%)	(1.9)	(5.1)	(5.3)	(7.1)	(5.5)	(4.5)	(10.1)	(8.3)	(7.8)
Other	159,073	1,310,944	3,977,999	81,187	1,217,009	2,324,647	150,463	3,406,746	3,611,549
(%)	(16.6)	(17.9)	(15.6)	(18.6)	(21.5)	(21.7)	(18.2)	(18.8)	(17.6)
Total	957,292	7,306,543	25,575,178	436,088	5,651,561	10,694,620	827,297	18,082,956	20,508,010
(%)	(100)	(100)	(100)	(100)	(100)	(100)	(100)	(100)	(100)

Source: U.S. Department of Commerce, 1982.
[a]Percent of column total.

beef and hog farms are most prominent among part-time operators who work 200 days or more off the farm.

2. Forty-five percent of full-time farms were of types covered by commodity programs compared to 24 percent for operators with full-time (200 days or more) off-farm employment. It is apparent from (1) and (2) that full-time farming and commodity programs interact positively.

3. For tobacco and beef farms, the fact that the share of total income is less than the share of total farms indicates that these farms have less income per farm than do other farms on the average. An exception is for beef farm operators employed full-time off the farm. For operators employed 200 days or more per year off-farm, income from all sources was similar among all types of farms.

4. Full-time farm operators had the highest total income, $26,720, from farm and off-farm sources in 1979. This compares with income of $24,520 for operators with part-time off-farm work and $24,790 for operators with full-time off-farm work. These findings broadly agree with the conceptual framework outlined earlier in Figure 17.1.

Table 17.4, from a random sample of 937 Ohio farmers in 1987, allows us to ascertain whether program benefits are low per dollar of output on smaller farms because the farms are small (hence participation in programs is too much bother) or because part-time operators prominent on small farms do not have time to participate. Results strongly suggest the reason is because the farms are small and not because they are part-time. For example, approximately 17 percent of operators on farms with sales of less than $10,000 participated in grain and dairy programs regardless of off-farm employment compared to 70–100 percent participation on mid-size to large farms. In contrast to clear differences in participation among farm sizes, no systematic relationship was found between hours worked off the farm and participation rate except on large farms where participation rates in pro-

Table 17.4. Percent of farmers within category who participate in program, Ohio, 1986

Hours worked off-farm by operator	Sales class of farm ($000)					
	$250 and over	$100–250	$40–100	$20–40	$10–20	Less than $10
	Percent in grain or dairy program					
None	88.5	68.2	60.3	52.5	42.6	17.5
Less than 800	83.3	71.4	83.3	33.3	46.2	17.7
800–1,600	100.0	88.9	91.7	50.0	50.0	15.8
Over 1,600	100.0	87.5	70.6	65.9	43.1	15.7
Total	88.4	70.5	66.7	55.7	43.6	16.7

Source: Unpublished worksheets from Lynn Forster, Department of Agricultural Economics and Rural Sociology, Ohio State University.

grams were high among those who worked the most off the farm. Sample size was small, however, on large farms. The higher proportion of aged operators on small farms could explain some of the differences noted in Table 17.4.

Table 17.5 also from the Ohio survey relates receipts to enterprise, off-farm work, and sales class. The table is included to provide additional detail but some cells with small sample sizes are subject to considerable error. Conclusions generally reinforce estimates from the 1979 Farm Finance Survey.

1. The dairy enterprise is prominent on full-time farms. Hog and cattle enterprises (in the "other" category) are prominent on farms where the operator is employed over 1,600 hours annually off the farm. (The "other" category is sometimes negative because it includes inventory changes.)

2. Receipts from enterprises covered by commodity programs are a greater proportion of total receipts on full-time farms than on part-time farms. Results are erratic but provide some indication that program enterprises are more prominent on large farms than on small farms. Ohio is not representative of the nation in this respect because it does not have the large livestock and poultry feeding operations and fruit and vegetable farms found in other states and which are not covered by programs.

3. Based on a poverty threshold of $11,000 per family, farms with no off-farm work by operators needed to be at least in the $40,000 to $99,999 farm sales class to avoid poverty. Social Security and income from other family members also contribute, of course. For operators employed 1,600 hours or more off the farm, average income was well above the poverty level for each class of farm.

4. Again, it is apparent that commodity payments are inconsequential for small farms. Program payments averaged approximately $400 per farm over all off-farm work categories on farms with sales of less than $10,000 per year.

Summary and Conclusions

Commodity programs play a central role in the economic viability of mid-size farms; off-farm income plays that role for small farms. Multiple job-holding and farm commodity programs have independently and inter-dependently influenced farm structure. The direct impact of multiple job-holding has been revolutionary and underrated; the influence of farm com-

Table 17.5. Average annual receipts per farm by hours worked off-farm and sales class of farm, Ohio, 1986

Off-farm work and enterprise	Sales class of farm ($000)											
	$250 and over	Percent of gross	$100–249	Percent of gross	$40–99	Percent of gross	$20–39	Percent of gross	$10–19	Percent of gross	Less than $10	Percent of gross
No off-farm work												
Program	81,575	8.0	14,720	9.1	6,359	9.6	2,292	7.7	1,254	8.7	406	15.0
Dairy	214,014	21.0	77,353	47.8	32,797	49.4	7,944	26.8	1,176	8.2	2,330	85.0
Soybean	133,848	13.1	26,425	16.3	20,466	30.8	6,902	23.3	4,221	29.2	1,201	44.2
Grain	224,615	22.1	34,468	21.3	19,591	29.5	8,020	27.1	5,243	36.2	1,361	50.1
Other	363,597	35.7	8,747	5.4	-12,819	-19.3	4,451	15.0	2,533	17.5	-2,584	-95.2
Gross	1,017,650	100.0	161,713	100.0	66,394	100.0	29,610	100.0	14,427	100.0	2,714	100.0
NFI[a]	121,559		32,213		15,586		7,170		4,244		1,940	
Less than 800 hours of off-farm work												
Program	144,662	9.8	17,854	11.6	6,957	10.2	1,034	3.7	1,134	8.1	470	19.8
Dairy	82,406	5.6	7,434	4.8	16,961	24.8	23,275	83.2	0	0.0	7	0.3
Soybean	326,183	22.2	29,575	19.2	19,579	28.6	6,149	22.0	4,279	30.6	768	32.3
Grain	371,605	25.3	54,055	35.1	23,496	34.4	2,361	8.4	3,806	27.2	2,372	99.8
Other	543,300	37.0	44,894	29.2	1,386	2.0	-4,859	-17.4	4,759	34.0	-1,240	-52.2
Gross	1,468,155	100.0	153,812	100.0	68,379	100.0	27,960	100.0	13,978	100.0	2,377	100.0
NFI[a]	-358,067		33,397		15,659		20,682		15,303		6,422	
800 to 1,600 hours of off-farm work												
Program	27,000	10.7	26,050	13.8	6,382	10.7	2,495	8.8	832	6.6	365	13.0
Dairy	0	0.0	31,955	16.9	8,284	13.9	3,562	12.6	0	0.0	0	0.0
Soybean	0	0.0	42,158	22.3	15,252	25.5	5,149	18.2	1,635	12.9	1,652	58.8
Grain	190,000	75.1	72,010	38.0	18,662	31.2	9,258	32.7	1,233	9.7	1,556	55.4
Other	36,000	14.2	17,176	9.1	11,143	18.6	7,882	27.8	8,976	70.8	-762	-27.1
Gross	253,000	100.0	189,350	100.0	59,724	100.0	28,347	100.0	12,676	100.0	2,810	100.0
NFI[a]	33,658		81,717		22,588		25,171		7,494		23,554	
Over 1,600 hours of off-farm work												
Program	81,831	11.7	19,070	13.8	5,759	9.9	2,334	8.0	994	6.9	414	11.8
Dairy	130,000	18.6	22,852	16.5	3,932	6.8	2,732	9.4	147	1.0	117	3.3
Soybean	0	0.0	16,118	11.7	13,323	22.9	10,742	37.0	5,107	35.6	927	26.5
Grain	196,982	28.2	57,048	41.3	20,135	34.6	9,377	32.3	4,944	34.5	614	17.5
Other	289,000	41.4	22,995	16.7	14,990	25.8	3,857	13.3	3,156	22.0	1,430	40.8
Gross	697,813	100.0	138,083	100.0	58,140	100.0	29,043	100.0	14,348	100.0	3,503	100.0
NFI[a]	164,821		37,773		43,326		25,206		27,590		30,070	

Source: Unpublished worksheets from Lynn Forster, Department of Agricultural Economics and Rural Sociology, Ohio State University.

[a]Net farm income plus off-farm income.

modity programs has been modest and overrated (see Spitze et al. 1980; Sumner, 1985).

Some arithmetic illustrates the importance of multiple job-holding. The labor-management share of all farm inputs is as little as 5 percent on large farms but under arbitrary, generous assumptions might reach 20 percent on small farms. That means that achieving U.S. median income of $29,458 in 1986 required a farm with 5 × $29,458 = $147,290 of sales. Alternatively, achieving average income ($22,673) on farms with sales of $40,000 or less would require a farm with sales of 5 × $22,673 = $113,365 if all income must come from the farm. Less than 300,000 farms were of that size or larger in 1986! The implication is that less than 300,000 of today's farms could earn a reasonable income from the farm alone.

The commodity program effect on farm numbers is much smaller than the off-farm income effect. Assuming each dollar of direct payments generated one additional dollar of receipts from government programs, then farms with sales of $40,000 and over on average benefitted more from commodity programs than from off-farm income. Such farms which owed their livelihood to commodity programs more than to off-farm income accounted for only one-fourth of all farms in 1986. However, it is important to note that in the absence of commodity programs, land value and other adjustments would occur until farms earned about the same return to labor and management as with the programs. Some farmers would be lost in this adjustment process. Based on the Census of Agriculture, approximately 37 percent of the 210,000 farms in the $100,000 to $249,999 sales categories are classified as grain-soybean, cotton, tobacco, or dairy farms relying heavily on income from commodity programs. Many of these would not survive without commodity programs although most have farm receipts that would appear to be large enough to earn a satisfactory income from farming alone. An end to commodity programs adds to the number of farms unable to survive and provide a reasonable return to operators in the absence of off-farm income and commodity programs. The implication is that the number of farms may be as much as ten times higher today than would have been possible without off-farm income and (to a much lesser extent) government programs. Of course, an alternative view is that part-time farms are not farms at all but merely rural residences of urban workers.

Data for Ohio indicate that part-time farmers are no more or less likely to participate in commodity programs than full-time farmers, other things equal. On the average for the nation, large-size farms receive a smaller percentage of receipts than do other farms from enterprises covered by commodity programs but participation rates in any one program for which an operator is eligible increase with farm size. This phenomenon helps explain why overall program benefits are smaller per dollar of total output on large farms than on all small farms but, among farms eligible for any one program, payments per dollar of output are greatest on large farms (see Tweeten 1984).

References

Forster, Lynn. 1988. Unpublished data from longitudinal survey of Ohio farm operators. Columbus: Department of Agricultural Economics and Rural Sociology, Ohio State University.

Sanford, Scott, Luther Tweeten, Cheryl Rogers, and Irving Russell. 1984. "Origins, current situation, and future plans of farmers in East Central Oklahoma." Research Report P-861. Stillwater: Oklahoma Agricultural Experiment Station.

Sonka, Steve, Robert Hornbacker, and Michael Hudson. 1987. "Managerial performance and income variability for a sample of Illinois grain producers." Mimeo. Urbana: Department of Agricultural Economics, University of Illinois.

Spitze, Robert, Daryll Ray, Allan Walter, and Jerry West. 1980. "Public agricultural food policies and small farms." Paper I of NCR Small Farms Project. Washington, D.C.: National Rural Center.

Sumner, Daniel. 1985. "The effects of commodity programs on farm size and structure." AEI Occasional Paper. Washington, D.C.: American Enterprise Institute.

Tweeten, Luther. 1984. "Causes and consequences of structural change in U.S. agriculture." NPA Report No. 207. Washington, D.C.: National Planning Association.

U.S. Department of Agriculture. 1987. *Economic Indicators of the Farm Sector: National Financial Summary, 1986.* ECIFS 6-2. Washington, D.C.: Economic Research Service.

——. 1988. *Farmline* 9 (No. 1). Washington, D.C.: Economic Research Service.

U.S. Department of Commerce. 1982. *Census of Agriculture, 1978.* Vol. 5, Part 6, 1979 Farm Finance Survey. Washington, D.C.: Bureau of the Census.

CHAPTER 18

Rural Development and the Well-being of Farm Families

KENNETH L. DEAVERS

The brochure announcing this symposium states: "The prevalence of off-farm work among farm households has effects on farm organization, the future structure of agriculture, and public policies to aid farm families and maintain rural communities." I understand my charge to be an assessment of rural development programs in assisting farm families.

As a starting point, I want to indicate the kinds of programs I include in the rural development category. For purposes of this chapter, only those programs that are meant to improve the competitive economic position of rural places and the economic returns to rural resources are included, whether their legislation provides explicit geographic targeting or not. The discussion excludes monetary and fiscal policies, other national policies (e.g., environment, deregulation) which have no particular geographic focus, and sectoral policies. I do this even though I recognize that these other policies may have large and often unintended spatial effects.

I find it convenient to think of rural development programs falling under two broad classes of policy.

Territorial Policy

Rural development policy has most often focused on strategies to ameliorate differentials in levels of economic activity, growth, and rates of

The author acknowledges the advice and counsel of several ERS-ARED colleagues. He is especially grateful to Calvin Beale, Tom Carlin, and Mary Ahearn for their assistance.

return between rural and urban "regions" (and to a lesser extent among rural places). Mobility of resources is an important way of redressing such differences. In fact, the U.S. economy has been characterized by its capacity to move capital across sectors and between regions (and worldwide) in response to changing market forces. Large numbers of people have followed as economic opportunities shifted. The movement of individuals from areas of low returns to areas of higher returns is not without substantial economic and psychic cost, and given the importance of "place" in our federal system, it has serious political costs as well. But public intervention to achieve more "balanced" growth is not necessarily without cost.

One way to understand the problem is in terms of the possible motivations for national rural development policy interventions. There are only two: efficiency and equity. The efficiency rationale typically involves asserting some form of market failure which results in underperformance of the rural economy. The political attractiveness of the efficiency rationale is that policies to improve efficiency imply that a higher level of national output can be achieved with the same level of inputs. Rural development policies that overcome market failures create more rural jobs, but they are not jobs lost to urban America.

A related argument attributes regional differences (especially rural poverty) to low-factor productivity resulting from environmental or infrastructure deficiencies in the region. An obvious solution to this situation would be to allow (encourage) interregional migration. But investments in a region's infrastructure might increase rates of return more. If so, rural infrastructure investment policies are motivated primarily by efficiency objectives.

The equity rationale, of course, is that whether or not the observed geographic distribution of development is efficient, the resulting differentials in incomes, jobs, and well-being are unacceptable. Even if correcting these distributional inequities involves real costs (e.g., a reduction in national output), rural development policy interventions are justified by this rationale.

While equity arguments have sometimes been a politically salient rationale for advocates of a national rural (or urban) development policy, they have seldom been dominant in the targeting of assistance offered by specific programs.[1] Thus, most programs developed to implement policy have been administered as a response to presumed market failures or inadequate infrastructure. But the analytical foundation for asserting wide-

---

1. Witness the Economic Development Administration which has made nearly 80 percent of the nation eligible for assistance, in part by legislative action blocking the redesignation of places whose most recent measures of economic stress would otherwise disqualify them.

spread failure of information or capital markets, or for preferring infrastructure investment to migration, is virtually nonexistent. Under these conditions it is not surprising that there is considerable skepticism among social scientists and politicians alike about the effectiveness of a place-oriented rural development policy that assumes each and every community assisted can and will grow, if only the "right set" of public investments is provided.

Most past federal programs specifically aimed at rural economic development (e.g., Appalachian Regional Commission, Tennessee Valley Authority, Area Redevelopment Administration, and Economic Development Administration) have devoted the majority of their funds to public infrastructure, largely to serve goods-producing firms. There is little reason, however, to believe that future growth patterns in the U.S. economy generally will favor large increases in the absolute number or share of goods-producing jobs. Thus, there is little reason to believe that the expansion or location of manufacturing enterprises in rural areas will play a major role in solving existing economic stress. This raises serious questions about the future effectiveness of rural policy that focuses primarily on financing traditional kinds of goods-producing, industry-serving infrastructure, and promotes programs of local "smokestack chasing." Future rural infrastructure needs are more likely to be for facilities that reduce rural disadvantage in access to information (and communication).

Rural economic policies need to reflect realistic assessments of a process of structural economic change taking place in the U.S. economy, and potential futures of individual rural areas — their place in economic space, and the degree or urbanization of their region. These policies need to accommodate futures of stability or decline, not just growth. The role of state government has been substantially enhanced by the difficulty of addressing the diversity of rural conditions with national policy and programs. At all levels of government, however, we have been unable to envision and unwilling to design rural policy that includes the reality of decline, preferring instead the myth of universal growth.

The great diversity of rural economies, and the fact that economic stress is not the experience of all rural communities, increases the importance of targeting the public funds available for rural economic development and effectively coordinating programs at the local level. But many rural communities lack the institutional capacity to mobilize local resources, to utilize federal and state programs, and to develop and carry out successful initiatives in cooperation with the private sector to stabilize or expand their local economies, or to plan for orderly decline. There is an important place for government-supported programs that facilitate a process of rural institutional capacity building, often called community development. Various models exist, including the federal-state-local partnership of the Cooperative Extension System.

Clearly, an achievable goal for U.S. policy that focuses on rural economic development for the 1980s and 1990s is coping with change. Such a policy is most likely to permit rapid overall U.S. growth, provide new opportunities to reemploy displaced rural (and urban) workers, and generate a political climate that makes public funds available for programs to ameliorate the economic stress of structural change.

Human Resource Policy

Out-migration from rural to urban areas was the dominant theme of U.S. population movement from the turn of the century until the 1970s. It is the dominant theme again in the 1980s.

The 25 years from 1945 to 1970 were a period of particularly rapid rural out-migration, largely because of the technological revolution in farming and the dramatic declines in the number of farms and farm population. It is not unusual to find rural counties in the Great Plains, the Corn Belt, and the deep South that reached their peak population in 1900–1910, and now have only 50 to 60 percent as many residents. Because young people are much more likely to move than older people (migration rates for people in their 20s are five times the rates of those in their 60s), the sustained period of outmigration has left the nonmetropolitan United States with a lower share of people of prime working age (20 to 44 years of age) than found in the metro United States. This is a serious constraint to future rural job growth for which there are not politically viable policy solutions.

Since many rural youth end up spending their working lives in urban areas, the success of rural educational systems has a bearing on the capability and skills of both our rural and urban work force. Unfortunately, in the United States average rural educational attainment is lower and the average high school drop-out rate is higher than in urban areas. Regional variations are noticeable, with the rural South exhibiting particularly serious educational disadvantage. These human resource problems also have their impact within rural labor markets. While cause and effect are not easy to sort out, and other factors are also at work, the relatively low-skill, low-wage occupational structure in rural areas is importantly related to the educational attainment of rural workers. In the manufacturing sector, the different occupational structure of rural firms has been a major source of slow job growth. Between 1979 and 1985, U.S. manufacturing employment declined by 6 percent. But white collar manufacturing employment actually grew by

10 percent, while blue collar employment declined by 15 percent. Because blue collar jobs make up 75 percent of nonmetro manufacturing employment, the decline in blue collar jobs has been disproportionately a rural labor market adjustment.

Most of the burden of the economic adjustments occurring in rural America falls on human resources — displaced industrial workers, displaced farmers and other proprietors, and members of their households. Problems of job loss are exacerbated by difficulties individual workers may face in shifting from production jobs to white collar jobs in the service sector. Skills gained in farming, mining, and blue-collar manufacturing employment frequently are of little direct use in the service sector. Also, pay scales are substantially lower in many parts of the service sector. Most who succeed in making the occupational transition may have to accept changes in job tasks. Many may have to move their residences to find new jobs.

Rural workers, particularly in agriculture, are more likely to have been self-employed — often in an enterprise spanning several generations — which may also make occupational shifts more difficult. Thus, human resource policies that equip people for major changes in occupation and that rely on broad multicounty, regional, and national labor markets in which to seek reemployment opportunities for displaced rural workers are critical to successful amelioration of current rural economic stress.

Unfortunately, not all displaced workers will make a successful transition to new private sector jobs. Older workers, those with work-limiting disabilities, and those who lack basic educational skills will be difficult (sometimes impossible) to place. For these people, as well as for many of the long-term rural poor, federal and state public welfare programs, not labor market programs, will determine their future well-being.

It seems to me there are at least three questions one might ask about the relevance of rural development programs to farm families:

1. Can rural development programs play a significant role in easing the financial stress among farm households, relieving some of the pressures leading to displacement among farm operators and their families, especially in the most farm-dependent areas?

2. What is the potential role of rural development programs in reducing poverty among farm households, both those currently dependent on off-farm income for their well-being and those still dependent on farming?

3. Is it likely that rural development programs will alter economic opportunities facing all farm households in a fundamental way, leading to a significant increase or decrease in part-time farming in the United States?

Rural Development and Farming Dependence

My view is that the role of rural development and rural programs for rural citizens generally is extremely important, but that for those farmers and other rural citizens living in highly specialized, farm-dependent counties such programs have much less potential. Many of the farm-dependent counties (Figure 18.1) are small and remote from metropolitan areas. Given the difficulties that these characteristics pose—insufficient size to achieve important economies of scale in public and private service delivery, absence of important agglomeration economies, and difficulty developing commuting linkages to expanding urban labor markets—the prospects of nonfarm job growth are limited. This is not a new problem for these areas, which have been unable for decades to diversify their economies and hold displaced farmers and new labor force entrants within their boundaries. It is useful to review how we got where we are.

At the beginning of World War II most of our rural citizens lived and worked on farms. But an agricultural revolution, fueled by changing technology and facilitated by public policy, created a surplus of farmers, leading to a massive exodus from the sector. Between 1945 and 1970, an average of 120,000 farms disappeared annually, leading to an average yearly farm

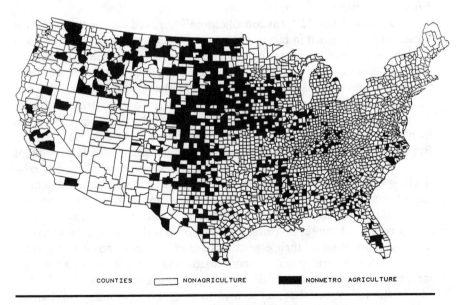

COUNTIES   ☐ NONAGRICULTURE   ■ NONMETRO AGRICULTURE

Figure 18.1. Nonmetro agriculture counties. (*Map from Bender et al. 1985*)

population decline of 600,000. In the end, we were left with less than one-third as many farmers as we began with.

In spite of significant declines in agriculture and extractive industry employment, 25 percent of our citizens remain in rural areas. In the 1960s and '70s a growing manufacturing sector provided new employment for rural workers, particularly for a generation of rural women whose labor force participation grew rapidly. During the same period rural areas also participated in the growth of the private service economy, which between 1969 and 1979 produced 55 percent of all the new jobs in rural America. Rural people now make their living from a wide-ranging set of activities not unlike those of urban Americans. Manufacturing, trade, and services are the dominant industries in rural areas. This transformation of the rural economic base from a primary dependence on natural resource activities, including agriculture, to a dependence on manufacturing, trade, and service has increased the diversity among rural areas.

Another aspect of rural diversity is that, in spite of widespread employment losses in rural manufacturing, agriculture, and natural resource–based economies in the 1980s, other rural areas have done relatively well. Job growth in the rest of rural America has exceeded 9 percent. Rural recreation-retirement counties have grown in population at more than four times the rate of the other nonmetro counties, capturing 85 percent of post-1983 rural population growth.

Post World War II farm consolidation improved the incomes of most families that remained in farming, and rural industrialization provided better jobs and higher incomes for many other rural workers. Other changes that modernized rural life were also taking place in the 1950s and '60s; expanded rural electrification and rural telephone service, improvements in rural educational systems, better transportation linkages to urban markets, upgrading of rural housing quality, etc. Collectively, these changes meant living in rural America did not necessarily imply social or cultural isolation. But most of our rural territory remains sparsely settled with few towns of more than 5,000 or 10,000 people, and most rural economies remain relatively specialized. In fact, the process of local economic development in rural communities after World War II involved moving from one economic specialization to another, as the dominance of natural resource–based industry receded. Many rural communities proved too small to achieve significant diversification of their economic base. The overall result was greater diversity among rural areas, but continued local dependence on a few major employers in a small number of closely related industries.

In the 1970s specialization seemed to be an asset for many rural areas. For example, mining and energy counties, riding the wave of rising energy prices and oil embargoes, experienced very rapid gains in employment and income. The economies of many other natural resource–dependent and farming areas were likewise buoyed by boom times in their basic industries. But boom and bust cycles have been frequent in the history of mining, forestry, and agricultural communities, and this time has been no exception.

Over the long-term, economic specialization is a serious handicap for rural areas, because structural decline occurring in a single sector can cause widespread dislocation threatening the viability of the entire community — there are simply no other expanding sectors to take up the slack when decline begins. For rural areas collectively, the problem of specialization is made worse by the fact that entire regions may share a common rural economic specialty. Thus, stagnation and decline are not confined to a small number of rural communities. They are particularly apparent in farming dependent areas of the Corn Belt and Great Plains. It is difficult to conceive of any feasible rural development policy that will stem the decline of many rural communities in this large region.

Overall Impact of Nonfarm Jobs on Farm Household Well-being

The importance of off-farm employment to the well-being of farm households is supported by trends in off-farm work, the share of farm family income attributable to this off-farm activity, and the dramatic decline in farm poverty in the last generation.

In 1950, 30 percent of all employed farm residents were working solely or primarily in nonagricultural work. (Figure 18.2) Given the extraordinarily liberal definition of a farm used at that time, which only required $50 of sales of farm products annually for qualification as a farm, it is not surprising that many people on "farms" already were primarily nonfarm in their work. Fully half of the farm women who regarded themselves as in the labor force were off-farm workers.

With each passing decade the reliance on nonfarm work has increased, both for men and women. By 1987, half of all employed farm residents were solely or primarily employed in nonagricultural industries. This proportion has reached 75 percent among women. The increase for farm men was much more modest, increasing from 26 percent in 1950 to 38 percent in 1987.

One major influence on the rise in the proportion of farm people with nonfarm work has been the rapid growth in the formal labor participation by farm women. In 1950, only 23 percent of farm women 14 years old and

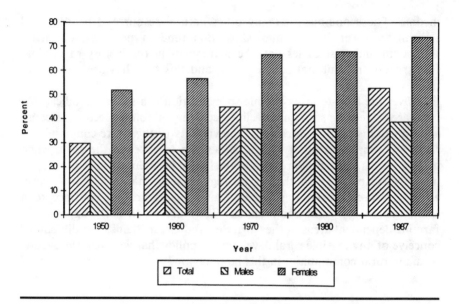

Figure 18.2. Nonfarm work of farm people. (*1950 to 1960 estimates from U.S. Bureau of the Census 1975. 1970 to 1980 estimates from* 1980 Census of Population Supplementary Report *1984. 1987 estimate from* Current Population Survey)

over were in the labor force, including those reported as unpaid family farm workers. Probably through a mixture of changed perception of women's roles and actual entry into the job market, 55 percent of farm women were in the labor force by 1987. Because working farm women are so heavily employed in off-farm jobs, this large growth in labor participation by farm women has contributed to raising the reliance of farm people on nonfarm income.

The importance of off-farm income can only be described as crucial for the nearly three-fourths of all farms that sell less than $40,000 of products annually. In 1986, these farms received 96 percent of their total cash income from off-farm sources. Thus, their access to cash income had very little to do with their agricultural activities. In sharp contrast, only 14 percent of the net cash income of farms selling $40,000 or more of products was off-farm income. Within this commercial-scale group, those farms with $40,000 to $99,999 of sales were dependent on off-farm income for 37 percent of their net cash income. The larger scale operations with $100,000 or more of sales had only 13 percent off-farm income in their net cash income. The latter farms numbered only a seventh of all farms, but provided over four-fifths of all U.S. agricultural output.

Over time, the combination of off-farm work, improved farm income (including government subsidies), and the exodus of many smaller-scale low-income farmers from agriculture has greatly reduced the poverty rate among farm residents. In 1960, 51 percent of the farm population lived in households in which the income from all sources was below the poverty level (Table 18.1), compared with 20 percent of the nonfarm population. Farm poverty dropped with remarkable rapidity during the next decade and was only 21 percent in 1970. There was further decline, with the rate reaching as low as 12 and 13 percent in several years of the 1970s. With the farm crisis of the first half of the 1980s, and the complications of the rural nonfarm recession, the rate rose again above 20 percent until 1986. In 1987, the farm poverty rate suddenly plunged to 12.6 percent from 19.6 percent a year earlier. The 1987 rate was nominally lower than the nonfarm rate (13.5 percent) for the first time, although this was not a statistically significant

Table 18.1. Poverty rates of persons by farm/nonfarm residence

Year	Farm (%)	Nonfarm (%)
1960	51.3	19.6
1961	43.7	20.0
1962	39.0	19.6
1963	39.6	18.0
1964	42.1	17.3
1965	34.7	16.2
1966	28.5	14.1
1967	25.9	13.5
1968	22.7	12.3
1969	20.2	11.7
1970	21.1	12.2
1971	20.9	12.1
1972	14.9	11.7
1973	13.4	11.0
1974	16.5	11.4
1975	16.4	12.1
1976	15.9	11.6
1977	17.1	11.3
1978	12.2	11.3
1979	13.2	11.6
1980	17.5	12.9
1981	23.0	13.8
1982	22.1	14.8
1983	23.7	15.0
1984	...	...
1985	20.3	13.8
1986	19.6	13.4
1987	12.6	13.5

Source: U.S. Bureau of the Census, years cited above.

difference. The magnitude of the decline in farm poverty from 1986 to 1987 may be partly a sampling aberration, but it shows up in both farm and nonfarm sources of income.

In sum, we have a literally defined farm population today whose employment is much more a mixture of farming and nonfarm work than was previously the case; the great majority of whose households have only minor amounts of farm income; and in which the incidence of poverty is much more similar to that of the nonfarm population than was true a generation ago, even though still somewhat on the high side in most years.

Farmer's Residential Location and Rural Development

Given that employment growth patterns in the United States strongly favor metro counties and adjacent nonmetro counties, the relevance of nonfarm rural development to farm households depends in large part on their residence in or access to these areas. Nearly 30 percent of all farms were in metro areas, according to the 1982 Census of Agriculture. Another 32 percent are in adjacent nonmetro counties. One would assume that households associated with these farms are well-positioned to combine farm and off-farm work to their benefit. In fact, it would be surprising if a large proportion of existing farms in the small sales class were not located in these counties.

The other group of rural counties that has shown strong employment and population growth in the 1970s and '80s is the retirement counties as defined by ERS (Figure 18.3). These 500 counties have absorbed 85 percent of all rural population growth since 1983, and had employment growth of over 20 percent from 1979 to 1987. Some 10 to 12 percent of U.S. farms are located in these counties. Again, the strong nonfarm employment growth in these counties should provide ample opportunities for farm families to increase their incomes with employment off the farm.

The question of a successful transition to nonfarm employment is not trivial. Thus, human resource policy that includes farm families as targets for training — not just displaced workers — is an important component of rural development policy for farm households.

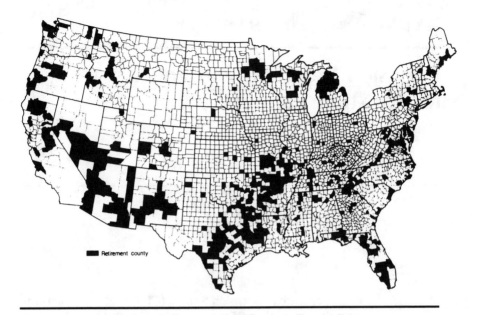

Figure 18.3. Nonmetro retirement counties, 1980. Nonmetro retirement counties are those in which the population 60 years and over grew by at least 15 percent from inmigration during 1970–80; nonmetro retirement counties of Matanuska-Susitna, Alaska, and of Maui and Hawaii, Hawaii, were omitted from this map. (*Map from U.S. Department of Agriculture, Economic Research Service*)

References

Bender, Lloyd D., Bernal L. Green, et al. 1985. *The Diverse Social and Economic Structure of Nonmetropolitan America.* Rural Development Research Report No. 49. Washington, D.C.: U.S. Department of Agriculture.

Current Population Survey, 1987, estimates for March. Washington, D.C.: U.S. Government Printing Office.

1980 Census of Population Supplementary Report, PC80-S1-15, March 1984, decennial census data from *Detailed Occupation of the Experienced Civilian Labor Force by Sex for the United States and Regions: 1980 and 1970.* Washington, D.C.: U.S. Government Printing Office.

U.S. Department of Commerce, Bureau of the Census. Various years. "Poverty in the United States." *Current Population Reports,* Series P-60, various numbers. Washington, D.C.: U.S. Government Printing Office.

_____. 1975. *Historical Statistics of the United States, Colonial Times to 1970,* Bicentennial Edition, Part 1, September 1975, tables D 75-84 and D 182-232.

CHAPTER 19

Extension Programs and Policies for Part-time Farmers

JAMES C. BARRON

The Cooperative Extension System (CES) is at a crucial turning point, more than 75 years after the Smith-Lever Act. The organization, structure, and composition of agriculture and rural areas is vastly different than it was in the early 1900s. Indeed it is quite different than it was in the 1950s and 1960s. Many small towns that were service centers for agriculture have declined or disappeared as the number of farms declined and their average size increased. The services are now obtained from larger towns and cities brought closer by good roads, telephone, and computer access. Some other rural towns have developed a new economic base from tourism, retirement communities, small manufacturing firms, or services for a broader rural population.

The CES has its roots in rural America, but as population and economic activity have moved to urban areas, Extension has sought to keep pace by offering programs tailored to urban and suburban audiences. The clearest rationale for this strategy is that a broad-based nonformal educational program on a national basis is not likely to survive if it only seeks to serve the 2 or 3 percent of the population who live on farms (U.S. Department of Commerce 1987).

Among the audiences in metropolitan and suburban regions are small and part-time farmers. They are a diverse lot and have various needs and pursue a wide range of objectives. Part-time farmers may be found scat-

The author appreciates the helpful comments of Harry Cosgriffe, Ronald C. Faas, Lois Bassett, Marvin Konyha, Richard Carkner, Bruce Florea, and Fred Woods.

tered throughout the nation, but are more plentiful in areas in close proximity to urban settings because that is where most of the nonfarm employment opportunities are located.

Should the CES be providing educational programs to part-time farmers? Why or why not? What are the consequences related to either decision? If the answer is yes, what is the nature of the demand and appropriate supply responses facing the CES? Not everyone favors providing educational programs as the following quote illustrates (Carter et al. 1981, p. 13): "Operators of part-time, small farms are also not prime candidates for greatly expanded public production and marketing research and Extension programs because they produce little farm output, have limited time to spend in farming, and are not easily reached by extension programs."

On the other hand, there are many people in the CES who believe that more Extension programming for small or part-time farmers is desirable for a variety of reasons. Part-time farmers are seeking educational assistance and Extension is being forced to respond in some way. In priority setting exercises, however, "small farms work has never been identified by directors as having a very high priority. . . . Furthermore, the ECOP subcommittees have never identified the need for more program development vis-a-vis small farms" (Konyha 1987).

A keyword search of the NARS data base (Narrative Accountability Reporting System data base used by the CES for state plans of work and reporting) shows that in the 1988–91 state Extension plans of work, there are 102 separate major programs with a variety of keywords such as part-time, small, or limited-resource farmers. These were distributed as follows among the regions:

South	13 states	58 programs (32 in 1890 institutions, 23 in 1862 institutions, and 3 joint 1862/1890 programs)
Northeast	5 states	14 programs
North Central	6 states	13 programs
West	4 states	8 programs
Territories	4 territories	9 programs

These programs are clearly not limited to part-time farmers and it is likely that in the 22 states without such identified program activities, they are also providing education to part-time farmers. All states also project for the four-year plan of work four to six impact-evaluation studies that will be carried out, but only two are shown that relate to small farms.

This chapter provides a brief historical perspective on the CES and its audiences as agriculture has matured during this century. The implications for CES of a heterogeneous set of part-time farmers are discussed, and issues of program development, staffing, and educational methods are raised. A final section addresses the issues that Extension must face as it decides how much of its resources to allocate to programs for part-time farmers.

Historical Perspective

Part of the ambivalence about Extension programs for part-time farmers may be explained by the evolution of Extension from serving an agriculture comprised of many small farms by today's standards to currently working primarily with large specialized farms.

The Morrill Land Grant Act of 1862 is frequently cited as a basis for Extension's agricultural programs with full-time commercial farmers because it specifically mentions agricultural learning. A full reading, however, shows that the scope was much broader, as shown by the remainder of the language which said, " . . . in such manner as the legislatures of the states may respectively prescribe, in order to promote the liberal and practical education of the industrial classes in the several pursuits and professions in life" (Caldwell 1976, p. 12). This authority opens up a very wide set of possibilities for all social and economic classes of people.

The Smith-Lever Act of 1914, which created the Cooperative Extension System, grew out of a movement to make agriculture more modern and scientific; i.e., efficient and progressive. The outreach function was designed primarily to serve agriculture to increase production per acre or per person (Jenkins 1980, p. 65). As the Extension system evolved, it has generally had an orientation to middle-class clients, and in agriculture those have been the commercial farmers. That is not to say it has been exclusively or narrowly confined to that clientele group. While created primarily to serve agriculture, the structure has allowed much greater flexibility (Jenkins, p. 7):

> Thus, from the very beginning the potential has existed for Extension to function appropriately as an educational institution dispensing the fruits of freely determined and conducted research while at the same time contradicting the single minded intentions which led to its being founded. Ultimately, the problem seems to be that the early supporters failed to grasp adequately the nature and potential of the educational institution they were creating.

By 1946, the seeds were planted for major changes in agriculture. The substitution of capital for labor accelerated rapidly and many farmers who had returned to the farm after the war found themselves having to look for other jobs or careers. As agriculture adopted the capital intensive technology that displaced labor, several things happened:

1. A massive labor migration off the farm took place. Much of it was out of the South and Appalachia, but no region was immune to this migration.

2. The size distribution of farms became much wider. Not all farms or farmers were equally able to use the emerging technology, but those who were began to grow in size of output and left the smaller farms behind. For example, the vertical integration of the poultry industry that occurred within five years in the late 1940s and early 1950s forced thousands of small poultry flocks out of business. What were left were large and low cost operations usually with the farmer providing only labor and buildings.

3. The predominant base of support for the CES came from the middle- and large-sized farms that now had electricity, more mechanization, and a host of other amenities and market services.

The rapid increase in new technology after World War II that left some small farmers behind did not go unnoticed. In 1955, Section 8 was added to the Smith-Lever Act which provided special funding for Extension programs for small or limited-resource farmers. In the 1960s, the CES began to face some issues about the audiences it was serving and for what purpose. Questions were raised about the kind of training and skill levels that should be required of county agents and of specialist staff. Who should receive priority in program development? Also, how could the system respond to emerging needs and new programs? There were no clear-cut answers to these questions and different states adopted a variety of approaches. Some work was being done with small and part-time farmers, but it was not a major emphasis. One estimate showed that about one-third of Extension's agricultural work was directed to low income and small farm operators, but there is no way to estimate how many were part-time farmers (U.S. Department of Agriculture, 1968, p. 6).

By 1974, the number of farms had dropped to 2.3 million and the substitution of capital for labor had reduced on-farm jobs dramatically. This was also a period when agriculture had large increases in production, and prices for farm products were relatively high. In the mid-'70s, farmers were responding as good profit maximizers and planting "fencerow to fencerow." Exports of agricultural products boomed and land prices increased sharply.

The Cooperative Extension System continued to largely direct its programs in agriculture to the commercial farms with little attention to small or part-time farmers. The skills and educational methods appropriate for the specialized farms were not the same as were required for the part-time farms. It was an upscale image that Extension was cultivating with the successful middle- and large-sized farms. These farms were now much larger than mid-sized farms were during the pre-World War II era. Part-time farmers were viewed as in transition into or out of farming, but were not very important in the overall production of food and fiber. The larger farms required more and more specialization both by the farmer and by the Extension professionals who worked with them.

Then came the 1980s. What goes up must come down. And down indeed went farm prices, exports, land values, and expectations. A significant decapitalization of agriculture took place and financial stress became severe. It is interesting to note the high level of concern for the plight of a few thousand farmers who failed financially in the 1980s as compared with almost no public notice of the many millions of farmers who were forced out in the 1940s and 1950s. One difference is that in the 1980s, the farmers who failed were by almost every measure successful farmers who fell victim to forces far beyond their control. They grew good crops, got high yields, used modern machinery and management techniques, and still failed financially.

Beginning in the 1970s, something else has been happening quietly in the background. After many years of steadily declining numbers of farms, the number of farms in many places has been increasing. This is not an isolated phenomenon. The total number of farms increased 7.1 percent from 1974 to 1978. In Washington's 39 counties only three had an increase in number of farms from 1969 to 1974. From 1974 to 1978, 30 counties showed an increase and from 1978 to 1982, 37 counties gained in farm numbers. Many of the new farms are smaller and many are part-time. Mid-sized farms have been disappearing by joining the large farm category or going out of business. Consequently, there is an emerging bimodal distribution of farms by size. Perhaps this trend affected the task force that produced "Extension in the '80s" (U.S. Department of Agriculture 1983), which recognized small farmers as an appropriate audience after a long series of official documents over the years that focused on commercial agriculture and economic efficiency. It also suggested that the CES should be concerned with programs to enhance job opportunities for people displaced in agriculture (USDA-NASULGC 1983). Section 8 of the Smith-Lever Act also provides for such programs. These programs could provide job opportunities for part-time farmers making the transition out of agriculture.

Extension programs for part-time farmers

The middle-sized farms in the past have formed the core audience and support for Cooperative Extension, but are declining in numbers, production, and overall importance. It is said that the large farms are turning away from Extension and searching for more and more specialized and highly technical information and assistance (Feller 1987, p. 315). County agents usually cannot provide the help because they are so few in number as to have to be generalists. Large farms are not retreating completely from Extension; they are instead bypassing the county agent and seeking advice directly from Extension specialists or researchers. They also seek help from agricultural consultants or field representatives of supply or processing firms, but many of those consultants rely on Extension information for their own work.

While large farms are requiring a new approach, small and part-time farmers are seeking education from Extension in increasing numbers. Many of them are well educated and skilled professionals in other fields and some have political clout that has generally not been associated with this category of farmers.

Part-time farmers are not a homogeneous set. For many it is a permanent situation and they plan to continue part-time farming and off-farm work. For others it is a transition into full-time farming while capital or other resources are acquired for the future. For still others, it is a way-station to leave agriculture and find full-time, off-farm employment.

These differences clearly present the CES with a segmented market for its educational programs. The market segments are defined by four elements: (1) resource allocations of part-time farmers, (2) part-time farmers' economic and social objectives, (3) the educational and technical level of the farmer, and (4) expectations for the future of the farm.

The resource allocations may vary widely. By definition a part-time farmer has a labor, and possibly a management, constraint. It would be a mistake, however, to assume that all part-time farmers are also small. There are farmers with full-time, off-farm jobs who own, manage, and provide part of the labor for quite large farms. If land and capital resources are plentiful, the most appropriate type of technology and method of farm operation may be about the same as for a full-time commercial farmer. These resource constraints will dictate different educational programs to adapt to the organization of the farm.

Educational programs need to recognize the farmers' objectives. Part-time farming may or may not be entirely for profit. Some part-time farmers do so as a hobby to get away from the stress or strains of other employment or perhaps for tax shelter reasons. The tax shelter benefits of farming, however, were greatly reduced by the 1986 Tax Reform Act so it can no longer be assumed that this is a primary motivation for part-time or other farmers. In some cases, it may be a simple means of providing some food for home consumption and some psychic value as well. For still others, it is an escape "back to the land" from modern society which has been a major impetus to an "alternative agriculture" philosophy and way of life. Some see it as a way to earn supplemental income in addition to the off-farm job and farm primarily for economic gain. It is important not to overlook a set of part-time farmers who are retired, whether from farming or something else, and farm for any of the reasons discussed above. Part-time farmers may have either high or low incomes. Some who have full-time, off-farm jobs are relatively well paid and do not have the capital constraints of low income earners.

The educational level and/or agricultural knowledge of the part-time farmer is important, but may or may not be a constraint. Some farmers are well informed about agricultural production, marketing, and management while others may need help understanding very basic concepts and principles. Some may be well educated in other areas and able to learn agricultural principles fairly quickly. For this audience, publications, articles, and other materials for self-learning may be quite useful.

What are the future expectations of part-time farmers? Will some want to move into full-time farming? Will others clearly not? What will they want the farm to be when their children grow up? Will their children decide to farm or not? What does the farmer plan to do in retirement? Will the farm be leased, sold, or passed on to the next generation? The farm decisions made presently can influence what the farm will be when that future time comes.

The challenge to the Extension educator is to understand these factors and to define effective educational programs that reflect these characteristics of the farm, the farmers, and their families. Producer satisfaction in light of his or her own objectives should be the goal of educational programs. The subject matter is merely a means to reach the end of producer satisfaction, although the educator sometimes loses sight of this. Extension specialists and agents need to be more aggressive, more visible, and more aware of the farmers' concerns. They need to become partners with the farmers in the educational process.

Extension programs should also focus on entry to and exit from farming. The University of Wisconsin has prepared an excellent guide for the would be part-time farmer who does not have much, if any, agricultural background (Hafs et al. 1987). Farmers moving out of agriculture also need assistance. Section 1440 of the 1985 Farm Bill provided $3.35 million to be targeted to eight states (Iowa, Missouri, Kansas, Nebraska, North Dakota,

Oklahoma, Mississippi, and Vermont) to assist displaced farmers. Other programs need to be developed to help farmers who wish to leave agriculture and explore alternatives based on interests, skills, mobility, and other factors. Michigan State University has developed such a program in cooperation with the state's role under the federal Job Training Partnership Act. This is a comprehensive program of counseling, training, and placement designed to meet the special needs of farm families and their employees making or contemplating a transition to new occupations.

It is important for Extension to package and deliver education in a form and at the right time and place to meet the needs of the various market segments. There are some serious internal differences of opinion on what the nature of those products should be. One group argues that the same information relevant to full-time commercial farmers is similarly appropriate for part-time farmers with differences only in scale of operation or application. Another group insists that a whole new and different body of knowledge and associated research program is needed. Either side may sometimes be correct, but in most circumstances, the truth is somewhere between these two extremes.

It is true that photosynthesis or ruminant digestion takes place in exactly the same way on full-time as part-time farms. It is not always the case, however, that the part-time farmer wants to maximize output subject to the constraints of available resources. Extension educators are usually used to thinking in terms of farmers who want to be efficient, make money, and generally operate in a maximizing framework. If the objectives of part-time farmers are different, then their production decisions will not follow the normal mode. The combination of inputs, the use of labor, the complement of machinery, and the timing of farm tasks could differ significantly from what would be expected on a full-time profit maximizing farm. Educational programs should be developed that both recognize and reflect these differences.

There are a variety of adjustments that can be made in the way programs are planned and carried out that will make them more suitable to part-time farmers. Changing the workweek is one way to more effectively reach part-time farmers. There is nothing sacred about a Monday to Friday workweek. It could be changed to Tuesday through Saturday (or even Sunday) for selected Extension staff who work primarily with small or part-time farming audiences. Most of the off-farm jobs will be on the normal workweek and if the Extension educator does all the office work and other preparation during the week, he or she can be available to conduct demonstrations, workshops, or farm visits on the weekend. Another alternative is a four-day workweek with longer hours.

Delivery methods ranging from traditional meetings and result demonstrations to modern electronic technology are possible. Video tapes for education are becoming widespread and Extension must exploit their effectiveness. They may be highly sophisticated or done in pretty rough-and-ready form, depending on the audience and the objectives. They have an advantage of being viewed at home by the farmer at a convenient time. Innovative ways of circulation or distribution should be explored with the possibility of local libraries or other locations as feasible circulation centers.

Computer programs with interactive programs allowing the user to insert his own constraints or assumptions are available for many topics. Electronic bulletin boards have the potential for use in education. It is possible with existing technology for an Extension specialist or county agent to operate an electronic bulletin board for a selected audience such as part-time farmers, and put on new information from time to time. It would allow the users to raise questions, suggest needs for additional information, and interact with Extension educators.

Master volunteers have been used in a variety of Extension programs and in the last few years several pilot programs have used master farmers to provide educational programs to small or part-time farmers. The volunteers are usually retired farmers who are expected to receive intensive training from Extension staff and in return work with other producers. These programs generally are focused on a limited subject matter such as Master Livestock Producers. There is potential for expansion of this concept.

A variation of the master volunteer approach is to use hired paraprofessionals who are trained in specific areas similar to master volunteers. Several states, in response to the recent financial situation in agriculture, appointed short-term Extension agents or paraprofessionals to provide one-on-one education to farmers and their families. They are hired for a fixed period of one to five years with no guarantee or expectation of a permanent position.

In certain areas, immigrants from abroad have settled and are seeking to become farmers on either a part- or full-time basis. Language and cultural differences pose challenges for educational programs for these groups.

Extension programs for part-time farmers should emphasize an overall systems approach to the farm operation. In the 1950s, Extension did this in a major way with Farm and Home Planning programs which involved both spouses and drew on agriculture and home economics program areas. These programs were designed to look at the entire farm, the mix of resources available, the alternative enterprises possible, and the combination of all. This approach gave way in the 1960s to more narrow disciplinary programs as commercial farms became more specialized and the need for even more technical subject matter pushed Extension people into specialization. In the 1980s, the "farming systems" approach has been rediscovered after it was developed for international agricultural development programs. When using this approach, it is important to relate the off-farm employment and the demand it makes on the farm family to the on-farm system. It would be easy to fall into the trap of ignoring those outside or off-farm constraints in the systems approach.

A study of small farm extension programs in the South was conducted in 1986 through interviews with program administrators in both 1862 and 1890 colleges (Ingram 1986). Demonstrations and personal contact were deemed to be the most important educational methods and a limiting constraint was professional and paraprofessional staff time. Marketing and financial management along with enterprise selection was identified as high priority educational needs.

Issues Facing the Cooperative Extension System

The question was raised earlier whether and to what extent Extension should provide part-time farmers with educational programs.

The CES was originally established for the primary purpose of promoting efficiency in agricultural production and marketing to raise the standard of living of farmers, thus contributing to national economic progress. This has remained a key objective of Extension programs. However, as a broad based educational arm of the land grant university system, all Extension programs have been much broader almost from the inception of the organization. In the last quarter of a century, Extension programming has been provided to disadvantaged sectors of society. What then are the issues facing Extension with respect to part-time farmers?

The first is an efficiency question while the second is an equity issue. Suppose the overriding goal of agricultural programs is more efficient production and marketing of farm products. In this case the return on Extension's resources would be higher if they are devoted to full-time commercial farmers. The simple fact is that is where the vast bulk of agricultural output is produced and hence holds more prospect for increased gain. The part-time farmers, most of whom are also small producers, do not produce enough to make much difference. The exceptions to this conclusion are, of course, those part-time farmers who are also large producers on a par with commercial farms.

Now let us partly relax the strong efficiency goal and introduce equity considerations. For our purposes that means that, all other things being equal, it would be socially desirable to assist people with lower incomes and who have less access to educational resources. For those with low income, limited land, limited capital, and low education, it would clearly be advisable for Extension to provide education if the equity criterion is invoked, but these are only a portion of the total population of part-time farmers. Some of them have total family net incomes that are equal to or exceed that of mid-sized, full-time farmers.

If we cannot use either the efficiency or equity criterion for an unequivocal policy decision, what about a political consideration? With the decline in numbers of middle-sized farmers, the potential defection away from Extension by the large farmers, and the rising numbers and possible influence of small and/or part-time farmers the implication is clear. If the traditional support base is eroding and a new one is at hand, it makes sense for Extension to capitalize on this opportunity. In some circumstances, the particular audience may be such that it will also meet either or both of the efficiency and equity criteria. It may be, in fact, the beginning of a new cycle. The part-time farmers may be the medium-sized or full-time farmer of tomorrow.

One response to the question is that the CES is a public institution with educational responsibility for programs including agriculture, and it cannot and should not discriminate by withholding its services from anyone who seeks them. This begs the question, however, of how to allocate scarce resources among competing demands that exceed the capacity of Extension to respond.

An ad hoc committee of the Joint Council on Food and Agricultural Sciences offered four principles as the basis for public programs in research and education for small farmers (U.S. Department of Agriculture 1979):

1. All farmers, regardless of size, should be assisted.
2. Simple equity requires that attention be given to those whose needs are greatest.
3. An agricultural system with small farms provides an opportunity to choose small-scale farming or to combine it with off-farm employment as a life-style.
4. Assistance to small-scale farmers will promote better management and more effective use of a significant body of the nation's natural resources.

Another issue is whether and to what extent Extension programs may affect the structure of agriculture. The entire complex of agricultural research and Extension has had a profound effect on the structure of agriculture through the development of new technology that made it possible for farms to get larger. A research and Extension program that is structurally neutral would develop and disseminate technologies that can be used by any size of farm (Knutson 1985, p. 67). Not all technologies are structurally neutral, however, and their adoption will be influenced by availability of existing resources, capital requirements, and technical skills of the farmer. It is generally the larger and more knowledgeable farmers who have the best access to Extension information that will adopt new technologies. In order to strive for more neutrality, Extension may choose to devote particular attention to small or part-time farmers to keep them from losing out competitively.

Harold Breimyer, in a perceptive note, suggests that we all have a stake in what the future organization and structure of agriculture will be. In short, his argument is that a broad mix of sizes and types of agricultural enterprises and firms is desirable. "Because access to knowledge is essential for the traditional independent farmer, the effectiveness of Extension's performance will continue to affect the ability of that farmer and his kind of farming to survive" (Breimyer 1976, p. 199). This argument provides support for Extension programs to all farmers regardless of size or full-time commitment to farming.

Conclusion

The question of how much of Extension's program activity should be directed to part-time farmers is unanswered. Clearly some is already taking place and it is likely that the amount will increase. The question of allocating resources among program priorities is one that each state Extension organization will have to deal with. Assuming that part-time farmer education will continue, there is much room for innovation and adaption to increase the effectiveness with which those programs are planned, delivered, and evaluated.

References

Breimyer, Harold F. 1976. "Future directions in agriculture," in U.S. Department of Agriculture, *Heritage Horizons: Extension's Commitment to People,* ed. C. Austin Vines and Marvin A. Anderson, 193–200. Madison, Wis.: Extension Journal, Inc.

Caldwell, John Tyler. 1976. "What a document . . . that land grant act!" in

U.S. Department of Agriculture, *Heritage Horizons: Extension's Commitment to People,* ed. C. Austin Vines and Marvin A. Anderson, 12–16. Madison, Wis.: Extension Journal, Inc.

Carter, Hal O., Willard W. Cochrane, Lee M. Day, Ronald C. Powers, and Luther Tweeten. 1981. "Research and the family farm." Paper prepared for the Experiment Station Committee on Organization and Policy, Ithaca, N.Y.

Feller, Irwin. 1987. "Technology transfer, public policy, and the Cooperative Extensive Service–OBM imbroglio." *Journal of Policy Analysis and Management* 6 (No. 3):315.

Hafs, Hubert, Jeffrey Key, Lawrence Tlachac, Jack Trzebiatowski, and William Saupe. 1987. "Part-time farming for rural residents of Wisconsin." Pub. No. A3090. Madison: Extension Service, University of Wisconsin.

Ingram, DeWayne L. 1986. "Small farms extension programs in Southern states." Gainesville: Institute of Food and Agricultural Sciences, University of Florida.

Jenkins, John W. 1980. "Historical overview of extension," in *Evaluation of Economic and Social Consequences of Cooperative Extension Programs,* unpaginated. Washington, D.C.: U.S. Department of Agriculture, SEA-Extension.

Knutson, Ronald. 1985. "A special report for the 1985 farm bill." Washington, D.C.: Office of Technology Assessment.

Konya, Marvin E. 1987. "Small farms." Issue paper prepared for the Extension Service, U.S. Department of Agriculture.

U.S. Department of Agriculture. 1968. "A people and a spirit." Condensation of a Report of the Joint USDA-NASULGC Study Committee on Cooperative Extension. Boulder: Extension Service, Colorado State University.

———. 1979. "Research, extension, and higher education for small farms." Report of ad hoc committee on small farms of the Joint Council on Food and Agricultural Sciences. Washington, D.C.: U.S. Department of Agriculture.

———. 1983. "Extension in the '80s." Report of the Joint USDA-NASULGC Committee on the Future of Cooperative Extension. Madison: Extension Service, University of Wisconsin.

U.S. Department of Commerce. 1987. "Farm population of the United States, 1986." *Current Population Reports,* Series P-27. Washington, D.C.: Bureau of the Census.

operators of small farms tend not to want to be bothered with commodity programs because of the high transaction costs associated with program participation.

3. Operators of small farms receive only a small percentage of their income from commodity programs and a very high percentage from off-farm employment.

4. Mid-sized farms are relatively more dependent on government programs than large farms. Therefore, termination of commodity programs would hurt mid-sized farms.

5. In the 1980s, off-farm income and, to a lesser extent, commodity programs have played major roles in retaining people on farms. The structure of agriculture would be quite different in the absence of off-farm employment and commodity programs.

6. Dairy, grain, and soybean farms covered by commodity programs are relatively prominent among full-time operators, whereas beef and hog farms are most prominent among part-time operators who work 200 or more days off-farm.

7. Multiple job-holding is an important means of helping farmers achieve current U.S. median income levels. Less than 300,000 of today's farms could earn a reasonable income from the farm alone.

While I can agree with many of the above points, I tend to hold a different opinion relative to the importance of commodity programs to the incomes of large farms. Tweeten does not indicate which commodity programs are referenced in Table 17.1. The numbers used appear to be transfer payments. If benefits from other programs were included (e.g., marketing orders, subsidized irrigation), the percentage of government payments going to the very large farms would perhaps be greater.

I also take issue with the statement that small farms (which represent 75 percent of all farms) are neither helped nor hurt much by commodity programs. There are a number of farm programs such as set-asides, allotments, and quotas, which cannot be evaluated in terms of income received. While these programs may not provide a large percentage of income, they may create incentives to farm or provide other supply control or demand enhancing benefits that proportionally benefit small farms more than large farms. Thus, although a farmer may not explicitly participate in a commodity program, he/she is an indirect recipient of any spillover effects which have been documented. For example, to the extent that commodity price support programs result in higher open market prices, the farmer may receive a higher price for his/her commodity than if there were no such programs. Further, the nonparticipating farmers can be free riders and take advantage of market structure, organization, and performance which leads to more efficient marketing. Although small farms may receive a small amount of income from commodity programs in both absolute and percentage terms, the marginal utility of that income may be enough to keep them involved in farming.

Extension Programs and Policies for Part-time Farmers

James Barron begins his discussion by tracing the evolution of the Cooperative Extension Service since its inception in 1914 to the present. He notes that early Extension programs were geared to commercial and/or middle size farms, with very few resources devoted to work on small farms. In the 1970s the number of farmers in many states and locales increased. Nearly all were small and many were part-time. In the 1980s many failures have occurred among the farmers that had traditionally been Extension's clientele. Many large-acreage farmers are turning away from Extension and searching for more specialized and highly technical information and assistance. Many other operators of large farms continue to use the Cooperative Extension Service as an information source; however, these farmers are bypassing county Extension agents and seeking advice directly from state Extension specialists. While Extension appears to be losing its traditional commercial farm audience, small and part-time farmers are seeking help from Extension in larger numbers.

Barron importantly identifies the new Extension audience (small and part-time farmers) as being diverse relative to information needs and suggests that Extension must formulate and implement a comprehensive program to respond to those needs. To illustrate the diversity that exists, Barron points out that for many part-time farmers, farming represents a permanent situation. For others it represents a transition into full-time farming and the off-farm job, and for some individuals it is a way-station for exiting agriculture and finding full-time, off-farm employment. The diversity in goals and objectives of part-time farmers suggests the need for flexible Extension programs and approaches.

Early Extension programs were geared to commercial farmers and profit maximization was the major objective. Therefore, Extension programs were geared to help farmers reach this objective. Barron suggests that part-time farmers may not be engaged in farming entirely for profits. Other important objectives for part-time farmers include (1) pursuing a hobby with which to get away from stresses and strains of other employment, (2) providing food for home consumption, (3) escaping back to the land from a "modern" society, and (4) supplementing income with off-farm employment.

Barron suggests that the Cooperative Extension Service should respond to the information needs of small and part-time farmers via a number of program adjustments, including (1) changing the workweek for selected Extension staff; (2) instituting a four-day workweek with longer hours; (3) using electronic technology, such as video tapes; (4) using electronic bulletin boards; (5) using master volunteers or master farmers to provide educational programs; (6) using paraprofessionals to provide one-on-one education to farmers; and (7) emphasizing an overall systems approach.

Most, if not all, of the program adjustments suggested by Barron are not new. Many state Cooperative Extension Services currently employ the program approaches suggested either on a formal or informal basis, with varying degrees of success. In tailoring future Extension programs to small and part-time farmers, we need to keep in mind that commercial farmers who are looking to county Extension personnel and in some cases state Extension specialists are also going to agribusiness marketing and management firms. There appears to be a need to further define and identify our emerging Extension audience as a means of tailoring programs and delivery systems to their needs.

Barron fails to mention the involvement of Extension in other rural development options but instead continues to focus on agricultural programs. I would suggest that Extension has the responsibility and expertise to work with a larger segment of rural America, a segment which impacts part-time farmers.

Within the land grant university system there appears to be need for an increased level of communication between research and Extension. Do we need more research and Extension programs that are scale neutral and/or structure neutral? Is a "farming systems approach" or "holistic approach" needed? If so, what organizational changes do we need to make in the land grant system? Are there disadvantages to the Extension team approach?

Rural Development Programs

Kenneth Deavers is no stranger in the rural development arena. "Choosing a Rural Policy for the 1980's and 90's" (Deavers 1987a) and "Rural Economic Conditions and Development Policy for the 1980s and 1990s" (Deavers 1987b) provide a picture of rural America that is painful to digest but no doubt accurate. Deavers sees a rural America that suffers from a number of problems including limited rural job opportunities and high unemployment, and reduced population growth and underemployment of human resources.

Slow rural job growth and high unemployment is documented by Deavers through the use of several statistics: (1) rural employment growth since 1979 has been slower than urban employment (4 percent versus 13 percent); (2) overall employment in farming dependent counties has been stagnant (no growth) for a number of years; (3) more than 1,000 rural counties had unemployment rates of 9 percent or higher in 1986; and (4) high unemployment rates are concentrated in the manufacturing counties of the South and East, the mining and energy counties of Appalachia, the Gulf Coast, and scattered areas of the Northeast.

Reduced population growth is evidenced by the following: (1) between 1983 and 1985, almost half (1,160) of all nonmetro counties lost population primarily through out-migration; (2) between 1985 and 1986, some 632,000 people moved out of nonmetro areas; and (3) population decline and out-migration are concentrated in the plains and western Corn Belt, and recently spread to the lower Great Lakes region and parts of the South.

Underdeveloped human resources is supported by the following findings by Deavers: (1) the 1985 poverty rate of the nonmetro population was 18.3 percent, compared with 12.7 percent of the metro population; (2) the metro poverty rate has been falling during the recovery from the recession of the early 1980s, but the nonmetro rate has not; (3) the nonmetro poor are more likely to be elderly, white, and reside in the South; and (4) nonmetro residents continue to lag behind metro residents in education. The gap for high school completion has persisted at about 10 percentage points since 1960, and the gap for college completion has widened since then. Furthermore, low educational attainment and high illiteracy and school dropout rates are especially common in the South, and low spending for public schooling in the South suggests that little progress is being made in reducing the region's educational disadvantage.

Deavers points out, as do many others, that rural development policy and farm policy are no longer synonymous. The farm population now makes up only 9 percent of the rural population in the United States. He suggests that other economic influences, besides those related to farming, now exert more important effects on the rural economy. He further suggests that the rural economy is no longer insulated from national and global economies, but has become an integral part of these economies. As a result, national rural policy will encompass a variety of policy elements. Deavers offers several policy choices:

1. Policies that facilitate a smooth and rapid movement of capital and labor from less to more competitive industries and/or locations.

2. Policies to protect certain industries as they become more competitive.

3. Policies that recognize the differences in interests of the farm sector and the territorial needs of rural areas.

4. Federal programs to improve the human capital endowments of rural youth and the rural work force as a means to overcome chronic underinvestment in rural human resources.

5. Regional rural development policies that recognize possible economies of scale, and offer the attractiveness of larger and more varied labor markets.

6. Public policy to facilitate the development of new rural enterprises by reducing information and transaction costs for private venture capitalists.

7. Public policy that builds the capacity of local institutions to access their comparative economic advantage, identify competitive opportunities, and obtain the public and private resources needed to exploit these opportunities.

Deavers correctly identifies a number of problems which current rural development programs may have very little potential for alleviating. For example, he asks, "Can rural development programs ease the financial stress associated with agriculture?" He noted that while many farmers under stress may be retrainable, the employment opportunities do not exist. Can these programs decrease the poverty rate among small farm households? Again, he suggests increasing employment opportunities to ease either social or financial stress of farm families.

Deavers doesn't believe that current rural development programs will significantly affect the structure or organization of economic development. He identifies the need for infrastructure and communications to move ideas and information rather than moving people as a means of economic development.

The problems of rural communities include unemployment, underemployment, higher school drop-out rates, an unskilled/uneducated labor force, poor infrastructure, few social and cultural opportunities, and a need for an economic development plan. These problems are similar in many ways to those in urban areas. Perhaps urban development is an appropriate thrust as part-time farmers increasingly turn to these areas for their economic and social needs.

Summary and Conclusions

The survival of rural America, both the farms and smaller communities, is dependent upon the expansion of income and employment opportunities in rural areas. A policy that focuses only on the farm sector is not likely to improve the income and quality of life of the rural masses. After all, the farm sector represents only 5.6 million of the over 63 million people who reside in rural areas.

Within the farm sector, off-farm employment, and to a lesser extent commodity programs, are essential to the economic viability of mid-sized and small farms. In terms of numbers, these farms represent over 75 percent of all U.S. farms. While off-farm employment is essential, we must not assume that such employment opportunities will always exist in the absence of rural development policies that encourages competitiveness both on the farm and in rural-based industry as well.

The Cooperative Extension System has played and will continue to play an important role in rural revitalization. Cooperative Extension recognizes the need to continuously review its programs and delivery methods based on the changing needs of its clientele. The most recent example of Extension's flexibility is "The Cooperative Extension System National Initiatives" (Johsrud and Rauschkolb, 1988) that identifies several national initiatives. The initiatives, when implemented, will address a number of critical issues important to rural residents, farm and nonfarm. The initiatives (listed here in alphabetical order) are (1) alternative agricultural opportunities; (2) building human capital; (3) competitiveness and profitability of American agriculture; (4) conservation and management of natural resources; (5) family and economic well-being; (6) improving nutrition, diet, and health; and (7) water quality. The identification of these initiatives is in itself evidence that Extension recognizes that its clientele and their information needs are undergoing continuous change.

Several critical issues identified under the National Initiatives provide some insight as to who Extension considers its current and future clientele and to some extent the types of programs needed. These issues (among others) include exploring nonfarm income sources, preparation and transition, preparing youth for responsibility, strengthening business and commodity support systems, developing long-term agricultural policy that considers both national needs and global realities and ensuring that the agricultural system has an adequate supply of competent professionals, dependence on too few income sources, growing service demands accompanied by diminishing resources, adjusting to the impact of change, and need for skilled community leadership.

Multiple job-holding farm families are important to rural and urban America. Their future depends on a rural development policy that takes into account both the farm and nonfarm sectors of rural America.

References

Deavers, K. 1987a. "Choosing a rural policy for the 1980's and 90's," in *Rural Economic Development in the 1980's: Preparing for the Future,* 377–95. Washington, D.C.: U.S. Department of Agriculture.

———. 1987b. "Rural economic conditions and development policy for the 1980's and 1990's." Paper presented at the international seminar *Agriculture and Beyond: Rural Economic Development,* Wye Plantation, Virginia.

Johsrud, D. Myron, and Roy S. Rauschkolb. 1988. "Cooperative Extension System national initiatives." Washington, D.C.: Extension Service, U.S. Department of Agriculture.

PART VI

Policy Issues
and
Research Needs

CHAPTER 21

Policy Issues and Research Needs

R. J. HILDRETH

The symposium has exposed a rich and diverse set of problems and opportunities — thus a rich and diverse set of policy issues as well as research needs. The linkage between policy issues and research needs is direct and well understood. Research and analysis could prevent unintended and perverse policy effects.

Identifying the problem is the start of both the policy process and the research process. Choices are made among alternative methods of dealing with an unsatisfactory situation during the policy process. Analysis aids the political process by pointing out the consequences of policy alternatives. But a very important contribution of analysis is political problem or issue identification. So, for both the policy as well as the research agenda, problem identification is vital.

What is the problem in multiple job-holdings among farm families in North America? Does a single problem exist or is there a nest of inter-related problems? It is my hypothesis that much of the growth of interest and concern about part-time farming (multiple job-holding among farm households) grew out of the concern about structural changes in farming and the economic and social well-being of low-income farmers. This concern came from a number of sources: worry about income levels of certain farm households, the agrarian value system (a good society has a large number of farmers), the possible economic and social decline of farm dependent communities, and a wide range of other sources.

The concerns came from society, not social sciences. Thus the concerns were not free of inconsistency. A literature grew as social scientists applied their skills and knowledge to the concerns. But social scientists have various perspectives of reality even within a single profession such as agricultural economics. Now may be a good time to give some attention to the definition of problems about multiple job-holding. Mary Ahearn and John Lee (Chapter 1) raised the question of problem focus in their paper at this conference.

"Are we a conference looking for an objective? Other than for the study of household and firm behavior, is there some social or policy objective or perceived problem that explains why we address a two-day conference to a vaguely-defined subpopulation we alternately call multiple job-holding households, part-time farms, and part-time farmers—and for which the only clear distinction is that they have some financial link to farming?"

My answer to their question is to say that there is not a single social- or policy-perceived problem, but as noted earlier, a nest of problems related to "a vaguely defined subpopulation" linked to farming. The nest of problems is created by part-time farmers or multiple job-holding farmers. I find evidence of multiple job-holding over time and space. Part-time farming and associated multiple job-holding for rural residents appears to be worldwide. Discussion at this symposium, both formal and informal, has illustrated the existence of multiple job-holding in the United States, Canada, Japan, and Western Europe. My personal, brief, and informal observations in West Africa, South America, the USSR, and China suggest the existence of multiple job-holding in these parts of the world. Much of the light industry in China, for example, takes place on farms and in rural areas due to government policy to control migration into the large cities.

I find evidence of part-time farming over time in the work of the French historian Braudel (1981). His three-volume work discusses civilization and capitalism from the fifteenth through the eighteenth centuries. Volume 1, *The Structures of Everyday Life,* contains a discussion of the interrelationship of rural and urban areas in all parts of the world. He points out that the inhabitants of towns during this period often spent only part of their lives in the towns, leaving homes and trades behind them to work in the fields at harvest time. The countryside also had its industrial activity and craftsmen. Braudel argues that this kind of relationship existed not only in Europe, but also in Russia, India, and China from the fifteenth through the eighteenth centuries.

Thus I expect that part-time farming is, has been, and will be a reality and part of most agricultural problems. Let me attempt to illustrate with a series of examples. The following format shows a problem and the elemental role of part-time farming.

Problem	*Element*
Financial well-being of farm families	Financial well-being of part-time farm families
Efficient allocation and use of agricultural resources	Influence of part-time farms on allocation and use of resources
Income distribution within agriculture and between agriculture and the rest of the economy (both static and dynamic)	Part-time farm share of income
Patterns of land use	Role of part-time farms
Decision processes of farm families	Similarities and differences of part-time farm families from other farm families
Allocation of tasks, time, and resources within farm families	Allocation by part-time farm families
Explanation of the price of feeder cattle in Central Missouri	The impact of part-time farm production
Improved efficiency of rural labor markets	Demand and supply of off-farm labor
Impact of rural economic development on agriculture	Impact on part-time farms and farmers
Impact of agricultural development on the rural economy	Impact of part-time farms and farmers
Emerging structure of farming	Role of off-farm jobs in preserving the family farm
Impact of farming on environmental quality, e.g., water quality and soil erosion	Part-time farming practices that impact environmental quality
Impact of tax change on agriculture	Role of income earned from non-farm activities
Impact of decoupled farm income transfers on agriculture	Impact on part-time farm families and their reactions
Rural family participation in local community activity and extension education programs	Role of transactions cost of part-time farmers compared to full-time farmers
Part-time farm participation in agricultural commodity program.	Different behavior patterns of part-time farms

These examples illustrate that part-time farming is a part of many research and policy problems, usually making the problems more complex and challenging for the researcher. This significance of a social problem is not necessarily correlated with complexity. Yet to ignore the part-time aspect of problems because they add to complexity and difficulty may well lead to unintended and perverse policy effects.

To evaluate the symposium I apply the quip, "Education is the process of moving from cocksure ignorance to thoughtful uncertainty." One criterion for a successful symposium is the increase in thoughtful uncertainty it creates. Applying this criterion, the symposium is a success. It is my observation that the discussion during the symposium has increased the depth and breadth of thought about the issues. Thinking more deeply and broadly about issues does not solve them, but is a means of guiding and directing the work that will contribute to their solution. Thus the benefit of this symposium will be realized in the work you do after you leave.

References

Braudel, F. 1981. *The Structures of Everyday Life: The Limits of the Possible,* Vol. 1 of *Civilization and Capitalism, Fifteenth-Eighteenth Century,* New York: Harper and Row.

Index